IE SEASONS

Groom is an academic and writer. He is Professor in English
University of Exeter and has written widely on literature,
c, and contemporary art. He is the author of a dozen books
editions, including *The Forger's Shadow* (2002), *The Union Jack*
6), and, most recently, *The Gothic* (2012). He lives on Dartmoor
his wife, two daughters, and a cat, and keeps a flock of Black
sh Mountain sheep. When he is not writing, he can be found
ing the hurdy-gurdy in local pubs.

ressively eclectic... Groom's book makes a plea for English people
ediscover and "to share the rhythms of their festive year" and
rs them means to understand and preserve the traditions of the
ntryside' *Country Life*

easury of obscure facts and folklore... On almost every page there
n "I didn't know that" moment' *Countryman*

s delightful book is a fragrant potpourri of ideas... As a cultural
ory it's an enjoyable and enlightening read' *BBC Country File*

standing... As well as being a fascinating journey through the
ory of the English year, *The Seasons* will no doubt serve as a power-
l in protecting and conserving many such practices that make our
calendar a richly textured cultural landscape.' *www.caughtbytheriver.net*

'A heartfelt exploration of the connections between the seasons and
England's traditions and folklore brims with fascinating revelations.'
Readers Digest

Also by Nick Groom

The Gothic
The Union Jack
The Forger's Shadow
Introducing Shakespeare
The Making of Percy's Reliques

THE SEASONS

A Celebration of the English Year

NICK GROOM

Atlantic Books
LONDON

The author and publisher would like to thank the
following for permission to reproduce copyright
material: Extract from 'Journey of the Magi' taken
from Selected Poems by T. S. Eliot © Estate of T. S.
Eliot and reprinted by permission of Faber and
Faber Ltd; Extract from Murder in the Cathedral by
T. S. Eliot © Estate of T. S. Eliot and reprinted by
permission of Faber and Faber Ltd; Extract from
'The Waste Land' taken from The Waste Land and
Other Poems by T. S. Eliot © Estate of T. S. Eliot
and reprinted by permission of Faber and Faber
Ltd; Extract from 'Autumn' taken from Collected
Poems by Philip Larkin © Estate of Philip Larkin
and reprinted by permission of Faber and Faber
Ltd; 'The Cyder Feast' from The Cyder Feast and
Other Poems by Sacheverell Sitwell, reprinted by
permission of Peters Fraser & Dunlop (www.
petersfraserdunlop.com) on behalf of the
Estate of Sacheverell Sitwell; 'The Minister' by
R. S. Thomas, from Collected Poems: 1945–1990, The
Orion Publishing Group Ltd, London, copyright
© R. S. Thomas, 1993; Sir Gawain and the Green
Knight translated by J. R. R. Tolkien, reprinted by
permission of HarperCollins Publishers Ltd ©
J. R. R. Tolkien, 1975.

Every effort has been made to trace all copyright
holders. The publishers will be pleased to make
good any omissions or rectify any mistakes brought
to their attention at the earliest opportunity.

Dedicated to Matilda and Dorothy
in the hope that the English seasons do not become history

As on this whirligig of Time
We circle with the seasons.

Alfred, Lord Tennyson,
'Will Waterproof's Lyrical Monologue'

CONTENTS

ACKNOWLEDGEMENTS

A book of this magnitude, and which has been in preparation for some years, means that I am indebted to many people who may not even have realized they were providing assistance when I questioned them on some recondite area of expertise. I am grateful to all my colleagues at the University of Exeter who have supported me in this project and responded to work-in-progress in seminars and lectures, in particular Regenia Gagnier, Andrew McNeillie, Ayesha Mukherjee, Henry Power, Angelique Richardson, and Jane Spencer. I would also like to thank library staff at the University of Exeter (both Tremough and Streatham campuses), as well as at the British Library and the Bodleian Library. Parts of this work were aired in early drafts in conferences and seminars at the following universities: Cambridge, Cardiff, Keele, Loughborough, Plymouth, St Andrews, and Sheffield; and I would like to thank the organizers and participants for these opportunities and for discussing the work candidly, most notably Nicholas Allen, John Brannigan, Matthew Campbell, Robert Macfarlane, Dafydd Moore, Becky Munford, Nicholas Roe, Adam Rounce, Jos Smith, Shelley Trower, and Julian Wolfreys. I also spoke on May Day at the Du Maurier Festival, and so would like to thank the organizers of that event. Margaret Bushell, Revd Anthony Geering, Peter Gilliver, John Goodridge, Jonathon Green, Michael Nath, Steve Roud, Ian Wilson, Richard Wright, Moon Farm (Devon), and Wren Music responded promptly to queries, while Elizabeth Gladstone and Richard Moore-Colyer have since provided additional information. I am particularly grateful to Helen Parker-Bray, who generously read and commented acutely on several sections, to the meticulous dedication and erudition of Ben Dupré, who copy-edited the text, and to James Nightingale, who carefully guided the book through production.

David Godwin and his team have provided reliable support over the years, and Toby Mundy and all at Atlantic generously backed this project through all its ebbs and flows. The Devonshire Arms, the King's Arms, the Oxenham Arms, and the Seven Stars have been essential allies, as have The Academy and Elegia (who provided sponsorship for the illustrations).

My most profound debts, however, are to my editor Angus MacKinnon, and the photographer Chris Chapman. Angus was tireless in suggesting revisions to the manuscript – drawing my attention to infelicities of style, inconsistencies in argument, and *non sequiturs*, while maintaining both his good humour and undimmed faith in the book. Any errors or inaccuracies that remain are my own. Chris's remarkable images were one of the inspirations for this project and it is a privilege to be able to place his photographs alongside my own text. I am very grateful for his permission to include them. Finally, I would like to thank my wife, Joanne, for putting up with my writing when I might have been playing in the garden with our children; I hope that when they read the book they will see why I thought that it was worth the sacrifice of a few summer afternoons.

NOTES ON THE TEXT

References

All sources have been checked against the originals where possible, and therefore quotations in this book can be treated as accurate and reliable; only in a handful of unavoidable instances is primary material taken from secondary sources. For both better and worse, folklore scholarship tends to be collaborative: A finds X and sends it to B, who adds Y and informs C, who publishes it as Z. The problem, of course, is that A might never have intended X to be published without further verification. With this chain of Chinese whispers in mind, I have always tried to trace the earliest and most reliable source. My findings frequently contest accepted scholarship; in such cases, I accept that other evidence elusive to me may subsequently arise – but in the meantime, I trust that readers will accept my citations as primary sources.

First printings have, in the main, been preferred to modern editions for the simple reason that the texts used in this study were often heavily revised. A few modern editions are standard, but some create as many problems as they solve. Thomson's *The Seasons* is, appropriately, the watershed text for this book, but while I have often used James Sambrook's edition, I have also referred to early printings of *The Seasons* where necessary. Any significant divergences are noted.

Notes are given as simply as possible: author/title/editor, date and (where necessary) volume number, and page number/folium/signature; full citations are given in the bibliography. All quotations from Shakespeare are given as act, scene, and line number from *The Riverside Shakespeare*, ed. G. Blakemore Evans *et al.* (1974), unless otherwise indicated.

Modernization

It is important in a book such as this, which charts the history of the seasons, to impart the literary flavour of earlier epochs and to enjoy the expression and orthography of bygone ages. Consequently, spelling has not been modernized except in cases where not to modernize would make the originals unfamiliar – lines from William Shakespeare being an obvious example. Likewise, typography has been modernized only where obsolete conventions such as the macron would obscure meaning; such revision has been indicated in the notes. After some thought, the 'vv' for 'w' has been modernized, as have usages such as 'u' for 'v' and 'i' for 'j' (and *vice versa*); this has meant that some of Edmund Spenser's deliberate archaisms have been lost, but I have reluctantly made this decision in the interests of consistency and accessibility. Despite these changes, it is hoped that the challenge of unfamiliar spellings will still be enjoyed by the reader as part of the puzzle of early English literature. The warning '*sic*' is very seldom used in direct quotation from historical sources as spelling was fluid before the early nineteenth century; when '*sic*' does appear, it usually notes a verbatim usage by a modern or contemporary writer, a typographical error, or an exceptional spelling open to misinterpretation. Square brackets '[]' indicate editorial elucidation, such as adding necessary punctuation.

Capitalization

The seasons spring, summer, autumn, and winter are not capitalized except when referring to personifications of the season, or if capitalized in quotations – although here the personification may in any case be ambiguous and the result of printing conventions; likewise 'nature' and 'Nature', and 'sun', 'moon', and 'earth'. Archaic capitalization is retained. 'Countryside', 'nature', and similar words are used in common-sense ways throughout, although their usage and meanings have been challenged by environmental writers such as Donna Landry and Timothy

Morton. Anyone who wishes to pursue these arguments should refer to the bibliography.

Religious Festivals

Religious festivals are given their most popular or generic names, although some confusion between the *Book of Common Prayer* and the Roman Catholic Church is inevitable; in such cases, no offence is intended and apologies are offered in advance if any is taken. Saints' day festivals are described as follows: the 'vigil' is the eve of the day, the 'feast' the day itself, and the 'morrow' the day after.

Dating

Caution has to be exercised when translating dates from old calendars to the present calendar. Many English weather proverbs were originally based on the Julian calendar, retained until September 1752. The country then switched to the Gregorian calendar: this meant that eleven days had to be dropped from the year (see Chapter 2). Consequently, Julian dating can be up to thirteen days behind Gregorian dating, and from 2100 the difference will be fourteen days. This means that English May Day celebrations before 1752 would have taken place on our current date of 14 May.

Some dates are, however, independent of these calendars and are calculated by solar and lunar events. Easter falls on the first Sunday after the Paschal full moon (see Chapter 6), which means that it can occur on one of thirty-five possible dates – hence it is a 'moveable feast'. This in turn affects the timing of other festivals such as Lent and Pentecost, which map onto the Julian and Gregorian calendars in different ways. Still other dates are calculated by month and week. British Summer Time (BST) begins on the last Sunday in March, and most bank holidays fall on Mondays.

Definitions

In the interests of clarity, the seasons in this book are aligned with the months according to the simple rule of thumb adopted by the Met Office: spring is March, April, and May; summer is June, July, and August; autumn is September, October, and November; winter is December, January, and February. There is no reason why seasons should commence at the beginning of every third month, and no reason why spring and summer should be longer than autumn and winter by a day or two, but it makes organizing the year in a work such as this manageable – and that is the spirit in which these divisions should be understood. Indeed, calendars tended to shift the dates into each quarter by ten days, so spring for example customarily began around 10 March. But the calendar has always ultimately been driven by practicalities rather than theory – which is why it has been periodically adjusted, whether by adding whole intercalated months in ancient times or the modern practice of adding or subtracting certain days. My minor generalizations are therefore infinitesimally small compared with the ways in which the calendar has been wracked over the centuries.

ILLUSTRATIONS

All photographs are © Chris Chapman and are used with kind permission.

FOREWORD

The Seasons makes no claim to be a definitive account of the English seasons, or of their weather, folklore, and festive customs. Indeed, I soon realized that such a complete account would prove an impossibly Herculean labour, never mind the equivalent and equally extensive histories of Wales, Scotland, and Ireland. I also realized that far from writing an extended note of regret or even an obituary, my supposedly dying and arguably dead subject – the cultural calendar of England – kept displaying vital signs: I discovered aggressively living traditions in nearly every corner of the country. This was most heartening, but something else emerged from such vibrancy: the more I wrote about the peculiarities of local customs, the more fragmented the big picture became. I wanted to preserve the particularity of these strong regional identities and not shoe-horn them into a grand overall argument concerning the decay of Englishness, but there was too much material, it was too local, and it was always changing. The concept of a unified England kept dissolving in my hands: what was said or done in one locale was quite different, and perhaps in contradiction to, what was done a few miles down the road. It was simply all too overwhelming, too prolix, and so I changed tack.

This book is now a hybrid study, a sort of antiquarianism for the present times: part history, part almanac and part polemic – both a restitution of waning lore and a rallying cry for national renewal. If English society has experienced the seasons as much as a series of cultural events as it has understood them as part of the cycle of the farming year, then the ground of current environmental debate should be shifted to include the study of literature, cultural history, and folklore. Historically this mixed seasonal culture was one of the things that once gave the nation a shared identity. But if this communal heritage is in terminal decline, vestiges of these representations nevertheless remain and continue to shape the ways in which we understand and appreciate the countryside of England. Consequently it is my firm belief that the analysis of climate change should not be confined to bio-scientists and meteorologists: the environmental crisis is a cultural issue too, with profound implications for how our society makes sense both of itself and of the landscape in which it has dwelt for millennia.

This book also has an aim that is a good deal more practical: to encourage much more involvement in the festive year, which for centuries has been extraordinarily rich and varied. This does not mean that there should be, say, tens of thousands of people chasing a cheese down Cooper's Hill in Gloucestershire every Spring Bank Holiday – there are locals enough doing that already. But why not go, cheer the runners on, and make a donation? 'They also serve who only stand a round.'[1] One of the many things I have learnt in the course of researching and writing The Seasons was that for all the enthusiasts, revivalists, and busybodies (myself included) organizing local events, performances, sessions, and competitions, there is as much to be said for simply turning up at the local pub during a carnival, fair, pageant, festival, annual celebration, or the like and steadfastly drinking from lunchtime until bedtime. To do so offers as much support for the cause as getting involved in all sorts of other, more complicated (and sometimes more compromising) ways.[2] It is sociable, it acknowledges the community, and it is like tipping a hat: you can say hello to one and all, thank the company, and then get on with spending money at the bar and keeping the pub solvent. And perhaps it is here, in this friendly fug, that you yourself might even start to plan your own locally distinctive celebration of the English seasons. If you do so, you will become part of a new and long-overdue devolution, that of England from Britain.

We need to re-establish English festivals as occasions for local communities, otherwise they will become prey to extremists or commercial exploitation. I am not a fanatic for English nationalist politics and am horrified by aggressive displays of 'popular' chauvinism that seem all too frequent in sports such as football. But I do admire the Scots, Welsh, and Irish for their independence of mind and culture within the larger identities of the UK and Europe, and I rue the extent to which the English, whoever we may be in the first decades of the twenty-first century, have allowed our bountiful harvest home of traditions to become subsumed and dissolved within the Union. We may not have our own parliament yet – a political anomaly for which there is no justification – but we do have our own seasonal culture of the year. That culture can redefine the very essence of Englishness as something that can be enjoyed across England by anyone who is prepared to listen to history and then learn the one lesson of folklore: that it is up to all of us to make it up.

Nick Groom
South Zeal,
St Frideswide's Day, 2012

Part I

I INTRODUCTION

A word spoken in due season, how good is it!

Proverbs 15: 23

Once, the annual cycle of the seasons must have seemed eternal and indomitable. The year moved from the birdsong and flowers of spring through summer's work of harvesting and husbandry to autumnal stock-taking and into the icy challenge of winter. Every year was different, but the pattern of the seasons was consistent – a consistency powerfully strengthened by a rich calendar of proverbial lore, annual rituals, and frequent festivities. Although the weather and the seasons actually had an element of unpredictability from year to year, they were nevertheless yoked to a calendar that marked their characteristics and their progress with absolute certainty.

But now everything is changing. The seasons are blurring, they no longer have such apparently distinctive beginnings and ends. Winters can be unpleasantly warm, and summers uncomfortably wet and windy, and the months are no longer so readily defined by what weather or fortune they might bring. And as the complex rhythms of our weather are changing – and with them our sense, once close and vital, of the seasons – we are also losing and forgetting that shared seasonal heritage too. Once common cultural references are forgotten, and twenty-first-century British society is becoming ever more remote from the social and economic realities of rural life. Modern agricultural practice and climate change have clearly had their unwelcome effects, but perhaps it is precisely because those shared reference points and memories are fading that the seasons now seem so unstable.

It is time then to reflect what we risk losing if we cannot make sense of the sun, rain, and tempest, or of snow, frost, and hail – if we cannot make sense of them, that is, beyond the immediate practicalities of the weather forecast. What of our relationships with solstices and equinoxes, with the first cuckoo of spring and the last swallow of summer, and with all our rich inheritance of axiomatic wisdom, national folklore, and traditional festivity? What of the extraordinary compendium that centuries, if not millennia, of worship and study and experience of the seasons – as well as straightforward, first-hand familiarity with the weather – have created and bequeathed to us? If we abandon – or are forced to abandon – our hitherto intimate relationship with the seasons, will our lives be any the less? Will we lose an arcane knowledge, a key to an understanding of ourselves and our own place within the natural world: a key that is irreplaceable?

This book will touch upon many subjects to argue that our daily experience of the climate and the calendar still bears the deep stamp of centuries of culture, history, religion, politics, and agriculture. Yet that stamp is not indelible, and we need now more than ever to be reminded of our cultural inheritance. So here there are chapters on the folklore, customs, and literature of each season mixed with, among other things, a history of the calendar, accounts of saints' days, early theories of the weather, the calculation of Easter, the arrival of the cuckoo, James Thomson's best-selling political-pastoral poem *The Seasons*, and a summary of the grievous impact of the Enclosure Laws.

How we have viewed that climate and calendar is a vast subject, but any book can only be so long, and I have reluctantly had to exclude chapters on a number of closely associated themes, among them the pastoral and picturesque, and their often deleterious effect on the countryside and our perceptions of it. Pastoral poetry evolved out of the Renaissance's fascination with all things classical, spinning a direct line from Hesiod, Theocritus, and, later, Virgil to the English countryside – finding perhaps its greatest exponent in Edmund Spenser. In essence, the pervasive cult of the pastoral attempted to overlay an ancient, classical, and largely bucolic view of the land onto the fields, woods, and common ground of sixteenth-century England. But although for the vast majority of its inhabitants the Elizabethan and Stuart countryside was less an Arcadia than a harsh and unforgiving working environment, a stranger to prancing satyrs, flute-playing shepherds, and the Mediterranean sun alike, the cult of the pastoral proved to be remarkably tenacious, subtly shaping the land and making the labouring rural population vanish from this vision of England – and indeed, the pastoral still survives in a popular if degraded form today.

Similarly, picturesque painting styles approached the natural scenery of late eighteenth-century England with expectations and preconceptions derived from Claude Lorrain, a French Baroque artist best known for his Italian landscapes. Moreover, science was at hand to help England conform to Claude's Mediterranean visualization. For those spectators who lacked the imagination to see as Claude might have seen, or for those painters who lacked the artistic skills to paint as he might have painted, there was the 'Claude glass'. This was a tinted convex mirror: the tinting enhanced colours, while the convexity flattened and miniaturized a natural scene into what appeared to be a two-dimensional composition, drawing all the elements together. Detail was lost, but harmony was enhanced: voilà, the picturesque, which drained history, tradition, and folklore from seasonal landscapes and replaced them with an oddly disengaged senti-mentality. To this was added a sometimes frankly bizarre obsession with the sublime, and much ink was spilt on ascertaining how many cows gave the best balance to a painting, the most tonally effective time of day or year to paint flowers and trees, or where best to situate a ruined temple or wild cataract in a composition. And once again, the actual population of the countryside was, quite literally, expunged from the picture, just as it had been physically removed by the Enclosure Acts.

In spite of all this, the seasons still remain not only integral to our identity as a nation today but their heritage also demonstrates that culture can be a vital guide as we march blindly down the dark road of environ-mental change. If we ignore or choose to forget the culture of the seasons that has accumulated over thousands of years, our very humanity risks being eroded forever. Traditionally, our identity has been firmly built on the weather. Televised weather forecasts are a constant reminder of the proximity of the nations, provinces, and regions that make up the British

Isles, of the island mentality, and of separation from Europe and the European climate. Samuel Johnson famously noted over 250 years ago that, 'It is commonly observed, that when two *Englishmen* meet, their first talk is of the weather; they are in haste to tell each other, what each must already know, that it is hot or cold, bright or cloudy, windy or calm.'[1] Weather is unpredictable and yet is continually being predicted, as if in an attempt to master it. But the weather does – or at least did – go through recognizable seasons, each with its own horticultural and agricultural role, and also each with its own character, history, and folklore. Together, they can map out the year, the countryside, and one's place in it. The disappearance of the seasons will therefore erode a shared sense of identity, the present will become cut off from the past, and the culture of the seasons, from Geoffrey Chaucer to T. S. Eliot, will become strange. The ground we walk upon will fundamentally change as familiar flora and fauna become less numerous and are replaced by more aggressive imports such as grey squirrels, ladybugs, and Spanish bluebells.

There is nothing new in this – many apparently indigenous animals and plants, from rabbits to roses, are imports – but the gradual abstraction of seasonal life is accelerating, and alongside it the human aspect, the festive calendar, increasingly appears to be in terminal decline:

> Merry Old England died in the country a great while ago; and the sports, the pastimes, the holidays, the Christmas greens and gambols, the archeries, the may-mornings, the May-poles, the country dances, the masks, the harvest-homes, the new-year's-gifts, the gallantries, the golden means, the poetries, the pleasures, the leisures, the real treasures – were all buried with her.[2]

This nostalgic lament for Merry England does not date from the early twenty-first century, nor even from the early twentieth century, but was written by the poet and radical Leigh Hunt in 1817. It is ironic that it was written before the Victorian age, which through revival and invention has furnished us with so many of the images and impressions, customs and celebrations that seem to characterize the festive year. Indeed, what the English today are often most nostalgic for are traditions that go back no further than the nineteenth century. Nearly all of the current Christmas traditions, for instance, are examples of Victoriana.

But whether some or other Christmas custom was a Victorian invention does not much matter: what is important is how we continue to value these traditions and the ways in which they connect us with both the seasons and our communities, great and small. After all, the glorious poetry of the calendar resides precisely in its flaws, disparities, contradictions, and errors. Indeed, the drift of the Julian calendar (see Chapter 2) meant that even as it was still developing, the Christian calendar was already one day awry by AD 136, and a further day every 128 years or so after that. So the emergence of English folk traditions tied to saints' days – such as rain on St Swithin's Day meaning that it will rain for another forty days – took place at a time when the calendar was perpetually slipping, with the result that calendar-based traditions are not even stable relative to each other. But this, in all its glorious confusion, is what we have inherited, and it still resists every attempt to impose homogeneity upon it. For every year is different. We may have a dry or wet summer, a warm or chilly winter. Harvests may be bountiful or crops may fail. Easter, determined by calculations of hair-raising complexity (see Chapter 6), may fall early or late – and in doing so exerts a huge influence on how we lead our professional and personal lives.

Even now, in this age of all-year strawberries, of aggressively changing flora and fauna, of apocalyptic anxieties about extreme weather and ecological crisis, the calendar can provide reassurance; its rituals and rhythms can still help us to understand the natural world in more 'natural' ways, by which I mean more historical and more cultural ways.[3] This is one of its many prodigious gifts, and so we must beware not to sentimentalize the land or fall victims to the nostalgia of the countryside. But if the seasons and the way we mark their progress do eventually become more remote and if we further loosen our cultural connections with them, what then? What will have been lost when we no longer hear the first cuckoo of spring, or even recognize the first flowers? The sobering answer is an immeasurable amount, and a large and vital part of ourselves. This book is first and foremost a celebration of England's seasons; I hope that it does not also prove to be a memorial to them.

2   THE YEAR

He appointed the moon for seasons:
the sun knoweth his going down.

———————

Psalms 104: 19

Where does our year come from? In one sense, the year exists independent of human society and history, reflecting the cycles of the sun and the moon, which in turn affect the earth's climate and are a key factor in long-term weather patterns. But in another sense the year is clearly a human invention – one of the most significant, if perhaps inevitable, inventions in history, and also one of the most successful. The seasons emerge from the solar, lunar, and calendar years as a rough compromise between nature and culture: between those things that happen independently of human engagement, such as the annual summer solstice, and those things that are dependent on that engagement – naming, recognizing, and celebrating the solstice as being somehow significant. We all know the order of the months of the year, and the number of days in each month, but there is no precise alignment of the months with the seasons, and neither is there a precise alignment of the seasons with the moveable feasts determined by Easter. Easter may be early or late, as calculated by the solar and lunar calendars, but spring too may be early or late – increasingly early, it should be said – depending on whether daffodils are out or cuckoos are calling. The tilt of the earth's axis and the earth's elliptical orbit create seasonal differences, but this only influences weather patterns over time: it does not determine the specific weather on a certain day or in a particular place, or even in a certain year or a particular era. Consequently there is an odd disjuncture when trying to map the months over the seasons: is May in springtime or the summer, should midsummer and midwinter be in the middle of their respective seasons, can autumn really begin as early as August?[1] The weather might 'feel like spring' or there could be 'an autumnal chill in the air', but such observations could apply to almost any season. The seasons are in any case slipping and sliding due to trends measured over decades and centuries, while climate change will dramatically increase the unpredictability of our weather patterns.

The moon orbits the earth approximately once every twenty-nine-and-a-half days (every 29.5306 days, to be precise). As it orbits, it is caught in the light of the sun, which can obviously only ever illuminate one side of the moon. Depending on one's position on earth relative to these stages of illumination, the moon appears to go through phases, waxing as a crescent, first quarter, gibbous, and full moon, and waning through gibbous, last quarter, crescent, and finally the dark moon. The cycle then commences again: traditionally the waxing crescent was known as the new moon, but the new moon is now defined as occurring in the middle of the dark moon phase. Twelve cycles of the moon roughly correspond to the annual cycle of four seasons, and because of the clarity of the moon's phases, the lunar cycle was a convenient early calendar and continues to be used as the Islamic religious calendar, or Hijri.

The lunar year does not, however, correspond with the solar year, which is the time taken for the earth to orbit the sun. This is where things become complicated. First, the earth's orbit is not a perfect circle with the sun at the middle, but is offset and elliptical. The earth also has a tilted axis of rotation – it does not spin on a precisely vertical plane but with a deviation of about 23.5 degrees; this was known at least as far back as ancient Egypt, when the Alexandrian astronomer Eratosthenes (276–194 BC) calculated within one tenth of a degree the tilt in the earth's axis. This tilt is what causes seasonal variation: it means that at different times of the year each hemisphere receives more or less sunlight; the northern hemisphere is inclined towards the sun in June and the southern hemisphere in December. Between these two solstices, there are two moments – the vernal equinoxes – when the equator is perfectly aligned with the ecliptic (the apparent cyclical path of the sun), and the effect of the earth's elliptical orbit means that at these times light from the sun may be of stronger or weaker intensity. The earth's orbit also fluctuates because the earth is not a perfect sphere and because it drifts and wobbles. The moon and every other planet in the solar system exercise some gravitational influence on the earth's orbit, pushing and pulling it out of true; furthermore the earth's oceans, themselves drawn to ebb and flow by the moon, can create a 'tidal drag' on the orbit and perturb the movement of the earth. The extent of these variations depends on how the orbit is defined: whether by measuring the earth's movement from and to a fixed position, this fixed point being calculated in relation to the stars – the sidereal year; or in relation to the earth itself, returning exactly to its own alignment in relation to the sun – the tropical year.

The average sidereal year, calculated for the year 2000, was 365 days, 6 hours, 9 minutes, and 9.7676 seconds; the average tropical year for the same period was 365 days, 5 hours, 48 minutes, and 45 seconds. That twenty-minute variation is not going to affect our everyday lives in any meaningful way, but this is not the case with the lunar year. The lunar year works out at just under 354.5 days long (354.3672 days precisely). This means that the lunar year moves much more swiftly than the solar year – by eleven or twelve days every twelve months. Following a lunar calendar means that within sixteen years the seasons are inverted: spring becomes autumn and summer becomes winter, and *vice versa*. After thirty-three years the lunar and solar years are again approximately in synchronization before the drift begins once more. This is why Ramadan, which is calculated using the Islamic Hijri, appears to be celebrated earlier every calendar year.

The convenience of the lunar cycle and the practical necessity of observing the solar year meant that most early societies developed a hybrid of the two – the luni-solar year. The solar year runs as follows:

21 March: spring equinox with twelve hours of sunlight, twelve hours of night-time (*equinox* meaning 'equal night')

21 September: autumn equinox, likewise

21 June: summer solstice and longest day (from *sol*, meaning 'sun', and *sistere*, 'stand still')

21 December: winter solstice and shortest day

The pagan Saxon calendar was a luni-solar system, which started on 25 December, just after the winter solstice. The names of the months were:

guili, yule, the first and last month of the year

se æftera geōla, 'the latter Yule' (after midwinter – January)

solmōnaþ (month of offering cakes, literally 'dirt-month' – February)

hreþmōnað (month of the goddess Rheda – March, later became hlȳda, 'Lide')

ēastermōnað (month of Ēostre, goddess of spring and twilight – April)

þrimilce (month of the three daily milkings – May)

se ǣrra līþa ('gentle', before midsummer – June)

þrilīþa (third midsummer – intercalated midsummer leap month)

æftera līþa (after midsummer – July)

wēodmōnað (month of the plants – August)

hālegmōnaþ (holy month – September)

winterfylleþ (winter-filled – October)

blōtmōnaþ (month of sacrifice – November)

se ǣrra geōla (before midwinter – December)[2]

There is also some confused evidence about ancient British festivals: the fire festivals of Beltane on 1 May and Samhain ('summer's end') on 31 October may be familiar to some, but there are also the festivals of Imbolc (lactation, the festival of Brighid) on 1 February and of Lammas (also known as Lughnasadh, from Lugh, the god of the harvest) on 1 August. Celtic revivalists have also added Ostara on 21 March and adopted the Welsh figure Mabon vab Modron, who is associated with hunting, poetry, and music, for the Autumn Equinox of Mabon.[3] Some of these names are familiar: guili or geōla is clearly Yule, for example, and Ēostre is the source of the popular name 'Easter' for the Feast of the Passion. The Saxon goddess Ēostre was linked by the Anglo-Saxon monk and chronicler the Venerable Bede to Ostara in De temporum ratione and Bede also mentions the festival of Litha, which has in turn been adopted, and popularized, by J. R. R. Tolkien in his Middle-earth writings. But other festivals listed here only survive as esoteric revivals, and the organization of the English year and the names of the months have other origins.

In the eighth century BC, Romulus – legendary wolf-child, founder of Rome, and slayer of his brother Remus – established Roman society along decimal lines. This meant that not only the numerical system but the vast majority of institutions and social organizations, from representation in the Senate to the military, had a base numerical factor of ten. Consequently, the early Romans favoured a ten-month lunar system. The months were named *Martius* (after Mars, the god of war, and aligned with the vernal equinox), *Aprilis* (perhaps a reference to pig farming), *Maius* (after a seasonal goddess), and *Junius* (after Juno, queen of the gods), before the seductions of decimalization rendered the remaining months *Quintilis*, *Sextilis*, *September*, *October*, *November*, and *December* (i.e., fifth, sixth, seventh, eighth, ninth, and tenth). Months were either hollow (twenty-nine days) or full (thirty days), thereby averaging 29.5 days, the length of the lunar month. The remaining sixty-one days or so needed to synchronize this decimal system with the solar year were 'winter days' that existed outside the named months.[4]

The days themselves were ordered by their proximity to the beginning of the month, the fifth or seventh day, and the middle of the month. These three markers were *kalends* (hence calendar), *nones*, and *ides*, and dates were calculated in terms of how many days they fell before one of these markers. (This system is further complicated today by the Romans not having a number zero, so the marker day is actually day one rather than day zero.) By such reckoning, the first half of March would be:

Modern date	Roman date
1 March	*Kalendis Martiis* [kalends of March]
2 March	*a.d. VI* Nonas Martias* [5 days before nones, where nones is 1]

* *a.d. [ante diem]* VI = 'sixth day before'

3 March	*a.d. V Nonas Martias* [4 days before nones]
4 March	*a.d. IV Nonas Martias* [3 days before nones]
5 March	*a.d. III Nonas Martias* [2 days before nones]
6 March	*pridie Nonas Martias* [day before nones]
7 March	*Nonis Martiis* [nones of March]
8 March	*a.d. VIII Idus Martias* [7 days before ides]
9 March	*a.d. VII Idus Martias* [6 days before ides]
10 March	*a.d. VI Idus Martias* [5 days before ides]
11 March	*a.d. V Idus Martias* [4 days before ides]
12 March	*a.d. IV Idus Martias* [3 days before ides]
13 March	*a.d. III Idus Martias* [2 days before ides]
14 March	*pridie Idus Martias* [day before ides]
15 March	*Idibus Martiis* [ides of March]

Despite the apparent complexity of this daily reckoner, it not only outlasted the Roman Empire, but survived for some two thousand years through the mediaeval period well into the Renaissance. Dating by the Roman kalends is famously invoked by Shakespeare in plays such as *Julius Caesar* – 'Beware the ides of March' – and in the proverbial rhyme:

> March, May, July, October, these are they,
> Make Nones the seventh, Ides the fifteenth day.[5]

The counting of days in numerical sequences known as *dies mensis* – that is, 'days of the month' – only gradually caught on.

The kalends survived then, but not the Romulan year. Numa Pompilius, who succeeded Romulus as king of Rome, added *Januarius* and *Februarius* and rearranged the days of the hollow and full months. This extended the designated year to 354 days, to which Numa added a day for luck: the Romans had superstitions about even numbers, hence his reform of *Februarius*, which at twenty-eight days was split into two oddnumbered parts. Leap months were occasionally added between the two parts of *Februarius*, and these could make the year up to 378 days long. The Numan year was therefore based on the lunar year and so ran ten or eleven days too fast; eventually the Roman year adopted the Greek model of regularly adding months every thirty years or so to average the year at 365 days. Numa may also have made January the first month of the year.

These intercalated months were, however, often overlooked, meaning that by Julius Caesar's reign the calendar was nearly two months adrift – an impossible situation that was hardly conducive to governing an empire. Caesar employed the Alexandrian astronomer Sosigenes, who introduced the Egyptian system of a year of 365.25 days: three years of 365 days and one leap year every four years of 366 days. Finally, to align the new calendar with the solar year, two long intercalary months were added to 46 BC, making that interminable year 445 days long: *ultimus annus confusionis*, 'the last year of confusion'. When it came to the months of the year, Caesar confirmed January as the first month to align the year more closely with the winter solstice, and arranged the months in a pattern alternating between thirty-one and thirty days, in which February had thirty days only in leap years and in other years twenty-nine days. As the historian Suetonius described the reform of the Roman calendar in AD 96, 'Caesar ... reorganized the calendar, which the pontifices had allowed to fall into such disorder, by intercalating days or months as it suited them, that the harvest and vintage festivals no longer corresponded with the appropriate seasons.'[6] The Senate honoured Caesar by renaming the month of *Quintilius* as *Julius*.

Unfortunately, after Caesar's death in 44 BC the frequency of leap years was erroneously increased to a three-year cycle – a confusion arising from counting days inclusively – until Augustus rectified matters in 8 BC by ignoring the next three leap years. Harmony was restored by AD 8 and, remarkably, this 'Julian' calendar has remained impressively stable ever since, requiring only one significant set of revisions. The Senate renamed *Sextilis* as *Augustus* in the emperor's honour, as it had proved an auspicious month for him. But the month of *Augustus* had only thirty days in the original Julian system, so this was raised to thirty-one days to put *Augustus* on the same footing as the month of *Julius*. February was again obliged to surrender a day and now only had twenty-eight days, twenty-nine in a leap year. Moreover, there was now a run of three thirty-one-day months over the summer and autumn, so the lengths of September and November were swapped with October and December. And that rather opportunistic fiddling has survived for two millennia to the present day.

The Julian calendar can be seen as a revolution in the ways in which individuals and human society conceived themselves in relation to time. Time had previously been understood in cycles of weather and therefore farming, or, as the writer David Ewing Duncan describes it, had been an instrument of power:

> But no more. Now the calendar was available to everyone as a practical, objective tool to organize shipping schedules, grow crops, worship gods, plan marriages and send letters to friends. Combined with the rising popularity of sophisticated sundials and water clocks, the new Julian calendar introduced the concept of human beings ordering their own individual lives along a linear progression operating independent of the moon, the seasons and the gods.[7]

There were other, equally long-lasting innovations. By the sixth century BC the Roman week was eight days long. This model, adopted from the Etruscans, was known as the nundinal week – meaning 'ninth': the *nundina* was the market day and a fixed point of reference. However, a seven-day week system had been established in ancient Babylon, coincidentally at about the same time as the inception of the Romulan calendar, and corresponding to the seven 'planets'. Eventually the two systems met under the Roman Empire, and after a brief and not surprisingly unsuccessful attempt to run the two systems alongside each other, the seven-day week was increasingly favoured from the first century AD. In AD 329, the seven-day week was officially proclaimed by the first Christian Roman emperor, Constantine the Great, who also introduced Sunday – *dies solis*, 'sun-day' – as a regular holy day in the week.[8]

This ancient seven-day week system, some 2,700 years old, is still at least half-recognizable today: Sol (sun) day, Luna (moon) day, Mars day, Mercury day, Jupiter day, Venus day, Saturn day. These planets clearly form the basis of Romance-language days of the week, such as the French *lundi*, *mardi*, *mercredi*, *jeudi*, and *vendredi*. In England, however, the Anglo-Saxons who settled Britain after the collapse of the Roman Empire combined the Babylonian-Roman-Christian seven-day week with their own Norse mythology, introducing Tiw, Woden, Thor, and Freya as substitutes for Mars, Mercury, Jupiter, and Venus, and these names seem to have been retained by Pope Gregory at the time of the conversion of Britain.

Constantine's adoption and semi-Christianization of the seven-day week clearly paid homage to the creation of the world in the first chapters of Genesis, but was not without controversy. Sunday now conflicted with the Jewish Sabbath (Saturday), itself observed by some Christians as a holy day, and many pagan Romans also held Saturn's day as sacred. Interestingly, though, Constantine's adoption of Sunday may well have placated the Roman Mithraists, pagans who worshipped the Sun and who had a discernible influence on nascent Christian institutions. Meanwhile in Egypt, Ptolemy produced an encyclopedia in the second century AD that remained a reference work for over a thousand years by virtue of its modelling of astronomical movements, and its calculation of months and years, eclipses and equinoxes.

Constantine had in fact already instituted major calendrical reforms at the Council of Nicaea in AD 325. This famous and long-running congress, at what is now Iznik in modern Turkey, effectively Christianized the Julian calendar by establishing specific dates for Christian festivals such as Christmas, and simultaneously adapted the Jewish luni-solar calendar prevalent in Judea in Christ's own lifetime to calculate the date of Easter – thereby creating 'immoveable' and 'moveable' feasts respectively. Constantine's aim was to reach a Christian consensus for Easter, declaring at Nicaea, 'By the unanimous judgment of all, it has been decided that the most holy festival of Easter should be everywhere celebrated on one and the same day.'[9] The argument was that without an agreed and reliable foundation for the most holy of days, Christianity would be condemned to sectarianism, heresy, and schism – as it had been in the first three centuries of its existence. More practically, if the Church was to have a state role, it had to secularize.[10]

The calculation of Easter is discussed in detail below (see Chapter 6). What was not, however, known at the time of the Nicaean Council was that the solar year is about eleven minutes longer than the Julian year, meaning that the solar year was advancing by about a day every 128 years and that by the time of the Council the calendar year was already nearly three days fast. In other words, settling Christmas Day, say, as 25 December simply compounded the error by fixing the wrong date.[11] But in the event it took nearly a thousand years for this to become apparent. By 1267, the English Franciscan friar and philosopher Roger Bacon had calculated that the calendar year was several days behind the solar year.[12] Not only did this mean that the months were slipping back into earlier seasons, but every holy day was being observed at the wrong time, making a mockery of the secular authority of the Church. Moreover, Constantine had determined that the Christian calendar had to some extent to depend on the luni-solar year, as Easter had to be calculated from the spring equinox (mid-way between the winter and summer solstices). But the Council had themselves fixed the spring equinox to 21 March, and by 1267 the true spring equinox was actually on 12 March: nine days before the official date. Bacon was not the first to notice this. Bede had divined that there was a problem, but was content to claim that God's time had precedence over human systems; and since the ninth century significant doubt had been cast on the accuracy of the Church calendar by scholars across Europe – notably by the memorably named Notker the Stammerer and Hermann the Lame. But Bacon was the first to go to the Vatican. His point being that natural time and God's time were (or should be) one and the same, he argued that:

> The errors I have mentioned are terrible in themselves, yet they bear no comparison to those which follow from the facts now stated. For the whole order of Church solemnities is thrown into confusion by errors

of this kind respecting the beginning of the lunation according to the Calendar, as well as by the error in determining the equinoxes. And not to refer to other years for evidence of this error, I shall state the case in this present year. . . . Wherefore the feast of Easter, by which the world is saved, will not be celebrated at its proper time, but there is fasting this year through the whole true week of Easter. For the fast continues eight days longer than it should. There follows then another disadvantage that the fast of Lent began eight days too late; therefore Christians were eating meats in the true Lent for eight days, which is absurd. And again then neither the Rogations nor the Ascension nor Pentecost are kept this year at their proper times. And as it happens in this year 1267, so will it happen the year following.[13]

Bacon, for his pains, was ignored, but others began to notice. The first popular printed 'Shepherd's Calendar' appeared around 1500.[14] The printing and dissemination of printed calendars and their study by astrologers, astronomers, theologians, and mathematicians inevitably drew attention to the glaring discrepancy between the Julian calendar and the solar year, which by 1500 amounted to nearly ten days. Chief among these problems was the reliability of the date of Easter – the major Christian festival. Christian astronomers had favoured the Metonic cycle for calculating Easter, a system based on the work of Meton of Athens in the fifth century BC. Meton discovered that nineteen solar years were equivalent to 235 lunar months, and this equation was used by Christian astronomers to create tables of Easter dates from the third century AD. However, this measurement drifted as well – by one-and-a-half hours in every cycle, or a day every 312.7 years – so by the sixteenth century it was four days adrift. The Metonic cycle was scrapped in the 1570s after the calculations of the Italian physician, astronomer, and chronologist Aloysius Lilius, and it was Lilius' work that inspired Pope Gregory XIII (1502–85) to reform the Julian calendar in 1582 and thereby establish the Gregorian calendar.

At the same time, the German mathematician and astronomer Nicolaus Copernicus had instigated an astronomical revolution by replacing the traditional geocentric model, in which the heavens revolved around the earth, with a heliocentric model, in which the planets, including the earth, revolved around the sun.[15] *De revolutionibus orbium coelestium* ('On the Revolutions of the Celestial Spheres') was published just before Copernicus' death in 1543 and was dedicated to Pope Paul III. Heliocentrism therefore had implications for the computation of the calendar in defining the solar year. Copernicus distinguished between the seasonal or tropical year, based on the cycle of the seasons and therefore on the length of time between the vernal equinoxes, 'when the planes of the equator and the sun's ecliptic intersect in the spring' – this roughly conformed to the Julian year – and the star or sidereal year, the time taken by the earth to complete an orbit of the sun and return to the same position, externally determined.[16] Copernicus not only found fluctuations in the lunar year, but also calculated that the earth's rotational tilt causes the tropical year to run about twenty minutes faster than the sidereal year – a phenomenon known as the precession of the equinoxes. Moreover, the earth's tendency to wobble on its axis also means that the tropical year is variable. He therefore favoured the sidereal year as the basis for his calculations.

———

Once the calculations had been accepted, calendar reform was in one sense very simple. Since its foundation, the Julian year had run slightly slow compared with the solar year. By 1582, this discrepancy amounted to ten days, so all that had to be done was to shift the calendar by that many days. October was selected as the month for the reform as it had comparatively few holy days or saints' days. Gregory therefore issued a papal bull proclaiming that at midnight on 4 October 1582 Roman Catholic countries should move straight to 14 October. The new Gregorian calendar would then follow and correspond to the Julian with one exception: to eliminate future Julian drift, leap years would be observed except in those years that were divisible by 100 but not by 400, when the leap day should be suppressed.

There was also another anomaly: there was no consensus over the first day of the year, just several contenders. The first of January had been instituted by Caesar and was incorporated in the Julian calendar: *Januarius* (or *Ianuarius*), from *ianua*, 'door', was associated with the two-faced god Janus – looking back at the old year and forward to the new year. The first of January was therefore traditionally favoured by the populace (*stylus communis*) and had been Christianized as the Feast of the Circumcision (*stylus circumcisionis*); it also had traditional festivities associated with it. Theologically speaking, however, Christmas Day had a strong claim as the first day of the year because of the birth of Christ (*stylus nativitatis*), and this was also the day on which the Papal Chancellery sometimes began its year (*stylus curiae Romanae*).[17] Alternatively, 25 March – the date of the Annunciation (*stylus annunciatonis*, or *stylus incarnationis*), nine months before the birth of Christ – was a plausible option, and was also close to the vernal equinox, the traditional New Year of the pre-Julian calendars. Good Friday and Easter Day similarly had claims. Gregory's decision was to make 1 January New Year's Day for 1583 and ever after.

Unfortunately, however, the new Gregorian calendar was not universally adopted. While it was straightaway accepted by Italy, Spain, and Portugal, some Catholic countries such as France, Belgium, and parts of the Netherlands did not act until December – which rather ridiculously meant sacrificing the major festival of Christmas Day. The English merchant and informant Thomas Stokes wrote to Queen Elizabeth's principal secretary, Sir Francis Walsingham, from Bruges just before Christmas was due to fall. He was amazed:

> Yesterday by proclamation from the Court, and proclaimed here in this town, 'that yesterday' was appointed to be New Year's Day and to be the first of January; so they have lost Christmas Day here for this year.
> – Bruges, the 23 December 1582, 'stillo anglea' [English style]; and here they write the 2 January 1583.[18]

The new Gregorian calendar was also ignored of course by Protestants in Germany and Denmark, and in England and its colonies. Interestingly, though, Walsingham did ask the mathematician, astrologer, and occultist John Dee to report on the 1582 Gregorian bull. Dee made a thorough investigation in a long treatise: 'A playne Discourse and humble Advise for our Gratious Queen Elizabeth, her most Excellent Majestie to peruse and consider, as concerning the needful Reformation of the Vulgar Kalendar for the civile years and daies accompting, or verifyeng, according to the time truely spent'.[19] The work was prefaced with some intellectual doggerel:

> As Caesar and Sosigenes,
> The vulgar kalendar did make,
> So Caesar's Pere, our true Empress,
> To Dee this work she did betake.

> To finde the Dayes superfluous,
> (which Caesar's false Hypothesis,
> Had bred; to Nature, odious:)
> Wherein, he found eleven amyss.

> For he, from Christ, Chief Root of time
> The time did try, by heavenly wit:
> No Councell can deme this a crime
> From CHRIST, to us, tear time to fit.

> ELIZABETH our Empress bright,
> Who in the yere of eighty three,
> Thus made the truth to come to light,
> And civile yere with heaven agree.

> But eighty foure, the Pattern is
> Of Christ's birth yere: and so for ay
> Eche Bissext shall fall little mys,
> To shew the sun of Christ birth day.

Three hundred yeres, shall not remove
The sun, one day, from this new match:
Nature, no more shall us reprove
Her golden tyme, so yll to watch.

The God of might, our father dere,
Whose rayng no tyme can comprehend,
Good time our Elizabeth grant here
And Bliss aeternall, at her ende.

Amen.[20]

Dee himself supported reform, although he refused to date the revision
back to the Council of Nicaea and argued for dating it from the time of
Christ ('Chief Root of time'), which would make a loss of eleven days,
rather than ten ('Christians should regard his [Christ's] birth as the
"Radix of Time",' according to Dee). In other words, Dee's was another
Protestant reformation against the perceived lies of Roman Catholicism,
even if it was admittedly inspired by a papal bull, although he later
moderated his demands to concur with the Council of Nicaea. He also
drafted a revised calendar for 1583, the *Annus Reformationis*, which would
be followed by 'Queen Elizabeth's perpetual Kalendar'. Dee's judicious
recommendation was to drop three days from May, one from June, and
three from both July and August: this was potentially far less disrup-
tive than a sudden change, and much more sagacious than the apparently self-flagellating zeal on display in France and Belgium that had
righteously cancelled Christmas 1582. Dee sent his results to the queen's
commission, and the queen herself may have appreciated the hand of
an earlier Englishman, the mediaeval philosopher Roger Bacon, in the
reform, thereby defusing some of the papist associations of the change.
An Act was read in Parliament in March 1583 – arguably reform was supported despite, and not because of, Dee – and the plan was approved
for implementation in May.[21] However, the archbishop of Canterbury,
Edmund Grindal, and other leading bishops refused to add their consent,

requesting further, procrastinating discussion. Thus the reform foundered. Dee fought on using astronomical, economic, and maritime arguments, but that was the last time that the matter was seriously debated in England for 166 years.[22]

While the Scots adopted the Gregorian reform in 1600 and the German and Danes accepted it in 1700 (although they continued to calculate Easter in their own way until 1775), the English and their colonies seemed to take a perverse pride in remaining loyal to the Julian calendar, distinguishing dates as being Old Style (OS, following the Julian calendar) or New Style (NS, following the Gregorian calendar). Indeed, nothing further was seriously proposed until 10 May 1750, when George Parker, the earl of Macclesfield, delivered a paper to the Royal Society which was published in the same year with the ponderous title *Remarks upon the Solar and the Lunar Years, the Cycle of 19 Years, commonly called the Golden Number, the Epact, and a Method of Finding the Time of Easter, as it is now observed in most Parts of Europe*. Macclesfield based his argument on the assumption that the Julian year of 365 days and 6 hours was adrift, and in doing so he relied upon Edmund Halley's calculation that the solar year was 365 days, 5 hours, 48 minutes, and 55 seconds long.

There things might have rested as an academic footnote, but for Philip Dormer Stanhope, earl of Chesterfield, aristocrat, man of letters, and leader of taste, taking up the cause. Chesterfield was perplexed that only England, Sweden, and Russia reckoned time outside the Gregorian reform: 'It was not, in my opinion very honourable for England to remain in a gross and avowed error, especially in such company; the inconveniency of it was likewise felt by all those who had foreign correspondences, whether political or mercantile'.[23] Chesterfield commenced a campaign to raise public awareness of the issue, writing pseudonymous articles for the weekly humorous magazine *The World* and drafting reformist legislation.

The response was lukewarm. Nevertheless in 1751 Chesterfield introduced a bill to Parliament: 'An Act for Regulating the Commencement of the Year, and for Correcting the Calendar now in Use'. As he later explained to his son:

I had brought a bill into the House of Lords, for correcting and reforming our present calendar.... It was notorious, that the Julian Calendar was erroneous, and had overcharged the solar year with eleven days.... I determined, therefore, to attempt the reformation; I consulted the best lawyers, and the most skilful astronomers, and we cooked up a bill for that purpose. But then my difficulty began; I was to bring in this bill, which was necessarily composed of law jargon and astronomical calculations, to both of which I am an utter stranger. However, it was absolutely necessary to make the House of Lords think that I knew something of the matter; and also to make them believe that they knew something of it themselves, which they do not. For my own part, I could just as soon have talked Celtic or Sclavonian to them, as astronomy, and they would have understood me full as well: so I resolved to do better than speak to the purpose, and to please instead of informing them. I gave them, therefore, only an historical account of calendars, from the Egyptian down to the Gregorian, amusing them now and then with little episodes; but I was particularly attentive to the choice of my words, to the harmony and roundness of my periods, to my elocution, to my action. This succeeded, and ever will succeed; they thought I informed, because I pleased them; and many of them said, that I had made the whole very clear to them; when, God knows, I had not even attempted it.[24]

Although Chesterfield was warned 'not to stir matters that had long been quiet', the bill was passed on 17 May and received royal assent on 22 May.[25] It was a victory for style: for the New Style.

As had happened in Europe in 1582, the consequence of this decision was to remove several days from the calendar in England, Wales, and the British colonies. Eleven days rather than ten were now needed to set things straight: Wednesday 2 September 1752 was followed by Thursday 14 September. The Act also stipulated that Easter would be calculated under the Gregorian system, and that the new year would begin on 1 January rather than 25 March. The details were carefully worked out: court dates, holidays, 'Meetings and Assemblies of any Bodies Politick or Corporate', elections and so forth were calculated according to the new method and so effectively took place eleven days earlier. However, rents, contracts, wages, and so forth were counted by actual or 'natural' days, so the eleven lost days did not directly cost anyone anything. Likewise, coming of age, indentures, criminal sentences, and the like were determined by natural days rather than the new dating system, as were markets and fairs. The Church of England was behind the reform, declaring 'The New Style the True Style'.

Despite the claims of popular history, there were no calendar riots following this legislation.[26] There were objections from various quarters, but these generally reflected a resistance to modernization and notions of rationalist or Newtonian time, an ill-informed confusion about when dates would now fall for rents and for fairs, or a conservative adherence to the old ways of the Church and a sense of what distinguished England from the continent.[27] The antiquary John Latimer, for example, reported that the Holy Thorn at Glastonbury, which traditionally flowered on Christmas Day, 'contemptuously ignored the new style [and] burst into blossom on the 5th of January, thus indicating that Old Christmas Day should alone be observed, in spite of an irreligious legislature'. Likewise, the *Gentleman's Magazine* for January 1753 reported:

> Glastonbury.—A vast concourse of people attended the noted thorn on Christmas-day, new style; but, to their great disappointment, there was no appearance of its blowing, which made them watch it narrowly the 5th of January, the Christmas-day, old style, when it blowed as usual.

The *London Daily Advertiser* of 5 January 1753 also claimed that a Holy Thorn in Quainton had not blossomed on 25 December NS – a non-event witnessed by over two thousand people – and the Holy Oak in the New Forest also adhered to the old calendar by blossoming on Old Christmas Day rather than New Christmas Day. However, the *Gloucester Journal* of 2 January 1753 confirmed that the real Glastonbury Thorn had actually blossomed according to the New Style.[28]

Most newspapers noted the change and moved on, perhaps pausing to make some droll observation. In the *Gentleman's Magazine* for September 1752, a correspondent quipped to 'Mr Inspector',

> I Write to you in the greatest perplexity, I desire you'll find some way of setting my affair to rights; or I believe I shall run mad, and break my heart into the bargain. How is all this? I desire to know plainly and truly! I went to bed last night, it was *Wednesday Sept. 2*, and the first thing I cast my eye upon this morning at the top of your paper was *Thursday, Sept. 14*. I did not go to bed till between one and two: Have I slept away 11 days in 7 hours, or how is it? For my part I don't find I'm any more refresh'd than after a common night's sleep.
>
> They tell me there's an act of parliament for this. With due reverence be it spoken, I have always thought there were [v]ery few things a *British* parliament could not do, but if I had been ask'd, I should have guess'd the annihilation of time was one of them![29]

There were some drawbacks to calendar reform. An incident was reported in Bristol on 6 January 1753 (that is, 26 December Old Style):

> Yesterday being Old Christmas Day, the same was obstinately observed by our Country People in general, so that yesterday (which was Market-Day according to the Order of our Magistrates) there were but few at Market, who embraced the Opportunity of raising their Butter to 9^d and 10^d a Pound.[30]

Because of the timing of rent days, hiring days, fairs, the sacred calendar, and so forth, the old dating could not realistically persist. As the poet and abolitionist William Cowper commented in 'A Fable', ''Twas April, as the bumpkins say, / The legislature call'd it May'.[31] Yet an adherence to the Old Style did survive a surprisingly long time. The folklorist Ella Mary Leather recorded a Herefordshire apostate in 1912 remembering:

'My grandfather always kept up Christmas on old Christmas day,' said W– P– of Peterchurch, 'none of your new Christmas for him; it must be the real Christmas, too, for the Holy Thorn blossoms, and the cattle go down on their knees at twelve o'clock in remembrance.' I have talked to many people who firmly believed this; though they had not seen it, their parents or grandparents have.[32]

On the other hand, there was the experience of the Revd Dr Waugh talking to his father's gardener, who informed him that the 'craws' (rooks) always began building twelve days after Candlemas. Waugh asked whether the craws counted by the Old Style or the New Style, 'just then introduced by Act of Parliament. Turning upon the young student a look of contempt, the old gardener said, "Young man, craws care naething for Acts of Parliament!"'[33]

In fact, English society still resolutely observes a vestige of the Julian calendar in one aspect of every citizen's – or at least every taxpayer's – life. The English year had begun on 25 March, and in one area continued to do so. The bankers refused to make 31 December the end of the financial year and were not even prepared to adopt 25 March (New Style). Instead, they refused to pay any taxes until 365 days had elapsed from the last date of taxation, which delayed the financial year until 5 April, Old Lady Day. Another adjustment of a day was made for the leap century in 1800, moving it to 6 April – and that was the last adjustment made: by 1900, the debates about 1752 had been forgotten. Henceforth, the financial year in England has always run for twelve months, including leap days. Today it runs from 6 April to 5 April the following year: effectively the Julian New Year, New Style.

Some also argue that there are continuing problems with the Gregorian calendar. As it stands, the year is indivisible: 365.25 cannot be easily divided into any units. So in a twenty-eight-year cycle the days drift by one day every year and two days after every leap year, meaning that events are never on the same day in successive years; likewise, weeks also move within months. Furthermore, there is no year zero in AD dating (now sometimes known as CE, 'Common Era' – another pointless abstraction), which means that new centuries and new millennia should really be celebrated in years beginning –01 or –001, and the new year does not properly begin until 1 a.m. on the morning of 1 January, as pedants such as the author of this book are keen to point out. The Gregorian calendar runs fast by 25.96 seconds a year, which counting from 1582 will be a whole day by AD 4909. And of course the days in each month, the last four of which are now erroneously named, are arranged in part to honour ancient, if not forgotten, Roman emperors.

Consequently, a World (or Universal) Calendar has been proposed. It would alternate the distribution of days in a month as trios of thirty-one, thirty, and thirty – which, ironically, rather reverts to the original Julian arrangement. In such a model each year and each quarter would therefore commence on a Sunday, and each month would always start on the same day. A 'Worlds Day' [sic], outside the weekly and monthly computation, would be added at the end of the year, and leap days would be added as extras at the end of June – features reminiscent of the earliest Roman calendars, the Romulan and Numan.[34]

Such an attempt to stabilize the fluidities and idiosyncrasies of the calendar would not only sunder further the relationship between the present and the past, but would also make the year, quite frankly, rather boring. Part of the attraction, the liveliness, the character of the calendar is its mutability, the restless movement of dates such as birthdays from one day to the next (with the occasional leap-frog), the mysterious rhythm of thirty- and thirty-one-day months, the oddity of February. It is not even as if the Gregorian calendar has become wholly accepted across the Western world. Not only does the Eastern Christian Church still calculate Easter differently to the Western Church, despite having adopted the Gregorian calendar, but there remain pockets of Paleoimerologites (Old Calendarists) adhering to the Julian calendar in Jerusalem, Russia, Serbia, and Greece. They are a good reminder of times past: perhaps, in putting culture before astronomy, the Old Calendarists have the right idea.

3 MONTHS AND DAYS

Behold the man, who did the heav'ns survey...
Whence winds arise, which o'er the ocean blow,
And into rage transform his peaceful brow;
By what magnetic pow'r and influence rare
The pond'rous earth suspends and rolls in air;
Why rising stars adorn the blushing east,
And lose their lustre in the dusky west;
Why the returning seasons of the spring,
Instruct the flow'rs to blow, the birds to sing;
Why the rich grape in yellow autumn swells,
And cheerfully the generous goblet fills.

Boethius, *De consolatione philosophiae*

Thirtie dais hath September,
Aprill June and November
Februarie twentie and eight alone
And all the rest have thirtie & one.

This familiar rhyme was first written down over 450 years ago in the Stevins Manuscript (*c*.1553–4).[1] A dozen or so years later a simplified version of the mnemonic was printed in Richard Grafton's introduction to the *Abridgement of the Chronicles of England* (1570):

Thirty dayes hath November,
Aprill, June and September.
February hath xxviii alone,
And all the rest have xxxi.[2]

It is a very handy summary of the Gregorian variations, and probably the only piece of traditional wisdom that so concisely covers the entire year. There is much proverbial lore for each individual season, month, and day (and it is here distributed under the various seasonal chapters), but the year itself receives limited attention and there are only a handful of short-hand accounts for the whole year. The agriculturalist and poet Thomas Tusser, for example, author of *A Hundreth Good Pointes of Husbandrie* (1557), later expanded into *Five Hundreth Points of Good Husbandry* (1573), wrote 'A sonet or brief rehersall of the properties of the twelve monethes afore rehersed':

As Janever fryse pot, bidth come kepe hym lowe:
And feverell fill dyke, doth good with his snowe:
A bushel of Marche dust, worth raunsomes of gold:
And Aprill his stormes, be too good to be solde:
As May with his flowers, geve ladies their lust:
And June after blooming, set carnels so just:
As July bid all thing, in order to ripe:
And August bid reapers, to take full their gripe.
September his fruit, biddeth gather as fast:
October bid hogges: to come eate up his mast:
As dirtie November, bid threshe at thine ease:
December bid Christmas, to spende what he please:
> So wisdom bid kepe, and provide while we may:
> For age crepeth on as the time passeth away.[3]

This is about as good as it gets. There is simply not enough room for every daily, monthly, or seasonal detail to be included if the complete year is to be encompassed within a few lines. Poets from the Elizabethan Edmund Spenser to the Romantic John Clare tended to write much more detailed monthly sequences – shepherds' calendars – to describe the annual cycle of natural change and farming activities. Anything more simplistic was either going to be poetic flim-flam, or comic. The late-eighteenth-century writer and editor George Ellis came up with perhaps the pithiest description of the annual cycle in 'The Twelve Months':

Snowy, Flowy, Blowy,
Showery, Flowery, Bowery,
Hoppy, Croppy, Droppy,
Breezy, Sneezy, Freezy.[4]

Much more recently, the comic duo Flanders and Swann and the poet Wendy Cope have come up with 'A Song of the Weather' and 'The English Weather' respectively – both somewhat darker in tone and more rain-sodden than Ellis's skit.[5] Shakespeare too jests briefly on the character of the months in *As You Like It*, perhaps alluding to a country maxim:

> men are April when they woo, December when they wed; maids are May when they are maids, but the sky changes when they are wives.[6]

Yet just moving from one month to the next entails various arcane obligations. In addition to pinching and punching on the first day of the month, 'Hares' should be the last word one says on the last day of a month, and 'Rabbits' the first word the next morning – and there are local variants dictating the number of times and precisely when the word should be said. Little about the monthly calendar is simple or straightforward.

————

Up to the middle of the nineteenth century, the British economy was primarily determined by the weather; it still exercises a significant effect today.[7] In the past, weather patterns would affect the harvest and consequently the material conditions of the lower and labouring classes, as well as having an impact on the higher echelons of society. Organization and experience – and an awareness of the latest scientific discoveries and innovations – were therefore crucial in planning and pursuing the farming year and in responding to both the weather and the contingencies of growing crops and raising livestock. This remains the case, as even modern weather forecasts can be extremely unreliable. But clearly one of the reasons that the clarity of the seasons is disappearing from the national consciousness is precisely because most of us are no longer involved in tending our own crops and stock, or in hunting, gathering, or gleaning: such activities are either no longer widely practised or even ruled unlawful, so the language and terminology withers, distinctions lapse, and culture disappears.

This is a great loss, for the English rural vocabulary is a treasury of striking words and phrases. 'Dilling', for instance, meant the youngest of a family or a brood – related to darling and dearling, and also possibly

the Anglo-Saxon diminutive -*ling*, as in gosling and kitling; it also meant
a favourite child, or the smallest: hence 'dilly-pig' for a tiny piglet.[8] Some
words one can guess at from their sound: 'flothering' (flowers that lie
straggling on the ground and need to be tied up), 'quiddle' (to suck, as
a child sucks her thumb), 'scranny' (wild, crazy, driving to distraction).[9]
Indeed, it is worth noting that English rural vocabulary was for centuries
an extensive and specialist lexicon, enabling subtle distinctions to be made
in categories of everyday rural work, from livestock and arable farming, to
hunting and the weather: 'scrails' and 'sprawts', for instance, are cuttings
left by hedgers, 'stelms' or 'stembles' are tree shoots that grow after old
wood has been cut down (and where the best nuts could be found), and
'it is come' described the process by which milk coagulated into butter
or cheese:

> Come, butter, come,
> Come, butter, come!
> Peter stands at the gate
> Waiting for a butter'd cake;
> *Come, butter, come!*[10]

This language weaves through the poetry of Michael Drayton, Thomas
Herrick, and John Clare – and of course Shakespeare was always alive to
the allure of the rural vocabulary: in *The Winter's Tale* he refers to ''leven
wether tods', meaning that eleven fleeces of castrated yearling rams make
up a 'tod', a statutory weight of 28 pounds.[11]

The demands of agriculture once meant that there was a huge market
in books offering advice for the farming year. These were known as
almanacs, and by the later seventeenth century they were outselling every
other publication by far – including the Bible. Almanacs combined three
varieties of essential information: first, the almanac proper gave details of
astronomical events, eclipses, conjunctions, and moveable feasts, based
on the calculation of Easter; second, the 'kalendar' listed days of the week
by date, months, and fixed festivals; and finally, the 'prognostication' was

the astrological forecast for the year. These three components were often sold within one publication that also included all sorts of other useful everyday information. Many of the earliest examples used symbols rather than letters, with pictures to indicate saints' days, feast days, or signs of the zodiac, but with increasing rates of literacy, and the growing complexity of farming, by the sixteenth century they could be purchased together in a pocket-book format with additional pages for notes and observations. Broadside versions – that is, large poster-size copies – were also available to display on walls.

Almanacs were essentially manuals for living and their primary purpose was to provide a timetable for husbandry, arable farming – sowing, planting, and so forth – and other necessary jobs. The moon was steadfastly believed to affect the planting of crops, so the lunar information contained in almanacs assisted farmers in planning their planting and slaughter around different phases of the moon, as is still the case today on some farms.[12] Almanacs also offered recommendations for domestic activities and home medical care, the moon, again, being efficacious in curing warts.[13] They also contained instructions for forecasting the weather. For example, the Jewish astrologer Erra Pater's *Pronostycacyon For Ever*, first published in 1540, and the mathematician Leonard Digges's *A Prognostication of Right Good Effect Fructfully Augmented*, published in 1555 and subsequently reissued as *A Prognostication Everlasting*, both provided instructions for weather forecasting based on which day of the week New Year fell. On the other hand 'Godfridus', the pseudonymous author of *The Boke of Knowledge of Thynges Unknowen* (1554), based his weather forecasting on the day of the week on which Christmas Day was celebrated.

These forms of divination of course went much further. Almanacs counselled on unlucky days – known as 'Egyptian Days' and recalling a prejudice against foreigners and gypsies that went back to Anglo-Saxon times – but beyond such suspicions, they were also important handbooks of astrology, a discipline that, in the sixteenth century, appeared to provide a reliable intellectual framework for accurate weather prognostication. Astrology was a science, a science based on observable effects: the effects of celestial bodies on the earth and therefore on its weather, and on its inhabitants. It was distinguished by being a long-established science with roots in the venerable centres of ancient civilization – Babylon, Greece, Rome, Egypt, and the Arab world. This meant that like any academic discipline, astrology was not a single, consistent tradition but a series of schools of thought that had developed through the ages: there are major differences, for example, between ancient, mediaeval, Renaissance, and indeed modern techniques for casting horoscopes. The English astrological tradition was derived principally from Ptolemy's *Tetrabiblos*, which dates from the second century AD, but Ptolemy's advances took over a thousand years to reach Britain, and so astrology was not a part of the Anglo-Saxon understanding of the world.[14]

General predictions in 'judicial astrology' covered major events such as eclipses and conjunctions, which in turn enabled projections to be made regarding the weather, harvests, epidemics, politics, and war – in other words, the overall state of society. Consequently, astrology inspired early meteorological record-keeping in, for example, John Goad's *Astro-Meteorologia, or Aphorisms and Discourses of Bodies Coelestial* of 1686.[15] Other branches focused on the needs of the individual. Careful attention to the moon, again, was not just recommended for farmers, for women, and for those afflicted by warts, but was required preparation for anyone planning a long journey.

Astrology posits a single astronomical system in which the sun and six 'planets' – the moon, Saturn, Jupiter, Mars, Venus, and Mercury – move across a map of the twelve constellations or 'houses' of the zodiac. The position of each planet within each house has different implications for those who fall under its influence, and these effects can be discerned by means of plotting the relationships between planets and houses in a horoscope. Astrology is therefore based on regular cycles of astronomical movements, and this regularity is moreover linked to the seasons and the weather in a principle of repetition: astrologers, as the British historian Keith Thomas describes them, 'assumed a division of the universe whereby the superior, immutable bodies of the celestial world ruled over the terrestrial or sublunary sphere, where all was mortality and change'.[16] The cycles of day and night, and of the seasons, were all produced by these celestial rhythms. It was clear, for instance, that if the tides of the oceans ebbed and flowed under the influence of the moon, then so did human fortunes. Such beliefs were doggedly adhered to well into the nineteenth century. 'He's a going out with the tide,' says Mr Peggotty of Mr Barkis in Charles Dickens's *David Copperfield* (1849–50), explaining:

> 'People can't die, along the coast ... except when the tide's pretty nigh out. They can't be born, unless it's pretty nigh in – not properly born, till flood. He's a going out with the tide. It's ebb at half arter three, slack water half-an-hour. If he lives 'till it turns, he'll hold his own till past the flood, and go out with the next tide.'[17]

Such lunar learning appeared to confirm the close relationship between human life and environmental cycles. Consequently, horoscopes could be cast not only to explain events in the past and the present, but also, because of the predictability of celestial movements, to discern what the future held.

Human moods and emotions likewise ebbed and flowed under these influences. The theory of humours linked anatomy and psychology to the weather and the seasons, and so the influence of the heavens on the human body was simply another factor in the great 'chain of being' – another proof of the connection between heaven and earth. It was understood that the four sublunary elements – earth, air, fire, and water – were constantly responding to the pull of celestial bodies, affecting human physiology and by turns physical and mental health. Even the new, rationalist, mechanical science seemed to support such conclusions with discoveries such as the regular circulation of the blood.[18] Astrology therefore fitted neatly into the Renaissance cosmology of the humours: it was required training for practising everything from medicine to botany, from psychiatry to ethnography – and also of course for meteorology.

Until the seventeenth century this was how the Western world explained the way it worked: astrology was science, and it was indisputable. As the Elizabethan explorer, historian, and poet Sir Walter Raleigh plaintively remarked:

> certainely it cannot be doubted, but the Starres are instruments of farre greater use, then to give an obscure light, and for men to gaze on after Sunne-set: it being manifest, that the diversitie of seasons, the Winters, and Summers, more hote and colde, are not so uncertained by the Sunne and Moone alone, who always keepe one and the same course, but that the Starres have also their working therein.
>
> And if we cannot denie, but that God hath given vertues to Springs and Fountaines, to cold earth, to plants and stones, Mineralls, and to the excrementall parts of the basest living creatures, why should we robbe the Beautifull Starres of their working powers? For seeing they are many in number, and of eminent beauty and magnitude, wee may not thinke, that in the treasurie of his wisdom, who is infinite, there can be wanting (even for everie Starre) a peculiar virtue and operation; as every herbe, plant, fruit, and flower adorning the face of the Earth, hath the like.[19]

Conflict arose, however, between astrology and Christianity as the Protestant Reformation began to saturate the nation's consciousness and the relationship between God and humankind fundamentally shifted. Many astrologers were devoutly Christian, from pre-Reformation Roman Catholics to seventeenth-century Quaker sectarians. They saw no contradiction between their science and their beliefs, not least because the signs of the zodiac and also of the sun and moon appeared in plenty of churches, and churches themselves were built facing the east and the rising sun.[20] But other churchmen claimed that storms and extreme weather were expressions of divine retribution rather than the inevitable outcome of celestial transits. In the words of John Hooper, sixteenth-century bishop of Gloucester and Protestant martyr, 'it is neither Sun, neither Moon, Jupiter nor Mars, that is the occasion of wealth or woe, plenty or scarcity, of war or peace' – it is God.[21] Likewise, for the Puritan polemicist Philip Stubbes, lunar, solar, and stellar worship of any complexion was simply paganism:

> who, hearing that . . . the sun, the moone, the starres, the signes & planets, doe give both good things and evill, blessing and cursing, good successe and evill successe, yea, life and death, at their pleasure . . . and that they rule, governe, and dispose al things whatsoever, yea, both the bodies and soules of man . . . who, hearing this, . . . would not fall from God and worship the creatures that give such blessings unto man? . . . why should not planets and starres be adored and worshipped as gods, if they coulde worke these effects?[22]

However, a more serious challenge to astrology came from the new astronomy, the unlikely ally of the Church in this case being the Renaissance polymath Nicolaus Copernicus. Under the Copernican revolution, heliocentrism had replaced geocentrism, the celestial skies were replotted, and the scientific basis for astrology was simply exploded. At the same time, it was increasingly evident that advances made in other areas of natural science had very little to do with the holistic, unified precepts of astrology – suggesting that perhaps one explanation for the centuries-long dominance of astrology was that the then fragmentary nature of medicine, biology, and meteorology meant that a theory of everything could usefully occupy the intellectual vacuum at the heart of Renaissance thinking. But with the new science the world was rapidly and irreversibly changing, and by the time of the English mathematician and natural philosopher Isaac Newton's discoveries, astrology had been reduced to a risible affectation, associated only with ignorant rustics and esoteric conmen. Still, belief in the influence of the zodiac persisted throughout the eighteenth and nineteenth centuries and still retains the power to entrance today.

Almanacs too have survived to the present, often with their ludicrous astrology intact. Popular guides included *The Kalender of the Shepherdes* (first translated from the French around 1500 and subsequently reissued and pirated), the *Speculum anni* (edited in its heyday by the appropriately named physician Henry Season), and the parodic and anti-astrological *Poor Robin* series, which ran from the mid-seventeenth century to the end of the eighteenth.[23] In the eighteenth century the most popular almanac was probably *The Shepherd of Banbury's Rules* (1744), originally published as *The Shepheards Legacy* in 1670. This was supposedly by John Claridge (or Clearidge), a shepherd, but the eighteenth-century revision was also attributed to John Campbell (1708–75), an historian known to Samuel Johnson. In addition to his serious historical works, Campbell published a not entirely serious treatise on longevity that claimed that a man could live to the age of 115 by inhaling the breath of young women; Campbell himself died aged sixty-seven.[24]

Despite their popularity, long-range weather forecasts were often given as little credence as John Campbell's secrets of a long life, and almanacs and astrological predictions were persistently satirized from the mid-sixteenth century onwards: in the seventeenth century *Poor Robin*, for instance, was simultaneously a Royalist calendar and a mock-almanac. The 1664 edition mixes details of national history with satirical comments on religious fanaticism, bawdy innuendo, and facetious humour: as 'Poor Robin' sagely remarks in 'Observations on February', 'Many people shall live, and many shall die, but those that die this month shall not live the next'.[25] The 1702 edition is more expansive, if no less droll:

> Cold wrinkled *Winter* ... is generally extreme Cold ... and some will run themselves into the Nooze of Matrimony for the Comfort of a warm Bedfellow: But let every one have a care how they Marry; for Women are Pictures out of Doors, Bells in their Parlours, Wild-Cats in their Kitchens, Saints in their Injuries, Devils being offended, Players in their Houswifry, and Housewives in their Beds.[26]

Likewise, on fiddlers:

> You and Ballad-Singers shall lead very merry Lives; and well you may, for none of you both seldom carry any Crosses about you. I prognosticate

there will be abundance of Weddings this Year, which will get you store of Money, besides Scraps; and where you will have the liberty to sing damnable Ballads, wicked Madrigals, and lowsy Lampoons, and those sung to as lamentable Tunes.[27]

There are also instructions 'To make a Chamber as Light by Night as by Day' by using a glow-worm in a jar.[28] But despite this drollery, *Poor Robin* also contains many details of familiar proverbial lore.

The most annihilating attack on professional astrologers was made by the Augustan poet and 'Scriblerian' novelist Jonathan Swift. Swift attacked John Partridge, who had been producing his almanac *Merlinus Liberatus* annually for over two decades. Writing under the name of 'Isaac Bickerstaff', supposedly a rival astrologer, Swift predicted the death of Partridge on 29 March 1708, and then at the end of that month published a completely spurious account of the poor man's demise. Partridge's objections – which amounted to publishing an insistence that he was still alive – were roundly satirized by Swift in another trenchant pamphlet. Partridge may have been alive and well, but was as good as dead to his public, and he swiftly lost his almanac franchise to pirate publishers.[29]

Come the end of the eighteenth century, weather lore was still being roundly mocked by none other than the poet and natural philosopher Erasmus Darwin, author of *The Botanic Garden* (1791) and paternal grandfather of the naturalist Charles Darwin, who strung together all the various predictors of bad weather into one meteorological rhapsody:

> The hollow winds begin to blow,
> The clouds look black, the glass is low;
> The soot falls down, the spaniels sleep,
> And spiders from their cobwebs peep.
> Last night the Sun went pale to bed,
> The Moon in halos hid her head;
> The boding shepherd heaves a sigh,
> For, see, a rainbow spans the sky.

The walls are damp, the ditches smell,
Clos'd is the pink-ey'd pimpernell.
Hark! how the chairs and tables crack,
Old Betty's joints are on the rack;
Loud quack the ducks, the peacocks cry,
The distant hills are looking nigh.
How restless are the snorting swine!
The busy flies disturb the kine;
Low o'er the grass the swallow wings;
The cricket too, how sharp he sings;
Puss on the hearth, with velvet paws,
Sits, wiping o'er her whisker'd jaws.
Through the clear stream the fishes rise,
And nimbly catch th' incautious flies;
The glow-worms, numerous and bright,
Illumin'd the dewy dell last night.
At dusk the squalid toad was seen,
Hopping and crawling o'er the green;
The whirling wind the dust obeys,
And in the rapid eddy plays;
The fog has chang'd his yellow vest,
And in a russet coat is drest.
Though June, the air is cold and still;
The mellow blackbird's voice is shrill.
My dog, so alter'd is his taste,
Quits mutton-bones, on grass to feast;
And see yon rooks, how odd their flight,
They imitate the gliding kite,
And seem precipitate to fall –
As if they felt the piercing ball.
'Twill surely rain, I see, with sorrow;
Our jaunt must be put off to-morrow.[30]

But Darwin's lines are nevertheless evidence that weather lore was still being taken seriously. It had to be: not only harvests, but a whole range of eighteenth-century industries depended on the weather. In textile manufacture, for example, rainfall was essential for washing and dyeing, but if frosts froze the streams, then business halted; on the other hand bleaching cloth required dry, sunny weather. Tanners, papermakers, and brewers all needed good rainfall, as did mills and foundries, whereas brick-making required warm weather to dry bricks before they went into the kiln, as rain and frost could damage unfired bricks. Building therefore slowed down after Michaelmas, 29 September, as did road-mending, which could itself lead to shortages of raw materials. Some trades picked up after Michaelmas when the harvests were in, brewing especially taking advantage of the new hops, and cider-making of apples.[31]

This scepticism, even contempt, for popular weather prognostication was in part an expression of frustration against unreliable forecasting. There was no lack of evidence. The mediaeval meteorologist William Merle, rector of Driby in Lincolnshire, kept a journal of relative temperatures, wind speed and direction, and weather events such as fog and rain, frost and snow, and thunder and lightning, for seven years between January 1337 and January 1344, during which time he also wrote a tract on Biblical and classical weather lore and subsequently compiled notes on making astrological weather predictions.[32] Ralph Josselin, a Puritan minister of Earls Colne in Essex in the mid-seventeenth century, kept a weather diary to account for God's attitudes to his parish. Such spiritual reckonings were favourite Calvinistic techniques for weighing sin against virtue in an individual or a community. The judgment of God was like a barometer – things certainly went up and down for the folk of Earls Colne in May 1648:

> May: 9: Among all the severall judgements on this nacion: god this spring in the latter end of April when rye was earing and eared, sent such terrible frosts that the eare was frozen and so dyed, and cometh unto nothing. . . .

May: 21: This weeke the Lord was good and merciful to mee and mine in our peace plenty health, outward enjoyments, in the season, which was exceeding comfortable, dry, warme, and some showers in some places the raine was exceeding violent, but with us temperate....[33]

The natural philosopher and polymath Robert Hooke read a paper on a 'Method for Making a History of the Weather' to the Royal Society on 7 October 1663 and kept a weather diary from 1672; the first rain gauge was developed in 1677.[34] The philosopher John Locke also kept such a diary and wrote to the Royal Society himself:

I have often thought that if such a Register as this were kept in every County in England, and so constantly published, many Things relating to the Air, Winds, Health, Fruitfulness, &c. might be collected from them, and several Rules and Observations concerning Extent of Winds and Rains &c. be in Time establish'd to the great Advantage of Mankind. From this solitary one there is little to be collected, besides the ordinary Observation, which I set down commonly every Morning, there seldom happen's any Rain, Snow, or other remarkable Change, which I did not set down.[35]

Meanwhile, the last six letters in Gilbert White's *Natural History of Selborne* (1789) are all concerned with the weather. It was inescapable – a reminder of one's place in God's earthly kingdom, or on an unruly planet that science was trying to put into rational order.

———

The weather and the seasons unfold as they will and we, the people, still experience them on a straightforward, everyday basis. There is, even in the twenty-first century, very little we can do to stop it raining or not raining for weeks on end, or to guarantee ourselves a suitably snow-sealed white Christmas. But other aspects of the year and its passage can be, and have been, much more closely controlled. When the days of the year were fixed by Constantine's adoption of the Julian calendar, time itself began to be structured in ways that regulated behaviour, thus paving the way for later religious orders. The sixth-century Roman saint Benedict of Nursia, for example, instituted what became known as the 'Rule of St Benedict': a set of stipulations to organize the activities of monastic communities for every hour of the day and every day of the year, ultimately for each holy day and saints' day. The 'Rule' was widely adopted across mediaeval Christendom and is still observed today:

> Having considered what is reasonable we lay down that during the winter (that is from 1 November [*a Kalendis Novembribus*] till Easter) the time of rising will be the eighth hour of the night. Thus they may sleep for a while after midnight and get up after digestion has been completed. The time that is left after Matins is to be used for further study by the brethren whose knowledge of the Psalter or of the readings is incomplete. From Easter till the aforesaid 1 November, the hour of rising should be so determined that there is a short interval after Matins, during which the brethren can go out for the necessities of nature. Lauds which follow are to be said as dawn is breaking.[36]

As the Christian year developed, it worked devotions and ritual activity and indeed the whole narrative structure of faith into the existing international calendar. At one level the model of the year presented the opportunity for an annual retelling of the cycle of life, death, and resurrection; at another level it could consolidate the established rhythms of the community through the seasons.

For the first thousand years of the English Church the year was a landscape repeatedly ritualized through annual activities such as Rogation Days, and by pilgrimages and processions of relics.[37] In this context, saints' days became significant landmarks in the calendar, gradually emerging as annual feasts established around a tomb or reliquary – altars were traditionally consecrated with holy relics, that is, actual physical remains of the saint. The Anglo-Saxons, and particularly the

Northumbrians and Cornish (known in the history of the Christian Church as the 'Insular Celts'), had been prolific in creating local saints, and saints' days were already an established feature of the English calendar by the time Rome developed protocols for canonization in about the tenth century. The Venerable Bede wrote a martyrology of 114 saints, and eighty-one saints' days are recorded in the 'Metrical Calendar of York', which dates from the late eighth century:

> At its beginning November shines with a multi-faceted jewel:
> It gleams with the praise of All Saints.
> Martin of Tours ascends the stars on the ides.
> Thecla finished her life on the fifteenth kalends.
> But Cecilia worthily died with glory on the tenth kalends.
> On the ninth kalends we joyfully venerate the feast of Clement.
> On the eighth kalends Chrysogonus rejoices with his vital weaponry.
> Andrew is rightly venerated by the world on the day before the calends.[38]

The devotional calendar – dating by saints' days – was a perpetual reminder of the Christian heritage and the folklore of early martyrs and gave a shape to the working year. Tusser, for instance, refers to these feasts in his *Hundreth Good Pointes of Husbandrie* in ordering the year's activities:

> From Aprill beginn, til saint Andrew be past:
> So long with good huswives, their dairies doe last.[39]

But the calendar of saints' days was also an accumulative tradition, and feasts could gather new associations. The king, for example, rallies his soldiers in Shakespeare's *Henry V* by predicting that the date of the battle will become an annual anniversary and a part of the pantheon of the saints:

> This day is call'd the feast of Crispian:
> He that outlives this day, and comes safe home,
> Will stand a' tiptoe when this day is named,

And rouse him at the name of Crispian.
He that shall see this day, and live old age,
Will yearly on the vigil feast his neighbors,
And say 'Tomorrow is Saint Crispian.'
Then will he strip his sleeve and show his scars,
And say 'These wounds I had on Crispin's day.'...
This story shall the good man teach his son;
And Crispin Crispian shall ne'er go by,
From this day to the ending of the world,
But we in it shall be remembered –
We few, we happy few, we band of brothers.[40]

The Feast Day of Sts Crispin and Crispinian, 25 October, is here insistently woven into the mythology of the nation. In fact, saints' feast days for
the apostles and evangelists tend to occur around the 25th of the month.
This was possibly to emphasize a monthly cycle between the conception,
nativity, and death of Christ, but could also have been influenced by the
regularity of Roman rural festivals at the same time. It was anyway a deliberate appropriation to ensure that the earlier cycle of agricultural celebration was fully Christianized. By the Middle Ages, the Catholic calendar had
ninety-five saints' days that were kept as holy days, which in turn encouraged the establishment of fairs and local celebrations in honour of the
parish saint.[41]

Particular dates in the liturgical calendar – the feasts of major or local
saints, or the anticipation of Lent – became occasions for revelry, and work
was prohibited on certain holy days such as Epiphany, Easter, Ascension,
Pentecost, Corpus Christi, and Christmas.[42] A sense of festival was virtually built into mediaeval church ritual. Carols (or 'caroles'), for instance,
were originally tunes for dance steps for specific saints' days. As Shylock
put it in Shakespeare's The Merchant of Venice:

What, are there masques? Hear you me, Jessica:
Lock up my doors, and when you hear the drum

And the vile squealing of the wry-neck'd fife,
Clamber not you up to the casements then,
Nor thrust your head into the public street
To gaze on Christian fools with varnish'd faces.[43]

According to the American feminist and activist Barbara Ehrenreich, contemporary celebrations included 'seasonal change, a calendrical event, the initiation of young people, a wedding, funeral, or coronation', and each event was keenly anticipated.[44] This rage for festivity may have been a response to attempts by the authorities to repress such merrymaking. The early Christian Church had legislated against carnivalesque revelries that were focused on saints' days, but celebrations were evidently widespread and by the early Middle Ages were tolerated within certain parameters: church holidays could be celebrated so long as the activities did not trespass on the sacred ground inside the church or within the church boundary. Likewise, 'Church Ales' (annual charity events for the parish) were forbidden to take place within church precincts from the middle of the thirteenth century, and in 1431 all dancing and carousing on such sites was banned by the Council of Basel. But 'traditions of merrie England' grew in popularity throughout the fifteenth century, and the British historian Ronald Hutton admits that he finds no obvious reason for the 'apparent greater investment in seasonal ceremony during the later Middle Ages' – although it is worth mentioning that many were customs of fairly recent vintage.[45] A taste for the ecstatic nature of revelry may have been a factor, but such mass hysteria during festivals seems to have been more characteristic of European revelry than English celebrations.[46] Rather, in the words of the Marxist historian E. P. Thompson:

Many weeks of heavy labour and scanty diet were compensated for by the expectation (or reminiscence) of these occasions, when food and drink were abundant, courtship and every kind of social intercourse flourished, and the hardship of life was forgotten.... These occasions were, in an important sense, what men and women lived for.[47]

Consequently, when church regulation amounted to prohibition, the festivities moved away from the church itself and took to the streets and fields, becoming more secularized, and increasingly mythologized as ancient survivals of mysterious old rituals.

But the regulation of the late Middle Ages was nothing compared with the repression of the Reformation and the eventual legislation of the Puritan Commonwealth under Oliver Cromwell. With that, as German sociologist Max Weber put it, Protestant asceticism 'descended like a frost on the life of "Merrie Old England"'.[48] 'Our holy days are very well reduced,' declared the antiquarian and early folklorist William Harrison in the mid-sixteenth century, and a century later the Nonconformist writer John Bunyan described 'Vanity Fair' in his Calvinist epic The Pilgrim's Progress (1678) as a place of festivity where Christian's companion Faithful is tortured and immolated.[49] It was inevitable that the killjoys would put a price on communal merrymaking, and sure enough by the late seventeenth century an English economist had estimated that each public holiday cost the country £50,000 in lost labour.[50] Consequently, several historians have argued that the regulation of festivity was a consequence of early capitalism and the Protestant work ethic, as summed up by Ehrenreich:

> The middle classes had to learn to calculate, save, and 'defer gratification'; the lower classes had to be transformed into a disciplined, factory-ready, working class – meaning far fewer holidays and the new necessity of showing up for work sober and on time, six days a week. Peasants had worked hard too, of course, but in seasonally determined bursts; the new industrialism required ceaseless labour, all year round.[51]

Thompson quotes an article from The London Magazine (1738) that explicitly recommends a controlled use of festivals as a form of social management:

> dancing on the Green at Wakes and merry Tides should not only be indulg'd but incourag'd: and little Prizes being allotted for the Maids

who excel in a Jig or Hornpipe, would make them return to their daily Labour with a light Heart and grateful Obedience to their Superiors.[52]

Thus, calendar festivals – the year – became an increasingly political affair after the Reformation, and figures such as the 'Lord of Misrule' and the outlaw Robin Hood came to preside over the revels, bringing with them murmurings of social discontent, encouraging on the one hand excess, on the other resistance and even rebellion.[53] The characteristic style of English celebration – the costumes and cross-dressing, blacking-up and masquerade, the songs and dances and games – all became ritualized, mythologized, and invested with layers of meaning and allusion, not least in popular protest and radical politics. Thompson again: 'a language of ribbons, of bonfires, of oaths and the refusal of oaths, of toasts, of seditious riddles and ancient prophecies, of oak leaves and of maypoles, of ballads with a political double-entendre, even of airs whistled in the streets'.[54] There was now, in the words of the historian of mediaeval theatre Meg Twycross, 'A solid barrier between the culture of gentility and the culture of the people'.[55] It is time to dismantle that barrier and reclaim the heritage of the nation.

4   THE WEATHER

Sunshine is delicious, rain is refreshing, wind braces us
up, snow is exhilarating; there is really no such thing
as bad weather, only different kinds of good weather.

John Ruskin, as quoted by Lord Avebury

England lies on the largest island of the British Isles: an archipelago, or collection of islands, in the North-east Atlantic. In addition to the general influence of the earth's rotational tilt, British weather and therefore the English climate is determined by the seas surrounding the islands: the North Sea, the Atlantic waters between Scotland and Iceland and off the coast of Cornwall, St George's Channel, and the English Channel itself. These seas affect the four principle winds: the north-west wind is a maritime polar wind blowing from the coast of Greenland across the Atlantic and is therefore wet and cool; the south-west wind is a maritime tropical wind from the equator across the Atlantic and is wet and warm; the south-east wind is the North African High, blowing mainly across land, and is dry and warm; and the north-east is the Siberian High, also blowing across land, and is dry and cool.[1]

In winter, cold air from the European and American continents and from the Arctic is warmed as it travels over the seas; in summer, however, the warmer air travelling north to Britain from Europe and the Mediterranean is cooled as it blows across the sea, and tropical air travelling from the Gulf of Mexico is likewise cooled by the Atlantic. As the geographer and meteorologist Robin Stirling explains, 'Even polar winds, during the summer, are less warmed by the sea than they would be if there were a land bridge from Scotland to Iceland'.[2] The North Atlantic Drift compensates in part for the effect of the seas on air temperature, being a continuation of the Gulf Stream that brings a current of warm seawater to European coasts. The momentum of the North Atlantic Drift is provided by other cold saline currents off Labrador and Greenland; the Greenland Current is, however, weakening, due to the melting Arctic ice that is reducing the salinity of the water, and this is likely to affect how far north or south the Drift may travel. At present, though, it is largely responsible for the mild, moist, variable nature of our weather, and Britain tends to be warmer than similar latitudes elsewhere. Peterborough in England, for example, is at about the same latitude as Saskatoon in Saskatchewan, Canada. The average temperatures in Saskatoon range from −17 °C (January) to 18 °C (July), and the lowest recorded temperature is −50 °C; the average temperatures for Peterborough are 0 °C (January) to 20 °C (July). But with such complex variables, it is hardly surprising that, even with supercomputers, attempts to model weather patterns cannot be relied on.

Despite the popular image of rain-soaked Britain, London's average rainfall is significantly less than that of Rome, Venice, and Nice, and the annual rainfall in tropical climates is over three times that of the British capital.[3] However, tropical climates have dry seasons and rainy seasons, with the dry seasons almost completely without rain; in England, there has been far less seasonal variation. April is usually the driest month, followed by March, June, May, and February – making spring on average the driest season (and it is increasingly becoming drier than it has been in the past).[4] November and December are the wettest months in most places in Britain; they have the most days on which it rains. July is by far the most thundery month. The driest part of the English year is therefore late winter to early summer, or February to June; after that the weather breaks with stormy July, and then the rains return in August. It is perhaps extraordinary that annual holidays are not arranged with this in mind, but the insistence on observing the August holiday, when Parliament is in recess and consequently the economy is relatively quiet, seems unbreakable, and is widespread across the Western world. This traditional recess dates back to the earliest days of our modern parliament, when MPs, as landowners, were required on their estates in August to oversee the critical activity of harvest, which could so easily be wrecked by rains or bad management. Over 300 years on, this break from government business continues, with all its implications for other areas of our lives

– for example, the dates of the school summer holidays, which likewise once helped to provide labour for the harvest. This is why most people take a holiday in a month that often has more rainfall than the previous five months; indeed, in some British calendars, August was considered the first month of autumn.

For most of us, any relationship with the characteristic weather of the seasons and its impact on farming exists now only as a potted weather lore – quoting an incomplete system of seasonal prognostication in an effort to predict daily variations. Perhaps only a partial account of cloud names has survived from a once much more comprehensive lexicon – lamb's wool sky, mackerel sky, mares' tails, overcast, rain cloud, stacken cloud, thunder cloud, and so forth: the images create a strange poetry. There are general cloud sayings – 'Mackerel sky and mares' tails, make lofty ships carry low sails', for instance, and 'When clouds appear like rocks and towers, the earth's refreshed by frequent showers' – and many more particular sayings, usually based on how various local landmarks appear.[5] But this is a meagre record of a rich past, and has since been replaced by the names proposed in 1803 by the chemist and meteorologist Luke Howard in a set of categories influenced by the taxonomy of Carl Linnaeus, the deviser of classification systems for plants and animals. It is to Howard that we owe the cloud names still used today: cirrus, stratus, cumulus, and nimbus, and their variations.

Howard sought to analyse the effect on clouds of different atmospheric conditions as a way of ascertaining 'present and ensuing phænomena' (that is, weather forecasting), and he acknowledged the traditions of weather lore, which he hoped to place on a more scientific footing:

> The want of this branch of knowledge [popular meteorology] renders the predictions of the Philosopher (who in attending only to his instruments may be said to examine only the *pulse* of the atmosphere) generally less successful than those of the weatherwise Mariner or Husbandman.[6]

While offering respect to the folklore of clouds and to the influence of contingency, Howard was also keen to come up with a complete and legible system rather than disconnected observations. Percy Bysshe Shelley was sufficiently inspired by Howard to write his poem 'The Cloud', describing the shape-shifting of clouds in response to the sun and the wind and the rain over a changing landscape, and the painter John Constable was also profoundly influenced by this new way of seeing. Constable sketched and painted several studies of clouds, and works such as The Hay Wain (1821) are characterized by a restless attention to the architecture of the sky.

But before Howard, and in the absence of a detailed folklore of clouds and the weather, what do we know of meteorological theories? The most famous English weather saying is of course 'Red sky at night, shepherd's [or sailor's] delight, red sky in the morning, shepherd's warning.' This is first recorded in the Bible and was, the Gospel of Matthew reports, allegedly quoted by Jesus.[7] In England, Jesus' saying appears in both John Wyclif's translation of 1395 and William Tyndale's translation of 1526, so it entered the proverbial tradition early. Thus in the 1611 translation, the King James Bible, Jesus responds to the Pharisees who seek a sign from Heaven:

> When it is evening, ye say, It will be fair weather: for the sky is red. And in the morning, It will be foul weather to day: for the sky is red and lowring. O ye hypocrites, ye can discern the face of the sky; but can ye not discern the signs of the times?[8]

Despite its geographical and historical remoteness, then, the Bible was a source of English weather lore. Biblical meteorology was predominantly a science of signs. This divinatory role for weather is declared in the first chapter of Genesis: 'Let there be lights in the firmament . . . for signs, and for seasons'. There was no weather in the Garden of Eden, but 'there went up a mist from the earth, and watered the whole face of the ground'. Yet after their expulsion from the Garden, God curses Adam to raise his own crops without the benefit of this perpetual hydration and irrigation: 'the LORD God sent him forth from the garden of Eden, to till the ground from whence he was taken'.[9] The critical effect of the weather on the harvest is therefore a consequence and ongoing reminder of the Fall. This theme is carried through to the Revelation of St John the Divine, when in the face of the Apocalypse the seasons disappear and the Tree of Life 'yielded her fruit every month'.[10]

Biblical weather is usually a punishment. The fate of Adam, his eldest son Cain, and the rest of mankind is to farm the land – 'thou shalt eat the herb of the field; In the sweat of thy face shalt thou eat bread' – and the agricultural cycle is characterized by years of plenty followed by years of famine. The weather in the Book of Genesis can be catastrophic: the Flood smites 'every living thing' and deluges the land for forty days and nights. After this God promises not to revisit this level of destruction on the earth again and confirms the new stability of the year by renewing the cycle of the seasons – 'while the earth remaineth, seed-time and harvest, and cold and heat, and summer and winter, and day and night shall not cease'; consequently, it was believed that the wind only blew after the Flood – it brought changes in the weather.[11] There are harvest celebrations in, for example, the Book of Deuteronomy: 'The Lord shall open unto thee his good treasure, the heaven to give the rain unto thy land in his season'.[12] But notwithstanding the sign of 'the everlasting covenant between God and every living creature' – the super-legible sign of the rainbow – Sodom and Gomorrah are destroyed by a wrathful rain of 'brimstone and fire', and Egypt too suffers a 'grievous hail' that destroys its harvest in one of ten devastating plagues.[13]

In the New Testament, an uncanny weather heightens the Passion of Christ, and of course the Apocalypse is the extreme weather event verily to end all others:

the sun became black as sackcloth of hair, and the moon became as blood; And the stars of heaven fell unto the earth, even as a fig tree casteth her untimely figs, when she is shaken of a mighty wind. And the heaven departed as a scroll when it is rolled together; and every mountain and island were moved out of their places.[14]

Elsewhere, however, the weather is more enigmatic and less of a scourge. The most intriguing remark by Jesus on the weather is probably that reported by John: 'The wind bloweth where it listeth, and thou hearest the sound thereof, but canst not tell whence it cometh, and whither it goeth'.[15] This comment undermines the divine practice of reading the weather as an expression of God's displeasure and an instrument of punishment, although Jesus' radical interpretation of the weather as being ambiguous was not pursued by later theologians. The early radical Protestant John Calvin had no doubt that bad weather was the result of bad behaviour: 'the inclemency of the air, frost, thunder, unseasonable rains, drought, hail or whatever is disorderly in the world are the fruits of sin'.[16] *The Storm* (1704), sometimes attributed to writer and journalist Daniel Defoe, follows this nonconformist line, reprinting a letter declaring that, 'this late great Calamity ... was sent upon us as a punishment for our Sins, [and] may be a warning to the whole Nation in general, and engage every one of us to a hearty and sincere Repentance; otherwise, I'm afraid we must expect greater Evils than this was to fall upon us'.[17] Yet this general attitude to bad weather as a divine punishment does not appear to have been reciprocated by good weather being considered as evidence that the divinity was well pleased with the situation on earth: bumper harvests were not theologically welcomed as the nation's just rewards.

The poet John Milton used these Biblical sources in his epic *Paradise Lost* (1667), in which the alternation of the seasons began after the Fall. Hence in the tenth book of the poem the movement of the sun and the seasons is carefully charted to show the declining state of humanity:

> The Sun
> Had first his precept so to move, so shine,
> As might affect the Earth with cold and heat
> Scarce tolerable, and from the North to call
> Decrepit Winter, from the South to bring
> Solstitial summer's heat.[18]

Consequently the sun,

> to bring in change
> Of Seasons to each Clime; else had the Spring
> Perpetual smil'd on Earth with vernant flowers,
> Equal in Days and Nights.[19]

Before then, there had been 'eternal spring' – and typically here Milton is marrying the Christian and the classical.[20] The belief in a lost paradise of perpetual spring goes back at least as far as the imagined Golden Age of the ancient Greeks. The idea was adopted by the Romans with poets such as Virgil and Ovid proposing that the cycle of the seasons began in the Silver Age, commencing a period of decline that led to the present.[21] Before then, it had been forever springtime; the seasons are therefore evidence that all is not right either in Eden, or in Arcadia.

––––––

The Christian Bible offered a moral vision of the weather profoundly centred on an interventionist god. But alongside the divine mechanics of the weather ran a classical system of meteorology that operated along different lines. Aristotle was the central thinker here, and his treatise *Meteorologica*, being 'the study of higher things' or 'meteors', was hugely influential and survived as a model of natural science until the seventeenth century. In his ratiocinative thought, Aristotle is the great example of deriving universal propositions from inductive reasoning based on our sensory perceptions, but *Meteorologica* is unusual within his work as it describes natural phenomena that the philosopher has not, and in some cases simply cannot, directly perceive or experience. Aristotle justifies his analysis of rainbows and comets and shooting stars by remarking that 'We consider that we have given a sufficiently rational explanation of things inaccessible to observation by our senses if we have produced a theory that is possible: and the following seems, on the evidence available, to be the explanation of the phenomena now under consideration'.[22] His interest in meteorological phenomena lies in analysing events that are natural but not as predictable as they are in other areas of natural science, such as astronomy.

In Aristotelian theory, the earth lies at the heart of the cosmos, and is surrounded by spheres of water, air, and fire. Beyond the sphere of fire is the moon; meanwhile the stars lie in aether, a mysterious fifth element of prime matter. The three meteorological spheres of water, air, and fire are influenced by the events in this fifth element. On earth, there are two basic processes or 'exhalations' (effectively evaporations): the sun heats the earth in order to draw up exhalations that are hot and dry, and also heats the sea to draw up exhalations that are cool and moist (vapours). As these exhalations move through the spheres, they give rise to different weather effects. Vapours produce clouds, rain, snow, hail, mist, dew, and frost: if a rising moist exhalation loses heat at a certain height, for example, it will turn to rain. Dry exhalations cause winds to blow as they ascend and can turn to shooting stars and comets (thunderstones); they produce thunder and lightning, and a dry exhalation trapped in the earth can cause earth-quakes. While the heat of the sun engenders these effects by drawing up exhalations, it also eventually dissipates them through its heat; exhalations are also cooled during the night, whereupon they fall back to earth.

The basis of this theory of the weather resided in the interaction of the various elements, meaning that meteorology in all its manifesta-tions was part of a greater scheme of qualities that were active, being hot or cold, or passive, being dry or moist. These qualities determined not only the character of each element, but also their effect on humans in the theory of humours and their consequent temperaments:

Fire	Hot	Dry	Yellow bile	Choleric
Air	Hot	Wet	Blood	Sanguine
Water	Cold	Wet	Phlegm	Phlegmatic
Earth	Cold	Dry	Black bile	Melancholic

The four cardinal winds were also linked to the elements, and therefore to humours, and consequently had physiological and mental effects. They had their own names, and effectively displayed their own vivid personalities: *Boreas* was the wintry north wind (earth), *Africus* (also known as *Notus* or *Auster*) was the moist south wind (water), *Zephyrus* was the fertile west wind (air), and the less common *Vulturnus* or *Eurus* was the hot and dry east wind (fire).[23]

All these relationships might be shifting and unstable, but it was clear from the time of early antiquity to the late Renaissance that changes in the environment – that is, meteorological effects – were likely to produce mood swings or even illness in particular individuals, all other things remaining equal. In fact, the theory survived in different forms through the eighteenth, nineteenth, and twentieth centuries. And it is not entirely without some foundation: Seasonal Affective Disorder (SAD) is a form of depression that can be affected by levels of melatonin in the brain, a condition brought about by low light conditions and which is therefore more likely to occur during persistent stretches of overcast weather, or in the winter. Aristotle remains with us in other ways too: his meteorological language survives when we describe the weather as 'the elements', as well as in images, for instance when we describe the morning dew as 'falling' and lightning 'striking'.

There were alternatives to the Aristotelian meteorological system. The Roman philosopher Lucretius argued in *De rerum natura* (*On the Nature of Things*) for an almost wholly chaotic system. Book VI of *De rerum natura* considers meteors: atmospheric phenomena, terrestrial phenomena, 'individual wonders', and the plague, which was itself a form of weather. Lucretius' system was based on the ancient Greek atomic theory devised by Epicurus and, according to American historian Edward Grant, presented a

cosmic vision based on an assumption of an infinity of worlds, each composed of atoms moving in an infinite void space. [Lucretius] assumed that each world comes into being by a chance coming-together of atoms in the void; eventually each world passes away when its atoms dissociate and move into the void to form parts of other worlds.[24]

What therefore distinguished Lucretian meteorology from Aristotelian meteorology was that for each weather event Lucretius attributed multiple causes and effects. It was a model based on perpetual disruption. In this, Lucretius provides an interesting precedent for late-twentieth-century 'chaos theory', which postulates among other things the 'butterfly effect' in which minuscule variations in calculation (such as rounding decimals up or down), although theoretically predictable, can have an unpredictable and potentially vast impact on systems such as the weather. Consequently, the profusion and fluctuation of these tiny variables make local weather forecasting of more than a few days ahead impossible.[25] Lucretius' own meteorological theory is driven by seemingly chaotic systems to the extent that the world appears perpetually on the brink of collapse: when 'the scudding clouds of heaven collide high in the air . . . everything is shaken with heavy thunder and seems to tremble, and the great walls of the all-containing world are torn and seem to leap apart'.[26] Although Lucretian thinking had little influence on mediaeval or Renaissance theology and natural philosophy, interest in his chaotic world-view revived in seven-teenth-century England during the Restoration following the turbulence and confusion of the Civil War years and the Commonwealth.[27]

If the Lucretian alternative to Aristotle was neglected in the early modern period, there were still plenty of responses to and adaptations of Aristotle.[28] The fourteenth-century French scholar Themon Judaeus, for example, queried in which region of the air rain was generated, whether it hailed more in the spring and autumn, whether thunder was fire being extinguished in a cloud, whether lightning was fire falling from a cloud, and whether typhoons and hurricanes were caused by hot and dry exha-lations.[29] The meteorological debate raged across the centuries and over Europe, and as different theories were contested, so too were they Christianized by thinkers such as Albertus Magnus and Thomas Aquinas. They also increasingly came under more sustained empirical scrutiny. The major English contribution here came from the Puritan theologian and controversialist William Fulke, who argued in *The Garden of Naturall Contemplation* (2nd edn, 1571) that 'within the globe of the earth, be wonderful great holes, caves, or dongeons, in which when ayer adondeth (as it may by diverse causes) this ayer, that cannot abide to be pined in, findeth a litle hole in or about those countries, as it weare a mouth to break out of: & by this meanes, bloweth vehemently . . . '. These underground wind tunnels had been distributed by 'the wonderfull wysdome of the eternall God' to keep the air circulating, 'Which were it not continually styrred, as it is, would soone putrifie, and being putryfied, would be a deadly infection to all that hath breathe upon the worlde'.[30] Fulke's model may have been based on Aristotelian theory, but for him the weather was both rational and divine.

Fulke's was the most significant work of meteorology written in English in the period and was, for instance, developed by the philosopher and natural scientist Francis Bacon, who described the 'breathing places of the earth' in his *History of the Winds* (published in Latin in 1622) as a system of subterranean conduits from which issued gusts and gales.[31] Once they had been generated, Bacon speculated on the plethora of potential influences on these winds:

> What [are] those things that are here upon the earth, or are there done do contribute towards the winds? what the hills and the dissolutions of Snow upon them? what those masses of Ice which swim upon the Sea, and are carried to some place? what the differences of soil and land (so it be of some large extent?) what Ponds, Sands, Woods, and Champion ground? what those things which we men do here, as burning of Heath, and the like, doth contribute to the manuring of Land, the firing of Towns in time of War, the drying up of Ponds and Lakes? the continual shooting off of Guns, the ringing of many Bells together in great Cities, and the like? These things and Acts of ours are but as small straws, yet something they may do.[32]

We may smile at the suggestion that bell-ringing causes gales, but Bacon was far ahead of his time in thinking about the effects of icy seas and atmospheric pollution causing meteorological disturbances.

The suggestion of a submerged otherworld that was the cause and being of environmental phenomena would return in new and influential ways at the end of the seventeenth century with the theories of the natural philosopher Thomas Burnet, but even then, in the 1690s, popular publishers such as John Dunton were still invoking thoroughly Aristotelian theories of meteorology, claiming that thunder and lightning were, as the historian of atmospheric sciences Vladimir Janković puts it, caused by a 'coagulation' of 'moist exhalations', which ignited the 'nitric ingredient'.[33] There was much speculation about comets and the 'ignis fatuus' or will o' the wisp, and bizarre weather events, glossed by Aristotelian explications, became a staple of modern folklore in fantastical works such as the antiquary and astrologer Joshua Childrey's *Britannia Baconica, or, The Natural Rarities of England, Scotland & Wales* (first published in 1661), and the history of lightning strikes given in *Admirable Curiosities, Rarities, and Wonders* (1684).[34] In a similar vein, the spa physician Thomas Short described battles in the sky involving the *Fata Morgana*, or heavenly mirage, in *A General Chronological History of the Air, Weather, Seasons, Meteors, &c* (1749).[35] But with the growing emphasis on the individual, personal identity, and psychological consciousness, there came a fascination with the effects weather and climate might have on the human body and especially the mind. As the sixteenth-century French physician André du Laurens put it, 'A grosse, darke, gloomish, stinking ayre, is very contrarie'.[36] How could meteorological conditions affect the way that people thought, and felt, and acted?

In the second century AD, the Graeco-Roman surgeon and philosopher Galen of Pergamon had refined the anatomical aspects of Aristotle's model and the humoural theory of health. In the context of the body, for instance, the heart or the liver performed the role of the sun in heating humours and producing vapours: the elements that made up the macrocosm of the earth and the heavens were mirrored in the microcosm of the body.[37] Galenic medicine provided the Western European standard for the next 1,500 years, during which time it developed a highly sophisticated humoural system based on the principle of correspondence. This posited that there were discernible patterns between the four humours, the four elements, the four directions of the wind, even the four Gospels. Such esoteric numerology was zealously attended to: there were seven days of creation and days in the week, seven planets, seven notes in a melodic scale, seven deadly sins or capital vices, and seven virtues, divided into cardinal and theological virtues; likewise there were twelve months, twelve apostles, and so on.[38] In mediaeval and Renaissance thinking, then, the world was interpreted through resemblance, rhymes, equivalences, and similitude. Representation was a form of repetition – a readable repetition: as the French thinker Michel Foucault suggested, 'The universe was folded in upon itself: the earth echoing the sky, faces seeing themselves reflected in the stars, and plants holding within their stems the secrets that were of use to man'.[39] Natural science had developed into a total method for comprehending the world.

There was a fundamental assumption in all of this that the human and natural worlds should ideally be in harmony, and that this could be revealed through analogies and correspondences. The better the state of this relationship, the more reliable the channels of communication between these worlds would be: portents would reveal knowledge to be unearthed. As the German physician and scholar Oswald Crollius declared, 'Is it not true that all herbs, plants, trees and other things issuing from the bowels of the earth are so many magic books and signs?'[40] And this theory of everything necessarily included the weather and the seasons and its effect on birds and beasts.[41] Hence the stormy omens in Shakespeare's *Macbeth*, in which the natural world and the supernatural world are revealed as being continuous with each other and bound together by the weather:

1. *Witch.* Thrice the brinded cat hath mew'd.
2. *Witch.* Thrice, and once the hedge-pig whin'd.[42]

Shakespeare was certainly most familiar with Renaissance weather theory. *Richard III* famously begins with an image of the seasons, which is immediately followed by the condensation of vapour into the sea. It is a classic example of Aristotelian meteorology:

> Now is the winter of our discontent
> Made glorious summer by this son of York;
> And all the clouds that low'r'd upon our house
> In the deep bosom of the ocean buried.[43]

In *The Tempest*, in contrast, Caliban curses Prospero, calling on rotten exhalations to rain down distempers on his head: 'All the infections that the sun sucks up / From bogs, fens, flats'.[44] The weather is also mysteriously bound up with identity. Hamlet, a character wreathed in psychological mists, is compounded of weather symptoms:

> O that this too too solid flesh would melt,
> Thaw, and resolve itself into a dew![45]

The dark and cloudy skies of Elsinore are, however, ever-changing in their meaning – floating signifiers, fanciful in their mutability:

> *Hamlet.* Do you see yonder cloud that's almost in shape of a
>   camel?
> *Polonius.* By th' mass, and 'tis, like a camel indeed.
> *Hamlet.* Methinks it is like a weasel.
> *Polonius.* It is back'd like a weasel.
> *Hamlet.* Or like a whale.
> *Polonius.* Very like a whale.[46]

This same scene is effectively repeated in *Antony and Cleopatra* as Antony prepares for his death, but here it is more sinister, more portentous:

> Sometimes we see a cloud that's dragonish,
> A vapor sometime like a bear or lion,

A tower'd citadel, a pendant rock,
A forked mountain, or blue promontory
With trees upon 't that nod unto the world,
And mock our eyes with air. Thou hast seen these signs,
They are black vesper's pageants.[47]

'Black vesper's pageants' were the gathering clouds of the evening sky.
So the same clouds that Hamlet mockingly describes to Polonius seem to
Antony to hold the secret of identity. The shapes in the sky pass through
a sublime spectrum, obscure and indecipherable – perhaps recalling the
enigmatic weather reported in the Gospel of St John.

Shakespeare was not the only one to mystify the heavens. Henry More,
one of the late seventeenth-century group of Cambridge Platonists, argued
that the Creation would be most dull if all plants revealed their use through
simple jingling correspondences, 'for the rarity of it is the delight'.[48] Still,
by the eighteenth century there was a grudging acceptance of the effect of
weather on human mood by no less a pragmatist than the great English
writer and lexicographer Samuel Johnson, as well as by the period's great
eccentric novelist, Laurence Sterne. In *Tristram Shandy* (1759–67), Sterne
described the lovable oddball 'my uncle Toby' as a 'humorous' gentleman:
that is, a man influenced by the humours. Indeed, 'His humour was of that
particular species, which does honour to our atmosphere'.[49]

The humoural theory of character rooted in Aristotelian and Galenic
thinking in fact continued well into the nineteenth century. The Romantic
poet John Keats's verse, 'The Human Seasons', is based on the humours:

Four seasons fill the measure of the year;
There are four seasons in the mind of man. ....[50]

Keats then describes the moods of the seasons, from 'lusty Spring, when
fancy clear / Takes in all beauty with an easy span' to the winter of 'pale
misfeature'. From its humoural designations, this is a poem that could
almost have been written in the early seventeenth century rather than

the early nineteenth, although perhaps Keats's dwelling on the mists of autumn reveals this to be a later poem. What is striking, though, is how the Romantic love affair with the literature of the Renaissance in general and with Shakespeare in particular inevitably revived old meteorological theories.[51] Although the science of the elements and correspondences now had far more of an aesthetic appeal than a practical application, Romanticism nevertheless revived antiquated attitudes and helped them survive the agrarian and industrial revolutions. This is one reason why Shakespearian versions of 'merrie England' and thereby old seasonal identities survived: Renaissance literature was saved for the nation's identity by the Romantics, and consequently the old pagan – that is, classical – seasons inhabit Romantic writing as the part of 'A motion and a spirit' that 'rolls through all things'.[52]

Part II

5 SPRING

Nothing is so beautiful as Spring –
    When weeds, in wheels, shoot long and lovely and lush;
    Thrush's eggs look little low heavens, and thrush
Through the echoing timber does so rinse and wring
The ear, it strikes like lightnings to hear him sing;
    The glassy peartree leaves and blooms, they brush
    The descending blue; that blue is all in a rush
With richness; the racing lambs too have fair their fling.

Gerard Manley Hopkins, 'Spring'.

In the 'Mutabilitie Cantos' of *The Faerie Queene* (1609), the Elizabethan poet Edmund Spenser describes the allegorical figure of Spring:

> So, forth issew'd the Seasons of the yeare;
> First, lusty *Spring*, all dight in leaves of flowres
> That freshly budded and new bloosmes did beare
> (In which a thousand birds had built their bowres
> That sweetly sung, to call forth Paramours):
> And in his hand a javelin he did beare,
> And on his head (as fit for warlike stoures)
> A guilt engraven morion [helmet] he did weare;
> That as some did him love, so others did him feare.[1]

Spring here is ambivalent, a time of rising, the Old English *spring*, from the Old German *spryng*, meaning 'to ascend'. Hence it is the beginning or dawn of the year, of flowers blossoming, trees leafing, birds singing, but also a rousing to action, a call to arms for love and war. Spring is traditionally associated with rebirth, fertility, sex, and conquest; with sowing and planting and putting to stud; and with major festivals such as the pagan celebrations of Ostara and Beltane, and the Christian season of Eastertide. In some older British calendars, spring began on 1 February OS or on Candlemas, 2 February, the date of the Purification of the Virgin, forty days after the Nativity. This festival of light, which also drew on the Roman festival of Lupercalia ('chaos'), marked the end of winter and the old year by processing with candles, thereby looking forward to spring and the new year.

Candlemas also significantly marked the end of sexual abstinence practised since Advent: it was unwise in agricultural economies to have heavily pregnant women or newborn babies in the late summer months when there was much work to be done at harvest, and such family planning led the Church to advocate celibacy in December and January, and then in Lent too. It is therefore not surprising how strongly associated with renewed sexual activity the season of spring became. Native birdlife seemed to bear this out: birds were supposed to find their mates on St Valentine's Day and according to mediaeval calendars stopped singing on 5 June, by which time their young had hatched. The naturalist Gilbert White of Selborne actually wrote in his diary for 10 June 1768: 'The nightingale, having young, leaves-off singing, & makes a plaintive, & a jarring noise'.[2]

Such associations are omnipresent and inescapable. On the one hand, they reflect the facts of agricultural life; the hagiologist Graham Jones notes that, 'There is no escaping the connection between the dependency of pre-Industrial societies on a good harvest for their survival, and concepts of fertility and motherhood.'[3] But on the other hand, spring brings with it wider cultural associations, some of which are not necessarily accurate reflections of the season's activities and characteristics. Spring evokes, for instance, images of newborn lambs – but as the naturalist and mystic Richard Jefferies observed in the late nineteenth century, 'Those that only roam the fields when they are pleasant in May, see the lambs at play in the meadow, and naturally think of lambs and May flowers. But the lamb was born in the adversity of snow.'[4] Today, this particular association is under even greater strain as many lambs, particularly lowland breeds, are born in January.

Nevertheless, spring is the time for flirting and lovemaking, and indeed singing about it – as do Shakespeare's pages in *As You Like It* (1599–1600):

It was a lover and his lass,
    With a hey, and a ho, and a hey nonino,

That o'er the green corn-field did pass,
    In spring time, the only pretty [ring] time,
When birds do sing, hey ding a ding, ding,
Sweet lovers love the spring.[5]

Or as Alfred, Lord Tennyson put it in the tripping trochees of 'Locksley Hall', written in 1835:

In the Spring a fuller crimson comes upon the robin's breast;
In the Spring the wanton lapwing gets himself another crest;

In the Spring a livelier iris changes on the burnished dove;
In the Spring a young man's fancy lightly turns to thoughts of love.[6]

The skipping metre is intrinsic to the meaning of these lines, which deliciously evoke the quickening pulse of impatient sexual desire. Indeed, spring is always the 'sweet' season, and perhaps not surprisingly it turns out that the word 'sweet' has sexual connotations. Hence Henry Howard, earl of Surrey, described it in the sixteenth century precisely as

The soote season, that bud and blome forth brings,
With grene hath clad the hill, and eke the vale.[7]

Clearly flowers spring to mind here too, and the Cavalier poet Robert Herrick eulogized the violets,

Welcome Maids of Honour,
    You doe bring
    In the Spring;
And wait upon her.[8]

But 'sweet' and for that matter 'flowers' had even more urgent sexual undertones than this pastoral bridal procession suggests. The phrase 'ful swete in bedde' goes back at least to the fourteenth century and 'to be sweet upon' meant to caress. In more subtle poetic hands, then, spring was a reminder of the earthliness and earthiness of human existence, and the seventeenth-century metaphysical poet George Herbert drew melancholy attention to this corporeal rhythm of carnality in 'Vertue':

> Sweet spring, full of sweet dayes and roses,
> A box where sweets compacted lie.[9]

That 'box where sweets compacted lie' is a reference both to the female sexual anatomy and to a coffin containing a corpse.[10] Such ambivalences – of love and war, of sex and death – haunt the culture of spring.

MARCH

In *Fantasticks: Serving for a Perpetuall Prognostication* (1626), Nicholas Breton, poet and contemporary of Shakespeare, describes the month of March thus:

> It is now March, and the Northerne wind dryeth up the Southerne durt: The tender Lippes are now maskt for feare of chopping, and the faire hands must not be ungloved: now riseth the Sunne a pretty step to his faire height, and Saint *Valentine* calls the birds together, where Nature is pleased in the varietie of love: the Fishes and the Frogs fall to their manner of generation, and the Adder dyes to bring forth her young: the Ayre is sharpe, but the Sunne is comfortable, and the day beginnes to lengthen: The forward Gardens give the fine Sallets, and a Nosegay of Violets is a present for a Lady: Now beginneth Nature (as it were) to wake out of her sleepe, and sends the Traveller to survey the walkes of the World: the sucking Rabbit is good for weake stomackes, and the dyet for the Rhume doth many a great Cure: The Farrier now is the horses Physitian, and the fat Dog feeds the Faulcon in the Mew: the Tree begins

to bud, and the grasse to peepe abroad, while the Thrush with the Black-bird make a charme in the young Springs: the Milke-mayd with her best beloved, talke away wearinesse to the Market, and in an honest meaning, kind words doe no hurt: the Foot-ball now tryeth the legges of strength, and merry matches continue good fellowship: It is time of much worke, and tedious to discourse of: but in all I find of it, I thus conclude in it: I hold it the Servant of Nature, and the Schoole-master of Art: the hope of labour, and the Subject of Reason. Farewell.[11]

The wind may be like a knife, but the sun is out and it is spring. Birds, amphibians, fish, and reptiles are all breeding. Flowers are appearing, new growth is showing, the thrush and the blackbird are singing, and baby rabbits are on the menu. It is a good time of the year to play football – real football, that is, not soccer. There is much to do for the forthcoming year, much to learn, much to look forward to, and much to ponder.

Once upon a time in old Rome, March was the first month in the year. This was because it holds the vernal equinox – around 20 March there are equal hours of sunlight and night-time – and because it is placed to mark the beginning of spring. Although spring takes time to get going, at least in England, there is in fact official recognition of March's springly status: British Summertime begins on the last Sunday in March.

March is named after Mars, Martius, the god of war, and Roman military campaigns traditionally began in the spring. But Mars was also an agricultural god, and this is why Spenser presents March as his rather awkward soldier-farmer figure:

> . . . sturdy *March* with brows full sternly bent,
> And armed strongly, rode upon a Ram,
> The same which over *Hellespontus* swam:
> Yet in his hand a spade he also hent,
> And in a bag all sorts of seeds ysame,
> Which on the earth he strowed as he went,
> And fild her womb with fruitful hope of nourishment.[12]

Echoing the start of military campaigning, March is proverbially a turbulent month that commences with that cutting wind. The Old English name for this equinoctial month was Hlȳda, meaning 'loud', from the noise of the wind, and this name survived the Norman Conquest as 'Lide'. In the late seventeenth century, the English antiquary John Aubrey could still note that 'The vulgar in the West of England doe call the month of March, Lide'. He also quoted the proverbial dietary advice,

> Eat leekes in Lide, and ramsins [wild garlic] in May,
> And all the yeare after physitians may play [i.e., be idle].[13]

It is even claimed that the Anglo-Saxon word Lide survived into Cornwall in the nineteenth century: 'Ducks wan't lay till they've drink'd lide water'.[14] More recently the word was revived by J. R. R. Tolkien in his Middle-earth writings to indicate three days of midsummer.[15] Harsh winds are characteristic of March, but good for all flora: 'March winds and April showers / bring forth May flowers'.[16] Indeed, the wood anemone, also known as the 'wind flower' (Anemone nemrosa), takes its name from Greek myth: the wind (anemos) sends the flowers at the spring equinox in anticipation of March winds. It is the time for bluebells too, also known in England as English jacinth and blue harebell, granfer griggles, and goosey ganders, fairy bells, and ding dongs. They begin to flower copiously in the spring when the light increases on woodland floors, often indicating undisturbed land.

Although February might grow milder and more clement as it wears on, if 'February makes a bridge ... March breaks it'. It is certainly likely to be stormy come St Winwaloe's Day, 3 March, following St David's Day and St Chad's Day – as recorded in a piece of weatherlore collected in the nineteenth century, warning householders to keep their roofing thatch in good order:

> First comes David, then comes Chad,
> Then comes Winneral as though he were mad.
>> White or black
> Or old house thack [thatch].[17]

Extreme weather certainly has been recorded in March. Hail, sleet, and snow are common, and blizzards are not unknown. In 1891 the Great Blizzard raged across southern England and Wales for four days, with snowdrifts in the West Country as high as twenty feet. Trains were buried in drifts – one sat immobile for two days before it was spotted and the passengers rescued. Several people froze to death, thousands of sheep and cattle died, and in the English Channel some 220 drowned in sixty-five shipwrecks. The snow was still visible on Dartmoor in June.

More usually, though, March is expected to be very wet: 'A bushel of March dust is worth a Kings ransome' – that is, a dry March is very good for farmers, as there is plenty of sowing to be done.[18] A cold snap in March is a 'blackthorn winter', stimulating the blackthorn to produce its distinctive white blossom, usually after the sallow and before the hawthorn. The weather also has a predictive aspect: according to *The Shepherd's Kalender* (*c*.1765), the weather on 10 March forecasts conditions for the rest of the year – 'Mists, or hoar frosts, on the tenth of March betokens [*sic*] a plentiful year, but not without some diseases' – and the prevailing wind on 21 March sets the wind for the ensuing summer.[19] Most notoriously, though, 'March comes in like a lion, and goes out like a lamb', a popular proverb today, first quoted in Francis Beaumont and John Fletcher's 1624 play, *A Wife for a Moneth*.[20]

But March is not so much associated with lions as with hares: Mad March Hares. If you are ever lucky enough to see hares fighting, you are likely to be witnessing a buck, or jack, after a reluctant doe, or gill, rather than bucks competing with each other in a bout of fisticuffs. The phrase 'hare-brained' dates from 1542, with the pointed comment 'undiscretely or harebrainlike, he would nedes in any wyse bee reputed and taken for an *Academique*'.[21] Shakespeare fondly presented the hot-head Henry Percy as 'A hare-brain'd Hotspur, govern'd by a spleen', and Lewis Carroll created perhaps the most enduring image of the Mad March Hare during the tea party in *Alice's Adventures in Wonderland* (1865) – both ludicrous and sinister: '[T]he March Hare will be much the most interesting,' reasons Alice, 'and perhaps, as this is May, it wo'n't be raving mad – at least not so mad as it was in March'.[22]

Yet for all its English eccentricity, the hare was anciently a taboo animal in Britain. Even to utter its name was unlucky, so dozens of sidelong ways of describing it were coined. A thirteenth-century verse from Shropshire lists seventy-seven such names for the Macbethian creature:

The hare, the hare-kin,
Old Big-bum, Old Bouchart,
The hare-ling, the frisky one,
Old turpin, the fast traveller,
The way-beater, the white-spotted one,
The lurker in ditches, the filthy beast,
Old Wimount, the coward,
The slinker-away, the nibbler,
The one it's bad luck to meet, the white-livered,
The scutter, the fellow in the dew,
The grass nibbler, Old Goibert,
The one who doesn't go straight home, the traitor,
The friendless one, the cat of the wood . . .
The hare's mazes . . .
The dew-beater, the dew-hopper,
The sitter on its form, the hopper in the grass . . .
The stag of the cabbages, the cropper of herbage . . .
The animal that all men scorn,
The animal that no-one dares name. . . .[23]

Today, however, hares have some sort of status and hare-coursing in England has been banned by law. For most people – in other words, those who do not have to deal with hare forms, or nests, in arable farmland – the hare is now a rather magical creature, far nobler than its distant domesticated cousin, the rabbit. They are not rare – the number of hares in Britain is at a healthy 800,000 – but they are in decline due to hedgerow removal, an increase in the rural fox population, and wide-scale arable farming, which regularly kills the young in their forms and which is also responsible for the collapse in partridge and skylark populations. Nevertheless, in an age where many animals have lost their majesty and glamour (in the old sense of the word), a glimpse of a lolloping hare is like a peep into Faërie. It appears to travel along the margin of reality – and so it is bad luck if a hare simply crosses one's path, as this can lead to entanglements in the Elfworld. The lean beast is haloed with strange beliefs: it is a shape-shifter and can change its sex; it is eerily vigilant and sleeps with its eyes open; it is a familiar of witches and a favourite likeness for them to assume.[24] The hare, with its mysterious and uncanny heritage, deserves our respect.

The calendar of March begins on St David's Day (1 March). His sign of the leek is seasonal fare, and was also of course worn in hats. This is noted by Shakespeare in *Henry V*: in the play the king admits his Welsh lineage, and the tensions between the English and Welsh ranks is characterized by an episode in which the Welsh Captain Fluellen forces the English yeoman Pistol to eat his leek; clearly by this time, then, St David's Day had become an occasion for the Welsh to antagonize the English and the English to retaliate.[25] This unfortunate custom survived the Commonwealth and Restoration, and was recorded in all its antipathy by the Dutch landscape painter William Schellinks in a visit to London in 1662:

> We saw some countryfolk carry such large leeks on their hats that their heads hung almost sideways because of them. And so on this day the Welshmen are greatly teased by the English, not only by calling them Taffey, Taffey, or David, David, but also by hanging out all kinds of dolls and scarecrows with leeks on their heads, and as they celebrate the day with heavy boozing, and both sides, from the ale, strong beer, sack and claret, become short-tempered, obstinate, and wild, so it is not often that this day goes by without mishaps, and without one or the other getting into an argument or a blood fight.[26]

Shortly afterwards, in 1667, Pepys was noting a supposed English custom of hanging Welshmen in effigy on this day.[27] More recently, however, it seems that this aggression has been channelled into Six Nations rugby matches. Still, fleas supposedly arrive in England on St David's Day and you are therefore advised to keep your windows shut.

The first day of March was also the Roman festival of women, Matronalia. This possibly provided the impetus for celebrating Mothering Sunday. On the fourth Sunday in Lent those living and working away would return to their home parish – the mother church – with flowers for their families from their employers' gardens; this claim has, however, been dismissed as fanciful, and leading historians such as Ronald Hutton identify the tradition as arising in the seventeenth century.[28] Whatever the origin, Mothering Sunday emerged in the Middle Ages, and was also known as 'Braggot' Sunday after a fermented honey drink still brewed by connoisseurs of Old English ales today. By the mid-seventeenth century it was established in the west of England, and in his collection *Hesperides* (1648) the poet Robert Herrick records the customary gift of a simnel cake on this day.[29] Mothering Sunday subsequently spread across the country, and survives today in competition with the more anodyne American version, Mother's Day. Mother's Day was first proposed in 1907 and is now established as the second Sunday in May; braggot is seldom drunk.

In Devon, the first three days in March are unlucky for planting – they are called 'blind days' – but there is conflicting advice for 1 March and 2 March: 'Upon St. *David*'s Day put oats and barley in the clay', and 'David and Chad sow pease good or bad'.[30] St Gregory's Day follows on 12 March, the date of this canonized pope's death in 604, although since 1969 Roman Catholics have observed his feast day on 3 September, which is when his episcopal consecration took place in 590. Perhaps oddly, Gregory the Great is as good as ignored by the festive calendar, this despite his prominence in sending the first mission to Anglo-Saxon England after his encounter with English slaves at a market, where he famously quipped, 'They are not Angles but angels'.[31] Indeed, this pope is clearly not held in any affection – except perhaps by those sowing onions, who once knew the day as 'Gregory-gret onion', or white peas: 'Sowe runcivals [large peas] timelie, and all that be gray: / but sowe not the white till, S. Gregories day' (1570).[32] St Benedict's Day, 21 March, is also, according to

John Ray's *English Proverbs* (1737), a pea-planting day: 'St. *Benedick*, sow thy pease or keep them in thy rick.'[33] In contrast, St Patrick's Day, 17 March, is a day for horses – 'On St Patrick's day / let all your horses play' – perhaps in recognition of St Patrick's adoption as the patron saint of Ireland.[34] Although St Patrick's Day occurs in Lent, it is a well-established feast and, like Sundays and various other days during the Lent season – the feasts of Sts Thomas Aquinas, Gregory, and Benedict – would not have been treated as a day of fast in earlier times. Furthermore, thanks to Irish emigration and commercial opportunism, it has become a global phenomenon. The day is certainly celebrated with gusto in England, encouraged by themed publicity packs sent to pubs by the Guinness Brewery. Indeed, St Patrick's Day is probably the most extreme example of the commodification of national identity as a regular international event, reducing Irishness to stout, whiskey, some kind of folk music, shamrock bunting, cuddly lepre-chauns, and the colour green.

St Cuthbert's Day, 20 March, is the date of Durham's annual fair, the antiquity of which predates the Norman Conquest, but the most impor-tant March fairs were the hiring fairs held on 25 March: this is Lady Day, which celebrates the Annunciation of the Blessed Virgin Mary.[35] Until 1751 in England, Lady Day was considered the first day of the year – not so much because March was originally favoured as the first month by the Romans, but because 25 March marks the moment of conception, being nine months before the Christmas Nativity. The first Good Friday, the date of Christ's Passion, was also symmetrically determined to be 25 March.[36] Despite its significance, though, Lady Day passed as a normal working day – it was, for example, a rent day if not necessarily a quarter day – and seasonal Christian celebrations were reserved for Easter, which of course falls during the spring, 22 March being the earliest possible date for Easter Sunday.

Lady Day is a reminder that the everyday English Christian calendar was not confined to saints' days. The identification of Lady Day as the first day of the year and also the anniversary of the first Passion was reinforced by theological speculation based around this date. Bede calculated that

18 March was the first day of the Creation, and this divine reckoning was confirmed by Ælfric in the tenth century, '*Se eaheteoða dæg þæs monðes þe we hata∂ martius þone ge hata∂ hylda wæs se forma dæg þyssere worulde*' ['The eighteenth day of the month that we [the clergy] call March, which you [the laity] call Lide, was the first day of this world'].[37] From this insight it can be calculated that 21 March, St Benedict's Day, was the day on which the sun, moon, and stars were established and time began, and that 23 March was the making of Adam. In the English tradition, the Fall then fell on 25 March as well.[38]

APRIL

Of all the months of the year, April and May are mentioned most often in poetry and proverbial wisdom, the calendrist Nicholas Breton remarking that 'The Poets now make their studies in the woods'.[39] The origin of the word 'April' is obscure – it may derive from Aphrodite (the ancient Greek goddess of love), or the Latin verb *aperire* ('to open'), or even from *alius* ('other', being originally the second month of the year after March). But its cultural associations are clear: April is the month of unpredictable and capricious weather, and of the return of migratory birds.

Perhaps the best-known lines invoking April occur at the beginning of the recognizable English literary tradition, at the outset of Geoffrey Chaucer's *Canterbury Tales* (*c.*1387), opening the 'General Prologue':

> Whan that Aprille with his shoures soote
> The droghte of March hath perced to the roote,
> And bathed every veyne in swich licour
> Of which vertu engendred is the flour;
> Whan Zephirus eek with his sweete breeth
> Inspired hath in every holt and heeth
> The tendre croppes, and the yonge sonne
> Hath in the Ram his halve cours yronne,

And smale foweles maken melodye,
That slepen al the nyght with open ye
(So priketh hem nature in hir corages);
Thanne longen folke to goon on pilgrimages.[40]

Chaucer describes the familiar April showers, although his suggestion that March is dry is somewhat at odds with vernacular wisdom. The wind is light, the crops begin to shoot, the sun is warm, the birds sing – and good Christians decide to go on pilgrimage. His point then is to mark the calendar months by the seasons and their relationship to the secular farming year before placing them in a religious framework of sacred homage.

Chaucer's depiction of April soaks through the history of representations of this month. Breton too makes a similar suggestion, describing how 'the Sunny showers perfume the aire' and marking the pearly dew. Nightingales, turtle-doves, and larks sing; trout and salmon are in the rivers; flowers bloom and the hawthorn and blackthorn blossom; colts frolic and lambs gambol. April makes the old feel youthful and the young feel chuffed: 'I hold it the Heavens blessing, and the Earths comfort'.[41] These aspects are likewise picked up in country sayings in collections such as Thomas Tusser's Five Hundreth Points of Good Husbandry (1573): 'Sweete Aprill showers / Do spring May flowers', an observation first recorded in 1560 and which has remained popular ever since.[42] The idea also lies behind Shakespeare's salacious lines in Antony and Cleopatra:

The April's in her eyes, it is love's spring,
And these the showers to bring it on.[43]

This is cultural meteorology: if the phrase 'April showers' derived from the pastoral fabrications of Chaucer and Breton, as well as proverbial remarks on the best weather to bring on the darling buds of May flowers, it also inevitably became common shorthand for describing April weather – no matter that April is in fact one of the driest months in England and is now becoming drier due to climate change.[44] Indeed, the so-called 'peasant poet' John Clare does not refer to April showers in his poem, 'The Days of April'. For him, April is a time for flowers: primroses, wood anemones, daisies, cowslips, pilewort (lesser celandine), sallow blossom, 'And wood larks dropping from the rich blue sky'.[45] He seems particularly taken by the song of the lark, which for Clare typifies spring: in the poem 'Larks and Spring', he writes how 'In every field they mount and sing / The song of Nature and of Spring'.[46]

Shakespeare, too, notes concisely the seasonal blooms, 'proud-pied April (dress'd in all his trim)' and 'well-apparelled April on the heel / Of limping Winter'.[47] He also represents April as a time of inconstant weather and hence, perhaps, of inconstancy in general:

> O, how this spring of love resembleth
>   The uncertain glory of an April day,
> Which now shows all the beauty of the sun,
>   And by and by a cloud takes all away.[48]

Even the urbane and metropolitan Augustan satirist Alexander Pope got out enough to notice the changeability of April's weather:

> Good God! what an Incongruous Animal is Man? how unsettled in his best part, his soul; and how changing and variable in his frame of body? The constancy of the one, shook by every notion, the temperature of the other, affected by every blast of wind. What an April weather in the mind![49]

Two writers, however, seem to have taken a somewhat peculiar view of April. Not for them the sunny showers or blossoming flowers, the flux of spring – or rather, something else overshadows this seasonal movement. In Samuel Taylor Coleridge's conversational poem 'Dejection', written on 4 April 1802, the poet listens to the howls of an Aeolian harp, set whining by scything gusts of wind:

Mad Lutanist! who in this month of showers,
Of dark-brown gardens, and of peeping flowers,
Mak'st Devils' yule with worse than wintry song,
The blossoms, buds, and timorous leaves among.[50]

April here is a wasteland of bare earth haunted by an everlasting winter
and stalked by things diabolical – a look askance towards the realm of
Faërie. And at the opening of Coleridge's 'Christabel' too, April is chilly,
again in the thrall of a winter that will not lift; it is fey and foreboding,
a dark time:

The thin gray cloud is spread on high,
It covers but not hides the sky.
The moon is behind, and at the full;
And yet she looks both small and dull.
The night is chill, the cloud is gray:
'Tis a month before the month of May,
And the Spring comes slowly up this way.[51]

This cold or unseasonal poetics is striking, and such inversion of seasonal
expectations can create unsettling effects: the familiar is made discon-
certingly unfamiliar, the seasons slip out of joint. At a much more minor,
domestic level, this accounts for the unease that unseasonal weather
brings with it: weather that goes against expectations can be merely dis-
appointing – no snow at Christmas – or it can induce a sort of madness.
Coleridge's contemporary Keats wrote similarly of April as a deathly month
in his 'Ode on Melancholy', a poem deeply entwined in sorcerous herbs,
poison berries, and suffocating flowers:

But when the melancholy fit shall fall
    Sudden from heaven like a weeping cloud,
That fosters the droop-headed flowers all,
    And hides the green hill in an April shroud....[52]

These lines rely for their initial impact on their contradiction of the habitual; this is not what we expect to happen in April. Furthermore, in challenging prevailing attitudes they suggest that there may be other, more sophisticated ways of comprehending the weather – ways that do not rely on the usual clichés but which ponder its unpredictability and mystery, that move everyday weather from the natural world into the realm of the supernatural. These weather effects make nature eerie and remote; they create a particularly unnerving atmosphere.[53]

Coleridge's most effective use of his unseasonal poetics is in 'The Rime of the Ancient Mariner', a poem that reveals how Anglocentric our reading of the weather is likely to be. The ship has passed the equator, and is eventually enmired in a nightmarish world on a rotting sea. The moon's beams shine out over this fervid main 'Like April hoar-frost spread'.[54] The image is startling – not only in the invocation of ice (precisely, rime) in the thick Pacific night, but in being an April frost. The image destabilizes our world picture: the ship has crossed the line, and so April has become one of the months of the autumnal equinox rather than of the spring. The year is waning: April is now marching towards the winter solstice and suddenly time feels like it is running backwards. The world has been turned upside-down, the months inverted. And so while a huge leap from Chaucer's imaginary English pastoral, it was but a small step from Coleridge's hallu-cinatory collapse of the seasons for T. S. Eliot to begin *The Waste Land* (1922) with the line, 'April is the cruellest month'.[55]

––––––

When the Ancient Mariner then finds his way through more familiar waters and eventually to his home ground, Coleridge promptly marks this shift in reality with the song of the lark. We are back within the English seasons, among the birdlife of April. Indeed, the return of migratory birds and the sudden crescendo of birdsong at this time of the year has exerted a cultural and ornithological fascination for centuries.

For Robert Browning, it was the chaffinch bursting into song that characterized the month of April:

Oh, to be in England
Now that April's there,
And whoever wakes in England
Sees, some morning, unaware,
That the lowest boughs and the brushwood sheaf
Round the elm-tree bole are in tiny leaf,
While the chaffinch sings on the orchard bough
In England – now![56]

The chaffinch can return as early as 5 February, though, and it is more likely that Browning meant the chiffchaff – the 'true herald of spring'.[57] The wheatear is actually the first of the spring migrants, but the chiffchaff can arrive by the second week of March and so is singing much earlier than the cuckoo. As Sir Edward, Viscount Grey – Liberal member of parliament, foreign secretary before the Great War, ornithologist, and author of *The Cottage Book* (1909) and *The Charm of Birds* (1927) – wrote:

> [the chiffchaff] is forerunner of the rush of songbirds that is on its way to us and will arrive in April, and thereafter enrich our woods, meadows and gardens with still further variety and quality of song. That is why the first hearing of a chiffchaff moves us so each spring. He is a symbol, a promise, an assurance of what is to come.[58]

Swallows come in early April, anticipating the spring, and curlews too. Grey again: 'To listen to curlews on a bright, clear April day, with the fullest of spring still in anticipation is one of the best experiences that a lover of birds can have. On a still day one can almost feel the air vibrating with the blessed sound.'[59] The 'drumming' of the great spotted woodpecker provides another sound of early spring – this is a territorial refrain made by tapping tree-trunks with its beak; the snipe also 'drums' in spring. The nightingale returns about mid-April, the cock birds arriving some ten days before the hens to mark their territories with song, most often at dawn and dusk. They will have stopped singing by the end of May.

The list goes on – redstarts begin to return at the end of April – and it is abundantly clear that the spring chorus of English birdsong has remained a natural phenomenon as well as a cultural shorthand for this time of the year and thereby inseparable from our idea of spring. And yet it is important to appreciate just how quickly this is changing. Birds are arriving at different times, not only because the English spring is warming up more quickly, but also because weather patterns across Europe and Africa are altering. Droughts in Africa in the Sahara, Sahel, and elsewhere can severely affect the feeding habits and survival rates of birds that migrate to the British Isles. In other words, this aspect of our national seasonal identity is intimately connected to regions thousands of miles away. Moreover, when the birds do arrive in Britain, they may find that their traditional habitats have disappeared. Blue tits, for instance, are suffering because their eggs are hatched to coincide with the caterpillar flush. But as caterpillars themselves are hatching some two weeks earlier due to climate change, fewer blue tit chicks are surviving: up to 80 per cent of a brood will starve.[60] The great tit, in contrast, has adapted to the early flush and now lays eggs two weeks earlier than thirty years ago. Similarly the blackcap, which used to arrive in about the third week of April, is now arriving earlier to take advantage of seasonal changes. It is only able to do so because it winters in Italy, so is at less risk of drought than the birds that migrate from Africa, such as the swallow. Butterflies themselves are appearing earlier, and some such as the red admiral no longer migrate but winter in Britain and are evident from late January, as opposed to mid-May. Bumblebees no longer hibernate and are spreading north. Even the hay-fever season has extended several weeks, now lasting from early March to early October.

Of course, some birds are benefiting from these changes, or are able to adapt more rapidly. Numbers of the flashing, incendiary kingfisher have increased due to milder, wetter weather, and the nightingale may also increase in dry Aprils and Mays. The blackbird has adapted well and extended its territory to compete with the ring ouzel and song thrush, which are faring less successfully. It is, however, becoming too warm for some North Atlantic birds: the puffin, for instance, is likely to move to cooler climes.

———

April has just a handful of significant dates, due in part to the Easter calendar that dominates this time of the year, St Mark's Day, 25 April, being the latest possible date for Easter. The other most significant traditional days of the month are All Fools' Day, 1 April, St George's Day, 23 April, St Mark's Eve, 24 April, and May Eve, 30 April. Old Lady Day, 6 April, is now the start of the financial year: rents were due and the date therefore became a day of moving, or flitting. The first three days of April are 'borrowing days' – that is, they are days supposedly borrowed by March and therefore have very bad weather. This tradition is unclear, but meddling with the days seems to have created some sort of meteorological disturbance. Still, 'If it thunders on All Fools' Day, / It brings good crops of corn and hay'.[61] Aside from that, Gilbert White noted that the wryneck 'pipes about in orchards. The first spring bird of passage'.[62] Aubrey recorded that at Droitwich there was a saltwater well sacred to St Richard that was traditionally garlanded on his day of 3 April.[63]

The story of how St George became the patron saint of England, and of how his bloody cross became part of the Union Jack flag, has been told at length elsewhere.[64] Suffice to say that although local celebrations can be dated back as far as the ninth century, the English love affair with the Syrian *megalomartyr* St George really began in the aftermath of the Norman Conquest and was driven by the popularity of warrior saints, or *milites Christiani*, during the Crusades and England's wars with the rest of the known world. Consequently at Cheddar in Somerset, for example, annual fairs have been held on 23 April since the reign of Henry III.[65] Indeed, evidence from 1244 suggests that Georgist festivities were already well established by this time: Henry III mandated

a dragon to be made in fashion of a standard, of red silk sparkling all over with gold, the tongue of which should be made to resemble burning fire, and appear to be continually moving, and the eyes of sapphires or other suitable stones, and to place it in the Church of St Peter, Westminster, against [in full view of] the King's coming.[66]

From at least 1399, St George's Day was officially recognized as a national holiday of sorts, and the more elaborate St George ridings or pageants were first recorded in 1408.[67] They may have involved mummers' plays, or some version of that tradition.

By the time of Henry VIII, St George's Day had been a significant event in the festive year for over a century – one could even be fined for not attending. Yet St George's Day ridings were not folk celebrations or carnivalesque events, but quite the opposite: they were a display of strength by the authorities and ruling powers.[68] Ridings were formal civic and guild events, equivalent to a Lord Mayor's show or communist May Day parade, consisting of processions, displays, devotions, and dinner. Nevertheless, at least some elements of traditional festivities were incorporated into them: at Norwich in the early 1500s St George was accompanied by 'the Snap', the mummers' hobby-horse appearing as a dragon.

St George occupied an unusual position after the Reformation: he was the national patron saint, his cross constituted the national flag, and he was the symbolic founder of the country's highest chivalric company, the Knights of the Garter. But St George also risked Protestant and Puritan displeasure by being classed as an instance of Catholic idolatry. Henry VIII tried to square this particular circle by declaring that while George should not be worshipped as a saint, he could still be celebrated as a person. It was not enough. Elizabeth I celebrated St George's Day in 1559 in grand style, but eight years later she abolished the event; thereafter, remaining Georgist festivities were incorporated into May Day.[69]

Despite the disappearance of the ridings, there were periodic attempts to revive the celebration of the day at a popular level. At the turn of the century, the balladeer and romance writer Richard Johnson's *Famous Historie of the Seaven Champions of Christendome* (1596–7) rewrote St George as a popular hero, and in *Henry VI, Part 1* Shakespeare noted the practice of lighting festive bonfires on St George's night:

Bonfires in France forthwith I am to make,
To keep our great Saint George's feast withal.[70]

Meanwhile, James I and VI took to the cult of St George with kingly enthusiasm, a fashion followed by his successor Charles I and consequently suppressed by Charles's nemesis, Oliver Cromwell. But George's fortunes did not sink completely during the years of the Interregnum. Although St George ridings were prohibited, his bloody cross became a standard of the Commonwealth – which is why it was all but ignored for generations afterwards, stained as it was with regicide and republicanism.

It was not until the nineteenth century that the folk cult of St George revived: the saint reminded the English of their Englishness, he was a folk hero of 'merrie England' and the central figure in many legendary mummers' plays, and he was also an exemplary Christian martyr.[71] St George therefore embodied the muscular Christianity of the British Empire as well as the egalitarian vision of early socialist movements, and was also a convenient model for the pocket-sized chivalry of the Boy Scout movement, of which he was made patron saint. But there was little common festivity attached to his veneration, and by the Second World War, a war fought as a resolutely British commitment with barely a mention of England, St George was again forgotten.[72] After the war, as British saints such as Andrew, David, and Patrick became increasingly revered and celebrated, George was steadfastly ignored by the general population until the end of the twentieth century, when a connection was made with association football. At the Euro '96 competition, English football supporters finally began to sport the cross of St George rather than waving the red-white-and-blue of the Union Jack, as they had done in 1966, and a popular version of Englishness began to be recognized and celebrated. A few weeks after Euro '96, as if in league with the new Zeitgeist, the Church of England revived St George's Day as a feast day.

Despite all this, however, little seems to happen on the day itself. Breweries are gradually catching on by providing gigantic novelty top hats and themed beer, and there is a high-street market for greetings cards and cheap-and-cheerful St George fancy dress, but beyond that and without the official sanction that would revive the ridings, there remains little sense of just what should be done on St George's Day. The folklorist Steve Roud discusses the English indifference to St George's Day with a sort of relieved and inverted pride, arguing that English identity is thankfully not being threatened with commercialization and commodification in the same way that St Patrick's Day has become an embarrassing international exercise in 'Oirishness'.[73] He is right in a way, but many feel that the English do need to do something to recognize their national day – otherwise the country will be condemned to rest the burden of its national identity on the hunched shoulders of a reliably under-performing football team. The neglected traditions, the literature and the culture of England's seasons are not just quaint archaeology. They need to be protected, preserved, and researched, and also to be restored, revived, and lived. If the English people, the lion that never roared, abdicate this responsibility, such expressions of national identity that remain will be appropriated by political extremists or taken over by commercial interests. It is time to act, and St George's Day seems to be a good day on which to do so. It could be a national day of local customs – some archaic, others yet to emerge. It could bring communities together by celebrating local diversity and character – individuality embedded in landscape and place, its history and its wildlife – all across the country. Rather than trying to kickstart a national celebration with one brand of beer and one red-and-white flag, St George's Day offers an opportunity to recognize difference and variety – strikingly appropriate to a saint who had a dazzlingly multifarious nature long before he was simplified into a mere dragon-slayer. Although St George only receives passing mention in the environmental activist group Common Ground's benchmark compendium, *England in Particular* (2006), making St George's Day a celebration of 'local distinctiveness' could provide a focus for many of the sort of initiatives the organization favours, from making parish maps filled with tiny communal and environmental detail to celebrating the two thousand-plus varieties of English apples by planting new orchards.[74] St George's

Day is, for instance, traditionally a good day on which to make dandelion wine: at the very least we should be aiming to celebrate it with such local vintages rather than with mass-produced keg beer. In doing so, we will begin to think again about how best to sustain both our communities and the environment.

In contrast to the bygone public spectacle of St George's Day, St Mark's Eve on 24 April was a much more private and intimate time. It was an occasion for premonitions in affairs of the heart, for having either sweet dreams or nightmares – the wraith of a future lover summoned to one's side – and also for forecasting death.[75] The customary vigil begins at midnight:

> On St. Mark's Eve, at twelve o'clock,
> The fair maid she will watch her smock,
> To find her husband in the dark,
> By praying unto good St. Mark.[76]

The eve of this feast day had traditionally been a time of dissipation, in truth perhaps a hangover from the feast of St George on 23 April, and the twelfth-century theologian Johannes Beleth complained that 'girls and boys, singers and gamblers' would spend the night before St Mark's Day in church, drinking.[77] But what they were doing there was divining mortality: descrying the ghosts of those who would die in the coming year. St Mark's Eve customs therefore tend towards the dark side of ritual, involving strictly observed silence, midnight rites, blades of grass symbolically plucked from graveyards, and similarly spine-chilling pursuits. Waiting in the church porch at midnight, which was first recorded in 1608, offered foretellings of death, but the price of such infernal knowledge was high. As late as the nineteenth century, 'an old fellow at Carthorpe' recalled in his rich Yorkshire dialect:

> 'Ah niver watched mysen, bud one James Haw used ti watch t' deead gan in an' cum oot o' Bon'iston Chetch iwery St. Mark Eve ez it cam

roond. He 'ed teea; he war forced tul 't, he c'u'dn't help hissen; he'd deean it yance, an' 'ed ti gan on wi' 't. Aye, an' he seed t' sperrits ov all them 'at war gahin ti dee that year, all on 'em dhrissed i' ther natt'ral cleeas, or else hoo mud he a'e kenn'd whau tha war? They all passed cleease tiv him, bud neean on 'em iwer gav' him a nod, na nowt o' that soart. Bud,' added he, almost in a whisper, 'them 'at duz it yance awlus 'ev ti deea 't; tha cann't he'd thersens back, they're forced ti gan iwery tahm St. Mark's Eve cums roond. Mun! it's a despert thing ti 'a'e ti deea, 'coz ya 'a'e ti gan, whahl at t' last end ya see yersen pass yersen, an' then ya knaw 'at yer tahm's cum'd an' 'at ya'll be laid i' t' cau'd grund afoor that daay cum twelve-month.'[78]

Keats describes the vigil in his fragment, 'The Eve of St Mark'. He notes the typical seasonal characteristics of the 'wholesome drench of April rains', but also the 'chilly sunset', a portent of doom – contrasting the thin spring weather outside with the virginal 'maiden fair' Bertha alone inside.[79] She sits reading, like so many of Keats's figures, in aesthetic opulence – it is unclear whether the embroideries in her chamber are material, or her own imaginings – but the mediaevalist prophecy of St Mark does carry an arcane weight, and warns of the appearance on the eve of St Mark of the ghosts of all who must die in the coming year.[80] Perhaps April really is the cruellest month.

MAY

The month of May is always the 'merry' month of May:

> There are twelve months in all the year,
>   As I hear many men say,
> But the merriest month in all the year
>   Is the merry month of May –

Or so the ballad of 'Robin Hood Rescuing Three Squires' has it.[81] If any month is synonymous with a season, it is May with spring. Its very name derives from a goddess of growth – the Roman Maia – and May began in the middle of the Roman festival of Floralia.[82] Sir Thomas Malory noted in the *Morte d'Arthur* that 'the month of May was come, when every lusty heart that is any manner of lover springeth, burgeoneth, buddeth, and flourisheth in lusty deeds', and Chaucer too found its blandishments a distraction from studying:

> the joly tyme of May,
> Whan that I here the smale foules synge,
> And that the floures gynnen for to sprynge,
> Farewel my stodye, as lastynge that sesoun![83]

May clearly has associations of rebirth, fertility, and sexual activity. It is a time fecund, opulent, and careless. Breton thinks that there is something in the May air – 'the sweetnesse of the Aire refresheth every spirit'. Sunbeams mingle with showers, rainbows kindle, the air is filled with birdsong – larks by day and nightingales by night – sleek deer roam the woods, mackerel and shad fill the sea. Food is tender and succulent: butter, sage, and peas; chicken, duck, and gosling; fresh cheese, and strawberries and cream.[84] The month is, according to Breton, the most sensuous: 'fayre weather makes the Labourer merry. . . . It is the moneth wherein Nature hath her full of mirth'.[85]

Likewise, Spenser regards May as a time for seasonal dainties, in an image recalling Sandro Botticelli's painting *Primavera* (c.1482):

> Then came faire *May*, the fayrest mayd on ground,
> Deckt all with dainties of her seasons pryde,
> And throwing flowres out of her lap around.[86]

Clare, writing some two centuries later of the disappearance of this idealized rural life, is, however, more carefully precise. His poem 'May' lists the countryman's observations that tell the arrival of the month:

The restless cuckoo absent long
& twittering swallows chimney song
& hedge row crickets notes that run . . .
& swathy bees about the grass . . .
To see the wheat grow green & long . . .
Or short not[e] of the changing thrush
Above him in the white thorn bush
That oer the leaning stile bends low
Loaded with mockery of snow
Mozzled wi many a lushy thread
Of crab tree blossoms delicate red . . .
Tender shoots begin to grow
From the mossy stumps below . . .
The yellow hammer builds its nest . . .
Bum barrels twit on bush & tree
Scarse bigger than a bumble bee
& in a white thorns leafy rest
It builds its curious pudding nest . . .
     May locks new come
& princifeathers cluttering bloom
& blue bells from the wood land moss
& cowslip cucking balls to toss.[87]

And later, in the nineteenth century, Robert Browning reminds us of the abundant, ever-changing birdlife:

And after April, when May follows,
And the whitethroat builds, and all the swallows![88]

But despite this expectation of sunshine and flowers and birds, May is often cold. This can be a good thing: 'Cold May and a winedye, / Barne filleth up finelye', the saying goes, and warm Mays were proverbially a risk to health – 'A hot May makes a fat churchyard'.[89] And it could certainly get cold and intemperate. The most violent hailstorm ever recorded in Britain took place in May 1697, recorded by the natural scientist Edmund Halley on 10 May in North Wales and North-west England, with a reprise on 15 May in Hertfordshire. The largest stones that fell were over five-and-a-half inches across – almost as big as a human skull – and at least one person was killed.[90] Towards the end of the month, 25 May was a day on which the weather patterns for the rest of the year would be predicted: 'If it rain on the 25th, wind shall do much hurt that year; / if the sun shine, the contrary'.[91]

So despite the sunny disposition of May, it is wise not to 'cast a clout' until May be out – in other words, not to dispense with winter clothing until the month is over. As the following advice from John Sowter's 1733 manual, *The Way to be Wise and Wealthy*, indicates: 'Leave not off a Clout. / Till May be out.'[92] This rhyme, which comes in a series of monthly proverbs, also reveals that despite the insistence of some commentators, this saying refers to the month of May and not to the appearance of blossom on the hawthorn or 'may' – which is surely far too early a time to go casting off 'clouts', or clothes, even today.[93]

The likelihood of bad weather, at odds with the floral image of May, is a repressed truth that returns in examples of the reputation that May has for being a dark and unlucky month. The first three days of the month, 1–3 May, were 'sharp days' on which no work should be started, women should not launder, men should not dig gardens. It was also a bad month to marry in: 'Marry in May and you'll rue the day'.[94] (Things were little better in June: the second of the month was also unlucky for marriage in England.) This tradition may be connected with the proverbial unluckiness of the last day of Floralia, 3 May – traditionally unlucky in ancient Rome and similarly the most unlucky day in Scotland. In Chaucer's poem 'Troilus and Criseyde', it is on 3 May that Pandarus tells Criseyde of Troilus' love, effectively condemning her. On the other hand, 8 May was the most popular day to marry in Christian Rome because of an appearance by the Archangel Michael, as reported by Lodowick Lloyd in his *Diall of Daies* (1590).[95]

———

Steve Roud, that indefatigable chronicler of customs, traditions, and superstitions, notes that May Day activities are second only to Christmas in the English festive calendar. They take place at all levels of society, and have also absorbed many folklorists, historians, antiquarians, and saloon-bar philosophers in remembering, researching, reviving, and reinventing them. Likewise, the scholar-editors Bonnie Blackburn and Leofranc Holford-Strevens note that 1 May has probably more traditional customs than any other day: bringing in the may, garlanding, singing May songs, and dancing around a maypole. Even the phrase 'going a-maying' is fluid, extending its meaning from collecting greenery to refer to any May-time custom (see Chapter 8).[96] May Day was also another All Fools' Day in some parts of England, notably the north, where May fools were known as May goslings. It was in addition the beginning of the London May Fair, a commercial market that ran for fifteen days from 1 May.[97] Greenwich Fair, which by 1761 was attracting 15,000 visitors annually, was also held around this time; Dickens described it in *Sketches by Boz* (1836–7) as 'a three days' fever, which cools the blood for six months afterwards'.[98]

Aside from May Day revels, the month has other carnivalesque festivities. The first Sunday after May Day – 'Low Sunday' – was the traditional day for Randwick Wap (it is now held on the second Saturday in May). First recorded in about 1703, this is a lord-of-misrule festival in which a mock mayor is elected to preside for the day over the Stroud village. The most notable of such events, however, is the Helston Furry Day and Floral Dance in Cornwall. This is held on Michael's Feast, 8 May, and commemorates a battle between Michael and the Devil.[99] The Devil's stone, hurled at the town, survives to this day in the courtyard of the Angel Inn. The Furry Dance music is first played as an overture on 1 May, and the celebrations proper begin a week later at 7 a.m. with a series of dances and singing:

> With Hal-an-Tow! Rumbelow!
> For we are up as soon as any O!
> And for to fetch the summer home,
> The summer and the May O!

> For summer is a-come O!
> And winter is a-gone O![100]

A huge processional dance then continues until about five o'clock in the evening. Helston's festivities were reported in the *Gentleman's Magazine* of June 1790, with the suggestion that Furry Day was a corruption of Flora's Day, although the name probably derives from the Cornish *fer*, itself derived from the Latin *feria*, a fair.[101] Helston Furry Day could also be a rare survival of Elizabethan 'Robin Hood' May Day festivals, as the song 'Hal-an-Tow' also incorporates a fifteenth-century Bristol sea shanty – perhaps a remnant of the national legacy of Elizabethan seafarers.

Brigg hiring fair (the 'statty') was held in the North Lincolnshire market town on the Friday before Old May Day – i.e., 12 May after 1752 and 13 May after 1800 – and some Old May Day festivals survive, notably Garland Day in Abbotsbury in Dorset. This was first described by the country historian John Hutchins in his *History and Antiquities of the County of Dorset* (1774).[102] Garlands of flowers were blessed in the parish church of St Nicholas and were then cast on the waves to bless the season's mackerel fishermen with a good catch. Although mackerel are no longer fished at Abbotsbury, the tradition survives as Garland Day: willow garlands of wild and garden flowers are laid on the village war memorial by local children.[103] Rye and Brighton also have mackerel rituals. At Rye the fishermen spit in the mouth of the first mackerel caught, whereas Brighton has its Bread and Cheese and Beer Day. The Brighton fishermen pray as the first nets are cast, and when ten nets have been spread, the skipper says,

> Watch, barrel, watch! Mackerel for to catch,
> White may they be, like blossom on the tree.
> God send thousands, one, two, and three,
> Some by their heads, some by their tails,
> God sends thousands, and never fails.[104]

In the early nineteenth century Derbyshire miners also celebrated Old May Day with garlands, dinner, and festivities. And in Lincolnshire at least, the Sunday nearest to 13 May was 'Rook Sunday' for eating pies filled with 'squabs', or baby rooks.[105]

The nineteenth of May was popularly known as St Dunstan's Day. Dunstan was abbot of Glastonbury around 940 and subsequently archbishop of Canterbury. According to Devonian legend – as opposed to Somerset hagiography – once, when he was brewing beer, Dunstan made a pact with the Devil to blight the orchards so that there would be no cider-apple crop and therefore a good market for his own beverage. Dunstan stipulated that the apple trees should be struck on 17, 18, and 19 May – the last date being St Dunstan's Day.[106] More edifyingly, Dunstan was also known for being tempted while he was making a chalice with a pair of tongs. A beautiful woman appeared whom he seized by the nose with the red-hot instrument: she was the Devil in disguise. The tongs are included in the arms of Tower Hamlets, and the well at which Dunstan was working and his anvil are at St Leonards-Mayfield School, formerly Mayfield Convent, in Sussex.

Oak Apple Day falls at the end of the month, on 29 May; it is also known as Royal Oak Day and Shick-Shack Day. This was a formal recognition of the restoration of Charles II after he had been proclaimed king on 8 May 1660, to coincide with his thirtieth birthday and in memory of the oak tree at Boscobel in Shropshire in which Charles hid after the Battle of Worcester – hence the pub name, the Royal Oak. The date of the anniversary was declared by Act of Parliament and the first annual celebration was noted by the diarist John Evelyn the very next year, 29 May 1661. Royal Oak Day appropriated some features of May Day and Whitsun, such as maypoles and garlands, in part because it was simply likely to be a warmer time of the year, but there is also some suggestive overlap between the supposed licentiousness of May Day and the Puritan attacks against it, and the sexual antics of the 'Merrie Monarch', Charles II, and his court. The oral historian Charles Kightly observes that after the Restoration, 'Oak Apple Day soon became so popular – especially in the Royalist north and west of England – that it absorbed many May Day and other customs'.[107] In other words, the sexual connotations of May Day were politicized by the Royalists. After years of Puritan rule and the regulation of sexual behaviour, this new Royalist libertinism was a clear way of showing support for the loose-moralled monarch and deliberately offending Puritan sensibilities. In other words, both maying and swiving were political acts that upheld the values of the constitutional Stuart monarchy against those of the republican Commonwealth. It was therefore another establishment festival: until 1864, Royal Oak Day was a holiday celebrated in the *Book of Common Prayer* – as were other political anniversaries such as the Martyrdom of Charles I on 30 January and Gunpowder Plot Day on 5 November.

Garland Day at Castleton in Derbyshire is a remnant of a Royal Oak Day festival; it is held on 29 May, or 28 May if 29 May is a Sunday. The pubs in the village take it in turns to make a three-foot-high garlanded frame; that evening, the Garland King and Lady ride the parish boundary, linking the festival to Rogation, and when they arrive at the garland pub, the new garland itself is placed over the King and there is a procession around the village to the 'Garland Tune'. Eventually, the King and Lady arrive alone in the churchyard and the new garland is pulled up the tower of St Edmund's Church; only the crowning posy, the 'Queen', remains. Great Wishford in Wiltshire, once known as Wishford Magna, also continues to celebrate Royal Oak Day as Grovely Rights Day.[108] This curious event begins at four o'clock in the morning with rough music to rouse the villagers, who leave at dawn to collect oak branches, some of which are taken to Salisbury Cathedral, and there is a procession of oak boughs through the village to the parish boundary.[109] The local pub – the Royal Oak, of course – has the Grovely motto inscribed on its sign: 'Grovely Grovely Grovely and All Grovely / Unity is Strength'. Aston-on-Clun in Shropshire's Arbor Day also possibly derives from Royal Oak Day. A distinctive black poplar tree was traditionally festooned with flags to commemorate the wedding of Mary Carter to John Marston on 29 May 1786. Black poplars, also known as Manchester poplars, are in serious decline across the country, and a revival of Royal Oak Day as Oak Apple Day would, if nothing else, be one way of drawing attention to their gradual disappearance. In Aston-on-Clun the tradition continued until the tree fell in 1995; a sapling grown from a cutting taken from the original has since been planted and the customary flags now surround it.

As trees are garlanded, the mowing season begins. St Walstan, an agricultural saint martyred with scythes, is celebrated on 30 May. His day marks the beginning of the reaping season according to the sixteenth-century agriculturalist Thomas Tusser:

> Set mowers a worke, while meddowes be growne:
> the lenger they stande, so much worse to be mowne.[110]

St Walstan's Day is therefore a final reminder of the grim mortality that stalks the spring.

Spring festivals celebrate spring, but they are also an attempt to arrest the season, to halt time at a moment of anticipated plenty – what is effectively a little re-enactment of the human condition in the Garden of Eden before the Fall. In doing so, they also reflect a conservative desire to preserve the old order and defeat the fickleness of the weather. Poetry, too, becomes a way of stalling change, a device to ensure a perpetual season – and therefore it tends to be Royalist poets, supporters of the threatened Stuart monarchy, even Catholic sympathizers, who inscribe the spring as a constant in English cultural life. Rather than focusing on the unpredictability of the weather, these poets canonize the permanence of the seasons – the most striking example of this being Robert Herrick's *Hesperides*:

> I sing of *Brooks*, of *Blossomes*, *Birds*, and *Bowers*:
> Of *April*, *May*, of *June*, and *July*-flowers.
> O sing of *May-poles*, *Hock-carts*, *Wassails*, *Wakes*,
> Of *Bride-grooms*, *Brides*, and of their *Bridall-cakes*.[111]

Consequently, our image of spring has in large part been conjured up by seventeenth-century political poetry written at a time when the identity of England itself was desperately under threat from civil war and religious extremism, and therefore yearning for a lost idyll that had never really existed. That is not to say that this inheritance should not be taken seriously: rather, we should be aware that this image of merrie England in the springtime is seventeenth-century nostalgia and can act as a powerful reminder of the ambitions of poets and writers to shape not only the world around them, but the future as well. And if our assumptions about spring have been sieved and sifted through literature and are therefore profoundly cultural, they are nevertheless a constant reminder to attend to the weather and the seasons and to notice the conformities and disparities with the experiences and fancies of the past. Whether or not the season lives up to our cultural expectations, and whether or not those expectations are realistic, they should still encourage us to take heed of changes caused by the climate and by the way we live today – otherwise, spring as we think we know it may never again return.

6   EASTER

Then there is a thing cal'd wheaten flowre, which the sulphory
Necromanticke Cookes doe mingle with water, Egges, Spice, and
other tragicall magicall inchantments, and then they put it by
little and little, into a Frying pan of boyling Suet, where it makes
a confused dismall hissing (like the Learnean Snakes [Hydra]
in the Reeds of *Acheron*, *Stix*, or *Phlegeton*), untill at the last by the
skill of the Cookes, it is transform'd into the forme of a Flap-jack,
which in our translation is call'd a Pancake, which ominous
incantation the ignorant people do devoure very greedily.

John Taylor, *Jack a Lent His Beginning and Entertainment* (1620)

Easter is a moveable feast. In 1818 it came as early as 22 March – something that will not happen again until 2285.[1] It is also sometimes as late as 25 April, a date consequently known as *ultimum Pascha*. From Easter come the dates for Lent – the forty days of fasting or abstinence leading to Easter, symbolic of Jesus' forty days in the wilderness.[2] These forty days are calculated differently according to custom and convention, but in the Western tradition Lent begins at midday on Ash Wednesday, which is forty days before Palm Sunday (the Sunday before Easter), and finishes in the afternoon on Maundy Thursday (at 'nones', the ninth hour, or 3 p.m.); consequently the first day of Lent can vary from 4 February to 11 March. In the Roman Catholic Church, however, Lent does not finish until Holy Saturday (Easter Saturday). And anyone who can be bothered to do the calculations will realize that Lent is actually therefore forty-four or even forty-six days long: this is because Sundays are technically not part of Lent.[3]

There is more. The three days preceding Lent constitute Shrovetide, and the three days of Easter – Good Friday, Holy Saturday, and Easter Sunday – are the Easter Triduum.[4] Hocktide is the Monday and Tuesday after Easter Monday, and can therefore fall from 30–31 March to 3–4 May. Ascension Day comes forty days after Easter, which means that the earliest possible date for it is 30 April and the latest 3 June. Ascension Day is immediately preceded by the three days of Rogationtide. Whitsun, or Pentecost, is the seventh Sunday after Easter, or the fiftieth day after Passover, and is the celebration of the manifestation of the Holy Spirit through the apostles:

And suddenly there came a sound from heaven as of a rushing mighty wind, and it filled all the house where they were sitting. And there appeared unto them cloven tongues like as of fire, and it sat upon each of them. And they were all filled with the Holy Ghost, and began to speak with other tongues, as the Spirit gave them utterance.[5]

Trinity Sunday is the first Sunday after Whitsun, between 10 May and 20 June, followed four days later by Corpus Christi.

Easter spins a cat's cradle of connected dates and what are effectively micro-seasons. These Eastertide feasts form part of the festive year that overlays the end of winter, the spring, and the first days of summer. And inevitably, these days have developed their own customs and traditions that run alongside the celebration of spring. This may not have always been the case: Easter was banned in England in 1647 by the Long Parliament, and in 1928 the British government discussed fixing the date of Easter to between 9 and 15 April on the grounds that the weather would be better during this period, despite all evidence being to the contrary. The Puritan ban on Easter was revoked, but amazingly the 1928 Act was passed. However, it has never been ratified by the World Council of Churches, and so instead, Easter and its orbiting festivals remain moveable feasts. But why is this, and how is Easter calculated?

––––––

The calculation of Easter was – and still is – a mysteriously opaque affair. It was established as a 'moveable' feast because Christ's Resurrection was recorded in the Gospels as occurring during the Jewish Passover festival. Passover, which lasts about a week, is a Jewish feast determined by the Jewish lunar calendar – that is, by phases of the moon – hence it did not correspond with the Roman Julian calendar of the time, and neither do any of the Gospels record an exact date for the Crucifixion or for the Resurrection according to the Julian system. All the witnesses agree, however, that Passover is significant and that Christ was crucified on the day before the Sabbath; consequently he rose on a Sunday, the first day of the week according to Jewish reckoning. But while Matthew, Mark, and Luke claim that this was the first Sunday after Passover, John calculates a different day based on the fact that Jesus' trial would have been held outside of Passover. All this is challenging enough, but since then the inevitable drift in the Jewish lunar year and the habit of adding intercalary months to make the Jewish calendar consistent with farming – the moment at which the barley harvest ripened could be used as a fixed calendrical point – have made retrospective dating impossible.

Perhaps this is why St Paul chastised those who absorb themselves in 'days, and months, and times, and years', for the temporal world is but 'a shadow of things to come'.[6] But as the years lengthened – literally, sometimes, in the case of the Jewish lunar year – and as the historic Jesus became more remote, earthly dates were needed to stabilize faith and to give a structure to worship that could be related to verifiable human events. Anniversaries and festivals could, moreover, fashion the sacred year by celebrating the life and works of Christ, and also by acknowledging the subsequent acts and sufferings of martyrs. Buttressed by the apparent stability of the Julian calendar, daily living in the terrestrial world became an increasingly regularized affair. The early Christian Church had no choice but to fall into step with the march of time.

The most obvious solution to calculating the appropriate day on which to celebrate the Crucifixion and Resurrection would have been for the Christian Church to have adopted the Jewish lunar year. There was, however, a strong antipathy against using another faith's calendar, laced in part, perhaps, by latent anti-semitism: 'We ought not,' wrote the Christian Roman emperor Constantine, 'to have anything in common with the Jews, for the Saviour has shown us another way; our worship follows a more legitimate and more convenient course (the order of the days of the week); and consequently, in unanimously adopting this mode, we desire, dearest brethren, to separate ourselves from the detestable company of the Jews'.[7] As the ambitions of the Christian Church increasingly lay in secular as much as in sacred kingdoms, it was certainly sensible to follow the established Julian calendar as far as possible. But the Julian calendar offered no clue in ascertaining a date for Easter. The compromise reached was therefore to reaffirm the relationship between the solar calendar and the Julian year by using the spring equinox as the basis for calculating Easter, and to play down the lunar aspects of the Hebrew calendar. Easter was therefore defined as the Paschal Sunday – the first Sunday after the first full moon after the equinox, unless this occurred at the beginning of the Jewish Passover. The evidence of the Gospels was therefore squared with the cycle of the solar year and the pragmatic necessity of fixing a precise date in the Julian calendar.[8]

In practice, however, it proved very difficult to calculate the relationship between the vernal equinox and the phases of the moon due to variations in solar and lunar years, not to mention the gradual drift of the Julian calendar itself. It is in fact a complicated business even today – Catholic astronomers currently use a fourteen-step algorithm that can predict Easter with a high, but not an absolute, degree of accuracy.[9] As we have seen, oblivious of these vertiginous complexities but all too aware of their own mathematical and astronomical shortcomings, the Council of Nicaea in AD 325 proposed a fixed date of 21 March to be used by churches as the date of the vernal equinox. It was a hopeful, if simplistic, suggestion – but it did inspire further research.[10] Subsequent to the Council of Nicaea, the calculation of Easter was determined using Alexandrian and Nicaean formulae by mathematical experts such as the sixth-century Scythian monk Dionysius Exiguus.[11] This sophistication was to be welcomed, but of more significance was that when Dionysius published his tables giving the dates of Easter for the years 532–627, he perhaps unconsciously introduced a major innovation in dating the years *anno Domini*, 'in the year of our Lord'. This is the origin of 'AD' dating (and now of the mealy-mouthed 'Common Era'). Bede duly adopted Dionysius' *anno Domini* system, thereby helping it to become established as the norm in the Western world.

This was all well and good, but, not for the last time, some parts of Christendom were slow to accept the Nicaean formula for Easter – not least Britain. Disparate sects in Ireland, Scotland, Wales, and parts of England such as Northumbria, Wessex, Somerset and Devon, and Cornwall have since been (erroneously) described as being in a mysterious tradition of 'Celtic Christianity'. Others more accurately describe these groups as examples of Insular Christianity to indicate their separation from the Continent and mainstream Christian thinking. Moreover, these sects had their own, often archaic, traditions, which included idiosyncratic ways of calculating Easter – not least because some held that the Crucifixion had taken place on a Thursday. In practice, this meant that when the Insular Christian King Oswiu of Northumbria married the Catholic Christian princess Eanflæd of Kent, some time between 642 and 644, they were occasionally obliged to celebrate Easter on different days. The Venerable Bede became quite exercised by the Paschal Controversy, writing in the next century (AD 731):

> it is said that in these days it sometimes happened that Easter was celebrated twice in the same year, so that the king had finished the fast and was keeping Easter Sunday, while the queen and her people were in Lent and observing Palm Sunday.[12]

Bede subsequently gives an account of the Synod of Whitby, the summit held in 644 and at which Oswiu presided over Ionan and Roman delegations who each argued their respective cases for determining when Easter would fall. Oswiu eventually agreed to conform to the Roman Church, although a hardcore of Insular Christians held out for another twenty-five years against this orthodoxy.

Bede also first recorded the name 'Easter'. According to him, 'Ēostre' was a Teutonic goddess celebrated in the name ēastermōnað (April). However, most European languages name the Paschal season from the Latin root, pascha; only English ('Easter') and German ('Ostern') possibly refer to Ēostre. Some subsequent folklore is – dubiously – attributed to Ēostre.[13] She is reputed to have been a goddess of spring and either twilight or the dawn. The hare was her familiar and she supposedly once rescued a wounded bird by turning it into a hare so it might survive the winter. Yet this was a transformation in outward appearance only, and so the hare found it could lay eggs – which it decorated and left for Ēostre each springtime.[14] Interestingly, at least one English nonsense song collected in the nineteenth century describes a hare being hatched from an egg, so there is possibly some lost folklore here.[15] Similarly, there are planting traditions at Easter, which some think derive from folk memories of the festival of Ēostre. After each harvest the moon's lover (or son) symbolically died; Ēostre celebrated his rebirth, and consequently this provided a template for the Christian Easter festival of death, incarceration in the tomb, and resurrection. Others claim that planting potatoes on Good Friday was symbolic of death and rebirth.[16] All that can be said for this is that if there are farming traditions to plant root crops when the moon is waning, then the surest way of guaranteeing this is to base planting lore around Easter, since, by the way that Easter is calculated using the lunar cycle, such days will always fall during a waning moon. In other words, the Christian festival of Easter and its luni-solar calculation have generated this Ēostran lunar folklore, not the other way round. And in any case, any Western folklore of the potato can only date from the last years of the sixteenth century, when it began to be grown in quantity – if less as an exotic and talismanic root vegetable and more as animal feed.[17]

––––––––

So much for the formal establishment of Easter. What of its festive traditions? Lent was a period of fasting, which meant no meat, eggs, or dairy products could be consumed; it was also a time of abstinence, which meant that no marriage or sexual act could be consummated. As an alternative to these proscriptions, simnel cakes were traditionally eaten during Lent – spiced fruitcakes with currants and almonds, sometimes decorated with eleven balls of almond paste to represent the eleven apostles (Judas Iscariot was not of course included in this reckoning – 'Eleven for the eleven who went up to Heaven', as the traditional English song 'Green Grow the Rushes, O' has it). Over time the rules of Lent were slightly relaxed – in 1538, for instance, Henry VIII permitted the consumption of dairy products – but the routine of Lent abstinence survived the Reformation as it was considered good for the national fish-trade. Lent then disappeared when Easter was abolished in the 1640s, before being reinstated shortly after the Restoration in 1664. Since then Lent has not been as zealously observed as it was in former times, but has developed into a salutary example of contemporary folklore. Lent is popular now for selective abstinence – giving up a little vice, such as alcohol, chocolate, or potato crisps – or alternatively, particularly in the Anglican Church, for adopting more charitable habits. What makes this a modern folk custom is that many people who are not regular church-goers nevertheless sacrifice something at Lent as an annual gesture to the culture of healthy eating, and as a moral alternative to self-indulgence.

The period immediately preceding Lent was Shrovetide: a period of preparation for shriving, confession, and absolution before the fast of Lent, but also a time for eating up everything out of larders and consequently a spur to customs and games associated with last-minute feasting. Egg or Egg Feast Saturday is self-explanatory, Shrove Sunday was Quinquagesima (the final Sunday before Lent and therefore fifty days before Easter, counting Easter itself), Collop Monday was the last day for eating meat, usually bacon and eggs, and Shrove Tuesday was the final chance to cook with eggs, flour, and milk – hence its popularity as 'pancake day', although there are local variations such as cockeels in Norfolk and doughnuts in Hertfordshire.[18] Pancakes are first mentioned by the poet William Warner in *Albions England* as 'Fasts-eve panpuffes' [i.e., 'fast's eve'].[19] As Shakespeare noted in *All's Well That Ends Well*, a play possibly first performed on Shrove Tuesday: 'A pancake for Shrove Tuesday, a morris for May-day'.[20] Pancakes on Shrove Tuesday were also noted a few years later in the lively social satire *Pasquils Palinodia* (1619):

> It was the day whereon both rich and poore,
> Are chiefly feasted with the selfe same dish,
> When every Paunch till it can hold no more,
> Is *Fritter-fild*, as well as heart can wish,

And every man and maide doe take their turne,
And tosse their Pancakes up for feare they burne,
And all the Kitchin doth with laughter sound,
To see the Pancakes fall upon the ground.

As was the forthcoming prohibition on sex:

When Country wenches play with stoole & ball,
And run at Barly-breake untill they fall,
And country Lads fall on them in such sort,
That after forty weekes they rew the sport.[21]

The shriving bell would ring to indicate confession; after the Reformation
this signal became known as the 'Pancake Bell' and the beginning of
the festival. Olney in Buckinghamshire appears to have hosted the first
recorded pancake race in 1445; after the race the pans were placed around
the church font during the Shriving Service. 'Shroving', meanwhile, presented children with an opportunity for some traditional begging exercises,
as recorded in Oxfordshire in 1895:

Pit-a-pat! the pan's hot,
    I be come a Shroving,
Catch a fish afore the net,
    That's better than nothing

Eggs, lard and flour's dear,
This makes me come a-Shroving here.[22]

Similarly, the day before Shrove Tuesday, also known as Hall Monday, was
an evening of mildly lawless children's games, especially in the south and
west of England: banging on doors and seizing chattels that would be
prominently exhibited the next day, or throwing shards of broken crockery
in doorways. On Shrove Tuesday itself a less edifying tradition developed

of destroying cockerels in various competitive ways – doubtless devised as a sort of ritual culling of young cockerels who had missed the pot on Collop Monday and would henceforth be a drain on domestic resources for the next month and a half. Stones were hurled at tethered cocks, cocks were thrown or threshed (they were buried to the neck or tied to a post and had sticks flung at them, sometimes by blindfolded competitors), and cockfighting was traditional on Shrove Tuesday – including at Westminster School.[23] Serious objections arose against cock-throwing and the like from the beginning of the eighteenth century and it was banned in the City of London as early as 1704. The last recorded instance of this exercise in brutality was in 1844; as for cockfighting, the RSPCA helped in a complete prohibition five years later in 1849.

Other Shrovetide revels included great unruly games of old-style football: 'real' football that has nothing to do with the preening antics of today's professional soccer matches. In Atherstone in Warwickshire the Shrovetide Ball Game has allegedly been played for over 800 years. To win, one simply has to be in possession of the ball at the end of the two-hour 'game'; the only rule appears to be that players are not permitted to kill each other. In Sedgefield in County Durham a similar game may have been in existence for nearly a thousand years; here the aim is to get the ball into a goal – originally a stream and a pond, now one of the local pubs. The Cornish version of these ball games is Cornish hurling. At St Columb Major, for example, two teams engage in ritualized play for about an hour before the contest proper kicks off, the aim being to get a silver ball over the parish boundary; the field of play is two miles across.[24] In 1602 the Cornish historian Richard Carew compared the ball to 'an infernall spirit: for whosoever catcheth it, fareth straightwayes like a madde man, strugling and fighting with those that goe about to holde him: and no sooner is the ball gone from, but hee resigneth this fury to the next receyver, and himself becommeth peaceable as before'. The match is repeated eleven days later; 'when the hurling is ended, you shall see them retyring home, as from a pitched battaile, with bloody pates, bones broken, and out of joynt, and such bruses as serve to shorten their daies; yet al is good play'.[25] For those in cities where exhausting games of football were not so practical, the excess of Shrove Tuesday spirits could easily escalate into minor rioting.

Everything was different the day after Shrove Tuesday. Ash Wednesday was originally named from blessing ashes with Holy Water and using them to anoint the congregation in preparation for their abstinence; this was abolished by Edward VI in 1548. As Lent commenced, some places had a final ceremony in which a Jack-a-Lent, or Jack o' Lent, was paraded as a scapegoat figure.[26] The custom, which dates from at least the mid-sixteenth century, required an effigy to be dragged around the parish and generally abused before being hung up somewhere prominent as a scapegoat. The emblematic poet Francis Quarles in *The Shepheards Oracles* (1646) described:

> how like a Jack-a-lent
> He stands, for boys to spend their shrovetide throws,
> Or like a Puppit, made to frighten Crows![27]

The ills of the locale heaped upon the head of Jack-a-Lent, the odd game of real football played out, and then all was quiet in the Christian calendar for a month.

Palm Sunday is the Sunday before Easter Sunday and therefore falls between 15 March and 18 April as a kind of rehearsal for May Day. The day commemorates Christ's entry into Jerusalem with 'palms', or rather local flora gathered by parishioners 'going a-palming'; these were used to decorate the church and make small personal tokens.[28] Box, cypress, hazel, yew, and willow were favourites, but the most popular switch for these displays was pussy-willow. Palm Sunday was banned in church by Edward VI in 1549, and after being revived in the brief Counter-Reformation, was banned again by Elizabeth in 1559; it remained, however, a secular tradition and has recently been reintroduced into some churches. Palm Sunday is also known as Fig Sunday, when children might be given figs and dishes prepared. At Hentland, King's Caple, and Sellack in Herefordshire, 'pax cakes' are distributed in church; the benefaction apparently dates from the fifteenth or sixteenth century.

Good Friday – named 'Good' as a synonym for Holy and also known as 'Long Friday' – was, before the Bank Holidays Act of 1871, one of only two annual holidays in England, the other being Christmas Day. Good Friday was not, however, a season of festivity but a day of devotion: a fast day and a day of charity. It therefore became unlucky to work – even to pare one's nails – and it was particularly ill-omened for blacksmiths to light their forges lest they be damned for making the sort of spikes that had crucified Christ. On the other hand, Good Friday was a lucky day for baking bread and collecting eggs, both of which would remain perpetually fresh. And the eggs could now be eaten again.

According to the *Oxford English Dictionary*, hot cross buns are first mentioned in the *Poor Robin's* almanac for 1733: 'Good Friday comes this Month, the old Woman runs / With one or two a Penny hot cross Bunns'.[29] More evidence appears as incidental detail in the true-crime confession of *The Trial, Conviction, Condemnation, Confession and Execution of William Smith* (1753), in which one of the witnesses declares:

> I am a Butcher, and I have had Dealings with Mr. *Harper* for many a Day . . . and he invited me to Dinner upon a *Good-Friday* Cake as we call it; for he was a right good neighbourly Man; and he invited five other Neighbours (for he loved friendly and good Company) to eat of this Cake. . . . Now you my worthy Lord must know, we have a Notion . . . in our Country, That if we do eat a Cake made purposely of *Good-Friday*, we shall never want Money nor Victuals all the Year round, which for as many Years as I can remember has always fallen out true.[30]

Hot cross buns baked on Good Friday were kept for their medicinal qualities and hung up in kitchens to bring good luck. The Romantic editor, folklorist and satirist William Hone recorded that,

> In the houses of some ignorant people, a Good Friday bun is still kept 'for luck,' and sometimes there hangs from the ceiling a hard biscuit-like cake of open *cross-work*, baked on a Good Friday, to remain there till

displaced on the next Good Friday by one of similar make ... 'no fire ever happened in a house that had one'.[31]

In Yorkshire dock pudding was eaten in the last two weeks of Lent. Known locally as Easter Ledges or Passion Dock, these were cakes made with oatmeal, nettles, onion, and dock leaves fried together. The annual World Dock Pudding Championship is now held in Mytholmroyd in West Yorkshire.

———

Thus to Easter Sunday, when it is good luck to wear one item of new clothing, just as it is at Whitsun and the New Year. Indeed, by the time the diarist Samuel Pepys was writing in the 1660s, this evidently meant that Easter had become the start of the fashion season:

> Pegg Pen is married this day privately.... This wedding, being private, is imputed to its being just before Lent, and so in vain to make new clothes till Easter, that they might see the fashions as they are like to be this summer; which is reason good enough.[32]

The English poet and dramatist John Gay also noted that high society was developing its own seasons:

> Nor do less certain Signs the Town advise,
> Of milder Weather, and serener Skies.
> The Ladies gayly dress'd, the *Mall* adorn
> With various Dyes, and paint the sunny Morn ...
> The Seasons operate on every Breast;
> 'Tis hence that Fawns are brisk, and Ladies drest.[33]

Easter Sunday is, however, most associated in the festive calendar with Easter eggs – arguably an ancient symbol of birth celebrated at the vernal equinox and adopted by the Christian Church as a symbol of resurrection. Eggs may also have associations with the vernal sun and the symbolism of rolling away the rock from the mouth of Christ's tomb – or possibly not. Pace-egging customs predominate in the north of England, and cover a range of activities involving eggs, the name 'pace-egg' being derived from the Latin *pascha* (originally from the Hebrew and Greek for 'Passover'), and corrupted into peace-eggs, paste-eggs, and pace-eggs. Since the 1790s, with food becoming comparatively more plentiful, eggs have been decorated and rolled down local hills – organized events now take place, for example, on Easter Monday at Avenham Park, Preston, or at Hoad in Ulverston, Cumbria.[34] Egg-rolling sometimes becomes a competitive game akin to marbles, or even combative like conkers, and survives, somewhat incongruously, as a seasonal staple of old-guard children's comics such as *The Beano* and *The Dandy*. The Pace-Egg mummers' play, meanwhile, was developed by eighteenth-century cotton-workers in Lancashire; it survived in Rochdale and has since been revived.[35] J. S. Fry sold the first chocolate Easter egg in England in 1873, and John Cadbury followed with his Easter eggs two years later.

In addition to eggs, Eastertime is now populated with rabbits, lambs, and ducklings, but traditionally the hare was the animal of the season, associated as it is with March and the springtime. Indeed, as we have already seen, some hares laid eggs which could be discovered on Easter Sunday; in other traditions, eggs would be hidden in a hare's form, or nest. This folklore is, as some of the eggs would be, scrambled, but it may be that the traditional Easter egg hunt is a remnant of a seasonal Easter hare hunt. The folklorist Roy Palmer notes a Hare Hunt in Leicester, first recorded in 1668, and every Easter Monday Hallaton in Leicestershire stages its Hare Pie Scramble and Bottle-Kicking match with neighbouring Medbourne.[36] Since 1771 the rector of Hallaton has provided a hare pie, drink, and bread. The dish is shared after the Easter Monday service and its remains are scattered in a field called Hare Pie Bank, where villagers scramble for pieces. The bread, meanwhile, is scattered in the Market Square, and the beer is decanted into 'field bottles' – actually three small barrels, one of which is empty. These bottles are then competed for in a huge scrum across a mile-long course bordered by Hallaton stream and Medbourne hedge.

There is also a tradition of 'lifting' or 'heaving' at Easter, in which typologically minded folklorists may find a reference to the Resurrection. The *Gentleman's Magazine* reported this custom in 1784:

> The men lift the women on Easter Monday, and the women the men on Tuesday. One or more take hold of each leg, and one or more of each arm, near the body, and lift the person up, in a horizontal position, three times. It is a rude, indecent, and dangerous diversion, practised chiefly by the lower class of people. Our magistrates constantly prohibit it by the bellman, but it subsists at the end of town; and the women have of late years converted it into a money job. I believe it is chiefly confined to these Northern counties [that is, Manchester].[37]

There is an element of Hocktide festivities in lifting, but Easter is in any case a traditional time for games, from communal skipping games that were once popular up to Good Friday, to real football matches – for example, at Workington, Cumberland, on Good Friday, Easter Tuesday, and the following Saturday, and dating from at least 1779. Since 1857 the Britannia Coco-Nut Dancers have danced through Bacup in Lancashire on Easter Saturday. They have blackened faces, white hats and stockings, skirts and breeches, and iron-soled clogs. Their five garland and two coconut dances traditionally came from sailors or Moorish pirates via Cornish miners looking for work in the North. The dances were adopted by millworkers, who added cotton bobbins to hands, waists, and knees. This tradition may be comparatively recent, but as early as the fourteenth century the Dominican friar John Bromyard was lambasting Easter festivities, perceiving in them the wiles of the Devil who had inflamed carnal appetites after the abstinence of Lent: women went about 'in their wanton array, frolicking, dancing'.[38] We should, I think, do our best to justify his fears.

Hocktide itself was the Monday and Tuesday a week after Easter.[39] The etymology of this unusual word is unclear, but it may have some rough equivalence with the Twelve Days of Christmas. Hocktide is a quarter day for rents, as first mentioned around 1175, and is also sometimes linked with Michaelmas. The festival was allegedly instituted by Alfred the Great as the symbolic replaying of the Anglo-Saxon defeat of the Danes. It was characterized by games of misrule, usually involving men pursuing – and possibly tying up – women on the Monday, and the women retaliating by chasing and tying up the men on the Tuesday. Some forfeit was extracted – such as a kiss – or those captured were lifted on a chair, or simply tossed up and down. Hocktide was well established by the late fourteenth century, and may lie behind the strange, ritualized courtship and patterns of seduction in the fourteenth-century alliterative romance of *Sir Gawain and the Green Knight*. Although these festivities were publicly criticized in the early fifteenth century, by the 1450s Hocktide revelries were contributing so much to church funds that they were reluctantly allowed to continue. But like so much else, Hocktide was suppressed by Edward VI, revived under Mary's Counter-Reformation, and then declined throughout the seventeenth century until Puritan extremists abolished it. Lifting or heaving traditions did, however, survive in the West Midlands until late in the eighteenth century, and a unique remnant of the original Hocktide is still celebrated in West Berkshire at the annual Hungerford Hocktide Court or Tutti Day in a set of elaborate and carnivalesque courtly rituals.

Rogationtide covered the Monday, Tuesday, and Wednesday immediately preceding Ascension Day, itself the fortieth day after Easter Sunday; it started, therefore, between 27 April and 31 May. St Mark's Day, 25 April, was also sometimes known as the Major Rogation, and the three days before Ascension were referred to as the Minor Rogations of Rogation Monday, Rogation Tuesday, and Rogation Wednesday.

It is possible that Rogation, from the Latin *rogare*, meaning 'to ask or beseech', was a custom based on the Roman festival of Robigalia celebrating the fertility of the spring, and that it was introduced to England from Gaul in the eighth century. Rogation was a time to fast and bless the fields, crops, livestock, and community of the parish, and so consequently it was an early example of what is now called 'beating the bounds', or walking the parish boundary to seek divine protection and God's mercy for the locale. On Rogation Days – also called Cross Days, Gang Days, or Grass Days – villagers 'ganged' or walked the parish boundary behind a cross, marking landmarks along the way, and often this marking actively involved the next generation: ducking children in streams or bouncing them on prominent rocks. Rogation was kept up after the Reformation and even through the time of the Commonwealth because the oral traditions and folk memories of boundaries were of crucial importance in maintaining local stability. But much of this traditional communal walking was swept away by Enclosure, which privatized common land and restricted access to the countryside (see Chapter 10). Nevertheless, beating the bounds survives in Devon, Kent, Yorkshire, and the city of Oxford, where the parish boundary of St Michael in the Northgate passes through Marks & Spencer's supermarket, and since 1976 it has been revived as an optional observance in the Anglican Church. More importantly, however, it has recently been encouraged by the environmental activist group Common Ground as part of their Parish Maps project and as a shared way of charting the territory of a community.

Ascension Day was also known as Holy Thursday in the *Book of Common Prayer*. It was the last of the Rogation Days in some parishes.[40] Ascension Day itself is an ancient Christian festival, and the notion of ascension is associated with aerial phenomena – and therefore with the weather, and consequently with rain: thus this is a popular day for dressing wells, or so the argument goes. Water drawn on this day would be lucky and medicinal, whereas drying clothes on Ascension Day is unlucky and is likely to cause a death in the family. In contrast, Whit Sunday, the seventh Sunday after Easter, celebrates the descent of the Holy Spirit among the disciples; it is also known as Pentecost, being fifty days after Passover. Trinity Sunday, the first Sunday after Whitsun, was fixed as a feast day in England in 1334 and remained popular after the Reformation because it did not refer to individual saints; a fifth of all churches dedicated in the mid-nineteenth century were to the Trinity. The Thursday after Trinity Sunday is Corpus Christi, at one time a very popular festival in England, introduced in 1264 and again in

1317 – it was characterized by street processions, pageants and the Corpus Christi or 'Mystery' plays. Whitsun was made a bank holiday in 1871, but a century later the Banking and Financial Dealings Act replaced Whitsun with the blandly named Spring Bank Holiday, the last Monday of May. This was ostensibly because Whit Monday could fall on any day between 11 May and 14 June, but by such formulaic legislation the nation is cut off from its past, its customs, and the cultural calendar.

Whitsun was always a popular holiday because of the likelihood of good weather. Easter could be unseasonably cold: possibly the worst Easter weather was in 1908, when despite Easter Sunday being late (19 April) there were severe frosts in Scotland and northern England and snow and hail in the south. Dr W. G. Grace took the crease for his final cricket match on Easter Monday of that year at Whitstable in Kent; there was snow lying on the outfield.[41] Whitsun, however, was the best part of two months later. Milk and cream were seasonal fare for Whitsun feasts, as were gooseberries and cheesecakes. As at Easter, it was important to wear new clothes at Whitsun – otherwise one might attract the unwelcome attention of disparaging birdlife. The weather could be relied on, and so Whitsuntide festivities tended to be more organized and more popular than other seasonal events.

Whitsun Ales, a seasonal variation on Church Ales, or charity events, were a popular way of raising money for the parish church in the sixteenth century. There was a minor revival of Church Ales at the Restoration; some of these lasted into the nineteenth century, and they may still occasionally be found today.[42] A Whitsun Morris dance is mentioned by Shakespeare in *Henry V*, and more commercial Whitsuntide events are also suggested by a broadside poster from 1758 advertising events to be held in Sunbury in Middlesex:

On Whit Monday, in the Morning, will be a Punting Match on the usual Terms. The first Boat that comes in to receive a Guinea. . . .
In the afternoon a Gold-laced Hat, Value 30s. to be cudgell'd for.
On Whit Tuesday, in the Morning, a fine Holland Smock and

Ribbons, Value One Guinea, to be run for by Girls or Young Women. And, in the Afternoon six Pair of Buckskin Gloves to be wrestled for. No entrance Money required.[43]

Whit Monday was also the traditional date for cheese-rolling at Cooper's Hill, Brockworth in Gloucestershire, although the date has since been transferred to the Spring Bank Holiday. Cheese-rolling is believed by some to be a rather surreal way for villagers to exercise their ancient grazing rights on the common, while others suggest its equally fanciful origins as a midsummer activity connected to rituals that sought to preserve the rays of the waning sun, akin to midsummer bonfires. Pseudo-pagan mysticism aside, cheese-rolling could just as easily be a riotous celebration of the season's fresh cheeses, which are ready in May. Thomas Hughes, best known as author of *Tom Brown's Schooldays* (1857), described eighteenth-century cheese-rolling at Uffington White Horse in present-day Oxfordshire in his 1859 novel *The Scouring of the White Horse*; it also takes place at Randwick in Gloucestershire.

Cheese-rolling regularly grabs the headlines as do-gooders and health-and-safety officials cringe while red-blooded Englishmen and women hurtle down precipitous slopes in pursuit of locally made dairy products. It is their choice to do so. The most remarkable Whitsuntide event, however, is surely Robert Dover's Olimpick Games. These games ran on the common land of Kingcombe Plain, Gloucestershire from about 1611 until the Civil War, and were reintroduced at the Restoration and continued until 1852, when Kingcombe Plain was enclosed. This land, now called Dover's Hill, was acquired by the National Trust in 1929; a one-off games was held in May 1951, then the event was revived again in 1966 and still continues to this day.[44] The 400th-anniversary Cotswold Olimpicks took place in 2012, and included tug o' war, a five-mile cross-country race, the Championship of the Hill, which consists of throwing the hammer, putting the shot, standing jump, and spurning the barre, and the ever-popular shin-kicking. It was undoubtedly the major sporting event of the year in England.

7   THE CUCKOO

O blithe New-comer! I have heard,
I hear thee and rejoice.
O Cuckoo! Shall I call thee Bird,
Or but a wandering Voice?

William Wordsworth, 'To the Cuckoo'

William Wordsworth's joyful cuckoo is still recognizable today. The cuckoo is a 'new-comer', returning each year to its old haunts to be heard. It is only seldom seen. It is perhaps barely a bird at all but 'a wandering Voice' – a bundle of associations, folklore, and superstition.[1] Wordsworth is particularly taken by the way that the call or voice of the cuckoo, rather than the song, dwells in certain forms of landscape – hills and dales rather than open plains. It inhabits these folds of the land and thereby the imagination: as he explained in his *Description of the Scenery of the Lakes* (1810), 'There is . . . an imaginative influence in the voice of the cuckoo, when that voice has taken possession of a deep mountain valley, very different from any thing which can be excited by the same sound in a flat country'.[2] But the ability of the cuckoo to fill the meadows and copses with its woody tones is not enough on its own to make it the poet's bird of choice for the rolling countryside: the cuckoo is also a bird with rich cultural trappings. Its distinctive voice echoes through custom and lore both as a bringer of good tidings and as a scornful, ill-omened cry. There is probably no other bird so much written and sung about in the English tradition as *Cuculus canorus*.[3]

The cuckoo is – or was – the popular bird of the spring season. The letters page of *The Times* traditionally alerts its readership to the first cuckoo heard every year – indeed, Kenneth Gregory's anthology of letters to *The Times* from 1900 to 1975 was titled *The First Cuckoo*.[4] The word itself seems to have derived from the Norman word *cucu* and the earlier form may have been 'gowk', which survives in some English traditions, but the first 'cuckoo' in English literature is in the birdcall refrain of the song 'Sumer Is Icumen In', which dates from around 1240:

Sumer is icumen in · Lhude sing cuccu ·
Groweþ sed and bloweþ med and springþ þe wode nu ·
Sing cuccu
Awe bleteþ after lomb · lhouþ after calve cu ·
Bulluc sterteþ · bucke verteþ
murie sing cuccu · Cuccu cuccu
Wel singes þu cuccu ne swik þu naver nu ·
Sing cuccu nu · Sing cuccu ·
Sing cuccu · sing cuccu nu ·

[Summer is a-coming in, loudly sing, cuckoo;
Grows the seed and blooms the mead (meadow) and springs the wood
   anew,
Sing cuckoo;
Ewe bleats after lamb, lows after calf the cow,
Bullock starteth, buck deer farteth,
Merry sing cuckoo: cuckoo, cuckoo;
Well sings the cuckoo: nor ever stop you now;
Sing cuckoo now; sing cuckoo;
Sing cuckoo; sing cuckoo now.][5]

The onomatopoeic 'cuckoo' in this song is, like the spring itself, the herald of the summer. But there is some confusion here: is it a bird of the spring-time or the summer? 'The merry Cuckow', in Edmund Spenser's description, is the 'messenger of Spring' (1594) – either proclaiming spring or alternatively appointed by spring to call the summer.[6] However, the writer and pamphleteer Thomas Nashe is more forthright in his 'Spring' song from *Summers Last Will and Testament* (1600):

Spring, the sweete spring, is the yeres pleasant King,
Then bloomes eche thing, then maydes daunce in a ring,
Cold doeth not sting, the pretty birds doe sing,
Cuckow, jugge, jugge, pu we, to witta woo.[7]

By the time of the popular eighteenth-century poet James Thomson's *Spring* (1728–46), the bird is unambiguously identified with the spring season: 'From the first note the hollow cuckoo sings, / The symphony of Spring'.[8] So the call of the cuckoo suggests the coming of spring, and mid-spring, and summer. This slip from 'The symphony of Spring' to 'Sumer is icumen in' suggests at the very least a fluidity in the perception of the seasons, but there is also a lack of precision, even dislocation, as to what distinguishes the spring from the summer. The seasons are not an exact science.

The traditional day of the first annual cuckoo in England is 3 April (Old Style: the Julian calendar), although the *Poor Robin* almanac for 1682 places the appearance of the bird slightly later in April – 'About the 8th, 9th, or 10th Days the Cuckow comes'.[9] The New Style Gregorian calendar presents the bird on 14 April, coincidentally almost exactly halfway through the spring if the spring is reckoned as March, April, and May. In Shropshire, Cuckoo Morning, when the cuckoo was first heard, became a Gaudy Day – a holiday for the miners. There are several more formal celebrations of Cuckoo Days across England, and although these are not necessarily in celebration of the bird's first appearance, they do suggest that the bird tends to have arrived by mid-April. Cuckoo fairs in Northamptonshire and Beaulieu Fair in Hampshire are, for example, held on 15 April, and the Cuckoo Feast (or Crowder Feast) in Towednack in Cornwall now takes place on the Sunday closest to 28 April. Cuckoo Day in Marsden in Yorkshire is also held at the end of the month, around 27 April, and features giant cuckoo puppets, a performance of a cuckoo play, and a cuckoo ball.

It is Heffle Fair, though, held in Heathfield in Hertfordshire on 14 April, that effectively sets the cuckoo's itinerary and with it the arrival of full-blown spring. The story goes that an old woman at the fair let a bird fly from her basket, and the bird flew up England 'carrying warmer days with him'.[10] This intrepid cuckoo arrived in Cheshire on 15 April, Worcestershire on 20 April, and North Yorkshire on 21 April. Rudyard Kipling describes the magical event in his 'Cuckoo Song':

Tell it to the locked-up trees,
Cuckoo, bring your song here!
Warrant, Act and Summons, please,
For Spring to pass along here!
Tell old Winter, if he doubt,
Tell him squat and square – a!
Old Woman!
Old Woman!
Old Woman's let the Cuckoo out
At Heffle Cuckoo Fair – a!

March has searched and April tried –
'Tisn't long to May now.
Not so far to Whitsuntide
And Cuckoo's come to stay now!
Hear the valiant fellow shout
Down the orchard bare – a!
Old Woman!
Old Woman!
Old Woman's let the Cuckoo out
At Heffle Cuckoo Fair – a! . . .[11]

Other fairs contend to record the flight of the first cuckoo of spring.
The archaeologist and folklorist Jeremy Harte notes that the cuckoo is
supposed to arrive at Wareham Fair in Dorset around 6 April 'to buy
himself a pair of breeches' before making off to Beaulieu Fair nine days
later 'to buy himself a great coat'.[12]

The cuckoo only sings in spring and early summer, during which time
the call of the bird changes to a sound more like a 'gowk' before it eventually falls silent. Ornithological antiquarians in the nineteenth century collected many local rhymes on the season of the cuckoo:

In April, come I will;
In May, I prepare to stay;

In June, I change my tune;
In July, I prepare to fly;
In August, go I must.[13]

A Sussex version of this rhyme continues,

If he stay until September,
'Tis as much as the oldest man can remember.[14]

Sometimes the cuckoo's calendar was adapted to local festivities. In
Tinwell in Rutland a May Day procession of girls and boys takes it in turn
to sing and dance at each house in the village:

Good morning, lords and ladies, It is the first of May,
We hope you'll view our garland, It is so smart and gay.

The cuckoo sings in April, The cuckoo sings in May,
The cuckoo sings in June, In July she flies away.[15]

Once the cuckoo's song ceases, summer is well underway and harvest time
is already near. Consequently, the departure of the cuckoo – or at least the
silencing of its call – was also a significant moment in the year. A rhyme
associated with Tenbury Fair in Worcestershire noted that

The cuckoo comes in April, and sings his song in May,
He buys a horse at Pershore Fair, and then he rides away.[16]

The implication is that if the cuckoo is heard after this time, it is because
he could find no horse to carry him away. The bird is also linked to buying
a horse variously at Orleton Fair in Herefordshire and Sawbridgeworth
Spring Fair in Hertfordshire on 23 April (OS: Old St George's Day).
    The association of the bird with the springtime and indeed May
Day is so strong that 'The Wise Men of Madeley', a renowned band of

Shropshire half-wits, tried to catch a cuckoo to ensure an eternal spring. Other examples of similarly daft behaviour come from Zennor in Cornwall, Borrowdale in Cumbria, and of course that legendary site of foolishness, Gotham in Nottinghamshire, where a hedge was set around the village to keep the cuckoo in.[17] Other versions of the tale relate that the people of Gotham fenced in a little tree to keep a cuckoo from the Sheriff of Nottingham, and indeed one of the local pubs is called the Cuckoo Bush Inn. Currently the National Trust is involved in supporting such activities:

> Every April the people of Marsden in West Yorkshire hold a Cuckoo Day. The event is based around a time-old legend in which the people of Marsden longed for eternal spring. A cuckoo was captured and put into a tower built by the villagers, but the bird flew away as the tower had no roof, thus taking eternal springtime with it. The National Trust jointly organises a Cuckoo Day with Marsden Community Association.[18]

Marsden Cuckoo Day traditions have also been attributed to folkloric depictions of nearby Austwick, which is known as 'Cuckoo Town' and whose inhabitants similarly tried to keep summer perpetual by building a wall around the village. Their plan was to keep the cuckoo in once it had arrived, but of course no matter how high they built the wall, it was never high enough to prevent the cuckoo from flying away. Apparently, the Marsden tower was a single row of bricks short of penning the bird and trapping the sunshine forever: 'nobbut just wun course too low'.

Flowers and insects are also connected with the season of the cuckoo. There are at least ten different species known as 'cuckoo flower' in different parts of the country that traditionally bloom with the arrival of the cuckoo, the best-known perhaps being *Cardamine pratensis*, and come mid-April the cuckoo-pint or pintle (*Arum maculatum*) is in flower.[19] 'Cuckoo spit' is produced by the froghopper insect (*Aphrophoridae*) and is a froth that acts as a protection over the nymphs or immature bugs; it is again associated with the arrival of the bird and is evident in late April, May, and early June.

Unsurprisingly, the instantly recognizable call of the cuckoo was a helpful reminder to working farmers within the agricultural cycle. 'When you hear the cuckoo shout, 'tis time to plant your tetties out' was the advice in the West Country – rather late, according to today's recommendations to plant potatoes in mid-March – while another saying collected by the seventeenth-century theologian and naturalist John Ray also pays close attention to the habits of the bird:

> When the Cuckow comes to the bare thorn,
>   Sell your cow and buy your corn:
> But when she comes to the full bit,
>   Sell your corn and buy your sheep.[20]

Similarly, the *Poor Robin* almanac of 1682 warns that when the 'Cuckow comes . . . you that keep Cows, provide Curds and Cream against her coming' – meaning that on arrival the cuckoo should be placated with a small offering lest it bring bad luck.[21] Other parts of the country were more superstitious. In Somerset one was advised to run around in a circle when hearing the first cuckoo to avoid idleness – a custom first mentioned by the poet and playwright John Gay in his *Shepherd's Week* (1714) – but one would be destined for a lean year if hungry when this occurred; in fact, individuals might spend the entire year doing whatever they were doing when first hearing the bird.[22] Consequently, having a pocketful of money on first hearing the call boded well, and in Cornwall, hearing a cuckoo on your right-hand side would bring prosperity.[23] The cuckoo could warn of – or bring – illness, disaster, or even death by calling over a house, or alighting upon a chimney or on rotten wood. It could predict how long one was likely to live – a belief going back at least to the fourteenth century – and was similarly used in predicting when one would find a partner.[24] In Northumberland and elsewhere, hearing the first cuckoo when walking on soft ground was good luck, but hard ground meant bad luck and could even be fatal. It was also very unlucky to kill the bird.

'Thou hast no sorrow in thy song, / No winter in thy year,' claimed the Scottish clergyman and writer John Logan in 1770, but in fact the cuckoo clearly has an extensive reputation as a bird of evil disposition.[25] The English clergyman, writer, and folksong collector Sabine Baring-Gould recorded a more sinister 'Cuckoo' song from Stoke Fleming near Dartmouth in the year 1892:

> The cuckoo is a pretty bird, she sings as she flies,
>> Her bringeth good tidings, her telleth no lies.
> Her sucketh sweet flowers to keep her voice clear,
>> And when she sings cuckoo the summer draweth near.[26]

This 'charming little song' quickly grows dark – the narrator is sent to the grave by her inconstant lover:

> The grave will receive me and bring me to dust,
>> An inconstant lover no maiden can trust.
> They'll court you and kiss you, poor maids to deceive,
>> There's not one in twenty that one may believe.

> Come all you fair maidens wherever you may be,
>> Don't hang your poor hearts on the sycamore tree.
> The leaf it will wither, the roots will decay
>> And if I'm forsaken I perish away.

A variation printed in the 1820s for children, no less, makes the predatory threat of the bird more explicit:

> The Cuckoo's a bonny bird,
> She sings as she flies,
> She brings us good tidings,
> And tells us no lies.
> She sucks little birds' eggs
> To make her voice clear,

And never cries Cuckoo!
Till spring time of the year.[27]

And despite the bucolic tones of Spenser and Nashe, Shakespeare too places the cuckoo in a world of ravenous violence in which nature preys on itself when in *King Lear* (1605) the Fool declares,

> For you know, nuncle,
> 'The hedge-sparrow fed the cuckoo so long,
> That [it] had it head bit off by it young' [*sic*].[28]

Of course the principal way in which the cuckoo would bring bad luck was with its mocking cry of 'cuckold': the words 'cuckoo' and 'cuckold' were closely associated and 'cuckold' too originates in the mid-thirteenth century. The association came from the imagined promiscuity of the bird that led it to lay its eggs in other bird's nests. This was also underlined by the association with springtime and flowers such as the cuckoo-pint or pintle, which was named after its phallic spike or *spadix*, 'pintle' being an archaic euphemism for male genitalia.

Chaucer consequently called the cuckoo 'ever unkynde' (*c.*1381), and Milton declared it 'the rude bird of hate'.[29] Shakespeare's many references to the cuckoo include the figure of Spring lamenting at the end of *Love's Labor's Lost*:

> When daisies pied and violets blue,
>   And lady-smocks all silver-white,
> And cuckoo-buds of yellow hue
>   Do paint the meadows with delight,
> The cuckoo then on every tree
> Mocks married men; for thus sings he,
>   'Cuckoo;
> Cuckoo, cuckoo' – O word of fear,
> Unpleasing to a married ear![30]

The cuckoo's promiscuity and its relationship to 'cuckold' was duly noted by Henry Ellis, principal librarian of the British Museum, in his 1813 edition of John Brand's antiquarian opus on *Popular Superstitions*. Interestingly, 'cuckold' could also mean the adulterer himself:

> I know not how this word, which is generally derived from 'Cuculus,' a Cuckow, has happened to be given to the injured Husband, for it seems more properly to belong to the Adulterer, the Cuckow being well known to be a Bird that deposits its Eggs in other Birds' nests.
>
> The Romans seem to have used Cuculus in its proper sense, as the Adulterer, calling with equal propriety the Cuckold himself 'Carruca,' or Hedge-Sparrow, which Bird is well known to adopt the other's spurious offspring.
>
> Notwithstanding this, it is still supposed that the word 'Cuculus' gave some rise to the name of Cuckold, though the Cuckow lays in other nests; yet the etymology may still hold, for Lawyers tell us that the honours and disgrace of Man and Wife are reciprocal: so that what the one hath, the other partakes of it. Thus then the lubricity of the Woman is thrown upon the Man, and her dishonesty thought his dishonour: who, being the head of the Wife, and thus abused by her, he gains the name of Cuckold, from Cuckow, which Bird, as he used to nestle in others' places; so 'twas of old the hieroglyphic of a fearful, idle, and stupid fellow, and hence became the nickname of such Men as neglected to dress and prune their Vines in due season.[31]

The connections are uncomfortable. The 1686 *Poor Robin* describes the state of affairs in a little morality tale that shows how the morals of the countryside remain in London as it expands into neighbouring Middlesex villages:

> Now Citizen a Journey makes
> To *Islington*, for to eat Cakes.
> With him his wife doth march along

To hear the Cuckow sing his song;
For if that he should go alone,
The Cuckow might be heard at home:
For Opportunity and Gold
Makes many a man be a Cuckold.
Yet Reader do not jealous be
With that which here is writ by me;
Nor think thy wife to be a whore,
Although he sings just at thy door;
For whatsoever he doth chat,
Wife may be honest for all that.
But rather thank him for his labour,
And think he calleth to thy Neighbor.

But there is few (I think) can tell
What Creatures Cuckolds are full well;
Or their sly subtile Nature conster,
To be born Man, but die a Monster.
Some People there be of this taking,
Think Cuckolds are of Womens making
But do not blame them for it, though
Perhaps that they were born it too:
Nor let none scorn to wear Hose yellow,
A Cuckold is a good mans fellow.[32]

The cuckoo, then, reflects the darker side of spring's traditional associations with sex.

If the cuckoo is considered to be over-sexed, it is also simple-minded (the two conditions may be connected: it thinks with its pintle).[33] This association therefore complements the tradition of All Fools' Day. Thus a cuckoo has meant a fool since the late sixteenth century, while a gowk has meant a fool since at least the seventeenth century:

April gowks are past and gone,
You're a fool and I am none.[34]

All Fools' Day itself appears to date from the late seventeenth century. Its origins are obscure, but it is perhaps based on the French custom, *poisson d'avril*, and was conceivably imported by the restored Stuart monarchy, which had held court in France during the Cromwellian Interregnum: All Fools is not referred to in earlier plays or diaries, although Chaucer does date his 'Nun's Priest's Tale' (a tale of tricking Chaunticleer) to 32 March. 'Fooles Holy Day' is mentioned by Aubrey in 1686–7 – 'We observe it on ye first of April' – and appears in an almanac for the first time in the 1692 *Poor Robin*.[35] Ronald Hutton dates the custom of sending the gullible to wash the lions in the Tower of London to 1698, and in the north of England, 'hunting or hounding the gowk' means sending someone on a fool's errand on 1 April:

The first and second of April
hound the gowk another mile.[36]

————

The rich folklore associated with the cuckoo places it firmly in the imagined countryside of English folk history and tradition, within the frame of the nation's identity as reflected by the changing seasons: merrie England in the springtime. But the bird is already a likely victim of climate change. Gilbert White, writing in Hampshire in the eighteenth century, recorded the earliest date that cuckoos had arrived as 7 April, and the latest as 26 April.[37] According to Sussex bird reports for the period 1966–96, however, the mean arrival date of the cuckoo at the end of the twentieth century was 7 April.[38] In other words, the earliest date that the call of the cuckoo was recorded some two hundred years ago has since become the norm.

But just as spring is no longer the certainty it once was, how many people today ever really hear a cuckoo from year to year? Numbers of cuckoos are steadily declining in England, with a 63 per cent drop over the past twenty-five years. Recent research has revealed that the birds fly to Britain from the African Congo: this spring migration is an extremely risky venture and the birds are affected by droughts and other adverse weather over two continents.[39] They then face further challenges when they do arrive in England. Cuckoos feed on caterpillar varieties such as the garden tiger moth, but again the indigenous population of these moths has fallen by 60 per cent since the 1930s.[40] Even the cuckoo's most notorious survival stratagem has its limitations. The birds have evolved the ability to lay mimic eggs so that their brood will be fostered, but each hen can usually only lay one type of mimic egg from the dozens of potential hosts that were once available (principally meadow pipit, dunnock, reed warbler, and pied wagtail). Individual cuckoo pairs are therefore reliant on the survival of other species – it appears that they cannot adapt to lay new mimic eggs. Consequently, these parasitic skills are not serving the cuckoo well because of the difficulties in locating the right hosts when habitats are disappearing and overall ornithological biodiversity is in decline. And if they do find a host, they will be jeopardizing the survival of that species too.

The cuckoo, then, is on the cusp of becoming a metaphorical creature rather than a real bird. Most of the nation's population go from year to year without hearing a cuckoo in the wild, but in the nation's memory – through those letters pages in *The Times*, through nature programmes on television and radio – the cuckoo remains alive as the harbinger of spring or summer. Most of the folklore surrounding the bird has been forgotten and cuckoo songs are rarely sung. Still, while no one is likely to use the word 'cuckold' in anger today, the phrase 'a cuckoo in the nest' does survive to remind us of the bird's less comfortable heritage. Yet in a generation or two, the sound of the cuckoo may well be as elusive as the nightingale is to us today. If that comes to pass, spring will become a more silent, less distinctive season, and another link with English history, folklore, and legend will have been lost.

Part III

8 MAY DAY

No sparkling jewels, rich and rare,
Compose her crown or deck her hair,
    And simple is her dress;
But then her innocence of mind
Consider'd, is above you'll find,
    High titled wretchedness.

'The Order of Chusing the May Queen', *May-Day: A Poem*.

It is midnight on 30 April. I have spent the evening in the Golden Lion, a pub in the Cornish fishing village of Padstow, and I am now standing in the street as part of a large crowd of people – mainly locals. There is little conversation, just a beery sense of well-being. A light drizzle is falling. Some voices are raised in drunken revelry and immediately a stern voice silences them: 'Respect for the 'Oss!' The Old 'Oss is about to awake.

We sing the 'Night Song':

Unite and unite, and let us all unite,
For summer is acome unto day,
And whither we are going we will all unite,
In the merry morning of May.

I warn you young men everyone,
For summer is acome unto day,
To go to the green-wood and fetch your May home,
In the merry morning of May.

From some weird stable within the Golden Lion comes the Old 'Oss, an uncanny creature. I only glimpse it as it passes me with stealthy intent: the Old 'Oss is black and beribboned and appears to be constantly shifting its shape, merging with and then re-emerging from the midnight darkness. It is waiting for the dawn.

Early next morning, I am woken by the insistent throb of the 'Day Song'. Out of my window I look down on a grass verge – young children are cavorting with an 'Oss, accompanied by drums and melodeons. Everyone

is dressed in white with sashes to show their allegiance: red for the follow-
ers of the Old 'Oss, blue for the Blue Ribbon 'Oss that takes to the street
later in the morning. The Old 'Oss is away somewhere, being led a merry
dance by its teaser. I walk down into the village to watch Blue Ribbon burst
wildly from the Harbour Inn and begin whirling with a dizzying energy,
goaded by its own teaser. An hour later I come face to face with the Old
'Oss down a crowded side-street in a strange dance of swirling chaos
amidst a mass of singers and musicians. The same song is sung, occasionally slowing to a mysterious refrain:

> Where is St. George, where is he O?
>> He is out in his long boat all on the salt sea O,
> And in every land O, that land that ere we go,
>>> And for to fetch the summer home, the summer and the May O,
>> For summer is acome O, and winter is ago.[1]

Eventually, the Old 'Oss meets with Blue Ribbon at a towering maypole.
They dance together in ritual combat. Spring is here.

———

The Padstow 'Oss is first recorded by writer and topographer Richard
Polwhele in 1803, and although Cornish hobby-horses date back at least
to the play *Beunans Meriasek* (1504), the Padstow ritual is very much a
nineteenth-century festival.[2] Indeed, the Blue Ribbon 'Oss was established
by Victorian temperance campaigners who wished to modernize the
event by offering a teetotal option to the festivities, although most of the
Blue Ribbon supporters now seem to have fallen off the wagon. But there
are strong elements of earlier customs too: the breaking of boundaries,
the maypole, and the greenery that garlands the streets are all pre-
Reformation ways of celebrating May Day.

The stirring of the Old 'Oss on May Eve may also be a folk memory of
30 April as a night for supernatural encounters, devilry, and beastly ritual:
fairies went about, witches were in the air, and goats held sabbaths until

the Queen of May finally appeared at midnight to banish winter. In some accounts the otherworld remains present a little longer. Restless and mischievous and downright evil spirits were thought to be particularly active at turning points of the year, and the first three days of May were proverbially unlucky: Queen Guinevere, of Arthurian legend, was seized by the Lord of the Summer Country on 1 May.[3] These beliefs may be because May Day festivities appear to retain elements of Beltane rituals. The first day of May is popularly the start of Beltane, the pagan festival celebrating summer, so named for the 'lucky fire' which dominates its rituals. Beltane fires were lit in the Central Highlands of Scotland on 1 May, as was described in the eighteenth century:

> There is [a] Druid temple, upon a rising ground, where, upon the first day of May, or Balden, a fire was kindled in honour of the god Belus, or Baal, and where delinquents, transgressing the rules of the Druids, were obliged to walk bare-foot upon hot cinders ... there is another custom which prevails amongst the youths upon this day, they kindle fires, and make up an image in form of an human body, and throw it into the fire, as a kind of sacrifice to Baal.[4]

Antiquarians interpreted these rites as remnants of open-air druidical worship, which still reverberated with echoes of human sacrifice. In one parish, a fire was lit and an oatmeal cake baked and divided into pieces, one of which was daubed with charcoal. The villagers were blindfolded and each picked a piece:

> Whoever draws the black bit is the *devoted* person who is to be sacrificed to *Baal*, whose favour they mean to implore, in rendering the year productive of the sustenance of man and beast. There is little doubt of these inhuman sacrifices having been once offered in this country, as well as in the east, although they now pass from the act of sacrificing, and only compel the *devoted* person to leap three times through the flames; with which the ceremonies of this festival are closed.[5]

Other parts of Scotland favoured 2 May (OS) for their 'bone-fires' as protection against the witches who roamed on that night. Jumping over the flames three times or keeping the ashes was usually considered good luck for the community, although the significance of these sacraments was magnificently over-interpreted by later anthropologists such as James George Frazer, who was responsible for *The Golden Bough*, which eventually grew to twelve volumes (1911–14). In a tenth-century account of Irish practices, cattle were driven through the embers or between the bonfires on May Day.[6] In Wales, too, it was recorded that 'the bonfires lighted in May or Midsummer protected the lands from sorcery so that good crops would follow'.[7] This may be linked to the custom of beating the bounds that in Cumbria, Northumbria, and Berwick-upon-Tweed took the form of riding the Marches on May Day.[8]

These bonfire customs meant that 1 May, which was also the Feast of Sts Philip and James, became a traditional time for moving livestock, and the date consequently became associated with closing town fields. According to Thomas Tusser, the sixteenth-century compiler of agricultural lore,

> At Philip and Jacob bid put of thy lammes [to separate grazing pasture]
> that thinkest to have any milke of their dammes.[9]

In the north of England, perhaps under the influence of Scottish customs, 3 May was favoured as a time for the ritual lighting of fires to protect the cattle as they moved to new grass, and this moment also marked the beginning of the dairy season. The third of May was the feast of the Invention of the Holy Cross, also known as St Helen's Day-in-the-Spring, or Ellenmas.[10] So in certain parts of the country – especially those that relied on livestock farming – Ellenmas may have been more significant than May Day itself.[11]

As late as 1794, witches in Banffshire were still being reported on 12 May to be riding about on broomsticks through the air, dancing on water, and stealing milk from cows. Of course, 12 May was Beltane Eve, Old

Style.[12] Revd Francis Kilvert was aware of the tradition, although he treated it with rather more circumspection. In his diary for 1870, he noted:

> This evening being May Eve I ought to have put some birch and wittan (mountain ash) over the door to keep out the 'old witch'. But I was too lazy to go out and get it. Let us hope the old witch will not come in during the night. The young witches are welcome.[13]

It is possible that these ancient British superstitions remain in the unluckiness associated with the spring and early summer, but it is worth emphasizing that there is little evidence of Beltane festivals being celebrated in England except at the borders with Scotland and Wales and at Ellenmas in the north. In a sense, then, the magical defences that were erected against these threatened supernatural incursions are as much barriers against the Scots and Welsh and their beliefs as they were protection against the denizens of the English Elfland. This is evident in Shakespeare's A Midsummer Night's Dream, which takes place on May Eve and is a concerted attempt to canonize the English otherworld, what could be called the realm of Anglo-Faërie, while deliberately resisting the supposed 'Celtic' superstitions of Scotland, Wales, and Ireland.

Hobby-horses were one defence. There do not appear to be significant hobby-horse traditions in Scotland or Ireland, although Wales has its Mari Lwyd (Grey Mare) ritual; but hobby-horses do make frequent appearances in English folklore, poetry and plays (including Love's Labor's Lost and Hamlet), and, of course, Morris dancing – from the Hooden Horse to Old Hob.[14] Apart from the Padstow 'Oss, however, there is only one other apparently surviving, and thriving, hobby-horse festival in England – in Minehead, Somerset. The Minehead Hobby Horse was first recorded in 1792. Like Padstow's Old 'Oss, it appears briefly on May Eve, but unlike the Padstow 'Osses is then at large for the next three days. Two or three horses usually go abroad, including the Sailors' Horse and the Town (or Show) Horse.[15] The Minehead hobby-horses are huge – about twelve feet across – accompanied by musicians playing traditional tunes over and over again, and are attended by 'gullivers' whose role is to seize willing victims to be presented to the creature. Moreover, in addition to the Padstow and Minehead beasts other hobby-horses are appearing throughout the country; if hobby-horses really are distinctively English, this revival perhaps indicates a reconnection with the festivities of the past, a renewal of the mischievous antics that lie scattered through the nation's history.[16]

The Padstow 'Oss and Minehead Hobby Horse are well known, but less well known is the tradition in Padstow of garlanding the streets. This too was a form of protection. In 1240 Robert Grosseteste, bishop of Lincoln, criticized priests who participated in 'games which they call the bringing in of May'.[17] Bringing in the may or going a-maying meant bringing in green boughs and blossom gathered on May Day, often hawthorn or 'may blossom', to cover streets and houses, inside and out. In *The Court of Love*, a verse once attributed to Geoffrey Chaucer, the anonymous poet describes how

> And furth goith all the courte, both most and lest,
> To feche the floures fressh, and braunche, and blome;
> And namly hawthorn brought both page and grome,
> With fressh garlantis partie blewe and white,
> And thaim rejoyson in theire grete delite.[18]

Foliage had a sacred importance, and bringing spring greenery to the home was a declaration of the common good, ensuring that human and natural worlds would exist in harmony throughout the year: it was a form of correspondence with the land. But as early as the eleventh century the Church had forbidden making trees the centre of sites of worship – St Boniface had, after all, been responsible for felling Thor's Oak, the holy tree of the Germanic tribes. Yet bringing in the may stubbornly persisted.[19] Indeed, it became synonymous with Englishness: in 1515, for example, Henry VIII went a-maying with Catherine of Aragon to Shooter's Hill, Greenwich, where they met with 'Robyn Hood' and his company. These merry men provided an archery display for the king and queen and their entourage (and a crowd of onlookers consisting of 'a great number of people'), before serving a banquet of venison in the woods and singing songs to the party when it was time to depart.[20] Maying, Robin Hood, Henry VIII, a picnic under the trees, and a sing-song: it was a thoroughly English day out.

Morris dancing, too, can be added to bringing in the may, Robin Hood, and hobby-horses as a seasonal English spectacle, as noted by Shakespeare in *All's Well That Ends Well* (1602–3): 'A pancake for Shrove Tuesday, a morris for May Day.'[21] This practice, which, despite what some Morris men and women might claim, dates from the mid-fifteenth century and became popular in the sixteenth century, often takes place around 1 May as a popular itinerant entertainment – there are Morris dancers at dawn on May Hill in Gloucestershire, at Nine Maidens on Dartmoor, and elsewhere.[22] Thomas Morley, court composer and father of the English madrigal, described the maverick unpredictability of the Morris thus:

> Ho who comes here all alone with bagpiping & drumming with
>   bagpiping & drumming?
> O the Morris tis I see tis the Morris daunce a coming.
> Hoe who comes here all a-lone with bagpiping and drumming,
> O the Morris tis I see, tis the Morris, daunce a coming.
> Come Ladies come come quickly, come away come I say, o come, come
>   quickly,
> & see a-bout how trim, how trim they daunce & trickly.
> and see about how trim they daunce & trickly.
> Hey ther a-gain hey ho ther a-gain, hey ho how yᵉ bells they shake it!
> now for our town hey ho, now for our town & take it.
> Soft a while not a way so fast they melt them: Piper, Piper, Piper!
> be hangd a while knave, looke yᵉ dauncers swelt then, yᵉ dauncers swelt
>   then.
> Out ther, out a while stand out you come to far, to far you come I say in,
> ther give the hobby horse more rome to play in,
> ther give the hobby horse more rome to play in, more rome to play in.[23]

All in good fun – but Morris dancing, like bringing in the may and similar seasonal pursuits, had already been roundly condemned by the Reformation. Most notorious, perhaps, in his assessment was the Puritan polemicist Philip Stubbes, who in *The Anatomie of Abuses* (1583) rails apoplectically at every imaginable and imagined vice, 'to be reade of all true Christians: but most needefull to be regarded in Englande'.[24] His comprehensive attack on the 'Lord of Misrule' is invaluable as it provides a wealth of historical detail that would otherwise have been lost:

> Then every one of these his menne, he investeth with his Liveries, of Greene, Yellowe, or some other light wanton colour. And as though that were not (baudie) gaudie enough I should saie, thei be decke themselves with Scarffes, Ribons and Laces, hanged all over with golde Rynges, precious stones, and other Jewelles; this doen, thei tye about either legge twentie, or fourtie belles, with riche hande kercheefes in their handes, and somtymes laied a crosse over their shoulders and neckes, borrowed for the moste parte of their prettie Mopsies, and loovyng Bessies, for bussyng them in the darcke. Thus all thynges sette in order, then have thei their Hobbie horses, Dragons and other Antiques, together with their baudie Pipers, and thunderyng Drommers, to strike up the Devilles Daunce withall, then marche this Heathen companie towards the Churche and Churche yarde, their Pipers pipyng, their Drommers thonderyng, their stumppes Dauncyng, their belles jynglyng, their handkerchefes swyngyng about their heades like madmen, their Hobbie horses and other monsters skirmishyng amongest the throng.[25]

Although early Protestants such as the Lollards had embraced the analogies between the common people and the greenwood, holding services beneath the leaves and taking trees for their pulpits, the Protestant Reformers perceived every form of ritual as superstitious and therefore potentially Catholic. In their ardent beliefs, they threatened to destroy the whole web of relations that embedded people within their environment. As the British historian Keith Thomas laments: 'Vehement Protestants, deeply sensitive to any apparent survivals of popery or paganism, were, like some of their mediaeval predecessors, strongly hostile to the notion that vegetation might have any protective power and were unsympathetic to the symbolic use of plants'.[26] On 1 May 1549, for example, Bishop Latimer was especially aggrieved when he learned that his Worcester congregation were too busy celebrating Robin Hood out among the trees to attend his sermon.

Remarkably, though, bringing in the may survived the Reformation. Elizabethans continued to attach nosegays to their horses and oxen, and poets such as Spenser found the celebration irresistible:

> Yougthes folke now flocken in every where,
> To gather may bus-kets and smelling brere:
> And home they hasten to the postes to dight,
> And all the Kirke pillours eare day light,
> With Hawthorne buds, and swete Eglantine,
> And girlands of roses and Sopps in wine.
> Such merimake holy Saints doth queme,
> But we here sytten as drownd in a dreme....

> To see those folks make such jouyance,
> Made my heart after the pype to daunce.
> Tho to the greene Wood they speeden hem all,
> To fetchen home May with their musicall:
> And home they bringen in a royall throne,
> Crowned as king: and his Queene attone
> Was Lady Flora, on whom did attend
> A fayre flocke of Faeries....[27]

Moreover, if Stubbes and his crew thought that maying was ungodly, for commentators such as John Stow it was quite the opposite – it was a way of communing with the Creation:

In the moneth of May, namely on May day in the morning, every man (except impediment) would walke into the sweet meadowes and greene woods, there to rejoice their spirites with the beaty and savour of sweete flowers, and with the noyce of birdes, praising God in their kinde.[28]

Similarly, there was devotion in the rhymes recited while a-maying:

> We've been rambling all the night,
>   And sometime of this day;
> And now returning back again,
>   We bring a garland gay.
>
> A garland gay we bring you here;
>   And at your door we stand;
> It is a sprout well budded out,
>   The work of our Lord's hand.[29]

Even the Holy Thorn at Glastonbury joined in, traditionally flowering for May Day as well as at Christmas.

Interestingly, the custom of garlanding houses and streets was not confined to country towns and villages. In the *Gentleman's Magazine* for 1754 a Mrs Pilkington records that horses were generously garlanded on urban routes:

> They took places in the waggon, and quitted *London* early on *May* morning; and it being the custom in this month for the passengers to give the waggoner at every inn a ribbon to adorn his team, she soon discovered the origin of the proverb *as fine as a horse*; for before they got to the end of their journey, the poor beasts were almost blinded by the tawdry party-coloured flowing honours of their heads.[30]

By the nineteenth century, this form of garlanding had become an annual feature of working equine culture, culminating in the foundation of the London Cart Horse Parade Society in 1886. There were other urban May Day celebrations as well. From the seventeenth century, May Day was the traditional celebration for milkmaids, who promenaded with pails and later large head-dresses made from silver plate, tankards, and teapots. Such garlands were noted by Samuel Pepys on 1 May 1667 and remained popular for another century – 'Isaac Bickerstaff', the pen name inspired by Jonathan Swift for writers contributing to The Tatler, wrote on 1 May 1710 that his milkmaid was 'dancing before my Door with the Plate of half her Customers on her Head'.[31]

Milkmaids shared the day with chimney sweeps, who were also decked out in ribbons and gilt paper. The peculiar figure of Jack-in-the-Green emerged from these festivities in the late eighteenth century. His part was originally played by a young sweep joining milkmaids' garland dances, but soon developed into an urban custom of its own to raise money for the child chimney sweeps. The poet laureate Robert Southey reported the phenomenon in 1820: 'he is in the middle of a green bush, which covers him all over, head and all, . . . ornamented with ribbons. . . . This Jack in the Bush is a comical sight, but I am sorry to say that it does harm by frightening horses'.[32]

The foliage selected for maying varied from place to place, depending on local habitats and regional variations in the weather – the writer and naturalist Richard Jefferies noted in 1885 that 'Spring dates are quite different according to the locality, and when violets may be found in one district, in another there is hardly a woodbine-leaf out'.[33] Two centuries earlier, the botanist William Coles noted in The Art of Simpling (1656) that, 'The common people formerly gathered the Leaves of Elder upon the last day of Aprill, which to disappoint the Charmes of Witches, they had affixed to their Doores and Windowes'.[34] Elsewhere, garlands made of hoops of rowan and marsh marigold are recorded: rowan was another prophylactic against the dark arts, whereas marsh marigolds were also known as may blobs, may blubs, or may bubbles, and were the 'herb of Beltane'; birch and sycamore, meanwhile, were popular in Cornwall. In nineteenth-century Cheshire, boughs of different trees were hung outside neighbours' houses to reflect the opinion of the women therein: 'A branch of birch signifies a pretty girl, an alder (or owler they call it) a scold, an oak a good woman, a broom a good housewife.... If gorse, nettles, sycamore or sawdust are placed at the door, they cast the worst imputation on a woman's character, and vary according as she be girl, wife, or widow'.[35] But hawthorn blossom – the 'may' itself – was the most popular; it too had associations of protection. Hawthorn growing in threes with oak and ash could open portals into the realm of Faërie – Thomas of Ercildoune (Thomas the Rhymer) met the Queen of Faërie under a hawthorn bush one May Day. Fairies themselves could be calmed by hanging ribbons from hawthorn, and it was wise to hang hawthorn around a cradle to discourage the fairies from replacing one's new baby with a changeling. Shakespeare's *A Midsummer Night's Dream* (1594–5) of course takes place on May Eve, the fairies' night, on which it was not only customary to gather greenery but also to play pranks.[36] Indeed, this play seems to be virtually the sole witness of English May-time fairy lore. Either Shakespeare made it all up, which is highly unlikely, or we have lost a huge wealth of English folk traditions.

But all the hedgerow bustle and May queenery associated with bringing in the may could not disguise the more carnal reputation of May Day. As on the Eve of St Mark and other propitious nights, May Eve afforded another opportunity for young women to predict whom they would love, court, and marry, and indeed Shakespeare's play has love games and sexual play at its heart. The madrigalist Thomas Morley's contemporary English pastoral (1595) has an undertow of this erotic tension:

> Now is the month of Maying,
> When merry lads are playing. Fa la la.
> Each with his bonny lasse,
> upon the greeny grasse. Fa la la.
>
> The Spring clad all in gladnesse,
> Doth laugh at winter's sadnesse. Fa la la.

And to the Bagpips sound,
The Nimphs tread out their ground. Fa la la.

Fye then why sit wee musing,
Youths sweet delight refusing. Fa la la.
Say daintie Nimphs and speake,
Shall wee play barly breake? Fa la.[37]

'Barley-break' was a game played by three couples based around swapping partners – the 'break'; it is mentioned in the courtier poet Sir Philip Sidney's *Arcadia*, the Cavalier poet and wit Sir John Suckling also writes about the game, and it appears frequently in the *Poor Robin* almanacs. The anonymous verse 'A Pleasant Countrey Maying Song' (c.1629), however, is the most explicit in its concluding scene of bucolic sensuality:

Thus the Robin and the Thrush,
Musicke make in every bush.
     While they charme their prety notes
     Young men hurle up maidens cotes.[38]

Similarly, Robert Herrick resorted to the bawdy euphemism of keys and locks in 'Corinna's going a Maying':

Many a green-gown has been given;
Many a kisse, both odde and even:
Many a glance to has been sent
From out the eye, Loves Firmament:
Many a jest told of the Keyes betraying
This night, and Locks pickt, yet w'are not a Maying.[39]

All of this could only lead to one thing: the sin of lust. Maying and May games were the work of the Devil. The historian and poet Robert Mannyng of Brunne (Bourne, in Lincolnshire) had stated in 1303 in *Handlyng Synne* that 'Daunces, karols, somour games, / Of many swych come many shames'. According to Mannyng, the Devil was ever in wait for those collecting flowers, tempting them to acts of carnality even on Sundays:

> ȝyf þou ever yn felde, eyþer in toune,
> Dedyst floure-gerland or coroune
> To makë wommen to gadyr þere,
> To se whych þat feyrer were;
> Þys ys aȝens þe commaundëment,
> And þe halyday for þe ys shent;
> Hyt ys a gaderyng for lecherye,
> And ful grete pryde, & hertë hye.[40]

Guardians of the morality of the nation were righteously indignant at the dissipation. The Calvinist translator Christopher Fetherston recounted in A Dialogue agaynst Light, Lewde, and Lascivious Dauncing (1582) how 'the abuses whiche are committed in your maygaymes are infinite': cross-dressing 'maymarrions', Morris men dancing 'naked in nettes' – 'what greater entisement unto naughtines, could have been devised?' Thus it was that 'tenne maidens . . . went to set May, and nine of them came home with childe'. The anonymous Vox Graculi (1622) likewise described how May Day encouraged 'young Fellowes and Mayds be so inveloped with a mist of wandring out of their wayes' and 'divers durty-Sluts' to roam at large.[41] The remorselessly Puritanical Philip Stubbes needed no further incentive to let his invective fly:

> Against Maie, Whitsondaie, or some other tyme of the yeare, every
> Parishe, Towne, and Village, assemble themselves together, bothe men,
> women, and children, olde and yong, even all indifferently: and either
> goyng all together, or devidyng themselves into companies, they goe
> some to the Woodes and Groves, some to the Hilles and Mountaines,
> some to one place, some to another, where they spende all the night
> in pleasant pastymes, and in the mornyng thei returne, bryngyng with

them Birch, Bowes, and braunches of Trees, to deck their assemblies withal: And no marvaile, for there is a great Lord present amongest them, as superintendent and Lorde over their pastymes and sportes: namely, Sathan Prince of Hel: But their cheefest jewel thei bryng from thence is their Maie pole, whiche thei bryng home with greate veneration, as thus, Thei have twentie, or fourtie yoke of Oxen, every Oxe havyng a sweete Nosegaie of flowers, placed on the tippe of his hornes, and these Oxen drawe home this Maie pole (this stinckyng Idoll rather) whiche is covered all over with Flowers, and Hearbes bounde rounde aboute with strynges from the top to the bottome, and sometyme painted with variable colours, with twoo or three hundred men[,] women, and children followyng it, with greate devotion. And thus beyng reared up, with hande kercheifes and flagges streamyng on the toppe, thei strawe the grounde aboute, binde greene boughes about it, sett up Sommer Haules, Bowers, and Arbours hard by it. And then fall thei to banquet and feast, to leape and daunce aboute it, as the Heathen people did, at the dedication of their Idolles, whereof this is a perfect patterne or rather the thyng it self. I have heard it credibly reported (and that *viva voce*) by menne of greate gravitie and reputation, that of fourtie, three score, or a hundred maides goyng to the Woode over night, there have scarcely the third parte of them retourned home againe undefiled.[42]

Dancing around a maypole holding ribbons is an abiding image of English May Day celebrations. But in fact ribbon dances only date from about 1830, and the earliest maypole dances, first recorded in the fourteenth century, were by the sixteenth communal dances of weaving, turning, and perhaps kissing. Nevertheless, for the outraged Stubbes they were heathen, Satanic, self-abasements before the 'stinckyng Idoll' of the maypole. To post-Reformation Puritans, maypoles looked wholly idolatrous – after all, this was a period when even a sprig of rosemary in a joint of meat could be condemned on religious grounds – and so come the Civil War the maypole was banned (1644).[43] The mechanist philosopher Thomas Hobbes followed the new orthodoxy, claiming in *Leviathan* (1651) that the maypole was based on the cult of Priapus: 'They [the heathens] had their *Bacchanalia*; and we have our *Wakes*, answering to them: They have their *Saturnalia*, and we our *Carnevalls*, and Shrove-Tuesdays liberty of Servants'.[44] Although maypoles were restored in 1660, the usually level-headed diarist John Evelyn objected to the waste of good timber and consequently, in his study of English trees and woodland, *Sylva* (1670), compared maypole dances with the excesses of ancient pagan rites:

> And here we cannot but perstringe those *Royotous* Assemblies of *Idle People*, who under pretence of *going a Maying* (as they term it) do oftentimes *cut down*, and *carry away* fine straight *Trees*, to set up before some *Ale-house*, or *Revelling-place*, where they keep their drunken *Bacchanalias* . . . I think it were better to be quite abolish'd amongst us, for many *reasons*, besides that of occasioning so much *wast* and *spoyl* as we find is done to *Trees* at that *Season*, under this wanton pretence, by *breaking*, *mangling*, and *tearing* down of *branches*, and intire *Arms of Trees*, to adorn their *Wooden-Idol*.[45]

A century later, Revd John William de la Flechere condemned the Madeley Wake in the same language: 'Seeing that I could not suppress these Bacchanals, I did all in my power to moderate their madness; but my endeavours had little or no effect: The impotent dyke I opposed, only made the torrent swell and foam, without stopping its course'.[46]

Aside from their theological objections to idolatry, the complaints of Stubbes and his contemporaries also reflected a disapproval of the wastefulness of spring festivities at a time when harvests were persistently failing. These agricultural disasters lasted almost a century – from the 1550s to the 1640s – and eventually helped to inspire the Royal Society's early interest in farming innovations, but at the time they also made the pastoral image of spring as a time of agricultural confidence look decidedly misplaced. Rather, the unpredictable weather that flattened and destroyed crops could be read in Biblical terms as an expression of divine displeasure at the corruptions of the world and the fickleness of human faith, and as a reminder of the Fall.

Many maypoles were destroyed from the time of the Reformation in 1535 until the Restoration in 1660, but the historian of paganism Ronald Hutton doubts the Puritan insistence that they were relics of ancient sex cults. The English maypole is not carved to represent a giant phallus, and in any case it is covered in foliage and ribbons. But for nearly 500 years over-enthusiastic commentators have presented maypoles as evidence of ancient English fertility beliefs – and in so doing are unwittingly echoing Stubbes. Such myths should be treated sceptically. Spring is a time in which there are obvious changes in flora and fauna. These changes are in turn celebrated in seasonal customs such as fetching greenery and making garlands; indeed, similar festive activities occur at other times in the year, notably at Christmas and on certain saints' days. Gathering foliage habitually takes place on common or waste land outside the usual environs of the community; consequently, maying is symbolically free from the constraints of normal moral behaviour and can develop into a sort of rural carnival. The strange, composite figures of the man-woman or man-beast that feature in this sort of festivity are common to both hobby-horse rituals and the Morris. But this does not necessarily imply a shared ritual significance drawing on the supposed practices of ancient cults: as Hutton argues, 'two of the simplest ways of expressing festive licence and signalling the existence of legitimate misrule have always been for the sexes to cross-dress or for people to put on animal skins or masks. Both indicate the suspension of the normal'.[47] Puritan theologians clearly recognized this, and as Keith Thomas points out, the Puritan polemicist William Prynne also condemned actors dressing as beasts on stage: 'What is this but to obliterate that most *glorious Image which God himself hath stamped on us*'.[48] And this may be one reason for the loss of the hobby-horse in mummers' plays.

What is significant here, then, is not how pre-Christian belief systems have allegedly survived but how cultural associations become naturalized. In other words, the culture of May Day that had evolved by the Reformation has since then profoundly influenced representations and imaginings of the springtime. Clearly one of the ways in which spring was imagined was as a heathen festival, and Puritan condemnation of this has been inverted by those who seek in folk customs the embodiment of pre-Christian beliefs. What they really embody, however, is the remnant of local pre-Reformation festivities that Puritan extremists found utterly distasteful.

Through this sort of cultural logic the season of spring became identified with sexual licentiousness, and so the language of spring in turn became the language of the erotic. This is strikingly demonstrated in eighteenth-century texts such as the *Merryland* series, a sort of natural history subgenre of the erotic that puts the 'whore' back into horticulture.[49] But it is an invention. Even taking into account the Julian slippage of the calendar, early May is cold and dewy – there are many customs about washing in the heavy dew (Mrs Pepys did so on 28 May 1667 and again on 10 May 1669).[50] This seasonal weather has meant that 1 May was never really a date conducive to casual, alfresco sex. Indeed, studies in population trends in Britain have shown that there was not an annual rise in births nine months after May Day; late summer was rather the more frequent time for conception.[51]

Notwithstanding all this, May Day still carries connotations of seasonal love-making. As an issue of *The Erotic Review* famously carried on its cover:

Hooray, hooray the first of May:
Outdoor sex begins today.[52]

And no matter how often seventeenth-century Puritans cut the maypoles down, still they went up again. 'An ugly thing . . . rough and crooked', said one preacher after his wife had taken the axe to a maypole and another had been erected in its place. 'Rough and crooked' it may have been, but the revels have continued.[53]

In the nineteenth century there were earnest endeavours to recreate old May Day festivities. As a way of balancing, or rather forgetting, the industry and empire that dominated society and the economy, the Victorian era turned to the mediaeval past in art, architecture, and literature, and celebrated, revived, and reinvented many examples of pre-industrial customs and traditions that remained in practice or memory. Previously children had carried a portable maypole around for their dances, in imitation of the adults. Now, however, May Day became a children's festival with garlands and singing – those who carried the garlands usually sang – and dancing around the maypole. Thus the culture of the maypole now became one of parents endorsing mock-mediaeval children's games:

> Come Lasses and Lads, get leave of your Dads,
> And away to the May-pole hey;
> For every he
> Has got him a she,
> with a minstrel standing by.... [54]

The May Queen, too, was a nineteenth-century invention, quite different from Elfland's Queen of the May: she was inspired by the American essayist and Anglophile Washington Irving's *Sketch Book* (1819) and *Bracebridge Hall* (1822), by Romantic poet and journalist Leigh Hunt, and later by the art critic and social reformer John Ruskin and by the poets laureate Wordsworth and Tennyson.[55] But despite this comparatively recent nativity, the May Queen was not wholly sentimentalized and there are darker notes here. Tennyson for one did perceive elements of sacrifice at the heart of the myth of the year's rebirth. In his poem 'The May Queen', the young girl who is crowned Queen of the May receives the honour as a death sentence: 'I shall never see / The blossom on the blackthorn, the leaf upon the tree'. Dancing around the maypole ensures her death – or at least a death of sorts (perhaps of her innocence?) – less than a year later:

> All in the wild March-morning I heard the angels call;
> It was when the moon was setting, and the dark was over all;
> The trees began to whisper, and the wind began to roll,
> And in the wild March-morning I heard them call my soul.[56]

We have come full circle, back to the menace of May Eve.

9   SUMMER

Now summer is in flower & natures hum
Is never silent round her sultry bloom
Insects as small as dust are never done
Wi' glittering dance & reeling in the sun
& green wood fly & blossom haunting bee
Are never weary of their melody
Round field hedge now flowers in full glory twine
Large bindweed bells wild hop & streakd woodbine
That lift athirst their slender throated flowers
Agape for dew falls and for honey showers
These round each bush in sweet disorder run
& spread their wild hues to the sultry sun.

John Clare, 'The Shepherd's Calendar'

Tennyson described the voice of the song thrush, mimicking the call of the bird:

> 'Summer is coming, summer is coming.
> I know it, I know it, I know it.
> Light again, leaf again, life again, love again,'
> Yes, my wild little Poet.[1]

Nature seems humming with life in summer. Shakespeare, too, has his Ariel sing of the buzzing bees and pendant blooms:

> Where the bee sucks, there suck I,
> In a cowslip's bell I lie; . . .
> Merrily, merrily shall I live now,
> Under the blossom that hangs on the bough.[2]

The poet Andrew Marvell appears positively intoxicated in *The Garden* (1681):

> What wond'rous Life in this I lead!
> Ripe Apples drop about my head;
> The Luscious Clusters of the Vine
> Upon my Mouth do crush their Wine;
> The Nectaren, and curious Peach,
> Into my hands themselves do reach;
> Stumbling on Melons, as I pass,
> Insnar'd with Flow'rs, I fall on Grass.[3]

Summer is the season of holidays and harvest, of picnics in the park and trips to the seaside, of music under sun or moon at Glastonbury or Glyndebourne, of bandstand recitals in market towns and Morris dancers arriving mob-handed in village pubs. Schools break up, Parliament goes into recess, industry slows – if not ceasing entirely for the old 'factory fortnight'. The season is marked by country shows and old fairs, and a bright thread of the carnivalesque runs through these events, but all this festivity is also twisted together with something darker. The turning of the summer solstice before the end of June leaves July and August already in anticipation of autumn, and of winter.

Shakespeare, in some of the most famous lines in English poetry, wrote in his Sonnet 18 of the swift passing of the summertime:

> Shall I compare thee to a summer's day?
> Thou art more lovely and more temperate:
> Rough winds do shake the darling buds of May,
> And summer's lease hath all too short a date.

The flowers that budded in May are buffeted by unexpected gusts and the 'summer's day' is never quite as lovely or as temperate – or as long – as might be hoped:

> Sometime too hot the eye of heaven shines,
> And often is his gold complexion dimm'd.

This is an odd sort of love song, for nothing beautiful will last:

> And every fair from fair sometime declines,
> By chance, or nature's changing course untrimm'd.

And when the beloved becomes central to the poem, the lines are haunted by mortality and transience:

But thy eternal summer shall not fade,
Nor lose possession of that fair thou ow'st;
Nor shall Death brag thou wand'rest in his shade,
When in eternal lines to time thou grow'st.

Thus the only permanence is in art – or more precisely, in Shakespeare's own sonnet:

So long as men can breathe or eyes can see,
So long lives this, and this gives life to thee.[4]

Summer is not simply nice and warm; it can be too hot, or too cold. The weather is unpredictable and often fails to live up to expectations or pre-dictions, and nature can overrun and mar beautiful things. Summer is also short-lived, and is haunted by the dead. See how quickly death steals into the summer idyll. There is a sense here of the Renaissance motto 'Et in Arcadia ego' – a phrase which is difficult to translate, but essentially means that even in Arcadia, Death is present and indeed uttering these words. Tennyson felt it too:

The woods decay, the woods decay and fall,
The vapours weep their burthen to the ground,
Man comes and tills the field and lies beneath,
And after many a summer dies the swan.[5]

Much has been written about Shakespeare's sonnets and the possible iden-tities of the figures that appear to be dramatized through the cycle, but what is more intriguing about these poems in the context of the English seasons is the degree to which they suggest that the weather and the seasons are poetic inventions. Shakespeare's sonnets keep returning to the representation of the weather and what it means: can the weather ever simply be just the weather itself, or in describing the weather do we inevitably bestow upon it some symbolic value? Shakespeare reveals this process in Sonnet 18, demonstrating how the summer risks becoming a heap of cultural images enlisted by the ulterior motives of love poetry. Indeed, he implies that real summers are utterly inadequate metaphors for describing conventional beauty.[6] Something is rotten in the state of summerland.

JUNE

According to Shakespeare's contemporary Nicholas Breton, June sees the muster of mowers and haymakers, the stacking of hay-cocks in the fields and preparations for harvest, the full leafing of the oak and the shearing of sheep, the partridge in season and venison pie and apples on the menu, and the brewing of cordials from roses and herbs: 'the Ayre now groweth somewhat warme, and the coole winds are very comfortable'.[7] Early summer continues the loveliness of late spring, and the name of the month of June is derived from Juno, both the Roman goddess of marriage and motherhood and a Latin term for a young woman ready for marriage. Not that anyone should be overhasty: in England, 2 June was an unlucky day for marriage.

June could also be a wet month. In the world of English proverbial wisdom it was not only likely to rain in June, but positively beneficial if it did: 'A dripping June brings all things in tune'.[8] All things, that is, except haymaking and possibly the harvest, which for a countryman like Thomas Tusser defined this time of the year:

> At midsummer, downe with thy brimbles and brakes:
> and after abrode, with thy forkes and thy rakes.
> Set mowers a worke, while the meddowes be growne:
> the lenger they stande, so much worse to be mowne.[9]

The weather had to be checked regularly and there is a rich lore for this time, although it is not always captured in the most elegant of couplets:

'If on the eighth of June it rain, / It foretells a wet harvest men sain'.[10] St Vitus' Day, 15 June, was another occasion for doggerel in anticipation of St Swithin's Day – 'If Saint Vitus's day be rainy weather, / It will rain for thirty days together'; rain was, however, desirable on St Peter's Day, 29 June, for improving the apple crop.[11] Unseasonal weather is certainly not unknown in June: on 4 June 1975 it snowed.[12]

But already in June the summer seems fully blown, and spring is past. As we have seen, birds traditionally stop singing on 5 June and some proverbial wisdom has them leaving at this time too: in Lancashire 'The first cock of hay / Frights the cuckoo away'.[13] Nevertheless, reed warblers are a feature of the season, and as the ornithologist Michael Waterhouse deftly puts it:

> The time to listen to them is on a fine day in June, when there is just enough breeze to make a slight rustling in the tall reeds that blends with the continuous singing of the birds. Then we know the world in which reed warblers live, and we feel the spirit of it.[14]

St Barnabus' Day, 11 June, was when mowing began in England – 'At Saint Barnabus the scyth in the meadow' – and white roses are worn in Staffordshire to honour the saint.[15] There may be an influence from the summer solstice here, the saint's feast day roughly coinciding with the solstice in Old Style Julian dating; this would account for the rhyme 'Barnaby bright, the longest day and the shortest night', and the tendency for St Barnabus fairs to be reckoned in Old Style and therefore to fall in the midsummer period.[16] Mowing also has strong sexual associations, 'rambling in the new-mown hay' being a euphemism for the slightly less modest innuendo of rolling in the hay. But that, too, had overtones of death: mowers looked like grim reapers in the meadows, intent on their levelling task – which could be a bloody business if the scythes met with any small mammals.

———

The summer solstice falls on 21 June: the sun rises in Greenwich at 3.48 GMT and sets at 20.20, giving 16 hours and 32 minutes of direct sunlight (and slightly more of indirect daylight). This has become a major festival for modern pagans, who gather at Stonehenge and other ancient sites to greet the rising of the sun on the longest day. English Heritage now provide 'managed open access' to Stonehenge from 8.30 p.m. on solstice eve until 8 a.m. on the morning itself. Nearly 20,000 attended Stonehenge for the summer solstice in 2010, thankfully far short of the astonishing 36,500 who turned up in 2009.[17] When I visited Stonehenge in 1986, I had to climb a barbed-wire fence in the dead of night to get near the stones. For my trouble I was caught by a security officer and reported to the Wiltshire police. That was the year after the 'Battle of the Beanfield', when the same police force had donned riot gear to arrest travellers who were planning a free festival there to celebrate the 1985 summer solstice. By 1989 English Heritage had introduced an annual four-mile exclusion zone, razor wire, helicopters, and searchlights to 'protect' the site.[18]

Although the current policy is an improvement, it has clearly brought its own problems. One of the reasons I went was simply to support the principle of access, but then I did not expect that within twenty-five years this would mean over 30,000 people celebrating there. Does this figure indicate a flourishing new belief system? One 'new age' website puts it thus:

> A celebration of life – standing amongst the towering stones with 30,000 others watching the sun rise on the magical midsummer morning. It's great to be able to stand inside the sacred circle of sarsens as our ancestors did as dawn appears over the Heel Stone – much better than from behind a fence. A traditional way to celebrate the longest day of the year.
>
> There's an amazing communal excitement at the solstice sunrise as the spiritual ancestry of this prehistoric temple is celebrated – with whoops of joy, drumming, horn blowing, cheering and applause . . . it makes you feel good to be alive.

This re-enacting of an ancient ceremony brings a mystical link, stretching right back through the aeons of time, producing almost a celebratory communion with our ancestors.

The mighty stones seem to breathe....[19]

It is difficult to divine any belief system at work here, unless sentimentalizing an archaeological site and mystifying the past for the purposes of having an early-morning party constitute a new religion. Little is known of the role of Stonehenge among the Neolithic peoples who built it or of the rituals, if any, that took place there – except that the site developed over hundreds of years and was used for the burial of bones and cremated remains. The likelihood is that such a major construction had multiple purposes. Recorded history, too, shows that Stonehenge has been in perpetual flux, shifting through the centuries as it comes under the scrutiny of antiquarians and archaeologists, writers, painters, counter-cultural agitators, and crackpots. Charles II, for example, tarried there on his escape after the Battle of Worcester (1651) and the standing stones consequently became a Royalist emblem comparable to the oak tree. The layout of Stonehenge provided the inspiration for the 'sacred geometry' in the town planning of Georgian Bath, and also, incidentally, the model for the traffic roundabout. Stonehenge was also a favourite picnic spot for Victorian day-trippers, who by 1857 could take a train direct from London: Charles Dickens visited and was able to hire a hammer and chisel there so he could take home a fragment of prehistory as a souvenir.[20] The megalithic mysticism so popular today is a relatively recent phenomenon, dating from the mid-eighteenth century. One of its effects has been to revive interest in celebrating the solstice, which otherwise would surely have little immediate impact on twenty-first-century life.

The English festive calendar, however, has a different emphasis in the ebb and flow of seasonal events. The solstice itself is not as important as Midsummer Day, 24 June, three days after the solstice: this is the feast day of St John the Baptist, the cousin of Christ – his nativity being six months before that of Jesus. This dating reflects the slight slippage at the winter solstice and Christmas Eve: the solar calendar and the festive calendar are three days adrift. This does not always seem to have been the case. Midsummer Mass was a major event in the Christian calendar and took place six months before the Midwinter Mass on 24 December. The word 'midsummer' itself was first used in Old English translations of Bede's *Ecclesiastical History* for the quarter of the year in which the sun rises at the solstice: '*æt middum sumere*'.[21] In other words, the early English Church was at this stage supposedly in accord with the solar year. But as we have seen, the Julian calendar had already drifted by three or four days when Bede was writing, meaning that there was a scale of discrepancy rather than a straightforward mismatch. The eventual aim of the Gregorian reform of 1582 was not to realign the Christian calendar with the solar year. Rather, the reform addressed one-and-a-half thousand years of temporal drift in order to provide a satisfactory and workable formula for calculating Easter within a calendrical religious framework – Easter being the major religious festival of the year, and the Christian calendar being a practical modern alternative to dating systems based on sun or moon worship. Hence the solstices, noteworthy as they are in the solar year, simply ended up preceding the religious festivals of Midsummer and Christmas, which were of more significance in the Christian calendar. There was, in short, a shift from days to dates.

At least that was the theory. In practice, the midsummer dates, the vigil and feast of St John the Baptist, were marked with characteristic celebrations that could be understood as being emphatically solar in symbolism and purpose. The 'Monk of Winchcomb', for instance, described the events surrounding Midsummer Eve festivities on 23 June in the thirteenth century as a striking mix of Christian dating and heathen festivity:

> Let us speak of the revels which are accustomed to be made on St. John's Eve, of which there are three kinds. On St. John's Eve in certain regions the boys collect bones and certain other rubbish, and burn them, and therefore a smoke is produced on the air. They also make brands and go about the fields with the brands. Thirdly, the wheel which they roll, which, with the rubbish they burn, they have from the pagans. . . .

The wheel is turned to signify that the sun then ascends to the highest point of its circle and immediately goes back.[22]

It is certainly tempting to see here the influence of ancient rites, although bonfires were lit and wheels, not to mention cheeses or eggs, were rolled on all sorts of occasions.

The antiquary John Aubrey invoked specifically the Roman myth of spring in analysing midsummer festivals. Proserpina was the daughter of Ceres, goddess of crops and farming, and was abducted by a lovestruck Pluto, god of the underworld. Ceres halted the world's agriculture forthwith and went searching for her daughter, lighting her way to the underworld with torches. Proserpina was released by Pluto, but only after she had eaten six pomegranate seeds. Having dined on the food of the dead, she was forever condemned to spend six months of every year in the underworld, whereupon the flora of the earth would mourn and die until she came again in – or rather as – the spring. For Aubrey, midsummer fires in Herefordshire and Somerset were indebted to this myth:

> on Midsommer-eve, they make fires in the fields in the waies: sc. [*scilicet*, to wit] to Blesse the Apples. . . . I doe guesse that this custome is derived from the Gentiles, who did it in remembrance of Ceres her running up and downe with Flambeaux in search of her daughter Proserpina, ravisht away by Pluto; and the people might thinke, that by this honour donne to ye Goddesse of husbandry, that their Corne, &c. might prosper the better.[23]

The sixteenth-century historian and surveyor of London John Stow also noted the enthusiasm for building bonfires at this time, but there is no indication that these fires are a survival of 'Celtic' celebrations of the solstice. Indeed, as the leading historians of the calendar Blackburn and Holford-Strevens put it, there is 'no evidence that Midsummer was a Celtic festival before the Middle Ages, though it certainly became one thereafter'.[24]

Midsummer was, however, certainly a moment when the year shifted and magic was in the air again. Gadshill in *Henry IV, Part 1* believed that fern seed gathered on Midsummer Eve had powers of invisibility, whereas Aubrey claimed that killing a snake on Midsummer Eve and drying its skin bestowed similar properties.[25] Sitting in a church porch on Midsummer Eve would give visions of those to be buried there in the year, much as would sitting there on the Eve of St Mark, and Midsummer Eve was likewise a time of divination.[26] St John's wort and orpine (the latter also known as midsummer men) were believed to have potent powers of divination at this time: a maiden who picked St John's wort on Midsummer Eve and found it still fresh in the morning would soon be married. Fortunes could be told on Midsummer Eve with eggs, or by cooking 'dumb cake', whereby the spirit of a future husband would appear to the cake-maker to share the cake with her. Finally, the midsummer moon could induce lunacy, as Olivia remarks of Malvolio in *Twelfth Night*, 'Why, this is very midsummer madness'.[27] No wonder the antiquary and engraver Joseph Strutt suggested that midsummer fires were 'made to drive away the dragons and evil spirits hovering in the air ... for "the dragons hattyd nothyng mor than the styncke of brenyng bonys"'.[28]

Because the evening was so long, the night so short, and the moon so antic, Midsummer Eve was a time of revelry. Stow described the enthusiasm for seasonal foliage in the sixteenth century even in the city of London, and the spectacle it afforded:

> On the Vigil of Saint *John Baptist* [23 June], and on Saint *Peter* and *Paule* the Apostles [29 June], every mans doore being shadowed with greene Birch, long Fennel, Saint Johns wort, Orpin, white Lillies, and such like, garnished upon with Garlands of beautifull flowers, had also Lampes of glasse, with oyle burning in them all the night, some hung out braunches of yron curiously wrought, contayning hundreds of Lampes light at once, which made a goodly shew, namely in new Fishstreet, Thames street, &c.[29]

St John the Baptist, like Mary Magdalene, is a saint of the wilderness rather than of farmed or cultivated landscapes. This may have encouraged such floral collections: most houses seem to have decorated the hearth with boughs and flowers throughout the summer as a seasonal alternative to lighting a fire, and in the Northumbrian town of Morpeth in the sixteenth century boys wore garlands at midsummer.[30] Similarly, midsummer cushions were cushions decked with local flora and displayed from Midsummer Day to Magdalene Day, 22 July. They seem to have been popular for about a century, from 1750 to 1850, and were noted by the poet John Clare, who planned to title his 1832 volume of poems *The Midsummer Cushion*.

These Midsummer Eve activities eventually brought about the Midsummer Watch, an exercise in law enforcement to curb the excesses of the night. However, this practice itself developed into a grand occasion as a procession of military might, veteran servicemen, and the ubiquitous Morris men. The procession survives in a similar form today as part of the Lord Mayor's Show. Stow again:

> the standing watches all in bright harness in every warde, and streete of this Citie, there was also a marching watch, that passed through the principall streets thereof. . . . The marching watch conteyned in number aboute 2000. men, parte of them being olde souldiers, of skill to bee captaines, Lieutenantes, Sergeantes, Corporals, &c. Wiflers, Drommers, and Fifes, Standard and Ensigne bearers, Sworde players, Trompiters on Horsebacke, Demilaunces on greate horses, Gunners with hand Guns, or halfe hakes Archers in coates of white fustian, signed on the brest and backe with the armes of the citie, their bowes bent in their handes, with sheafes of arrowes by their sides, Pike men in bright corslets, Burganets, &c. Holbarders, like the Bilmen, in Almaine Rivetes, and Aperns of Maylein greate number; there were also divers Pageantes, Morris dancers, Constables. . . .[31]

Sources such as Stow suggest that the days between St John the Baptist's Eve, 23 June, and St Peter's Day, 29 June, came together in one general midsummer festival. Giant wicker men roamed the streets of Old England:

one sixteenth-century commentator, the literary critic George Puttenham, wrote – though to little effect – to dispel their stature: 'midsommer pageants in London, where to make the people wonder are set forth great and uglie Gyants marching as if they were alive, and armed at all points, but within they are stuffed full of browne paper and tow, which the shrewd boyes, underpeering, do guilefully discover and turne to a greate derision'.[32] The annual midsummer pageant at Chester had four giants, as well as hobby-horses and effigies of animals. The giant's wife was included in Coventry, while a dragon joined the giant at Burford in Oxfordshire and was still processing through the town well into the eighteenth century. The social anthropologist James George Frazer recorded with rather too much satisfaction that,

> The last survivor of these perambulating English giants lingered at Salisbury, where an antiquary found him mouldering to decay in the neglected hall of the Tailors' Company about the year 1844. His bodily framework was of lath and hoop, like the one which used to be worn by Jack-in-the-Green on May Day.[33]

Midsummer fires are still lit at Whalton in Northumberland on 4 July: the custom is called the Whalton Baal Fire, *baal* or *bel* meaning 'sun'. At the other end of the country, there was a tradition of wrestling and hurling, and then lighting midsummer fires on the hills of West Penwith in Cornwall: 'dancing in a ring around the blazing fires, or pulling each other for good luck over the embers, that they might extinguish the fires by treading them out, without breaking their chain, or rather ring'.[34]

South Petherton in Somerset, meanwhile, held its annual fair on the day of the wool merchants' favourite saint, John the Baptist, as did the Cotswold town Stow-on-the-Wold from 1268 and Dorchester in Dorset from the 1330s; and a charter was granted for the prior and convent of Sempringham in Lincolnshire for the vigil, feast and morrow of St John the Baptist.[35] There were also midsummer fairs such as the Summer Gams in Horkstow, again in Lincolnshire, and a fair in Cambridge on Midsummer

Common, which still runs to this day. More recently, midsummer has seen the reinvention of the Cornwall snake dance, a simple communal dance based on the mediaeval farandole.[36] Some midsummer fairs took place on dates which had meaning for a specific parish. The translation of St Werburgh to Chester – 'translation' being the technical term for moving the relics, or corporeal remains, of a saint – took place on 21 June. St Werburgh thenceforth became the patron saint of the city and was subsequently commemorated with a fair lasting from her feast day until Midsummer Day. St Peter's and St Paul's Day, 29 June, was also included within the general midsummer festivities. At St Paul's Cathedral, the dean and chapter traditionally wore a garland of red roses on this day, and if they had not had a fair already, many places marked the end of the midsummer season with a St Peter's and St Paul's fair day combining trading with revelry. In 1156, for instance, 'customs, markets, tolls and fairs on either feasts of St Peter' were recorded at Bath and Wells for the Abbey of Sts Peter and Paul, which were extended to a fair on the 'vigil, feast and morrow' of the saints and the seven days following.[37]

In Appleton Thorn in Cheshire, a tradition of 'Bawming the Thorn' has been observed since the nineteenth century, although it draws on earlier midsummer customs. On St Peter's and St Paul's Day, local children garland a hawthorn with ribbons, flags and flowers, dance around it, and sing:

> The Maypole in spring merry maidens adorn,
> Our midsummer May-Day means Bawming the Thorn.
> On her garlanded throne sits the May-Queen alone,
> Here each Appleton lad has a Queen of his own.
>
> [Chorus]
> Up with fresh garlands this Midsummer morn,
> Up with red ribbons on Appleton Thorn.
> Come lasses and lads to the Thorn Tree today
> To Bawm it and shout as ye Bawm it, Hooray!

So long as this Thorn Tree o'ershadows the ground
May sweethearts to Bawm it in plenty be found.
And a thousand years hence when tis gone and is dead
May there stand here a Thorn to be Bawmed in its stead.[38]

The hawthorn in question is supposedly a descendant of the Holy Thorn of Glastonbury, brought by Adam de Dutton, a Norman knight returning from the Crusades via Glastonbury, in thanks for his safe passage.

As the festivities of St Peter's and St Paul's Day fade, midsummer is over, June is ended, and the season is already waning. Spenser's *Shepheardes Calendar* ends nearly every month at evening, sometimes, as one critic observes, 'with the distinctly English inflection of inclement weather or chilling dews'.[39] His 'June' ends thus:

But now is time, I gesse, homeward to goe:
Then ryse ye blessed flocks, and home apace,
Least night with stealing steppes do you forsloe,
And wett your tender Lambes, that by you trace.[40]

JULY

In the Roman calendar, the name of this month was of course changed from *Quin[c]tilis* (fifth) to *Julius* to honour Julius Caesar. In English this was rendered 'July', which until the middle of the eighteenth century was pronounced to rhyme with 'truly'.[41] Moreover, the lilt of a verse such as this – 'A swarm of Bees in May, is worth a load of hay: But a swarm in July, is not worth a fly' – would actually be recited with the emphasis on the second syllable, rendering the last phrase 'is not worth a flea'.[42]

July is considered to be the height of summer – but not nearly so temperate as June. There is violence in the air. Nature is red in tooth and claw: stags fight, sparrow-hawks hunt down partridge, and ferrets catch rabbits; fowlers annihilate sparrows; and the corn is cut down by reapers. Most significantly, though, July is characterized by thunder-storms. For Nicholas Breton, the Jacobean annalist of the months:

> Now begins the Canon of heaven to rattle, and when the fire is put to the charge, it breaketh out among the Cloudes: the stones of congealed water cut off the eares of the Corne: and the blacke stormes affright the faint-hearted.[43]

The astrologer John Gadbury likewise described July as the 'thunder month' in his regular almanac *Ephemeris* (1696):

> July is called the THUNDER-MONETH. It was a Custom at *Malmsbury-Abbey*, to Ring the great Bell, call'd St. *Adam's Bell*, to drive away THUNDER and LIGHTNING.... The Old *English* in time of THUNDER were used to Invoke St. BARBARA.[44]

For some, such as eel-gatherers, the thunder was welcome as it stirred up their prey. The poet and dramatist John Marston wrote in *The Scourge of Villainy* (1599):

> They are naught but Eeles, that never will appeare
> Till that tempestuous winds or thunder teare
> Their slimie beds.[45]

For most, however, the thunder was a fearsomely destructive threat. The month of July in 1808 was so hot that the *Gentleman's Magazine* reported that at least seven people died from the excessive temperature. That heatwave finally ended on 15 July with thunder-storms of such ferocity that one of the pinnacles of Gloucester Cathedral was destroyed and violent hailstorms devastated the South-west, with jagged fragments of ice up to a foot long falling from the sky.[46]

The date of 15 July is of course better known in England as St Swithin's (or Swithun's) Day, popular for carrying the best-known piece of saints' day weather lore in the country. If it rains on St Swithin's Day, it will rain for forty days:

> St Swithin's day, if thou dost rain,
> For forty days it will remain;
> St Swithin's day, if thou be fair,
> For forty days 'twill rain no more.[47]

Rain before the harvest could spell disaster – the effects of which are coolly dissected in Thomas Hardy's novel *The Mayor of Casterbridge* (1886) – and consequently weather prognostication and prayers to tutelary saints were taken very seriously by agrarian communities and still survive in popular folklore today. Unfortunately, however, the example of St Swithin's Day, renowned as it is, dramatically demonstrates the insoluble complications that are inherent in our calendar, and emphasizes that the calendar itself is the result of centuries of cultural history, rather than a stable, divinely sanctioned instrument of prognostication.

Swithin (d. 863) was bishop of Winchester from at least 854, appointed in the reign of King Æthelwulf of Wessex (839–55). The feast of St Swithin is 15 July, which commemorates the anniversary of his translation from the outside to the inside of Winchester Old Minster on that day in 971. Accounts of what happened next differ slightly. There is a tradition that on the day of translation there was a heavy downpour, revealing the saint's powers over the weather. This suggests that the story is a warning against the dangers of translating holy remains and relics, which were often sold or stolen. However, a more detailed version is given by William of Malmesbury, writing about 1125. Swithin had apparently chosen his own burial plot to be a sort of posthumous mortification of the flesh:

> On the point of bidding farewell to earthly life, on his authority as bishop he ordered those present to inter his corpse outside the cathedral, where it should be exposed both to the feet of passers-by and to the dripping of water from the eaves.[48]

As this plan had been thwarted by St Swithin's translation to the dry interior of the building, he caused it to rain for forty days until he was reinstalled outside. Weather forecasting on St Swithin's Day is therefore an example of Biblical meteorology that reads the signs and portents on a particular day to see into the divinely ordained future. If only, however, it were that simple.

Contrary to tradition, St Swithin's remains were never returned to ostentatious humility outside the minster. Instead, he was moved twice within the cathedral and relics were sent abroad. He was a major English saint, and the cult of St Swithin remained a powerful presence in Winchester until the Reformation, when his shrine was destroyed – so that scotches the idea that commands from beyond the grave dictated where his mortal remains should lie.[49] But there are also much more significant problems with the St Swithin tradition. St Swithin's Day was originally 2 July, the day on which he was buried in 863. This was his feast day in England, at least until 1149, and remains so on the continent. Stavanger Cathedral in Norway is dedicated to St Swithun (the local spelling), and interestingly there is a Norwegian proverb about the saint that likewise indicates his weather wisdom:

On St Swithun's day
if the clouds are stacked
it lasts to St Olaf's day [29 July].[50]

Irrespective of this, it transpires that the early Christians already had weather lore for 2 July several centuries before St Swithin. This meteorological tradition invoked the early Roman martyrs Processus and Martinian, and predicted that if it rained on their shared feast day it would rain throughout the summer and drown the corn: this association perhaps survives in another piece of weather lore, which predicts, 'If the first of July it be rainy weather, / 'Twill rain more or less for four weeks together'.[51] Such a claim is strikingly close to the St Swithin's Day forecast, except that Processus and Martinian's lore was based on Roman farming practices and Mediterranean weather patterns in about the second century AD. Nevertheless in England, when St Swithin's Day was moved to 15 July to celebrate the saint's translation, this migration carried with it the established associations of rain.

The history of St Swithin's Day therefore places the saint's day itself rather late in the narrative, and the story of his proverbial weather wisdom therefore runs as follows. From late June and early July, farming communities are anxious about the imminent harvest and vigilant for rain. A number of sayings therefore emerged or were adapted from Roman lore in the earliest days of the Christian Church, to seek some foreknowledge of the incoming harvest. These sayings were focused on the beginning of July and consequently gravitated towards Processus and Martinian, who were later eclipsed by St Swithin when he became a more identifiable candidate for intercession as an English bishop rather than a pair of obscure Roman saints. When the feast of St Swithin was then subsequently moved to 15 July, St Swithin retained his status as a rain saint, and so the weather lore associated with him shifted by nearly a fortnight. So although the prediction that rain on St Swithin's Day would last for forty days is quoted in an early fourteenth-century manuscript, even by then it had become hopelessly remote from the original date, and indeed country, that had generated the advice.[52] Finally, both the old St Swithin's Day (2 July) and the new St Swithin's Day (15 July) are Old Style dates – to give them modern equivalences requires adding at least twelve days, which would take new St Swithin's Day to 27 July.[53]

Explanations of the St Swithin's Day proverb often appear in British newspapers around 15 July. These accounts argue that the jet stream settles in mid-July, which sets British weather patterns until about the end of August: a southerly jet stream pulls depressions to Britain from over the Atlantic, resulting in wet weather, but a more northerly jet stream can attract subtropical fronts from the Azores.[54] This is ingenious, but completely ignores the erroneous dating of St Swithin's Day – it is, in effect, an example of recruiting science to prove a misinterpretation of cultural history.[55] Perhaps we should return to old St Swithin's Day, as calculated in New Style, for our weather forecasting – although how that more authentic date will fare in these days of climate change is anyone's guess. There are also alternative, less contentious, but perhaps in the end less useful prognostications: if the deer rise up dry and lie down dry on St Bullion's Day, 4 July, there will be a good goose harvest.[56]

Apples, meanwhile, rely on being christened – or rained upon – by St Swithin's Day before they are ready for picking, and there is a similar tradition for them on St Peter's Day, 29 June. On account of St Swithin's identification with the rain and with cider – and conceivably related to the Byzantine complications of his dating – he is also known as 'the drunken saint'.[57] Finally, old St Swithin's Day has a sort of coda in the 'dog days', the season that precedes the rising of the Dog Star, Sirius. During this time the sun was believed to increase its heat and make these days the hottest of the year. The result of this was to induce sickness in humans and madness in dogs. St Swithin's rains permitting, the forty dog days ran from 3 July to 11 August in ancient Rome; more recent estimates begin the dog days on 19 July and end them on 28 August.[58]

After the complexities of Roman martyrs, early Anglo-Saxon bishops, saintly translation, calendrical shifts, wet weather, and canine incalescence that are inscribed on the palimpsest of St Swithin's Day and the dog days, the rest of July is comparatively straightforward in terms of the festive calendar. There is a late-season garland day in Cornwall to celebrate St Thomas Becket on the Monday after 7 July. This required garlands to be gathered at the Bodmin Riding, which were presented to the local priory; the festival was revived in 1974 as the Bodmin Riding and Heritage Day. Garlands and rushes were also taken into Cumbrian churches broadly around this time as a harvest custom. These rituals survive in Warcop on 29 June, Ambleside on the first Saturday of July (originally on the Saturday nearest to St Anne's Day, 26 July), Great Musgrave on that same first Saturday in July, and Urswick on 29 September. All of these rush-bearing ceremonies begin with a procession that leads into the church to lay rushes and garlands on the flagstones. Rush-bearing was first recorded in Grasmere in 1680, and a report of this event on 21 July 1827 identified some illustrious members of the congregation:

> In the procession I observed the 'Opium Eater' [i.e., Thomas De Quincey], Mr. Barber, an opulent gentleman residing in the neighbourhood, Mr. and Mrs. Wordsworth, Miss Wordsworth, and Miss Dora Wordsworth. [William] Wordsworth is the chief supporter of these rustic ceremonies.[59]

The feast day of St Margaret is 20 July, which coincides with the birth of babies conceived between All Saints' and Advent. St Margaret was generally represented as a shepherdess – she worked with sheep after being cast out from her father's house – and so became patron saint of sheep farmers, as well as of childbirth and midwives, but her day could also be a wet day, with the risk of 'Margaret's flood'. Interestingly, the feast of another female saint, Mary Magdalene, frequently represented as a repentant prostitute, is at about the same time – 22 July – suggesting some overtly sexual associations of this time of the year. But the Magdalene is also the saint of the garden from her meeting with Christ there after He rises from the tomb, and further affinity with nature is shown in her association with healing herbs, and following her retreat into the wild, in depictions of her as a woman of the wilderness. In English folklore this connects Mary with Maid Marian of the greensward, and in one early outlaw ballad, Robin Hood visits a chapel consecrated to Mary Magdalene in Barnsdale, South Yorkshire.[60] Another enlightened female saint, Anne, the mother of the Virgin Mary, was also celebrated at this time, on 26 July. Anne's popularity grew in the fifteenth century, possibly as a consequence of an increased emphasis on family stability following years of plague and poor harvests, and also as female literacy and economic activity increased: Anne was characteristically depicted teaching her daughter to read.[61]

The feast of St James the Greater, 25 July, is traditionally the start of the oyster season, and at Whitstable in Kent the Oyster Festival, which includes a Blessing of the Waters, is still kept around this time – although with the change to the Gregorian calendar most places shifted the oyster season to 5 August, or Old St James's Day. Oyster shells had firm associations with St James, and were used as tokens by pilgrims. The nineteenth-century writer and publisher Robert Chambers notes that in London,

> In the course of the few days following upon the introduction of oysters for the season, the children of the humbler class employ themselves diligently in collecting the shells which have been cast out from taverns and fish-shops, and of these they make piles in various rude forms. By the time that old St James's Day (the 5th of August) has come about, they have these little fabrics in nice order, with a candle stuck in the top, to be lighted at night. As you thread your way through some of the denser parts of the metropolis, you are apt to find a cone of shells, with its votive light, in the nook of some retired court, with a group of youngsters around it, some of whom will be sure to assail the stranger with a whining claim – *Mind the grotto!* by which is meant a demand for a penny wherewith professedly to keep up the candle. It cannot be doubted that we have here, at the distance of upwards of three hundred years from the Reformation, a relic of the habits of our Catholic ancestors.[62]

Some customs, however, remain unchanged: 'Whoever eats oysters on St James's day will never want money' – meaning that they are most expensive on that day. Those who could not afford new-season oysters could at least look forward to brewing beer: 'Till St James his day be come and gone, / You may have hopes [hops] or you may have none'.[63] In the month of the 'drunken saint', that was some comfort. And the end of July, lest we forget, has since the twelfth century been marked by swan-upping: a census of the swans of England. One nick to the beak meant that they belonged to the worshipful Company of Dyers, two nicks identified the Vintners' swans, and unmarked swans are the queen's brood. In practice, however, the queen only claims ownership along certain parts of the Thames and its tributaries, and as for dyers and vintners, they no longer feast on roast swan.

Priddy Fair in the Mendips is supposed to be a traditional sheep fair on the village green – one of the last in the country. Sadly, things have changed. I arrived after a delightful journey through the countryside at its early August best, ready to take a few steps back into the golden age of English country fairs. Priddy was certainly well attended, although not by farming types: these were the small-town yeomanry of Somerset from Wells and Weston. It did not bode well, and so when I got to the green through the rambling village, I was not surprised to find that the grass had all but disappeared beneath a fun fair. The over-amplified soundtrack of enforced festivity was inescapable: there were waltzers and centrifugal wheels and even a place you could win a goldfish in a bag by throwing darts at gigantic, perforated playing cards – a sideshow I admit I had not seen for many years. There was also a van selling DVDs of bloodsports: bare-knuckle boxing, hare-coursing, and the like. The goldfish aside, it was oppressive. And there was a huge police presence.

Eventually at the far end of the fairground, behind all the sputtering machinery, there were about 120 sheep pens along the perimeter of the green, with some six or seven hundred sheep divided into lots. And at the very extremity of the green, there was an intense auction being held. It was almost completely drowned out by the thunderous thud of the fair, but everyone in this tight gaggle was focused on the slight and restless figure of the auctioneer. Lots were sold at dizzying speed. It was soon over and the auctioneer and the sheep farmers immediately dispersed. Only the empty pens were left.

That was the real Priddy, I remarked to a garrulous Cornishman. He was there on his holidays – a regular visitor. We talked about sheep awhile, but his real interest was in the horses up in yonder field. 'When's the auction?' I asked. 'Don't they ride the horses around the green anymore?' 'I've never seen no auction: it's like, private, you know.' I understood him and made for the field.

I was only a few hundred yards away from the village green, but the fairground noise had all but disappeared and now I was surrounded by dozens of horses: bays, piebald, skewbald, a few greys, and even a spotted stallion. Most had extravagantly long feathers and were held on ropes; occasionally bareback riders cantered behind the vans and boxes. There was a lot of tack on display, and a few puppies, rabbits, chickens, and the like. There were also a lot of people pretending not to sell things. Conversations were held in murmurs and punctuated by furtive glances, hands were grasped; the older men were less cautious, spitting on their palms and slapping them together. It was all nods and winks – and a great relief to get away from the coarseness of the fun fair, where everything was too explicit. I was offered a few ponies, quiet like. Maybe next year.

As I returned home, I thought I probably would buy a horse from a fair like this too. Partly just recklessness and the desire to be part of a 600-year-old tradition, but also because there is a joy in seeing these horses handled by the men and women and boys and girls who had tenderly reared them from foals. They love them ferociously, but would sell them for a song. That's not at all how I keep my own livestock, and so perhaps I should learn something from that.

———

St Laurence's (also Lawrence's) Day, 10 August, was a popular date for fairs and Priddy Sheep Fair was originally held on this day from 1348 until about 1785 (the parish church is dedicated to the saint); it is now held about a week later. Like the fairs in Wilton, Skipton, Corby Glen, and others elsewhere, Priddy is ostensibly a sheep fair, but it began life as Wells's midsummer fair; the event migrated from Wells in the mid-fourteenth century because of the Black Death and never returned.[64] Coincidentally, the meteor shower of the Perseids begins around 10 August and is most active on the night of 12 August – by their proximity to St Laurence's Day, these shooting stars are known as the 'fiery tears of St Lawrence'.[65]

And the name 'August'? Augustus Caesar held his first consulate in the month of *Sextilis* in 43 BC and made Egypt a province of Rome exactly thirteen years later. It was his lucky month. Consequently, *Sextilis* was renamed *Augustus* in honour of the emperor and to peg his status at the same level as that of Julius Caesar, for whom the month of *Quintilius* had been renamed *Julius*. Thus the vanity of imperial Rome still lives with us today in those names, July and August.

August is the month of harvest, a month crowned, as Spenser has it, 'With eares of corne'.[66] The summer is waning, autumn is coming, and August is one of the wettest months of the year – 'the first rain after Priddy Fair is the first rain of winter'.[67] But there is still time for late harvests and gleaning: 'Drye August and warme, / doth harvest no harme'.[68] The work of the summer is done, and Breton ruefully notes that 'the Alehouse is more frequented then the Taverne … The Pipe and the Taber is now lustily set on worke, and the Lad and the Lasse will have no lead on their heeles'.[69] Traditional harvest festivities predominate, including fairs and country shows, and there is gossips cake to eat and furmety to drink.[70] The month also gradually became associated with the arrival of families of migrant workers, who would help to bring in the harvest and, in Kent, pick hops. The agricultural reformer Arthur Young noted in his *Farmer's Kalendar* (1771) that 'Plenty of hands should, on all accounts, be provided for this important business: women do it as well as men: it is a work rather of care than of labour'.[71] By the twentieth century 'this important business' had become a sort of working holiday, not always without friction between local rural labourers and the temporary workforce from the towns and cities.

If the weather was kind, the harvest could begin at the end of July in time for the 'loaf-mass' of St Peter ad Vincula (St Peter in Chains, 1 August) – the blessing of the bread made from the new corn. Lammas, the loaf-mass, derives from the Anglo-Saxon *hláf-maesse*, and is linked to *hláf-diġe* and *hláf-weard*, Anglo-Saxon terms for which the literal translations are 'loaf-kneader' and 'loaf-guardian', and which give us the modern English words 'lady' and 'lord'. Lammas therefore has a venerable enough heritage without having to claim that it is an Anglo-Saxonization of *Lughnasadh*, the 'Celtic' festival celebrating the victory of the sun god over the god of the earth – although admittedly the ritual of celebrating the first fruits of the harvest may have had ancient origins.[72] Neither does Lammas Day have anything to do with lambs – the 'lamb-mass' is an eighteenth-century antiquarian fallacy that rather charmingly influenced nineteenth-century claims that tenants of York Minster were bound to bring live lambs into the cathedral for Lammas Day high mass.[73] The use of bread at Lammas-tide in church is not an unbroken tradition either but a reintroduced custom. In 1945 a campaign was launched to re-establish Plough Sunday, Rogation Sunday, Lammas-tide, and Harvest Thanksgiving with specially written services; it was taken up by several parish churches.

The celebration of the first new loaf was also marked by the removal of fences that had been erected on Lammas meadows at Candlemas, 2 February – common land that had been kept free of stock, growing hay that could then be cut and stored for the winter. Lammas was therefore an important day for reaffirming local rights by mowing communal meadows. It also marked the start of haymaking – hence the ballad 'Lord Livingston' begins with the observation,

> It fell about the Lammas time,
> When wightsmen won their hay.[74]

Lammas was not a quarter day, but was nevertheless a traditional day for the payment of rent and therefore all that went with it, such as changing jobs and moving house. It was also a popular day for fairs to celebrate the year's first wheat harvest – 'the feast of first fruits', as the *Anglo-Saxon Chronicle* has it.[75] The fair at Highworth in Wiltshire dates from a 1257 charter for St Peter ad Vincula's vigil, feast, and morrow – it became the biggest cattle-market in the county – and a similar three-day fair was established at Exeter, a 'pleasure fair'.[76] Since at least 1300 Lammas has also been known as the 'Gule', or neck, of August, and 'Latter Lammas' meant 'never'.[77]

'After *Lammas* corn ripens as much by night as by day', and the ensuing month continues to be given its shape and structure by farming and fishing.[78] St Sidwell, an agricultural saint, is celebrated around this time, on 31 July or on 2 or 3 August, and 5 August is St Oswald's Day, Oswald being patron of shepherds and sheep (and also, according to Aubrey, colloquially known as St Twosole). After 1752, 5 August was also Oyster Day (Old St James's Day):

> Greengrocers rise at dawn of sun –
> > August the fifth – come haste away
> To Billingsgate the thousands run, –
> > 'Tis Oyster Day! – 'tis Oyster Day![79]

A week later, the grouse season begins on 12 August, the 'Glorious Twelfth' – confirmed by the Game Act of 1831, which created 'close seasons' (times when game should not be under threat and allowed to breed and establish) and game licences.[80]

Following St Laurence's Day, the Assumption of Mary, 15 August, was also popular for fairs and was known as 'Mary in Harvest'.[81] Mary's maternal status chimed with associations of nurture and sustenance, and this may account for her appeal to farming communities, which relied on social cohesion to survive and thrive.[82] There was an annual fair on the Feast of Assumption from 1298 in Weare in Somerset, and from 1221 Salisbury had a two-day fair for the vigil and feast of the Assumption held on 14 and 15 August.[83] All hoped for good weather on the day: 'If the sun shine on the 15th, it is a good token of a mild winter'.[84] There were also much rougher festivals: the Revels at Tutbury in Staffordshire were a riotous assembly celebrated by a minstrels' court presided over by the beggarly king of the minstrels. After much drinking and singing the event climaxed with attempts to win an enraged bull by cutting skin from it as it charged about. Not surprisingly, the inhabitants of Tutbury succeeded in having the Revels abolished in 1778.

Harvest Home was the end of the annual agricultural cycle, and marked by more celebrations: Horkey in the east of England, Mell Supper in the north, the Harvest Frolic in the west. These were often accompanied by guisers or similar mummers' performances. An 1845 account from Norfolk by the popular novelist Captain Marryat records that:

> To-morrow the men have a harvest-home dinner, and the next day they put apart to get drunk; such being the invariable custom of the county. I proposed last year that they should get drunk on the day of the harvest dinner, but they scouted the idea – they would have a day for intoxication entirely. Such was the custom. It was true that they would lose a day's wages, but they must do as their forefathers had always done before them.[85]

Aside from Lammas, these festivities were not linked to any specific date but were dependent on the successful gathering of the harvest and therefore the weather. The anthropologist James George Frazer argued that, as corn was a Greek staple in the Homeric age and possibly the oldest crop cultivated in Western society, ritual beliefs surrounding the figures of the Corn-mother and Corn-maiden in Germany and Britain are the remnants of a prehistoric cultural heritage. In parts of Scotland and the north of England reapers ritually cut the last corn, sometimes blindfolded, and made it into the figure of a child. This kirn (corn) baby, kirn doll, or kirn maiden brought good luck to individuals, households, and livestock. In Yorkshire a sheaf of corn was burnt – 'burning the Old Witch'.[86] In Devon and Cornwall a sheaf of ears was made into 'the neck', which was then celebrated with a haunting chorus, as recorded by the nineteenth-century folklorist William Hone:

> On a fine still autumn evening the 'crying of the neck' has a wonderful effect at a distance, far finer than that of the Turkish muezzin, which Lord Byron eulogizes so much, and which he says is preferable to all the bells in Christendom. I have once or twice heard upwards of twenty men cry it, and sometimes joined by an equal number of female voices. About three years back, on some high grounds, where our people were harvesting, I heard six or seven 'necks' cried in one night, although I

know that some were four miles off. They are heard through the quiet evening air, at a considerable distance sometimes. But I think that the practice is beginning to decline of late, and many farmers and their men do not care about keeping up this old custom.[87]

The corn-women of the harvest also generated another allegorical figure: that of the Harvest Queen. Milton alludes to this custom in *Paradise Lost*:

> Adam the while
> Waiting desirous her return, had wove
> Of choicest flowers a garland to adorn
> Her tresses, and her rural labours crown,
> As reapers oft are wont their harvest-queen.[88]

Frazer points out that these primitive rituals require no priest to organize them but were communal and could take place anywhere. They honoured some general spirit of harvest rather than a specific god, and were magical rather than propitiatory – they did not rely on the power of sacrifice or prayer but were ceremonies that corresponded in some way to a desired end.[89] They also personified the harvest in the figures of corn-mothers, maidens, witches, or more recently, corn-dollies (first mentioned in England around 1598), and effectively anthropomorphized the crop in the figure of the Harvest Queen.[90] Although such customs seem to have virtually disappeared with mechanization in the nineteenth century, the Harvest Queen migrated to London costermonger markets and survives to this day among the Pearly Kings and Queens of London, whose traditions themselves date from the late nineteenth century. The influence of the Harvest Queen on the Pearlies can be seen in the floral patterns of their pearl buttons, and in their annual celebration in October of the Harvest Festival in St Martin-in-the-Fields in Trafalgar Square and St Paul's in Covent Garden.

The end of the harvest in England was usually celebrated in the last week of August with church wakes, public entertainment, and enthusiastic drinking.[91] This helps to account for the rise of St Bartholomew's Day Fair, commencing 24 August, as the crowning event of the season. Fairs were held throughout the late summer and early autumn, often on feast days, among them St Barnabas', 11 June; Lammas-tide, 1 August; Mary's Nativity, 8 September; the feast of the Exaltation of the Holy Cross, 13 September; and St Matthew's, 21 September.[92] Appleby Horse Fair in what was once Westmorland and is now Cumbria received its charter from James II in 1685 and lasts from Thursday to Wednesday in the first week of June. Fairlop Fair was a huge fair held a month later that was based around an ancient oak tree in Epping Forest; the tree was eventually blown down in 1820 and some of the wood was used to make the pulpit and reading desk of St Pancras Church on Euston Road, London. Scarborough Fair, established in 1253, began on 15 August and at its height lasted for a staggering forty-five days. England's oldest horse fair, Lee Gap Fair, dating from 1139, is held at West Ardsley in Yorkshire; it was originally two three-day fairs that merged into a single event running from 13 August to 8 September. The novelist Henry Fielding, writing in 1751, thought that it had been most advantageous when 'the Diversions of the People have been limited and restrained to certain Seasons'; this was, however, no longer the case:

> this Perversion [is now] carried to so scandalous an Excess ... especially in and near the Metropolis, where the Places of Pleasure are almost become numberless.... And these are carried on, not on a single Day, or in a single Week; but all of them during half, and some during the whole Year.[93]

For Fielding, the rhythms of the year were being eroded by the new, leisured society that demanded all-year festivity.

Although Appleby Horse Fair is still probably the largest horse fair in Europe, Lee Gap Fair has now reverted to its two original fairs, the First of Lee on 24 August and Latter Lee on 17 September, while Fairlop and Scarborough both came to an end in the nineteenth century. Many other local and regional fairs have disappeared, and with them have gone local history, identity, and customs. This is in part due to the long decline of English agriculture, something that has inevitably reduced the frequency and size of fairs. Common land has been enclosed and traditional grounds have been built over, thus removing possible sites. The Reformation also played its part by trying to insist that all parishes held their annual fairs or festivals on the first Sunday in October. Most significantly, though, there were radical changes in the seasonal rhythm of work. The move from an agrarian economy, where periods of intense activity such as the harvest were followed by others of relative idleness, to the regular factory working hours of the industrial revolution – and very long hours at that – meant that there was simply no longer any opportunity to attend the great fairs. Previously they had been a day on which the labourer could, for a time, forget his lot – although as the eighteenth-century labouring-class 'Thresher Poet' Stephen Duck ruefully observed:

> Our Master joyful at the welcome Sight,
> Invites us all to feast with him at Night.
> A Table plentifully spread we find,
> And Jugs of humming Beer to cheer the Mind;
> Which he, too generous, pushes on so fast,
> We think no Toils to come, nor mind the past.
> But the next Morning soon reveals the Cheat,
> When the same Toils we must again repeat:
> To the same Barns again must back return,
> To labour there for room for next Year's Corn.[94]

But in the industrialized working week it was Sunday rather than local saints' days that became the prescribed day of rest, and Sunday was not a day for visiting fairs. The Society for the Reformation of Manners, established in 1787 by the abolitionist and philanthropist William Wilberforce along the lines of similar seventeenth-century moral organizations, sought to enforce church-going on Sundays and forbade dissolute behaviour – but of course only among the poor.[95] The festive calendar was religiously eroded, and as one MP put it in 1800, 'if a company of strolling players make their appearance in a village, they are hunted immediately from it as a nuisance, except, perhaps, there be a few people of greater wealth in the neighbourhood, whose wives and daughters patronize them'.[96] All this has meant that, at worst, fairs have ceased to exist; at best, they have become predominantly fun fairs. Brigg Horse Fair in Lincolnshire, which dates back to the thirteenth century, almost collapsed with the foot-and-mouth outbreak of 2001 and the loss of its site to a superstore; it has now been successfully relocated and revived, and amazingly remains primarily a horse fair.

The staunchest supporters of these fairs have been gypsies, the Romany people, and the travelling community. Part of their identity is woven from fairs and festivals, and creates for these events a distinctive and robust atmosphere. This character connects the remaining tradition-al fairs with the sparkling attractions of the circus in Dickens's novel Hard Times (1854) and the vivacious banter of Shakespeare's pedlar Autolycus (The Winter's Tale, 1609–10). If these fairs are allowed to dwindle, it will not only break another link with the English past but will also corrode the rich and itinerant culture of gypsies, Romanies, and travellers today, and become yet another example of the persecution of difference and the homogenization of society.

This urge to uniformity is already evident in the August Bank Holiday, which has to a large extent replaced the ancient diversity of traditional summer fairs. The first Bank Holidays Act (1871) allowed the Bank of England to close on certain days, meaning that bills and promissory notes were payable on the following day without penalty. Christmas Day and Good Friday were already established, to which the Act added Easter Monday, Whit Monday, the first Monday in August, and Boxing Day. The Banking and Financial Dealings Act (1971) turned Whitsun into the Spring Bank Holiday and changed the date of the August Bank Holiday in England to the last Monday in August. New Year's Day was added in 1974, and May Day only in 1978.[97] So now the majority of the population have the same days off. Nevertheless, festive celebrations do vary. The archetypal August

Bank Holiday event is probably London's Notting Hill Carnival, which has been running since 1965: it is a huge and dazzlingly diverse annual event – only Rio's Mardi Gras is bigger. Open-air music festivals have also relentlessly gained in popularity, the longest established being the Reading Festival, formerly Reading Rock, which also happens to take place over the August Bank Holiday weekend. Glastonbury, meanwhile, is the largest green-field music festival in the world and, with Reading, effectively bookends the summer by taking place at the beginning of the season, towards the end of June.[98]

Notting Hill Carnival and outdoor rock festivals may be the most popular seasonal gatherings of twenty-first-century England, but they are dwarfed by past events such as St Bartholomew's, or Old Bartlemy's, Fair. This was the most famous – or notorious – of the annual fairs. Henry I granted the original charter in 1133 for a three-day cloth fair in the church-yard of St Bartholomew the Great, West Smithfield. But as London grew, so did Bartholomew Fair, and it became a huge event in the city streets, not least because it was hard by Cock Lane with its many blandishments in the shape of brothels and bawdy houses. Old Bartlemy's gradually drew fringe events, from 'Dogs that dance the Morrice' and re-enactments of St George slaying the dragon to public executions: Bartholomew Fair was where the 'Guardian of Scotland' and rebel Sir William Wallace was executed in 1305 by being hanged, drawn, and quartered, and subsequent-ly Reformation and then Counter-Reformation martyrs were burnt there too.[99] Notwithstanding such endorsements from the state, the Puritan Richard Brathwaite attacked the event in 1631 for moral turpitude:

> No season through all the yeere accounts hee more subject to abhomination than Bartholomew faire: Their Drums, Hobbihorses, Rattles, Babies, Jewtrumps, nay Pigs and all, are wholly Judaicall. The very Booths are Brothells of iniquity, and distinguished by the stampe of the Beast.[100]

Bartholomew Fair survived the Interregnum, however, and by the time Pepys visited in 1664 it was a fourteen-day event. All manner of goods could be purchased there – from cheeses to horses to pedlary – and its circus performances included, for Pepys, 'the best dancing on the ropes that I think I ever saw in my life'.[101] Bartholomew Fair was a subculture with its own language: a 'bartholomew boar' or 'pig' was an overweight gentleman, so named after the plentiful hog roasts; later, a 'bartholomew doll' or 'baby' was, frankly, an overdressed trollop, after the gaudy dolls sold there.[102] In the eighteenth century Old Bartlemy's took a historical turn and revived old 'mystery plays' that may have been performed in the fair's earliest days, and in 1752 the opening of the fair switched to 3 September. Fifty years later, in 1802, the poet William Wordsworth and his sister Dorothy were taken there by their friend, the aspiring writer Charles Lamb. Wordsworth never forgot it:

> What a hell
> For eyes and ears, what anarchy and din
> Barbarian and infernal – 'tis a dream
> Monstrous in colour, motion, shape, sight, sound.
> Below, the open space, through every nook
> Of the wide area, twinkles, is alive
> With heads; the midway region and above
> Is thronged with staring pictures and huge scrolls,
> Dumb proclamations of the prodigies;
> And chattering monkeys dangling from their poles,
> And children whirling in their roundabouts;
> With those that stretch the neck, and strain the eyes,
> And crack the voice in rivalship, the crowd
> Inviting; with buffoons against buffoons
> Grimacing, writhing, screaming; him who grinds
> The hurdy-gurdy, at the fiddle weaves,
> Rattles the salt-box, thumps the kettle-drum,
> And him who at the trumpet puffs his cheeks,
> The silver-collared negro with his timbrel,
> Equestrians, tumblers, women, girls, and boys,

Blue-breeched, pink-vested, with towering plumes.
All moveables of wonder, from all parts
Are here, albinos, painted Indians, dwarfs,
The horse of knowledge, and the learned pig,
The stone-eater, the man that swallows fire,
Giants, ventriloquists, the invisible girl,
The bust that speaks and moves its goggling eyes,
The waxwork, clockwork, all the marvellous craft
Of modern Merlins, wild beasts, puppet-shows,
All out-o'-th'-way, far-fetched, perverted things,
All freaks of Nature, all Promethean thoughts
Of man – his dulness, madness, and their feats
All jumbled up together, to make up
This parliament of monsters. Tents and booths
Meanwhile – as if the whole were one vast mill –
Are vomiting, receiving, on all sides,
Men, women, three-years' children, babes in arms.[103]

In 1840 Bartholomew Fair changed sites to Islington, which was where it eventually ground to a halt in 1855.[104]

The Saturday night following St Bartholomew's Day is the annual Burning of Old Bartle in West Witton in Yorkshire. An effigy is carried through the village:

On Penhill Crags he tore his rags
Hunters Thorn he blew his horn
Capplebank Stee happened a
misfortune and brak' his knee
Grassgill Beck he brak' his neck
Wadhams End he couldn't fend
Grassgill End we'll mak' his end

Shout, lads, shout! [*Respond with* 'Hip, Hip.'][105]

When the effigy reaches Grassgill End, it is stabbed, doused with paraffin, and burnt. 'Bartle' clearly refers to Bartholomew, but the precise details of the event are a mystery. The folklorist Charles Kightly suggests that Bartle Burning is a folk memory of the Reformation, when the locals tried to save an effigy of St Bartholomew from destruction by Protestants by carrying him away. The Protestants pursued the idol along the route described, where it met with various mishaps before being seized and destroyed.[106]

After Priddy rain and Mary's sunshine, St Bartholomew's Day is also a significant date for weather prognostication. The forty days of rain from St Swithin, if they have come to pass, are over – 'All the tears that St. Swithin can cry, / St. Bartlemy's mantle wipes them dry' – but it is towards autumn and winter that the year now looks. 'If St Bartholomew's Day be fair and clear, / Then a prosperous autumn comes that year'; at the same time, 'At St. Bartholomew / There comes cold dew'.[107] Summer is over. The yellowhammer is still singing in late August, but most other birds except the wren and the robin are silent by then, and the green sandpiper has arrived, which Grey describes as the herald of autumn.[108] Rudyard Kipling noticed this sense of passing too in his poem 'The Long Trail':

> There's a whisper down the field where the year has shot her yield,
>   And the ricks stand grey to the sun,
> Singing: 'Over then, come over, for the bee has quit the clover,
> 'And your English summer's done.'[109]

Perhaps the most striking moment of summer melancholy, though, comes early in the career of Charles Dickens, in the 'London Recreations' passage of *Sketches by Boz* (1839). Dickens describes an old couple, working their garden in late summer. The image of autumn presses on the scene so insistently that it is almost impossible to resist – but somehow Dickens extends this gentle portrait of human mortality into one of mutually dependent love and support, rooted in the garden. It is a response to the challenge of Shakespeare's Sonnet 18 – indeed, one has no doubt that this married couple once quoted Shakespeare's lines at each other. Dickens's answer to the intricate Arcadian shadows woven by Shakespeare is gently to drain away the metaphorical import of the season until there is nothing left but a fretful acknowledgement that the death of one will leave the other alone:

> On a summer's evening, when the large watering pot has been filled and emptied some fourteen times, and the old couple have quite exhausted themselves by trotting about, you will see them sitting happily together in the little summer-house, enjoying the calm and peace of the twilight, and watching the shadows as they fall upon the garden, and gradually growing thicker and more sombre, obscure the tints of their gayest flowers – no bad emblem of the years that have silently rolled over their heads, deadening in their course the brightest hues of early hopes and feelings which have long since faded away. These are their only recreations, and they require no more. They have within themselves the materials of comfort and content; and the only anxiety of each, is to die before the other.[110]

Part IV

10   A LAND ENCLOSED

There were three men came from the West,
Their fortunes for to try;
And these three men made a solemn vow:
John Barleycorn must die.

———————

Traditional

James Thomson's *The Seasons* was first published between 1726 and 1730. It was quite simply the most popular book of poetry in the eighteenth century, and in the hundred years between 1750 and 1850 went through over 300 editions; it was also frequently quoted in Samuel Johnson's landmark reference book, *A Dictionary of the English Language* (1755–6), and so became a standard model for the written word. *The Seasons* not only introduced its readers to the beauties of the indigenous English landscape but actually inspired its readers to follow in Thomson's footsteps and visit the places, or the sorts of places, he described.

The Seasons had another major impact: it became a huge influence on later writers and artists. In 1798 Coleridge found a copy of it left in a country hostelry for the benefit of visitors to the area. This was precisely the aim of Coleridge's collaboration with Wordsworth, *Lyrical Ballads*, published that very year: bonding literature to real people and real places. John Clare, meanwhile, described the discovery of Thomson's *The Seasons* as 'one of the great literary moments of his life'.[1] He was inspired to write poetry in 1806 after he had read *The Seasons*, aged just thirteen. Thomson was also acclaimed by the painters J. M. W. Turner and John Constable: lines from 'Summer' were used as an epigraph by both, and the first sixteen lines of 'Winter' were particularly praised by Constable.[2] Thomson is, in an important sense, the origin of Turner's 'elegant pastoral'.[3]

Thomson admitted his ultimate debt to Virgil's *Georgics*, and consistent with classical models, he personified the seasons and treated them as muses. National identity was also writ large in Thomson's innovative schemata of the seasons. There are frequent invocations of the new British national identity in the poem – effectively new since the Act of Union between England and Wales, and Scotland, in 1707. Thomson, who was Scottish, deliberately wrote the poem as a celebration of the newly minted Britishness, and it became a key text in uniting Britain. The poem focused on instances of common endeavour: wealth, commerce, liberty, and law; freedom, patriotism, and prosperity; the Empire and the Navy; the register of British Worthies; the progress of recent political history; and the ancient history of bards and Druidic groves. James Thomson, lest it be forgot, wrote not only the political poem *Liberty* (1735–6), but also the imperial anthem 'Rule, Britannia' (1740).

There is in Thomson much detail of indigenous seasonal flowers and birdlife and weather, but the poem's structure is chaotic in many respects, as is its style. Thomson's approach is one of a heightened sense of the visual, of minute observation. This mania for minutiae also accounts for the distinctive vocabulary of the poem, which is replete with Latinisms and archaic scientific terms: water is 'irriguous' and 'turgent', and a tempest is 'glomerating'. Thomson is fond of such words – 'nitid', 'gelid', 'efflux', 'relucent', 'pellucid', 'turbid', 'uvid', 'luculent', 'illusive' – and many similar terms pepper the lines, sending readers scurrying for the dictionary.[4] When such vocabulary is applied, say, to an account of a walk in the countryside, the effect is severely disorientating.

While *The Seasons* mixes ancient philosophy and classical pastoral in a rambling and chaotic panoramic sweep, it also celebrates the latest advances in empirical science. The pragmatic philosophy of John Locke and the mechanistic physics of Isaac Newton had helped to develop systematic new models for understanding perception, the senses, the intellect, and the imagination – and it was Thomson who attempted to fit all of these intricate models together. This enthusiasm for the new sciences encouraged Thomson to keep rewriting his four-part poem as terrestrial and meteorological theories, for example, developed: so *The Seasons* has little stability as a single text – it kept evolving in response to new ideas, and the poet strives to shape all these different structures of thought into one simultaneous whole. But what is perhaps most striking about *The Seasons* in the context of the culture of the English seasons is what is left out and how little Thomson takes from communal calendar customs. The more he tries to incorporate empirical science and philosophy, the more he disconnects the pastoral from the traditional cycle of the year, and from agricultural labour. This is a paltry record of festivity.

The poem consequently – if inadvertently – dramatizes eighteenth-century culture colliding with the environment, the jarring encounter between the new science and nature. Yet despite Thomson's popular appeal for over a hundred years, his influence on the Romantics did not last and he was eventually superseded. Wordsworth praised *The Seasons* generously, but really the poem was impossibly abstract, far too wordy – and in any case, Romantic science sought to retain the phenomenal wonder of the world, not reduce it to arithmetic. The Romantics did, however, recognize in Thomson's *The Seasons* the sensibility of leisure; the tendency to treat the countryside as a huge park for middle-class outings; and the ever-present impulse to celebrate trade, colonial expansion, and the national interest. There was no sympathy in the Thomsonian vision of natural England for the plight of the rural labouring class. It is as absent from Thomson's poem as, by and large, is any reference to rustic culture, festive traditions, agricultural proverbs, weather lore, saints' days, and the entire framework, which was then still sturdy, of the sacred year. For all the accumulation of empirical and perceptual detail, there is virtually nothing on the traditional annual cycle. *The Seasons* therefore presents a land devoid of its agrarian workforce: it is a poem that removes rural people from the countryside. Why? Because *The Seasons* is an anthem to improvement and progress, a hymn to the agrarian revolution and entreprencurship. And Thomson's sinister vision was realized within two or three generations by a landslide of Enclosure Acts, which physically removed the unimproved common people from the homesteads, hamlets, and villages that had supported them for centuries. Agricultural labourers and their communities were made to disappear as England was reconfigured. And with them went a thousand years of folk culture.

————

For centuries, much of the land in England was common: traditionally farmed on a collective basis, usually in three different ways. Arable fields were strip-farmed, which meant that strips were individually owned but opened up to common pasture over the winter; common meadowland was shared annually among the strip farmers in various permutations and also opened to common pasture over the winter; and the common proper, or waste, was a perpetual shared pasture that included communal, uncultivated spaces such as woodland.

From the sixteenth century, however, landowners began to apply for permission to enclose common land to improve agricultural efficiency, prevent the spread of infection and disease among livestock, and capitalize on economies of scale: these were the Enclosure Acts. Permission was granted by an individual Act of Parliament for each application. For two hundred years Enclosure was a gradual process, but the second half of the eighteenth century and the first half of the nineteenth saw private enclosure galloping ahead. The process was further accelerated by the General Enclosure Act of 1801 and a subsequent Act in 1836 streamlined the procedure. For the thousands of rural labourers deprived of their shared land rights, things would only become more difficult. By 1914, 6.8 million acres, or 21 per cent of the country, had been privatized in this way.

Enclosure stripped any rights of common use or access from the land. The early twentieth-century Liberal historians J. R. and Barbara Hammond compellingly described the consequences of this cataclysm, comparing the life of a rural labourer in an unenclosed village with life afterwards.[5] Before Enclosure, a labourer could provide for his family by working for wages, by farming strips and common meadows, and by foraging the waste. After Enclosure, the labourer would have no opportunity for small-scale farming, raising stock on communal fields, or any form of scavenging. He would have lost the intimate ties to the land that might have bound his family to a place for generations. He was now solely a wage-earner – a landless labourer – and probably still confined to his parish by the Settlement Act, which prevented those receiving poor relief from moving to more generous parishes. There was no minimum wage and little provision for domestic farming. The rural poor were pauperized and, in many cases, institutionalized in the workhouse. And as they died in despair, with them vanished a wealth of folklore, tradition, and ritual that formed the intricate culture of rural life. Nearly everything was lost to the demands of progress and market forces.

Among the ancient rights to go were those of gleaning and gathering. In late summer, grain could be gleaned from harvested fields, and small game, nuts, fruit, and fuel could be gathered from areas of common ground. Livestock such as pigs could also be left to feed on the waste before the winter. These were rights that provided a significant economic and dietary supplement: it is estimated that gleaning could amount to the equivalent of six or seven weeks' wages.[6] Gleaning also attracted little local customs. Farmers would indicate in different ways whether a field was fair for gleaning, and gleaning parties, usually composed of women and children, might use these opportunities to learn songs and step-dances while moving from one field to the next. Children would become familiar with local field systems, as well as local history, folklore, and traditions, which could in turn be connected to the significant dates in the farming or festive calendar. Sows put on the waste and conceiving in September, for instance, would farrow in time for St Antony's Day on 17 January – a neat symmetry as St Antony is considered a protector of swine and other livestock and is usually depicted with a piglet. The day therefore united agricultural practices and the Christian year, nature and culture. Moreover, participating in these activities was a confirmation of one's identity within a community, as they showed that the agricultural husbandman had a calendar that was as significant for him and his family as was the hunting year for the nobility.

So the increasingly widespread practice of Enclosure in the eighteenth century not only revolutionized farming for a growing population and provided a mobile workforce for the industrial revolution, but also eroded common rights, destroyed centuries-old ways of life, and offered little recompense to the small farmers, cottagers, and squatters who found themselves with nowhere to raise crops, graze livestock, or gather wild fruit and nuts and winter fuel. Of course the stated reason for Enclosure was to improve efficiency, and, along with Enlightenment farming innovations that applied modern methods to raise livestock and crops, it eventually led to huge surpluses. But this too had a devastating impact on the poor as prices were kept artificially high to prevent these profitable new markets collapsing – hence the Corn Laws. Corn, milled into flour for bread, monopolized food markets and became the staple foodstuff, and the rich variety of native fruits, berries, and nuts, as well as small game, and the associated practices of gleaning, foraging, and trapping that had marked the seasons, were eventually forgotten. The culture of the seasons across the country became more and more fragile. Enclosure, market forces, the industrial revolution, and urbanization had profoundly changed the land, its shared use by rural communities, and its defining role in the imagination and culture of the British people – many of whom were now starving to death.

The General Report on Enclosures (1808), drawn up for the Board of Agriculture by Arthur Young, presented a comprehensive account of these changes. In the account for Bedfordshire, for example, Young reported:

> The common was very extensive. I conversed with a farmer, and several cottagers: one of them said, inclosing would ruin England; it was worse than ten wars: Why, my friend, what have you lost by it? *I kept four cows before the parish was inclosed, and now I do not keep so much as a goose. And you ask me what I lose by it!*[7]

Another example from the same county described the wider effects:

> This parish [Sandy, Bedfordshire, enclosed in 1797] was very peculiarly circumstanced; it abounds with gardeners, many cultivating their little freeholds, so that on the enclosure there were found to be sixty-three proprietors; though nine-tenths, perhaps, of the whole belonged to Sir P. Monnoux and Mr. Pym. These men kept cows on the boggy common, and cut fern for litter on the warren, by which means they

were enabled to raise manure for their gardens; besides fuel in plenty: the small allotment of an acre and a half, however good the land, has been no compensation for what they were deprived of. They complain heavily, and know not how they will now manage to raise manure. This was no reason to preserve the deserts in their old state, but an ample one for giving full compensation.[8]

Much of the notorious 'Black Act' of 1723 had been designed to protect landowners' property and estates, making it a capital offence, for example, to cut down trees in a garden or orchard and to break fishponds.[9] This complemented earlier legislation that punished many minor offences, from stealing a horse to pickpocketing a shilling, with the death penalty; after 1741, taking a single sheep could also lead one to the gallows. An analysis of a single Old Bailey session in January 1715 has shown that the individual thefts of a silver tankard and silver spoon, 'a large quantity of Cambricks', 600 pounds of sugar, four pewter spoons and a copper furnace, and the theft of a bed, two blankets and a rug sent five separate prisoners to execution.[10] Murderers only accounted for about 10 per cent of those executed – the other 90 per cent were victims of this 'Bloody Code'.[11]

Although in the face of such legal bloodthirstiness judges and juries were often less than zealous in finding defendants guilty of petty crimes liable to lead to capital punishment, attitudes did not change appreciably when it came to defending land privatized by Enclosure. Game Laws redefined taking game as poaching, punishable by penalties ranging from imprisonment and public whipping to hard labour or military service; by 1816 the penalty for being found in a forest, chase, or park equipped for poaching – a man might, for example, have been carrying a net – was seven years' transportation.[12] The Malicious Trespass Act (1820) likewise protected new enclosed property by punishing damage to buildings, hedges, fences, trees, or woods with a fine equivalent to about three-and-a-half months' labouring wages or hard labour. The hunting set were of course specifically exempted from this legislation.[13]

Faced with shocking levels of rural distress, agriculturalists in the

1790s argued that dietary reform could alleviate the sufferings of the poor. Cheap cereals such as oats were proposed and the government began actively promoting the economic advantages of potato cultivation.[14] It was the English equivalent of Marie-Antoinette's imperious dismissal, 'Let them eat cake'.[15] Potatoes were animal meal and reduced the lowest classes of society to the level of beasts: 'We will not be fed on meal, and chopped potatoes, like hogs!' they protested.[16] Although potatoes were grown in Lancashire, they were considered to be barely edible and were at best a supplement to pigswill.[17] Boiled potatoes very rarely made it into the dining room in England, and some rural workers hated potatoes with a venom usually reserved for Catholicism. Indeed, in Lewes in East Sussex, citizens chanted 'No Potatoes, No Popery' during an election hustings in 1765.[18] In the same year, in Horsted Keynes in Sussex, nobody knew or cared how to plant potatoes, and an old fellow from outside the county used to visit each year on Old Lady Day to do so.[19] Nobody in England wanted to eat potatoes in preference to bread, which was endorsed by the Lord's Prayer and had an almost miraculous genesis through the action of yeast; wheat also had a profound, healthy symbolism that seemed to connect this manna from Heaven with the ripening sun.[20] In contrast, potatoes were sinister, subterranean, and believed to cause leprosy and scrofula.[21]

Changes in the food supply were therefore more instances of the labouring classes being alienated from the old seasonal cycle of sowing and harvesting indigenous crops – this time by the very food on which they were forced to subsist. Little comfort remained:

> Go to an ale-house kitchen of an old enclosed country, and there you will see the origin of poverty and poor rates. For whom are they to be sober? For whom are they to save? (Such are their questions) For the parish? If I am diligent, shall I have leave to build a cottage? If I am sober, shall I have land for a cow? If I am frugal, shall I have half an acre of potatoes? You offer no motives; you have nothing but a parish officer and a workhouse! – Bring me another pot – .[22]

The suppression of public festivities in the wake of the Reformation 250 years earlier had had a similar effect. The Puritan Richard Rawlidge wrote in 1623 describing how the repression of the sixteenth century had directly contributed to a culture of excessive private drinking.[23] In previous generations,

> people scorned to be seene to goe to an Ale-house, but at all festival times in the yeare, and at other times also they used other exercises ... as that commendable exercise of shooting, and of Beare-baiting, stoole-ball, foot-ball, wasters [fencing swords], and such like: but now in these our wofull dayes of sinning those publicke exercises are left of, by the reason that the Preachers of the land did so envay against them, as Lords of misrule ... but when that the people generally were forbidden their old and antient familiar meetings and sportings, what then followed? Why, sure Ale-house hunting: ... so that the people would have their meetings, either publikely with pastimes abroad, or else privately in drunken Ale-houses, wasting and consuming: The Preachers did then reprove dalliansey, and dancings of maides and young men together; but now they have more cause to reprove drunkennesse and whoring, that is done privately in Ale-houses: now whether of these two is the worst let any man judge it rightly; for the publike Recreations being laid of, now almost every street is full of such Alchouses, and Citizens and others resorting to them.[24]

Celebration had moved from the church grounds to public spaces. When the ritual year was first dismantled in the sixteenth century, amusements and entertainments had moved indoors; they also became more solitary and more extreme.[25] Much had been reinstated with the Restoration, but now a century later the land had been taken away as well. The village pub was about the only place left to go, the last remnant of a festive community.

In the face of such hopelessness, Clare's desperate poem 'Helpston' imagines Enclosure as an allegorical monster stalking the land, taking away labour and food, old trees and ancient woodlands, identity and freedom:

> Now all laid waste by desolations hand
> Whose cursed weapon levels half the land
> Oh who could see my dear green willows fall
> What feeling heart but dropt a tear for all
> Accursed wealth o'er bounding human laws
> Of every evil thou remainst the cause
> Victims of want those wretches such as me
> Too truly lay their wretchedness to thee
> Thou art the bar that keeps from being fed
> And thine our loss of labour and of bread
> Thou art the cause that levels every tree
> And woods bow down to clear a way for thee.[26]

The writer and poet Oliver Goldsmith had already described the devastating effects of 'improvement' in *The Deserted Village* (1770), one of Clare's acknowledged sources.[27] He portrays an eerily abandoned village: a village become extinct by an unholy union of Enclosure and landscape gardening.[28] Farming has collapsed, with disastrous consequences for local habitats, flora, and fauna – brooks are choked, paths overgrown, the ground ruined. The poem mixes local remembrance with a melancholy sense of loss through social predation – the crumbling village now stands as a terrible *memento mori* for modern farming practices, which themselves go hand in hand with the indulgences of the pastoral.

> The man of wealth and pride,
> Takes up a space that many poor supply'd:
> Space for his lake, his park's extended bounds;
> Space for his horses, equipage, and hounds:
> The robe that wraps his limbs in silken sloth,
> Has robb'd the neighbouring fields of half their growth;

His seat, where solitary sports are seen,
Indignant spurns the cottage from the green;
Around the world each needful product flies,
For all the luxuries the world supplies.
While thus the land adorn'd for pleasure all
In barren splendour feebly waits the fall.[29]

The village's inhabitants have fled, driven to migrate to North America. Enclosure and landscaping have achieved an idealized pastoral encapsulation of a countryside unperturbed by the inconvenience of the rural classes, and undisturbed by the arduousness of their work, the celebration of their culture, or the expression of their needs. They have been painted out of this landscape: 'The country blooms – a garden, and a grave'.[30]

11 AUTUMN

In heaven it is alwaies Autumne, his mercies are ever in their maturity.

John Donne, Sermon No. 8
(Christmas Day, 1624)

The folklore of autumn treats it as twilight. Its evenings lengthen, giving time enough to mourn the passing of the year; flowers wither and die and the leaves fall from the trees; it is a time for cheese, apples, mushrooms, and bonfires. Cider should only be made as the moon begins to wane, corresponding to the season marking the waning of the year. There is a faded and melancholy beauty in autumn, noticed by the metaphysical poet John Donne:

> No spring, nor summer beauty hath such grace,
> As I have seen in one autumnal face.[1]

The precocious eighteenth-century mediaevalist poet Thomas Chatterton also felt this, invoking the plaintive image of autumn fruitlessly gilding the dead leaf with the empty majesty of decay:

> Whanne Autumpne blake and sonne-brente doe appere,
> With hys goulde honed guylteynge the falleynge lefe.[2]

Keats remarked, as if in response, that autumn reminded him of Chatterton – Chatterton being the embodiment of a lost English past: the dream of the heraldic pageantry of the Middle Ages, the power of the Gothic imagination. So much had been lost with the untimely death of Chatterton, and autumn was the natural season of mourning – at least it appeared so for Keats.

But John Keats is of course the laureate of autumn for another,

simpler reason: his ode, 'To Autumn'. The poem reads like a finely con-
densed digest of poetic imagery:

> Season of mists and mellow fruitfulness,
>   Close bosom-friend of the maturing sun;
> Conspiring with him how to load and bless
>   With fruit the vines that round the thatch-eves run;
> To bend with apples the moss'd cottage-trees,
>   And fill all fruit with ripeness to the core;
>   To swell the gourd, and plump the hazel shells
>   With a sweet kernel; to set budding more,
> And still more, later flowers for the bees,
> Until they think warm days will never cease,
>   For Summer has o'er-brimm'd their clammy cells. . . .[3]

Yet for all its apparent seasonal detail, 'To Autumn' is an oddly
un-Romantic poem: its imagery does not transcend the individual
scenes to reveal some greater truth. Keats defines the season as a series
of impressions: there is no poet in the poem, no 'I' or 'eye' to guide the
reader, no individual personality – the poem is unclear, retreating into its
own mists. Furthermore, there is simply no evident method to the ode; it
resists any organizing structure, repudiates any methodical approach to
writing poetry; it also questions wider assumptions about the relationship
between writing and the environment.

What is really offered in 'To Autumn' is a series of vignettes that
challenge a reader to disagree and expose them as autumnal clichés:

> Who hath not seen thee oft amid thy store?
>   Sometimes whoever seeks abroad may find
> Thee sitting careless on a granary floor,
>   Thy hair soft-lifted by the winnowing wind;
> Or on a half-reap'd furrow sound asleep,
>   Drows'd with the fume of poppies, while thy hook

> Spares the next swath and all its twined flowers:
> And sometimes like a gleaner thou dost keep
>   Steady thy laden head across a brook;
>   Or by a cyder-press, with patient look,
>   Thou watchest the last oozings hours by hours.

All of these line-by-line details are suspect: Keats is meticulously delivering autumn as a cultural construct while simultaneously providing the means with which to dismantle that construct. Keats, for example, knew that cider presses flow copiously – what they do not do is ooze 'hours by hours'. Consequently 'To Autumn' demands that its readers seek out the reality of rural experiences, such as cider-making, winnowing, reaping, harvesting, and gleaning in order to measure them against pastoral platitudes – but unfortunately readers have done precisely the opposite and taken the poem at face value. They have ignored the poem's call to nature and have instead, perversely, turned 'To Autumn' into the very thing that it is not: autumn. 'To Autumn' is not a poem about autumn; it is a poem about how autumn is imagined, and the problems that this might entail:

> Where are the songs of Spring? Ay, where are they?
>   Think not of them, thou hast thy music too, –
> While barred clouds bloom the soft-dying day,
>   And touch the stubble plains with rosy hue;
> Then in a wailful choir the small gnats mourn
>   Among the river sallows, borne aloft
>   Or sinking as the light wind lives or dies;
> And full-grown lambs loud bleat from hilly bourn;
>   Hedge-crickets sing; and now with treble soft
>   The red-breast whistles from a garden-croft;
>   And gathering swallows twitter in the skies.

The problem here, for Keats, is that a pastoral vision of the country, and countryside, ignores the repression, suffering, and state-sanctioned violence of post-war Britain after the defeat of Napoleon in 1815. 'To Autumn' is fundamentally influenced by the Peterloo Massacre – the terrible events of 16 August 1819 when magistrates ordered cavalrymen to charge a peaceful political gathering on St Peter's Fields, Manchester, resulting in several civilian deaths and hundreds of casualties; the first fatality was a two-year-old child.[4] Peterloo was a defining moment in the history of English democracy, but few admit that Keats's poem, written within five weeks of Peterloo, is mourning the brutal regime of Lord Liverpool's government. Indeed, some critics have tried to separate 'To Autumn' from its historical context entirely, and others have erroneously placed it in the pastoral tradition, so strong is the desire, the need, to root Romantic poetry in an idealized English countryside rather than understand how this poem in particular challenges rather than endorses those pastoral clichés.[5]

So despite this, 'To Autumn' has been enlisted as descriptive of an English idyll, and every serious poet who has written about autumn since Keats has felt the need to respond to him in some way – to answer to his 'poetic' representation of the seasons rather than considering his argument that politics is inescapable, and that repressive government actions in Manchester will reverberate in the Hampshire countryside like a 'wailful choir'. These later responses may simply be a straightforward acknowledgement: Tennyson in 'In Memoriam' echoes 'Where are the songs of Spring? Ay, where are they?' in his lines 'I dreamed there would be Spring no more, / That Nature's ancient power was lost'.[6] Other allusions may be less obvious, more antagonistic. Philip Larkin seems barely able to admit to Keats's existence in his own poem 'Autumn', and so refers to the ode with deliberate distaste in the pettish comment about trying to find a lawyer's office 'at the back of the fog'.[7]

Larkin's line is supposed to be a sharp rejoinder to the 'Season of mists and mellow fruitfulness', but it is also a cheap shot because, despite the profound qualms that Keats voices about the associations of autumn, there is a real question here – why does Keats open his poem in a mist? Fogs, low cloud, sea frets, and mists can occur in every season, so why the opening statement that mists define the autumn? Admittedly, in Milton's *Paradise Lost* (1667), Death is manifested as autumnal mist before crystallizing into endless winter – 'Vapour, and mist, and exhalation hot, / Corrupt and pestilent . . . ice / And snow and hail and stormy gust and flaw . . . thunderous clouds . . . ponent winds'.[8] Nevertheless, after Keats misty morns are autumnal even when it is not actually autumn: the nineteenth-century writer and countryman Richard Jefferies, for instance, describes 16 July 1879 as 'Morning misty and still[,] exactly like autumn'.[9]

Keats has inadvertently made autumn misty, whether the mistiness occurs in September, October, or, for that matter, July. Is mist merely a metaphor for the twilight, for passing, for transition, for the lost? Keats's mistiness is there precisely because autumn, or rather his critique of the representation of the season, is very difficult to perceive. One craves the clarity of a refreshing shower or the sharp definition of a long drought or the drifts of meaning that gather and collect from a raging blizzard – even if these too, of course, are so many more seasonal clichés. But mist is actually much more specific than that: it is another definition of the English.[10] In Shakespeare's *Henry V*, the Constable of France puts English character down to weather and beer – both induce a fog:

> . . . where have they this mettle?
> Is not their climate foggy, raw, and dull,
> On whom, as in despite, the sun looks pale,
> Killing their fruit with frowns? Can sodden water,
> A drench for sur-rein'd jades, their barley-broth,
> Decoct their cold blood to such valiant heat?
> And shall our quick blood, spirited with wine,
> Seem frosty?[11]

'To Autumn' is, in other words, about the condition of England in 1819.[12]

Before Keats, mist was a mystery. Renaissance revenge tragedies, such as John Webster's *Duchess of Malfi*, written in 1612–13, are pervaded by a sinister mist, *Macbeth* (c.1606) begins in a fog, and Satan is described as a mist three times in Milton's *Paradise Lost*. Like English identity, like nature, mist is never there for independent scrutiny. It is a 'meteor', insubstantial and elusive, a perceptible obscurity.[13] The seventeenth-century philosopher John Locke compares language to mist in his influential *Essay Concerning Human Understanding* (1690):

> [words] interpose themselves so much between our Understandings, and the Truth, it would contemplate and apprehend, that like the *Medium* through which visible Objects pass, their Obscurity and Disorder does not seldom cast a mist before our Eyes and impose upon our Understandings.[14]

Language is a social medium for the pragmatist Locke, but it is never transparent, never easy. Language is flawed and fallible, tied up in contingencies and contexts, obscure and often opaque: it lacks definition.

Thus, through Keats mist condenses into the prevailing component of an English autumn. The nineteenth-century art critic Henry Twining, for example, describes the 'Picturesque Character of Fogs' in *The Elements of Picturesque Scenery* (1853):

> ... there are certain circumstances connected with thick mists which impart to the representations of them a peculiar interest; – the phenomena of the atmosphere have descended to the earth's surface, and the light grey tints of distance are brought into connection with the objects immediately around us....
>
> Fogs have further an interesting connection with the seasons and the weather. The fertilizing abundance of the dews, the hoar-frost which sometimes clings to the branches in such profusion as to weigh them down, and to alter the characteristic features of the tree, the dripping of water from the twigs till the soil beneath is saturated with moisture, whilst the surrounding parts are dry, the presence of pools and lakes as well as the winding course of rivers marked by the sheets or ribands of vapour which float above them, even the clouds of steam which at times

surround the panting animals, – are all incidents dependent on that peculiar condition of the atmosphere which engenders fog.[15]

The French sociologist Émile Boutmy alluded to this painterly mist in his essay *The English People*, first published in 1901. Boutmy reinvents Aristotelian climate theory to analyse the political and psychological effects of national meteorology on the English physique:

> In these big, white-skinned bodies, bathed in an atmosphere of perpetual moisture, sensations are experienced far more slowly, the 'circulus' of reflection takes longer to complete. Their impressions and perceptions are certainly less numerous and acute. Like their sensibili-ties, their physical imagination – I mean the faculty of consciously visualising sensations – is lethargic and dull. This is one of the reasons why surgical operations are more successful on an Englishman than on an Italian, for instance – the former excites and agitates himself far less than the latter.[16]

Capitalizing on this pseudo-medical insight, Boutmy argues that the fog of England explains everything from the bravery of the British Grenadiers, whose spirit is so soaked through that they are too sodden to recognize the possibility of flight, to the style of English landscape painting in which only certain colours can penetrate the gloomy haze, and also of course the imagination of English poets, which is apparently bereft of any meaning-ful external visual stimulation. Keats has been caught in a mist of his own making that has sentimentalized his poetry; the English countryside, too, has been sentimentalized – shrouded in a haze that diffuses the politics and economics out of rural life so that only an aesthetic mist remains. The landscape that seems so essentially English is one that has been wholly mystified.

Swallows flock and leave in September, anticipating the onset of autumn; with house martins and swifts they migrate to sub-Saharan Africa. Swallows are, according to Izaak Walton, the author of *The Compleat Angler* (1653), 'half year birds, and not seen to flie in *England* for six months in the Year, but about *Michaelmas* [they] leave us for a hotter Climate'.[17] It is a sure sign that summer is over – in the words of the poet Algernon Charles Swinburne:

> Swallow, my sister, O sister swallow,
> How can thine heart be full of the spring?
> A thousand summers are over and dead.
> What hast thou found in the spring to follow?
> What hast thou found in thy heart to sing?
> What wilt thou do when the summer is shed?[18]

The chiff-chaff, however, renews its song in September, not in the full-throated notes of March, but in a more melancholy, more dulcet tone, expressing itself, as the ornithologist and politician Sir Edward, Viscount Grey, put it, 'in a subdued repetition of the song – a sort of quiet farewell before the chiff-chaff leaves us on its long journey southwards'.[19]

September is therefore a time of leaving, a time of change. Nicholas Breton, Shakespeare's contemporary and the author of *Fantasticks: A Perpetuall Prognostication* (1626), noticed how the sun goes into its long decline, the meadows are left bare, the apples fall from the trees. It is also a time to gather for the winter – 'I hold it the Winters forewarning, and the Summers farewell': wood and coal are collected and charcoal is burnt, and much fruit and many vegetables are sold by costermongers.[20] The agricultural writer Thomas Tusser also asks for moderation in September until all the produce is safely stored:

September blowe softe,
till fruite be in lofte.[21]

Tusser's contemporary, the Elizabethan poet Spenser, imagines September
'heavy laden with the spoyle / Of harvests riches', and carrying a 'knife-
hook' in one hand and a 'paire of waights' in the other – the symbols of
justice.[22] This incongruous iconography derives from the association of
September with the renewal of the legal term for the 'lawyers' harvest'
– a significant characteristic of the season, and also a reminder of the
corresponding renewal of school, university, and parliamentary terms.
Hence 'Paper, pen, and inke are much in request', and legal, academic, and
bureaucratic cultures are revived. St Michael's Day falls on 29 September,
and Michaelmas, one of four, now defunct, legal terms, remains the name
for the autumn term at Oxbridge and at a handful of other universities.

Meanwhile, although in some places connoisseurs start eating oysters
again in August on St James's Day, the popular season opens once the
month has the letter r in it, as the 1676 *Poor Robin* notes:

From *Billingsgate* we now have Oysters
Are in their operative moystures
For when the Month hath got an R in't,
Ass-trologers do see so far in't
That they affirm, and that most truly,
They'r better than in *June* or *July*.[23]

In Pyefleet Channel by Mersea Island in Essex the new season is marked by
the mayor of Colchester proposing the loyal toast in gin and gingerbread.
Colchester has had rights over dredging these oysters since 1256, and since
1577 there has been no dredging permitted between Easter and Lammas to
conserve stocks.

Before Michaelmas, though, there was a series of seasonal celebrations, often fairs. The dating of fairs varied with the theological, political,
and economic climates. For example, there are four sheep fairs a year

at Wilton in Wiltshire, currently occurring on Thursdays in August, September, October, and November. Originally in 1300, however, the Wilton fairs were held in the week from 14 to 21 September – in the seven days leading up to St Matthew's Day. By 1414 a town fair was pitched from 19 to 22 July, and soon afterwards, in 1433, sheep fairs were held on either side in May and September. In 1496 St Giles's Day, 1 September, was adopted as a three-day event, as was St George's Day, 23 April, but the St Matthew's Day fair disappeared at the Reformation with the dissolution of monasteries (1536–9) as it was run by the local abbey. Yet the Wilton fairs continued, and at their height were selling 100,000 sheep. After 1752 the fairs kept the Julian calendar and so were shifted to 4 May and 12 September – that is, the Old St George's Day and the Old St Giles's Day. These dates settled in the nineteenth century to 5 May and 12 September, before being revised again to a modern day-of-the-week and week-of-the-month pattern in order to fit the working week of the later nineteenth century and auctioneers' schedules in the twentieth century – rather than keeping the vigils, feasts, and morrows of saints' days.

The first of September was St Giles's Day, and the day for St Giles's Fair at Winchester. This fair, granted a charter in 1079, was one of the four major fairs in England – the others being St Ives in Huntingdonshire, Northampton, and Boston in Lincolnshire. At its height the fair ran for twenty-four days, but it began to decline after the fifteenth century. A St Giles's Fair is today held in Oxford on the Monday and Tuesday following the first Sunday after 1 September, although this is not a fair by charter – it was originally an annual market or local wake originating in about the 1620s and tied to the nearby St Giles's church. When I attended as a student in the 1980s, I was astonished to find that there were sideshows of tattooed and bearded ladies, as well as the chance to meet 'The Smallest Man In The World', who seemed very happy with his lot. Yet within a year or two, these attractions had gone, replaced by more politically correct entertainments. St Giles's Day is also known as St Partridge Day since this is the opening of the partridge season, which lasts until 1 February.

Wakes Monday – the Monday following the first Sunday after 4 September – is Old St Bartholomew's Day and marks the performance of the Abbots Bromley Horn Dance, Abbots Bromley being on the edge of Needwood Forest in Staffordshire. This was first recorded in 1532. In 1686 the antiquary and naturalist Robert Plot described 'within living memory, a sort of sport . . . call'd the *Hobby-horse dance*'. The dance was named

from a person that carryed the image of a *horse* between his leggs, made of thin boards, and in his hand, a *bow* and *arrow*, which passing through a *hole* in the *bow*, and stopping upon a *sholder* it had in it, he made a *snapping* noise as he drew it to and fro, keeping in time with the *Musick*: with this *Man* danced 6 others, carrying on their shoulders as many *Rain deers heads*, 3 of them painted *white*, and 3 *red*, with the Armes of the cheif families (viz. of *Paget*, *Bagot*, and *Wells*) to whom the revenews of the Town cheifly belonged, depicted on the *palms* of them, with which they danced the *Hays*, and other *Country* dances. To this *Hobby-horse dance* there also belong'd a *pot*, which was kept by turnes, by 4 or 5 of the *cheif* of the *Town*, whom they call'd *Reeves*, who provided *Cakes* and *Ale* to put in this *pot*; all people who had any kindness for the good intent of the Institution of the *sport*, giving pence a piece for themselves and families; and so *forraigners* too, that came to see it: with which Mony (the charge of the *Cakes* and *Ale* being defrayed) they not only repaired to their Church but kept their *poore* too: which *charges* are not now perhaps so cheerfully boarn.[24]

A contemporary, the lawyer and antiquarian Sir Simon Degge, added that he remembered the event from before the Civil War.[25] Plot records that the dance took place on New Year's Day and Twelfth Day, but it would also seem to be a version of the ritual wearing of deerskin and horns described by Shakespeare in *As You Like It*.[26] The dance has changed little since the seventeenth century, although it now takes place on Wakes Monday, commencing at 7.30 a.m. The horn dancing is characterized by a hay (or winding dance) followed by an imitation of rutting stags, which is reminiscent of late mediaeval 'brawls' – dances that mimicked animal or human activities.[27] The same antlers that Plot witnessed are still used today, and one set has been carbon-dated within eighty years to 1065.

The fourth of September is also the date of Barnet Horse Fair, known as the 'costermongers' carnival'. The fair once commanded a twenty-acre site, and as late as 1952, 620 horses were traded there. Urban development has engulfed this part of Hertfordshire, however, and the fair is now held at Greengates Stables for just three days. Barnet Horse Fair was roundly condemned in 1867 by the investigative journalist James Greenwood. His account is worth quoting at length:

> My first impression was my last, and still remains – viz., that Barnet Fair is a disgrace to civilisation. I have witnessed a Warwickshire 'mop' fair; I have some recollection of 'Bartlemy;' I was at Greenwich when, on account of its increasing abominations, the fair that so long afflicted that Kentish borough was held for the last time; but take all these, and skim them for their scum and precipitate them for their dregs, and even then, unless you throw in a very strong flavouring of the essence of Old Smithfield on a Friday, and a good armful of Colney Hatch and Earlswood sprigs, you will fail to make a brew equal to that of Barnet. It is appalling. Which-ever way you turn – to the High Street, where the public-houses are – to the open, where the horse-'dealing' is in progress – to the booths, and tents, and stalls – brutality, drunkenness, or brazen rascality, stare you in the face unwinkingly. Plague-spots thought to be long ago 'put down' by the law and obliterated from among the people, here appear bright and vigorous as of old – card-sharpers, dice-sharpers, manipulators of the 'little pea,' and gentlemen adept at the simple little game known as 'prick the garter.' Wheels-of-fortune and other gaming-tables obstructed the paths. 'Rooge-it-nor, genelmen; a French game, genelmen; just brought over; one can play as well as forty, and forty as well as one. Pop it down, genelmen, on the black or on the red, and, whatever the amount, it will be instantly kivered! Faint heart never won fair lady, so pop it down while the injicator is rewolving! Red wins,

and four half-crowns to you, sir; keep horf our gold is all we ask; our silver we don't wally!' Not in a hole-and-corner way this, but bold and loud-mouthed as goods hawked by a licensed hawker.

Disgusting brutality, too, had its representatives in dozens. There were the tents of the pugilists, where, for the small charge of twopence, might be seen the edifying spectacle of one man bruising and battering another; there was the booth of the showman who amused the public by lying on his back and allowing three half-hundredweights to be stacked on the bridge of his nose; there was the gentleman who put leaden pellets in his eyes, and drove rows of pins at a blow into a fleshy part of his leg; and there was a lean and horrible savage (a 'Chicksaw,' the showman said he was, 'from the island of High Barbaree') who ate *live rats*. Decidedly, this was the show of the fair. An iron-wire cage, containing thirty or forty rats, hung at the door, and beside it stood the High Barbarian, grinning, and pointing at the rats, and smacking his blubberous lips significantly. The sight was more than the people could stand; they rushed and scrambled up the steps, paying their pennies with the utmost cheerfulness; and, when the place was full, the performance was gone through to their entire satisfaction. The High Barbarian really did eat the rats. He set the cage before him, and, thrusting in his hand, stirred the animals about till he found one to his liking, then he ate it as one would eat an apple.[28]

The Nativity of the Virgin Mary, 8 September, is the date for a fair once held, for example, at Watton-on-Stone in Hertfordshire, where it lasted for three days: the vigil, feast, and morrow.[29] Thomas Tusser, meanwhile, recommended this day for preparing the spice saffron: 'Pare saffron, betwene the two S. Mary daies, / Or set or go shift it, thou knowest the waies' (the two feasts of Saint Mary were 15 August and 8 September).[30]

Holy Cross Day, 14 September, the day on which the passion flower traditionally blossoms, is also the day on which the Devil goes out nutting, so it is wise not to do so oneself.[31] The poet John Clare wrote to William Hone:

On Holy rood day it is faithfully & confidently believed both by old & young that the Devil goes a nutting on that day & I have heard a many people affirm that they once thought it a tale till they ventured to the woods on that day when they smelt such a strong smell of brimstone as nearly stifled them before they coud escape out again – & the cow boy to his great dissapointment finds that the devil will not even let his black berrys alone & he believes them after that day to be poisend by his touch.[32]

There are various local beliefs associated with the Devil gathering nuts: sometimes he helpfully holds down branches to assist nutters; at others he encounters the Virgin Mary on the same business and they compete for nuts, giving as they do so names to local landmarks such as the Devil's Nightcap, at Alcester in Warwickshire. These warnings against diabolical encounters presumably originated in the same way that condemnations of gathering the may arose: like 'maying' and 'rambling in the new-mown hay', 'nutting' was also a euphemism for casual sex. Once the Devil had nutted, however, it was theoretically safe to go out, although some authorities such as Tusser recommended delaying the nutting season until after Michaelmas.[33]

If anyone was prevented from nutting, there was always Sturbridge (or Stourbridge) Fair in Worcestershire to visit, which commenced on the same day. Between the end of the sixteenth century and the mid-eighteenth century this was the largest fair in the country. The main trade of Sturbridge Fair was wool and hops, but it soon expanded to include every conceivable commercial interest. Daniel Defoe described it thus:

It is kept in a large Corn-field, near Casterton, extending from the Side of the River Cam, towards the Road, for about half a Mile Square. . . .

It is impossible to describe all the Parts and Circumstances of this Fair exactly; the Shops are placed in Rows like Streets, whereof one is called Cheapside; and here, as in several other Streets, are all sorts of Trades, who sell by Retale, and who come principally from London with their Goods; scarce any Trades are omitted, Goldsmiths, Toyshops, Brasiers, Mercers, Drapers, Pewterers, China-Warehouses, and, in a Word all Trades that can be named in London; with Coffee-Houses, Taverns, Brandy-Shops, and Eating-Houses innumerable, and all in Tents and Booths, as above.[34]

Sturbridge Fair was granted its original charter in 1211 and ran until 1933. At the height of its success and popularity it lasted for an extraordinary thirty-five days. Similarly, Southwark Fair – memorably recorded by William Hogarth – was established in 1462 by charter of Edward IV to run from 7 to 9 September. After 1752 it started on 18 September, supposedly for three days, but in the event lasted for up to a fortnight – before its demise in 1762.

St Matthew's Day, 21 September and usually the equinoctial eve, was also a time for fairs. At Bury St Edmunds in Suffolk, the church, later cathedral, of St James received a charter for its fair in 1135, but as St James's Day fell during the harvest, Henry III shifted the fair to St Matthew's Day. Likewise, Cricklade in Wiltshire had a St Matthew's Day fair from 1257, as well as fairs on the third Wednesdays of April and July, although the April fair was later held on the second Thursday of April. Nottingham's charter dates from 1284, and was granted by Edward I. The charter was for fifteen days but actually ran from 2 October for twenty-one days:

> besides the fair that they have for eight days at the Feast of St Matthew the Apostle, have for ever another annual fair in the said town, to begin on the eve and day of the feast of St. Edmund, the king and martyr, to continue the twelve following days.[35]

This fair became known as the 'Goose Fair' some three centuries later to reflect its sale of geese for Michaelmas. A four-day Goose Fair is now held on the first Wednesday in October.

In addition to all this, there were major fairs at Michaelmas, 29 September, such as Egremont Crab Fair in Cumbria, which now takes

place on the nearest Saturday to 18 September and still includes traditional sports such as climbing the greasy pole, pig's bladder football, and the
World Gurning Championship. In his *Historie of Great Britaine* (1611), the
mapmaker and topographer John Speed described the fair at Yarmouth in
Norfolk that started at Michaelmas: 'there is Yearly in September the wor-
thiest Herring Fishery in Europe, which draweth great concourse of People,
which maketh the Town much the richer all the Year following, but very
unsavoury for the time'.[36] William Camden, the antiquary and herald, also
remarked on this event: 'it is almost incredible, what a great and throng
Fair here is at Michaelmas, and what quantities of herring and other fish
are vended'.[37] This autumn herring fair lasted even longer than Sturbridge
Fair – a pungent forty days, from Michaelmas to Martinmas. Tavistock
Goosie Fair in Devon was also originally at Michaelmas but is now held
on the second Wednesday in October. It is the subject of the dialect song
'Tavvystock Goozey Vair' written by C. John Trythall in 1912:

> An' uts 'Aw thun, whur be 'e gwaine, an' wot be 'e doin' of there?
> 'Aive down yer prong an' stap down long, tes Tavvystock Goozey Vair.'[38]

Songs about fairs keep the events in popular consciousness even if they
decline in reality: sadly, live geese are no longer sold at Tavistock because
of outbreaks of fowl pest in the 1950s and 1960s.

The season Michaelmas to Martinmas – October to November – had
a special significance. Michaelmas was one of the four quarter days of the
English business year and therefore not only a day on which rent was due
but a date also associated with changing employment and moving lodgings
– a 'flitting day'. This was particularly acute at Michaelmas because, by
the First Statute of Labourers (1351), a worker could go to be hired at the
nearest market town on the day after Michaelmas Day – that is, on 30
September – which was when pay rates were set at the statute sessions;
sessions were also held at Martinmas and occasionally at Whitsun.
Therefore, fairs held during this period were hiring fairs or 'mops'; similar
days occurred during the year on Lady Day, May Day, and Ascension Day,

for example, at Rig Fair in Wem in Shropshire.[39] Thomas Hardy describes the scene in *Far from the Madding Crowd* (1874) when Gabriel Oak takes himself off to Greenhill Fair:

> At one end of the street stood from two to three hundred blithe and hearty labourers waiting upon Chance – all men of the stamp to whom labour suggests nothing worse than a wrestle with gravitation, and pleasure nothing better than a renunciation of the same. Among these, carters and waggoners were distinguished by having a piece of whip-cord twisted round their hats; thatchers wore a fragment of woven straw; shepherds held their sheep-crooks in their hands; and thus the situation required was known to the hirers at a glance.[40]

In the nineteenth century, Marlborough in Wiltshire hired on the Saturday before Old Michaelmas and the Saturday after 10 October; meanwhile Kirkby Stephen, then in Westmorland, had hirings on Whitsuntide and in November.[41]

Geese were traded at St Matthew's Day and Michaelmas fairs as a winter staple – their fat being good both for cooking warming winter stews and for keeping out the cold when rubbed on the chest – and at one time, the goose was identified with Michaelmas as much as eggs are with Easter today, if not more so. The bird had associations with paying quarterly rents at this time of the year, and therefore with financial solvency: 'If you do not baste the goose on Michaelmas Day, you will want money all the year'.[42] Accordingly, eating goose at Michaelmas was believed to be good for domestic security. Moreover, the customary gift of a goose from a tenant farmer to his landlord developed into a tradition of giving small presents at this time of the year:

> And when the tenauntes come to paie their quarters rent,
> They bringe some fowle at Midsommer, a dish of Fish in Lent,
> At Christmasse a capon, at Mighelmasse a goose:
> And somewhat else at Newyeres tide, for feare their lease fly loose.[43]

Goose was also a patriotic dish. Elizabeth I was supposedly dining on goose on St Michael's Day in 1588 when she was informed that the Spanish Armada had been defeated. She consequently decreed that the victory should be celebrated annually thereafter with a goose dinner.

But Michaelmas was a time to prepare for the winter season in ways other than simply reserving goose dripping. It was the earliest date on which horses and cattle would be brought down from upland grazing pastures, perhaps reflecting Michael's strong equine associations. These livestock movements harked back to an ancient farming system based on the managed migration of flocks and herds, pre-dating the large-scale arable cultivation seen in the communal working of common open fields that later dominated the mediaeval period. Michaelmas was also a day on which to attend to associated chores as well, as Tusser advised:

> Saint Michel doth bid thee, amend ye marsh wall
> the breck & the crab hole, the foreland & all.[44]

Blackberries should not be eaten after Michaelmas because the Devil will have touched them (or even spat on them), but candle-making began, and oak trees cut at Michaelmas could forecast the character of the next year. And of course Michaelmas daisies flowered on this day.

OCTOBER

October is the end of the wheat-sowing season, celebrated by seed cakes, pasties, and frumenty (or furmety), which was a gruel made of milk, wheat, and sweet spices, occasionally laced with alcohol – in which form it was the bane of Michael Henchard in Hardy's *The Mayor of Casterbridge*. The tireless Tusser corroborates the seasonal fare:

> Wife somtime this week, if the weather hold cleere
> an end of wheat sowing, we make for this yere.

Remember you therfore, though I do it not:
the seede Cake, the Pasties, and Furmenty pot.[45]

Spenser describes October as 'full of merry glee' and the time for crushing grapes for wine-making, and Breton remarks upon the falling leaves, fat pigs feasting on acorns, rutting deer, corn markets, hunting, and commerce.[46] It grows wintry: 'Muffes and Cuffes are now in request', some play indoor sports to keep warm, others cuddle in the cold, and fauna disappear: 'the Titmouse now keepes in the hollow tree; and the black bird sits close in the bottome of a hedge'. It is a grim month: 'I hold it a Messenger of ill newes, and a second service to a cold dinner'.[47]

The Anglican Harvest Festival service takes place around 1 October, a religious custom introduced by Robert Stephen Hawker, the vicar of Morwenstow in Cornwall. On 13 September 1834 he wrote to his parishioners to inform them that there would be a 'sacrifice of thanksgiving' to give thanks for the harvest: 'Let us gather together in the chancel of our Church and on the first Sunday of next month [October], and there receive, in the bread of the new corn, that blessed Sacrament, which was ordained to strengthen and refresh our souls'.[48] Within a few years this innovation had captured the imagination of the country, perhaps stirring memories of old Lammas-tide services, and subsequently a special service was written.

The autumn fair season continued – in some cases still continues – from September into October. Several of these fairs were originally Michaelmas Day fairs that shifted into October with the 1752 calendar reform – an interesting example of how the calendar of livestock rearing, which had once been organized around saints' days, came to be seen as best farming practice and to influence the shape of the festive year and, accordingly, the dates on which animals were taken to market. Old Michaelmas fairs were held on or around 10 October: more goose fairs, mop fairs for hiring labour, and runaway fairs for those who changed their mind after mop fair employment. The Monday after Old Michaelmas Day, for instance, was Pack Monday Fair at Sherborne in Dorset – as described in detail by the journalist and folklorist William Hone in 1826 from an eye-witness account.[49] 'Tap-up Sunday', meanwhile, took place on St Catherine's Hill in Guildford in Surrey on the Sunday preceding 2 October; it was known as 'Tap-up Sunday' because anyone was allowed to sell beer there or 'open a tap'.[50] The Translation of St Ethelreda, also known as Æþelðryþ or Audrey, was also celebrated by a fair on 17 October following a charter granted to the Monastery of St Ethelreda by Henry I.[51] At this fair 'St Audrey lace' was sold – St Ethelreda had died in 679 from throat cancer, which she attributed to her youthful vanity in wearing necklaces. Intricate lace collars were therefore worn in remembrance of the saint and known as 'St Audrey' or 'Tawdry' lace. Gradually, however, these pieces of lacework became cheaper, more showy, and indeed tasteless – and so gave us the modern meaning of 'tawdry'. In October 1826 the farmer and political journalist William Cobbett visited the fair at Weyhill in Hampshire, which specialized in hops and cheese, and Swineshead in Lincolnshire had a cheese and onion fair in the same month. On the Eve of St Dennis, 21 October, there is still an oyster feast at Moot Hall, Colchester, following the opening of the oyster season in September. Meanwhile, Scottish cattle were sold at St Faith's (St Fay's) outside Norwich in October – the eighteenth-century parson James Woodforde regularly made this outing to inspect the livestock.

There are some late fruits at this time of the year that traditionally need to feel the frost. Damson and medlar, for example:

> These two keep summer in their lips
> Till their slow fruit the hoar-frost sips,
> That mouth of winter on deep summer
> Bears sweet plenty from sad drouth.[52]

Sloes, the blackthorn berry, should also be harvested for sloe gin after the first frost in October, although it has to be said that in recent years waiting for a frost in October may be fruitless. The sloe – 'which', as William Cobbett recalled, 'I have eaten many times when I was a boy until my tongue clove to the roof of my mouth and my lips were pretty well glued together, is astringent beyond the powers of alum' – is a native fruit that has been consumed in quantity since the Iron Age.[53] A minor revival of such native fruit festivals has been introduced by Common Ground, and the group's Apple Day, first celebrated on 21 October 1990, led directly to the rediscovery of many apple varieties thought to have been extinct, as well as to the founding of mother orchards for all regional varieties in, for example, Cheshire, Gloucestershire, Devon, and Hertfordshire. Apple Day has in turn inspired Damson Day in Westmorland, Plum Day in Pershore in Worcestershire, Pear Day at Cannon Hall Museum in South Yorkshire, and others; it is now preceded by All Fruits Eve.[54] As for sloes, they are also a staple of winter birds, and so if any remain after gin-making, they will be eaten by the song thrush, mistle thrush, blackbird, fieldfare, and redwing.

St Luke's Day, 18 October, was another day for love divination, and often a period of warm weather after the first snaps of autumnal chill – 'St Luke's Little Summer'. This date also inevitably had its own fair, which in the case of St Luke's was held at Charlton, now a suburb of London but previously in Kent. Daniel Defoe described Charlton as 'a Village famous, or rather infamous for that yearly collected Rabble of Mad-People, at Horn Fair'. The origins of the Horn Fair supposedly lay in an episode in which King John, fond of travelling incognito and mixing with his people, was unfortunately caught in flagrante with an accommodating but married subject by her irate husband. The cuckolded spouse was recompensed with money and an estate of local land, and subsequently established the Horn Fair in ironic recognition of his fortune. St Luke's is the parish church, and it would appear to be no coincidence that this saint is usually represented by a horned ox. Traditionally, the Horn Fair began with a motley procession of characters, many of them cross-dressed and/or carrying horns, who re-enacted the king's misbehaviour. Rams' horns were worn by all and sundry, and hung on all the fair booths. Everything for sale was either made from horn or had horns – even the gingerbread men sold at the fair by comfit-makers were horned. Defoe was not at all impressed by the day's horny shenanigans:

the Rudeness of which I cannot but think, is such as ought to be suppress'd, and indeed in a civiliz'd well govern'd Nation, it may well be said to be unsufferable. The Mob indeed at that time takes all kinds of Liberties, and the Women are especially impudent for that Day; as if it was a Day that justify'd the giving themselves a Loose to all manner of Indecency and Immodesty, without any Reproach, or without incurring the Censure which such Behaviour would deserve at another time.[55]

As London expanded, the Horn Fair attracted crowds from neighbouring Greenwich and Deptford. It managed to last until 1872, when it was abolished following the 1871 Fairs Act.

But there is now, at the end of the month, menace in the air – and it is not just because of the violent insinuations of Horn Fair. Thomas Hardy described the 'Last Week in October':

> The trees are undressing, and fling in many places –
> On the gray road, the roof, the window-sill –
> Their radiant robes and ribbons and yellow laces;
> A leaf each second so is flung at will,
> Here, there, another and another, still and still.
>
> A spider's web has caught one while downcoming,
> That stays there dangling when the rest pass on;
> Like a suspended criminal hangs he, mumming
> In golden garb, while one yet green, high yon,
> Trembles, as fearing such a fate for himself anon.[56]

Bonfires were lit on St Crispin's Day, 25 October, and it traditionally rains on 28 October, the feast of Sts Simon and Jude – 'Aswell as I know twill raine upon *Simon* and *Judes* day next'.[57] Yet this was a mere prelude to the most frightening night of the year: Hallowe'en.

Hallowe'en is All-Hallows Eve, the Vigil of All Saints' Day: 31 October.[58] The festival has 'Celtic' associations: in Ireland, this was the first night of Samhain ('summer's end'); winter began when the sun went down and bonfires were lit to mark the season. These fires were not only for symbolic purification: as at Lammas-tide, livestock were driven from autumn pastures into barns for the winter, passing through the embers or between bonfires, and it is commonly held that this may have helped to rid them of parasites. Animals not likely to survive the winter, but which would nevertheless consume fodder, were slaughtered for Samhain feasts. This was, then, another turning point in the year. As the anthropologist James George Frazer describes it,

> Witches then speed on their errands of mischief, some sweeping through the air on besoms, others galloping along the roads on tabby-cats, which for that evening are turned into coal-black steeds. The fairies, too, are all let loose, and hobgoblins of every sort roam freely about.[59]

In the popular imagination Hallowe'en consequently became celebrated as a time when spirits and witches were abroad. It was an opportunity for seasonal games such as apple-bobbing, and love divination with apple skins, pips, nuts, and various food with charms hidden inside. In the Cheviot Hills in Northumberland, Hallowe'en is Nut Crack Night, during which nuts were used to tell fortunes; in Lancashire apple pips were favoured. The last Thursday in October is Punky Night in Hinton St George in Somerset: local children carry lanterns made from mangel-wurzels or pumpkins and sing the 'Punky Night Song'. These lanterns, called 'punkies' and sharing their name with the local form of the will o' the wisp, might have their origins in Hallowe'en mummers' plays performed by guisers – the Antrobus Soul-Cakers, a mumming group in Cheshire, for example, perform around Hallowe'en. More seriously, Hallowe'en is 'Mischief Night' in parts of England – originally a night of harmless pranks and practical jokes. Most nineteenth-century folklorists assigned Mischief Night to May Day Eve, although it shifted to 4 November in the 1950s and in England is strongly associated with Hallowe'en, and its celebration has lately spiralled into more riotous behaviour. Miggy or Mizzy Night in York, Liverpool, and other northern cities is now characterized by a heavy police presence on the autumn streets.

Surprisingly, perhaps, there is little other lore attached to Hallowe'en in England, and it has only recently become the foremost celebration of all things supernatural. Moreover, there is no evidence of Hallowe'en being a supernatural festival in early Scotland or Wales either, although Samhain clearly had supernatural elements in Ireland. The calendar historians Blackburn and Holford-Strevens comment that 'In most of England ... Hallowe'en was even more alien than Hogmanay until the late twentieth century, when it began to encroach on Guy Fawkes Day as both safer for children than domestic fireworks and more profitable than the collection of near-worthless pennies'.[60] Far more significant in England was All Souls' Day, 2 November, when children would go souling – asking for money for 'soul cakes' as a way of remembering the dead.

The folklorist Steve Roud argues that Hallowe'en had faded almost entirely from the festive calendar until the American tradition of 'trick-or-treating', itself a version of soul-caking, was noticed in films of the 1970s and 1980s and thereby reintroduced. This has made it very much an autumnal children's festival. Although this 'New Hallowe'en' has been criticized as a mandate for begging with menaces, the level of parental supervision prevalent on the night means that it is a relatively safe time for children to be on the streets in the early evening.[61] New Hallowe'en has also generated an enthusiastic demand for cheap knick-knacks: costumes are everywhere offered for sale and fancy-dress for hire, and there is a ready market for gruesome paraphernalia from rubber skeletons and severed hands to sweets that look like enucleated eyeballs and miniature, jelly-filled brains. The season is now marked by such ghoulish fripperies; nevertheless, a sense of the mysterious, fateful darkness of late October can sometimes still be felt on a cold autumn night. As T. S. Eliot put it:

Since golden October declined into sombre November
And the apples were gathered and stored, and the land became brown
sharp points of death in a waste of water and mud.[62]

All Saints' Day, 1 November, also known as All-Hallows, Hollantide, and Hallowmas, is the Christian celebration of all the saints and martyrs, including all those who are unknown to the martyrologists. It was originally observed in May, but migrated to 1 November in the eighth century. All Saints' Day is also the eve of All Souls' Day, 2 November, although in practice the laity have tended not to distinguish much between All Saints' Day and All Souls' Day. Both presented the opportunity to venerate one's ancestors and were a reminder of the communal identity of Church and family. The latest date for taking livestock down from upland pasture was also probably 1 or 2 November, a month after Michaelmas. Bringing the stock down from the fields and quartering it for the winter on All Saints' or All Souls' Day was a symbolic way of invoking the protection of the company of Heaven: both saints and individual family members were the guardians of all those in the long-house, farmers and stock lodged together.[63]

All Souls' Day or Soul-mass Day, 2 November, dates from the eleventh century – prior to that, ancestors were remembered on the Monday after Pentecost. All Souls was a way of ensuring that those in Purgatory – in other words, those who had died without the last rites being administered – could be aided on their way to Heaven. This was effected by prayers, candles, and especially by ringing church bells. Purgatory had of course no place in Protestant theology, and so All Souls was suppressed in 1559 following the Reformation. Nevertheless, folk memory remained troubled by Purgatory and its population of unquiet and restless spirits. Traditional soul-cakes were still being baked and offered to visitors at the end of the seventeenth century, at least by papists, who shared them with the refrain:

> A SOUL-CAKE!
> A SOUL-CAKE!
> Have Mercy on all Christen Souls, for
> A SOUL-CAKE![64]

Other souling rhymes, though, were more sophisticated. For example:

> Soul! Soul! for a soul cake!
> I pray, good missis, a soul cake!
> An apple or pear, a plum or a cherry,
> Any good thing to make us merry.
> One for Peter, two for Paul,
> Three for Him who made us all.
> Up with the kettle, and down with the pan,
> Give us good alms and we'll be gone.[65]

All Saints' and All Souls' were also good days for long-term weather prognostication: 'On all-hallows day cut a chip from the beech tree; / if it be dry the winter will prove warm.' Likewise,

> If ducks do slide at Hollantide,
> At Christmas they will swim;
> If ducks do swim at Hollantide,
> At Christmas they will slide.[66]

Such soothsaying could be defended in the most esoteric terms. An almanac for 1664 confirmed the efficacy of the two days at the beginning of November for predictions thus:

> It is common among the countrey people, to judge of the following winter by the quarter wherein the winde shall be on the first of November. But that which is more observable is the second of November, which to the Arabian Astrologers was a Critical day, from which they could know something in general concerning the disposition of the aire in rain, thunder and lightning. For if Jupiter, Venus, and Mercury were then Occidental, or retrograde, they judged much rain to be in that year. They also had an eye to Saturn and Mars, whether of them were the stronger; as also what society they had with the other Planets, chiefly with Mercury;

that so they might judge the better concerning the following changes of the aire.[67]

However, Shakespeare diverges from common opinion in his mention of All-Hallows in the first part of *Henry IV*: 'Farewell, the latter spring! Farewell, All-hallown summer!'[68] This may refer to a warm spell of weather at this time of the year, which might be interpreted as a meteorological recognition of the religious significance of All-Hallows. In other words, the weather could emphasize the spiritual importance of particular days or dates.

Hard on the heels of All Saints' and All Souls' comes Gunpowder Treason Day, 5 November, better known as Squib-Night, Plot Night, the Fifth, Guy Fawkes Day, and Bonfire Night. This commemorates the failed attempt to blow up Parliament (not to mention King James I and VI as well) on 5 November 1605, as recorded in an eighteenth-century miscellany:

> Come let us remember the 5th of November
> > The gunpowder Treason Plot,
> Can any give reason that gunpowder treason
> > Should ever be forgot.[69]

An Act passed by Parliament in 1606 required attendance at church on the morning of 5 November for social prayers and a reading of the Act. Very soon, Gunpowder Treason Day had become a popular and strongly Protestant festival, celebrating the foiling of a major Catholic conspiracy – in addition to Guy Fawkes, ten other conspirators were executed, all of whom were papists. So later in the century the day became an opportunity to denounce the marriage of Charles I, James's successor, to the Catholic Henrietta Maria.

Because of its extreme Protestant bias, Gunpowder Treason Day was the only festival not abolished in 1647 after the defeat of Charles I by the Parliamentarians, and was virtually the only day on which church bells were rung for the next dozen years of the Commonwealth. The celebration continued after the Restoration in 1660 and was celebrated with ferocious enthusiasm when James, duke of York and later James II, converted to Rome in 1673 – the public response being to burn the pope in effigy.[70] Some attempts were made to suppress Gunpowder Treason Day when the Whigs tried to prevent James's claim to the throne – a political emergency known as the Exclusion Crisis (1678–81) – but despite efforts to abolish the festival at James's accession in 1685, the day predictably became more popular still. William of Orange duly landed on Gunpowder Treason Day in 1688 to begin the Protestant Glorious Revolution that swiftly brought the Stuart monarchy to an end.

As Gunpowder Treason Day developed, the parading and burning of effigies did not confine itself to Guy Fawkes and the pope – usually Pope Paul V (1552–1621); immolation was also extended to political figures (most of whom, from Tom Paine to Tony Blair, have ended up on the fire), international enemies, and unpopular local personages. In New England, 5 November was known as 'Pope Day' and was the only English festival kept by the Puritan settlers. Effigies of Guy Fawkes, the pope, and the Devil were zealously burnt by unruly crowds until by the mid-eighteenth century the authorities were forced to curtail the celebrations.[71]

Back in old England, however, Gunpowder Treason Day was a mass event that continued to grow in popularity and dangerous exuberance, encouraged by its status as a national holiday until 1859. It was also long believed that Gunpowder Treason Day was a day on which normal life was suspended and the usual laws did not apply. 'Guy riots' annually raged across the country, from Croydon to Exeter, and there were disturbances in Oxford, Cambridge, and London as late as the 1950s and 1960s. A second verse of the memorial rhyme 'Remember, remember / The fifth of November' was recorded in 1890, and seems to refer back to mob festivities of the seventeenth and eighteenth centuries:

> A stick and a stake
> For King James's sake,
> Please give us a coil, a coil.

If you don't give us one, We'll take two,
The better for us, sir, And worse for you.[72]

The escalation of Gunpowder Treason Day in the mid-nineteenth century meant that it became a serious threat to public order. William Howitt recalled in 1841 that:

> every town and village in the kingdom used to be in a state of utter riot and confusion on fifth of November morning. Great fires were burning in every open place; guns, blunderbusses, pistols, key-guns firing in all directions; squibs and crackers bouncing and fizzing everywhere under feet; rockets soaring over head. Mobs of lads carrying round the image of Guy Faux; and men and lads in every place, shouting, scuffling, making all the uproar, and doing all the mischief possible.[73]

Organized bonfires and spectacles were therefore established, but many of these remained edgy events liable to ignite in violence, and so often families remained at home and held their own private firework displays.

Lewes in Sussex famously retains a flavour of the old-style Gunpowder Treason Day. The event is in part a modern carnival with, for example, a fancy-dress competition, but at its heart it is clearly a Protestant ritual from another age. The festival is based around seven Bonfire Societies, each leading torch-lit parades in different parts of the town in remembrance of seventeen local Protestant martyrs executed during the Counter-Reformation, and culminates in the burning of effigies of Guy Fawkes and Pope Paul V. It is principally a local event and the Lewes Bonfire Council in fact emphasizes how uncomfortable the night is likely to be (cold, wet, crowded, limited transport arrangements, restricted access to pubs, and so forth) as a way of deterring tourists, even urging 'people from outside the Lewes locality to celebrate in their own area'.[74] Nevertheless, community events on 5 November are increasingly popular due to the expense and perceived danger of back-garden fireworks, and the inescapable influx of visitors has certainly calmed the Lewes bonfire celebrations in recent years.

Autumn is a popular time for West Country carnivals, and several of these are based around 5 November. On the Friday nearest to the date (previously the Thursday), Bridgwater in Somerset has a two-hour carnival procession. This supposedly began in 1605 in the wake of the Gunpowder Plot and was first described in 1860. In 1880 it ended in a riot, necessitating subsequent reorganization into a pageant, which today is attended by some 150,000 people, five times the town's population. Even a tiny village such as Sticklepath in Devon has a spectacular annual 5 November Fireshow that mixes giant puppetry and pantomime in a carnivalesque celebration; it attracts a regular audience of 3,000 – seven-and-a-half times the village population. Ottery St Mary, also in Devon, has a full carnival parade that precedes the processions of flaming tar barrels that are carried along the streets throughout the evening. That makes it sound rather polite: the barrels are in fact small infernos, and the men carrying them run full-pelt down side-streets into the village square. The spectacle of a huge, flaming creature careering towards you is awe-inspiring. Tight crowds of onlookers suddenly scatter like ash in the wind. It is a strangely lonely moment – social conditioning evaporates and all one is left with is a visceral dread of the raw intensity of fire. It is tempting for some to cling here to the myth of Samhain fires, but there is no evidence that Samhain festivals survived in England, either as Hallowe'en bonfires or transferred to Gunpowder Treason Day.[75] Indeed, the tar barrels of Ottery St Mary seem to have begun in the mid-nineteenth century.[76] But the same families have been running the barrels since then and the right to do so is carefully preserved – so what is at stake here is that English traditions do not need to garner cultural authority by scraping acquaintance with old 'Celtic' festivals. The intense experience of running and facing the burning barrels proves that English traditions can summon more than enough stunning power by reworking English customs and folklore.

In contrast to the fire festivals across the rest of the country, in Shebbear in Devon it is a local custom on 5 November for the bellringers to pull discordant peals, and then to leave the bell-tower to overturn the Devil's Stone outside the churchyard. This Devil's Stone is a huge boulder, and its presence in the village is a geological impossibility, suggesting it was deposited there for some ancient and now lost reason. The tradition itself certainly seems ancient, and is perhaps connected with the dedication of the church to St Michael, the Devil's scourge.[77] There may also be a connection here with Ringing Night, 4 November, in which bells were once rung in anticipation of Gunpowder Treason Day, and which continues in some parishes in Cornwall. Coincidentally, the Taurids, a meteor shower, also occur at this time, climaxing around 3 November.

———

The eve or vigil of St Martin, 10 November, was a day for weather prognostication: 'If the 10. day be cloudy, it denunciates a wet; if dry, a sharp winter'.[78] For John Clare, 'St Martins Eve' was a dreary time of the year:

> Now that the year grows wearisome with age
> And days grow short and nights excessive long
> No out door sports the village hinds engage
> Still is the meadow romp & harvest song
> That wont to echo from each merry throng....

There is little birdsong save the 'lone and melancholly crane', and the swallow and martin have deserted the countryside; all the fruit has been picked, it is raining, and children are pent up indoors waiting for the weather to improve. The only amusement is to be had in sitting by the fire and gossiping while the wind blows outside:

> While in the chimney top loud roared the gale
> Its blustering howl of outdoor symphonies
> That round the cottage hearth bade happier moods arise
> And circling round the fire the merry folks
> Brought up all sports their memory could devise
> Playing upon each other merry jokes....[79]

The early nineteenth-century comic poet Thomas Hood put the matter rather more bluntly in his poem 'No!', which, after a lengthy jeremiad complaining about everything that is wanting in the month, concludes 'No shade, no shine, no butterflies, no bees, / No fruits, no flowers, no leaves, no birds, – / November!'[80]

St Martin's Day proper, 11 November, also known as Martinmas or Martlemas, was the herald of winter: 'At Saint Martin's day / winter is on his way'.[81] Consequently it was the traditional date for slaughtering cows and pigs, whose meat would be preserved for the winter by salting or smoking – hence the proverbial wisdom on the inescapability of fate, 'His Martinmas will come, as it does to every hog'.[82] Meat preserved at this time was 'Martinmas beef', and what could not be preserved – offal, for example – would be consumed at Martinmas feasts. This late bounty seems to have influenced Spenser's depiction of November as a glutton

> . . . grosse and fat,
> As fed with lard, and that right well might seeme;
> For, he had been a fatting hogs of late,
> That yet his browes with sweat, did reek and steem,
> And yet the season was full sharp and breem.[83]

The slaughtering tradition certainly pre-dates the Norman Conquest and may be much older: the Old English name for the month was blōtmōnaþ, 'blood month' or 'the month of sacrifice', referring to the slaughter of animals. With little else to do but eat tripe and talk, those with a weather-eye might observe that 'If the wind is in the south-west at Martinmas, it keeps there till after Candlemas'.[84] However, there was also the chance of a 'St Martin's summer', a spell of warm weather at this time of year, as noted by Shakespeare in the first part of *Henry VI*:

> Expect Saint Martin's summer, halcyons' days,
> Since I have entered into these wars.[85]

There were also yet more November celebrations. Elizabeth I, the Protestant daughter of Henry VIII, had succeeded to the throne on 17 November 1558. In 1568, church bells were rung to commemorate the tenth anniversary of her accession, and in 1576 the date became a holy day with its own prayers. Inevitably, it also became a secular event with music, pageantry, bonfires, and fireworks to celebrate the great return of Protestantism after the Counter-Reformation of Mary I; this meant that effigies of the pope and the Devil were once again burned in effigy – particularly in 1712 when Paul V, the pope who had excommunicated Elizabeth and who was seen as a particular enemy of England, was canonized. Other villains imagined to be threatening the constitution, such as the Pretender (James Stuart, the Stuart claimant to the throne) and later his son Charles Edward (also known as Bonnie Prince Charlie), were also burnt on the day. By another happy astronomical coincidence, the annual meteor shower of the Leonids is at its peak around this time.

The Elizabethan and Jacobean writer Nicholas Breton's account of November notes that it is the season for hunting woodcock, pheasant, and mallard and for the cook and comfit-maker to prepare for Christmas; it is also the time when butter and cheese rise in price, the nobility feast themselves while 'the poore die through want of Charitie', and there is chilling cold and rain, and high winds. His account of seasonal food is a reminder that parkin – oatmeal gingerbread – is a November cake that later became associated with Gunpowder Treason Day, especially in the north – it was made by Dorothy Wordsworth on 6 November 1800.[86] And even today, by the time November comes, Christmas is being anticipated in the kitchen. The Sunday before Advent and twenty-fifth after Trinity – that is, between 20 and 26 November – is 'Stir-Up Sunday' for mincemeat and plum-pudding mixtures.

Breton also remarks on the high winds characteristic of November. These were never as bad as on 26 November 1703, when the Great Storm hit England. It has been estimated that this catastrophe was equivalent to a Category 3 hurricane, with winds gusting at 120 mph and waves breaking sixty feet high. Eight thousand people died, including a tenth of the Royal

Navy's servicemen. The devastation was on a vast scale: buildings were destroyed and church spires blown off; chimneys toppled and killed, among many others, the bishop of Bath and Wells and his wife; and windmills were set ablaze from the friction created as their sails spun around. The diarist and advocate of reforestation John Evelyn noted of the millions of trees that had been blown down:

> methinks I still hear, and am sure feel the dismal Groans (happening on the 26th of *Novemb.* 1703.) of our *Forests*, so many thousands of goodly *Oaks* subverted by that late dreadful *Hurricane*, prostrating the Trees, and crushing all that grew under them, lying in ghastly Postures, like whole *Regiments* fallen in *Battel* by the Sword of the *Conqueror*.[87]

The Eddystone Lighthouse disappeared, along with its crew and even its architect, Henry Winstanley, who had arrived especially that night to enjoy the furious spectacle and oversee any subsequent repairs. By comparison, the greatest English storm in today's living memory, that of October 1987, may not have been as severe, but the wind still gusted up to 100 mph, 19 million trees were felled, and nineteen people killed.[88] So much for the season of mists and mellow fruitfulness.

Part v

12 WINTER

I wonder if the snow *loves* the trees and fields, that it kisses them so gently? And then it covers them up snug, you know, with a white quilt; and perhaps it says 'Go to sleep, darlings, till the summer comes again.'

'Lewis Carroll', *Through the Looking-Glass, and What Alice Found There*

The great mystery of TIME, were there no other; the illimitable, silent, never-resting thing called Time, rolling, rushing on, swift, silent, like an all-embracing ocean-tide, on which we and all the Universe swim like exhalations, like apparitions which *are*, and then *are not*; this is forever very literally a miracle; a thing to strike us dumb – for we have no word to speak about it.[1]

Thus spake the historian and man of letters Thomas Carlyle in 'The Hero as Divinity' (1840) – and so we move mysteriously, inexorably towards the end of the year.

———

The Old English *winter* derives from the Old High German and Gothic for 'wet', but its cultural meteorology is one of bitter cold, frost, snow, and darkness. It is a season in which the sun is absent, or at best remote – pale and weak, spreading a thin watery light over the landscape. In his Sonnet 97, Shakespeare develops this theme by adopting the yearly cycle as an index of the relationships explored throughout his sequence of poems:

> How like a winter hath my absence been
> From thee, the pleasure of the fleeting year!
> What freezings have I felt, what dark days seen!
> What old December's bareness every where!
> And yet this time remov'd was summer's time,
> The teeming autumn, big with rich increase,
> Bearing the wanton burthen of the prime,

Like widowed wombs after their lords' decease:
Yet this abundant issue seem'd to me
But hope of orphans, and unfathered fruit,
For summer and his pleasures wait on thee,
And thou away, the very birds are mute;
   Or if they sing, 'tis with so dull a cheer
   That leaves look pale, dreading the winter's near.[2]

The sonnet gathers up seasonal expectations and runs them backwards: absence is akin to winter, which denotes the end of the year – freezing, dark, barren; before then, autumn was rich with the harvest, yet melancholy at the passing of the summertime; and before even that, summer – remote summer – has gone, chorused in his time by birdsong but now dead and in his majesty irreplaceable as the year declines and falls into desuetude. The lines are regressive, full of woe, populated by widows and posthumous orphans, affrighted trees and lonely birds of omen. Summer seems not only impossibly distant, but gone forever, remembered only in mourning and in cold amazement that so little of it remains in the waste land. There is no mention of spring.

This image of winter guided the imagination so powerfully that a few years later, in 1622, Bishop Lancelot Andrewes wrote these myths of winter into his account of the Nativity and the coming of the Magi:

It was no *Summer progresse*. A cold coming they had of it, at this time of the yeare; just, the worst time of the yeare, to take a journey, and specially a long journey, in. The waies deep, the weather sharp, the daies short, the sun farthest off *in solsitio brumali*, the very dead of Winter.[3]

This is Judea read through the icy despair of a harsh English winter. The profound point of winter is 'the dead of winter', as it is of the night – such terms subtly structure the identity of the seasons: there is no 'dead' of spring, there are no 'depths' of summer, there is no 'prime' of winter.

Andrewes's lines were of course famously adapted by T. S. Eliot, who was well aware of the meteorological import, for his 'Journey of the Magi' (1930):

> 'A cold coming we had of it,
> Just the worst time of the year
> For a journey, and such a long journey:
> The ways deep and the weather sharp,
> The very dead of winter.'[4]

Bethlehem very occasionally has a dusting of snow, but the temperature drops below freezing only very rarely. Yet from the perspective of England we read the winter weather differently – whether in Eliot's lines, Christmas cards showing the Nativity in a snow-capped stable, or snow globes that depict the scene in 3D, a mere shake away from a swirling blizzard.

The imposition of a national seasonal stereotype on other territories is not unusual to the imperial way of thinking. The Romans imagined that the uncultivated lands at the edges of their empire were effectively in a state of everlasting winter to which they had become inured, as explained by the Stoic philosopher and statesman Seneca the Younger:

> Consider all the nations beyond the scope of Roman civilization, I mean the Germans and all the nomadic tribes that oppose us in the region of the Danube: they are oppressed by unending winter and a gloomy sky, and grudged sustenance by a barren soil; they keep off the rain by means of thatch or leaves, they range over marshes frozen with ice, they catch wild beasts for food. Do you think they are unhappy creatures? There is no unhappiness for those whom habit has brought back to nature; for little by little what they begin from necessity becomes a pleasure. No homes, no resting-places do they have except those that fatigue assigns for the day; their food is fit for beggars and must be gained by hand, the harshness of the climate is fearful, no clothing covers their bodies; this state, which you regard as disastrous, constitutes the life of so many tribes.[5]

This seasonal way of mapping the world is also reciprocal. It is evident in poets such as Robert Browning and Rudyard Kipling, for example, growing restless for English springtime when they are abroad, and even in Rupert Brooke's longing for 'some corner of a foreign field / That is forever England'.[6]

Back in England, wintry weather is not, however, all metaphor. There really are frosts and it really does snow. In the coldest years, the River Thames itself has actually frozen, and not only was the ice thick enough to walk on, it could carry the weight of a whole fair. These were the Thames 'frost fairs' – fairs in the spirit of St Bartholomew's Fair that spontaneously took to the ice.

Thames frost fairs date back to the middle of the twelfth century, but the first proper event was held in the winter of 1683–4, recorded in detail by John Evelyn on 24 January 1684:

The frost continuing more and more severe, the Thames before London was still planted with booths in formal streets, all sorts of trades and shops furnished, and full of commodities, even to a printing-press, where the people and ladies took a fancy to have their names printed, and the day and year set down when printed on the Thames: this humour took so universally, that it was estimated the printer gained £5 a day, for printing a line only, at sixpence a name, besides what he got by ballads, etc. Coaches plied from Westminster to the Temple, and from several other stairs to and fro, as in the streets, sleds, sliding with skates, a bull-baiting, horse and coach races, puppet-plays and interludes, cooks, tippling, and other lewd places, so that it seemed to be a bacchanalian triumph, or carnival on the water, whilst it was a severe judgment on the land, the trees not only splitting as if lightning-struck, but men and cattle perishing in divers places, and the very seas so locked up with ice, that no vessels could stir or come in. The fowls, fish, and birds, and all our exotic plants and greens, universally perishing.[7]

The fair became legendary, seeming thereafter to happen once every generation: 1715–16, 1739–40, 1767–8, 1788–9, and during the 'Frost of the Century' in 1813–14.

The Great Frost of 1740 was the most severe winter hitherto recorded in England. The philanthropist Robert Marsham, second Baron Romney, kept a diary, recording that the song thrush did not sing until March and the hawthorn only blossomed in June.[8] The Great Frost provoked food scarcity and famine. As the pseudonymous writer 'Icedore Frostiface' put it:

> great Numbers take the Advantage of warming themselves upon the Ice, and endeavor to live upon the harden'd Water, for fear of Starving upon Land. No Wonder if we see half of *London* running into the *Thames*, and Towns arising out of her Ruins on that Element. . . . No Wonder if among the great numbers of Printers, Engravers, Goldsmiths, Toymen, Coffee-Men, Raree-Shew-Men, Sellers of Gin and Gingerbread, you see a poetical-historical-philosophical Astrologer, endeavouring to catch your Curiosity, and vend those Wares which are no longer saleable elsewhere; especially as, by the Help of Engraving and Printing, he stands a fairer Chance to perpetuate the Memory of this remarkable Year, than any other of the Professions singly and alone.[9]

The Great Frost also froze the Thames, and again one of the great draws of the 1740 frost fair was to have one's name printed on a specially composed souvenir verse – the whole text actually printed on the ice by 'the noble Art and Mystery of Printing':

> Behold the liquid *Thames* now frozen o'er
> That lately Ships of mighty Burthen bore;
>
> Here you may print your Name tho' cannot Write
> 'Cause numm'd with Cold: Tis done with great Delight!
> And lay it by that Ages yet to come
> May see what things upon the *Ice* were done.[10]

Likewise January 1814 proved to be viciously cold – the decade 1812–21 being the coldest since the 1690s. A frost fair was again established on the frozen river and lasted until 7 February. A regular account of the spectacle was given in *Frostiana*, which continued the ice-print tradition by proudly announcing on its title-page that it was 'Printed and published on the Ice on the River Thames, February 5, 1814, by G. Davis'. *Frostiana* described both the beginning and the demise of the event from the ice itself:

Tuesday, Feb. 1. . . . . Many were induced to venture on the ice, and the example thus afforded, soon led thousands to perambulate the rugged plain, where a variety of amusements were prepared for their entertainment.

Among the more curious of these was the ceremony of roasting a small sheep, which was *toasted*, or rather burnt, over a coal fire, placed in a large iron pan. For a view of this *extraordinary* spectacle, *sixpence* was demanded, and willingly paid. The delicate meat when *done*, was sold at *a shilling a slice*, and termed *Lapland mutton*. Of booths there were a great number, which were ornamented with streamers, flags, and signs, and in which there was a plentiful store of those favourite luxuries, *gin*, *beer*, and *gingerbread*.[11]

Monday, Feb. 7. – Large masses of ice are yet floating, and numerous lighters, broken from their moorings, are seen in different parts of the river; many of them complete wrecks. The damage done to the craft and barges is supposed to be very great. From London-bridge to Westminster, Twenty Thousand Pounds will scarcely make good the losses that have been sustained. While we are now writing, (half past 2 p.m.) *a printing press has been again set up on a large* ICE-ISLAND, between Blackfriars and Westminster-bridges. At this *new printing-office*, the remainder of a large impression of the *Title-page* of the present work is now actually being printed, so that the purchasers of FROSTIANA, will have this additional advantage.[12]

The frost fair of 1814 proved to be the last, despite the severe winters of 1940, 1947, 1963, and 2010, when temperatures were sometimes lower than in 1814. But the Thames no longer freezes. Sir John Rennie's new London Bridge, which was opened in 1831, had wider arches than the old bridge and therefore allows the river to flow more swiftly, greatly reducing the likelihood of it freezing. The Thames is also warmed by cooling water from power stations and the tidal flow is consequently more vigorous, and the riverbed has been dredged, which allows for a deeper inflow of salt water.[13] London is also a heat island: concrete and tarmac effectively work as storage heaters and the vast expansion of the city has dramatically affected its microclimate: London is 2 °C warmer than the surrounding green belt. Finally, despite our occasional hard winters, climate change is making such extreme and protracted cold less likely.[14]

DECEMBER

December is Christmas: it is impossible to dissociate the two, especially in England. The whole month looks forward to Christmas Day, 25 December – quite professedly in the sense that Advent begins on 1 December – and post-Christmas there are Twelve Days of further celebration, stretching beyond the New Year. At least there used to be. Christmas has in fact changed dramatically over the centuries, and the fading of the Twelve Days, for instance, is symptomatic of those changes. Christmas-tide is not Keats's 'drear-nighted December' but the winter that William Cowper describes in The Task: 'Oh Winter! . . . King of intimate delights, / Fireside enjoyments, home-born happiness'.[15] Like Easter, then, Christmas deserves separate consideration and so has a following chapter to itself, along with the Twelve Days, while here we will focus on the months of winter.

Nicholas Breton, the irrepressible seventeenth-century commentator on the months and seasons, notes the feasting and self-indulgence of December: the rearing of 'Capons and Hennes, beside Turkies, Geese and Duckes, besides Beefe and Mutton'; the puddings of 'plummes and spice, Sugar and Honey'; the entertainments – 'Musicke now must bee in tune, or else never: the youth must dance and sing, and the aged sit by the fire'. It was a sort of seasonal madness: 'I hold it the costly Purveyour of Excesse, and the after breeder of necessitie, the practice of Folly, and the Purgatory of Reason'.[16]

But December was also a time of restraint. Sexual abstinence was strongly encouraged from Advent, 1 December, to Candlemas, 2 February, to purify the body before Christmas but also, more practically, to plan pregnancy and birth. As the historian Graham Jones puts it:

> The prominence of sexual behaviour in early law codes, strange to us now, highlights crucial concerns about the precarious balance between demand and supply of the necessities of life, and the dependence for social stability on clarity of kinship and legitimacy. Summer babies had a better chance of becoming healthy children, but also pregnant women were no use in the harvest, so there were practical reasons, too, for abstinence after the start of Advent.[17]

Consequently there is very little sexual euphemism and innuendo at Christmas compared with other times of the year, such as May Day, and, kissing under the mistletoe aside, Christmas remains an oddly chaste celebration.

There were in any case other festivities in the month before Christmas itself. The first of December was St Eligius' Day: Eligius, also known as Loy or Eloi, was the patron saint of blacksmiths and celebrated from the mediaeval period until the nineteenth century, when St Clement was instead adopted. Five days later, St Nicholas's Day, 6 December, commemorated a fourth-century bishop of Myra in Turkey. Among his miracles was saving children, including the resurrection of a few lads who had been diced up and salted to be sold as pork by an unscrupulous innkeeper. Hence Nicholas became the patron saint of children. The antiquary John Aubrey recorded that:

the School-boies in the west [of England]: still religiously observe
St Nicholas day (Decemb. 6th), he was the Patron of the Schoole-boies.
At Curry-Yeovill in Somersetshire, where there is a Howschole (or
schole) in the Church, they have annually at that time a Barrell of good
Ale brought into the church; and that night they have the priviledge to
breake open their Masters Cellar-dore.[18]

This is the tradition of 'barring out', popular in schools from Tudor
times to the late nineteenth century. During Shrovetide and on
St Nicholas's Day the pupils locked out the staff and made various
demands. Such a spirit of misrule is also evident in the election of Boy
Bishops, which some cathedrals still practise today: selecting a young
chorister to officiate at various ecclesiastical events from St Nicholas's
Day until Holy Innocents' Day, 28 December. There is some evidence that
St Nicholas's Eve, 5 December, was also a convivial celebration in the sixteenth century:

The v day of Desember was sant Necolas evyn, and sant Necolas whent
a-brod in most plases, and all Godys pepull received ym to ther howses
and had good chere, after the old custum.[19]

St Nicholas also reputedly saved three daughters from prostitution by providing three bags of gold – hence his patronage of pawnbrokers is signi-
fied by three golden globes, a sign that remains familiar in high streets.
He is consequently particularly associated with market places and urban
commerce, which may help to explain his degeneration into that icon of
Western capitalism, Father Christmas (see Chapter 13).

The eleventh of December was Old St Andrew's Day (St Andrews-
tide being 30 November, NS). Andrew is the patron saint of Scotland, as
well as Patras, where he was martyred, and Russia, but he also appealed
to Northamptonshire lace-makers, to whom he was 'Tander', so named by
the same process of contraction that led to St Oswald becoming 'Twosole'
and St Audrey 'Tawdry'. The lace-makers celebrated Tander by drinking,

eating, and cross-dressing, according to the nineteenth-century folklorist Thomas Sternberg:

> Of all the numerous red-letter days which diversified the lives of our ancestors, this is the only one which has survived to our own times in anything like its pristine character . . . drinking and feasting prevail to a riotous extent. Towards evening the sober villagers appear to have become suddenly smitten with a violent taste for masquerading. Women may be seen walking about in male attire, while men and boys have donned the female dress, and visit each other's cottages, drinking hot 'eldern wine', the staple beverage of the season.[20]

The prevalence of festivities during December is in part to compensate for the winter solstice, which occurs on St Thomas's Day, 21 December: 'St Thomas grey, St Thomas grey, / The longest night and shortest day'.[21] (The old calendar gave St Lucia the longest night – '*Lucy* light, the shortest day and the longest night'; her day is now 13 December, which by coincidence is when the Geminids annual meteor shower is at its most active.[22]) Giving provisions or doles to the poor and needy was customary on St Thomas's Day to ensure that everyone enjoyed a good Christmas, although sometimes the poor and needy could actually 'go Thomasing', or seek charity themselves. It was also the day for slaughtering pigs and preparing pork for the Christmas season: 'St. Thomas divine, / brewing, baking, and killing of fat swine'.[23]

As with the summer solstice, however, the Christian year played down the significance of the solar year in order to emphasize the calendrical dating of sacred festivals. The days before Christmas Day were relatively quiet: the halcyon days. These are named after a mythical Mediterranean bird, the 'halcyon', that builds its nest a week before the winter solstice on 14 December. Building the nest takes a week, and in another week she lays and hatches her eggs; during this time the sea is calm for the bird and her brood.[24] In contrast in ancient Rome, the capital of paganism, the riotous festival of Saturnalia ran from 17 to 24 December to celebrate Saturn, the god of the harvest. Saturnalia was followed on 25 December by *Mithrae dies natalis Solis Invicti*, the birthday of the Unconquered Sun, usually simply known as *Sol Invictus*, the Unconquered Sun.

———

St Stephen's Day, 26 December, is better known in England as Boxing Day, which was declared under the Bank Holidays Act of 1871. The *Oxford English Dictionary* dates the name 'Boxing Day' to 1833, but seasonal boxes occur much earlier, and the practice of making a winter cash donation to servants goes back at least to the beginning of the eighteenth century and may have originated in the 1620s with apprentices and servants collecting tips. In the nineteenth century, according to the footman diarist William Tayler, gangs of 'sweeps, beadles, lamplighters, watermen, dustmen, scavengers (that is the men who clean the mud out of the streets), newspaper boy [sic], general postmen, twopenny postmen and waits' would roam the streets playing music and expecting monetary hand-outs for their trouble.[25] The Christmas box does still survive in some areas, where one is expected to tip the postman, milkman, dustman, and paperboy or girl. Children also went speculatively begging on this day, a practice known as 'Stephening'.

St Stephen's Day is the traditional day for bleeding horses, a practice mentioned by the sixteenth-century agriculturalist Thomas Tusser, and also for 'Hunting the Wren', a custom that may also take place on New Year's Day or the Twelfth Day of Christmas.[26] This controversial ritual involves catching a wren and confining it in a wooden cage on the end of a long pole, around which songs are sung and mumming plays are performed; it is not really an English custom, being more prevalent in Ireland and Wales, and on the Isle of Man. However, an English folksong, 'The Cutty Wren', has become associated with the Wren Hunt, supposedly dating the institution to the fourteenth century and glossing the words as a symbolic account of Wat Tyler and the Peasants' Revolt of 1381. This is wrong, if romantic: 'The Cutty Wren' was actually first recorded in the eighteenth century as a Scottish song, and therefore is an example of invented – or appropriated – English folklore.[27]

Holy Innocents' Day or Childermas, 28 December, marked Herod's mass infanticide in Bethlehem in an attempt to kill Jesus. Children were traditionally permitted to play in church on this day, but Childermas was generally considered an unlucky day, and a perilous time to start anything new or engage in anything potentially dangerous. The Cornish antiquary Richard Carew noted in 1602, 'talke not of Hares ore such uncouth things, for that proves as ominous to the fisherman, as the beginning a voyage on the day when Childermas day fell, doth to the Mariner'.[28] This superstition lasted at least until the mid-nineteenth century. Holy Innocents' Day also marked the end of the reign of Boy Bishops, who had ruled from St Nicholas's Day.

Ringing out the old year and ringing in the new happens on New Year's Eve, 31 December, as noted by the Romantic essayist and humorist Charles Lamb in 'New Year's Eve' (1821):

Of all sound of all bells (bells, the music nighest bordering upon heaven) – most solemn and touching is the peal which rings out the Old Year. I never hear it without a gathering-up of my mind to a concentration of all the images that have been diffused over the past twelvemonth; all I have done or suffered, performed or neglected – in that regretted time. I begin to know its worth, as when a person dies.[29]

But the celebration of the New Year has only recently become a major festival in England. Indeed, Robert Chambers, publisher of the popular Book of Days, wrote in 1864:

As a general statement, it may be asserted that neither the last evening of the old year nor the first day of the new one is much observed in England as an occasion of festivity. In some parts of the country, indeed, and more especially in the northern counties, various social merry-makings take place; but for the most part, the great annual holiday-time is now past. Christmas Eve, Christmas-day, and St Stephen's or Boxing Day have absorbed almost entirely the tendencies and opportunities of the community at large in the direction of joviality and relaxation.[30]

The eighteenth-century parson James Woodforde would clearly stay up on New Year's Eve, drinking and horsing about, and the practice of kissing and singing to welcome in the New Year was noted in England by the American novelist Nathaniel Hawthorne in 1856.[31] But there is a general lack of English traditions for New Year's Eve and Day. Chambers and Lamb explain why: New Year's Eve comes too soon after the seasonal exhaustion of Christmas, and New Year's Day always carries with it a sense of mortality – as Lamb moodily puts it, New Year is the date from which 'all date their time, and count upon what is left'.[32] New Year's Day did not become an English bank holiday until 1974, in part to justify Scotland having an additional national holiday on 2 January: for many Scots Hogmanay was, and for some still is, more significant than Christmas. For the English, New Year's Day had been an unofficial day off for years due to the tendency to toast the New Year at midnight or one o'clock, but there's little else that goes on apart from a remnant of the carnivalesque in fancy-dress parties.

JANUARY

Gunter's Confectioner's Oracle (1830) has no doubt of the culinary riches of January:

> January is perhaps of all the months in the year the most favourable to enjoyments of the table: then it is, that the gastrologist, vigorous, in high spirits, and with a voracious and insatiable appetite, is a most welcome guest at the tables of – the RICH!...
>
> January is Nature's spoilt-child: all her gifts are laid under contribution by a cook of genius. Beef, veal, mutton, pork, venison, hare, pheasant, plover, the black cock, partridge, wild goose, duck, woodcock, &c., troop up to the great city, dead or alive; and in battalions that

serve only to entrance with delight the assembled forces of *bon-vivans*, to whom gold will render them an easy and immediate sacrifice. Cauliflowers and celery rear their tender and delicately juicy heads, merely for the pleasure of being decapitated. At this period, truffles are poetry. And now it is, that a householder must either give good and frequent dinners, or permit himself to be thrown without the pale of society, with, to use an animating figure, the pitchfork of universal resentment. When the appetite is both excellent and discriminating, the dinner must be abundant and admirable, – anything short of these qualities, is at all times a fault, but, in January, it is a moral assassination!

Talk not to me about presents at this time of the year: there are gifts which are to be valued more, than gold, silver, or precious stones, – I mean good dinners.[33]

Breton, two hundred years earlier, also noted drinks of apple and nutmeg, grape, and ale, and the market trade in young oxen and rams, coneys and poultry, woodcock, pheasant, and hare – even 'the proud Peacocke leaps into the pye' – and hares are traditional food throughout the winter, as is confirmed by a sixteenth-century cookery book: 'A Hare is ever good / but best from October to lent'.[34] It is a good month to follow the hunt, less good for fishing, bleak for anyone working outside, and foul for travelling. But it is an expensive month: 'I hold it a time of little comfort, the rich mans charge, and the poore mans misery'.[35]

January is an Anglicization of the Roman month *Januarius*, itself derived from *janua* meaning 'door' and associated with the two-faced god Janus. So despite the early Roman year originally beginning around the vernal equinox in March, once the month of January was introduced, it clearly became the first month of the year, a transitional time between the old year and new, the past and future. The new year therefore emerges from the depths of winter.

As the first month of the year, in popular reckoning, if not formally in England until January 1753, this was a keen time for predictions. The writer and courtier Lodowick Lloyd claimed in *The Diall of Daies* (1590) that the early days of January revealed the 'nature and state' of the succeeding months according to the following pattern:

2 January	September
3 January	October
4 January	November
5 January	December
8 January a.m.	June
8 January p.m.	May
9 January a.m.	August
9 January p.m.	July
10 January a.m.	October
10 January p.m.	September
11 January a.m.	December
11 January p.m.	November
12 January	the whole year [36]

Erra Pater's *Pronostycacyon For Ever* (1540) proposed an alternative system, based on the day of the week. For example,

> In the yeare that Janyvere, shall enter upon the sondaye, the wynter shalbe colde, and moyst, and the somer shall be hote, and the tyme of harveste shalbe wyndy, and rayny, with great habundaunce of corne, of all gardyne fruyte and herbes. There shalbe lytell Oyle habundaunce shall be of allmaner of fleshe. Some great newes shall men here spoken of Kynges of prelates of the churche and other erthly prynces. Great warres and robboryes shall be made, & many yonge people shall dye.[37]

Sunshine on St Vincent's Day, 22 January, ''tis a token bright and clear of prosperous weather all the year', and likewise the Conversion of St Paul, 25 January, was a reliable indicator:

Yf that the daye,

 of S. Paule be cheare

Than shall betide,

 an happy yere.

Yf it do chaunce,

 to Snowe or rayne

Than shall be deare,

 all kynde of grayne.

But and the wynde,

 than be a lofte

Warres shall vexe,

 this Realme full ofte.

And yf the Clowdes,

 make darke the skye

Both Neate amd Fowle

 that yeare shall dye.[38]

There was also more general advice: to eat a hen in January if you wished to live through the year, and cut wood on 30 or 31 December or 1 January. On 15 January, 'The Slug makes its appearance, and commences its depredations on garden plants and green wheat'.[39]

 Birds, too, were noticeable in the bare countryside, denuded by hungry scavengers: 'the Blackbird leaveth not a berry on the thorne, and the garden earth is turned up for her roots'.[40] The curlew could be heard, 'just enough to revive memory of the past spring and to stir anticipation of the next one', and the mistle thrush sings from January and effectively marks the beginning of the year's cycle of birdsong. The ornithologist and statesman Sir Edward, Viscount Grey, describes its call: 'there was boldness and mildness as well as sweetness in the tone ... there was weather in his song'.[41] The mistle thrush traditionally sings loudest in wet and rough weather, and is consequently known as the 'storm cock'.[42] Geese, too, were about and were favourite predictors of weather. In the seventeenth century, it was remarked that the goose 'hath a shrewd guesse of rainie weather being as good as an

Almanack to some that beleeve in her' and weeks of frosty weather could be divined from geese flying in formation.[43] The robin is also heard, its song seeming to chime with the season. The naturalist and writer William Henry Hudson described it thus:

> His song, indeed, never seems so sweet and impressive as in the silent and dreary season. For one thing, the absence of other bird-voices causes the robin's to be more attentively listened to and better appreciated than at other times, just as we appreciate the nightingale best when he 'sings darkling' – when there are no other strains to distract the attention. There is also the power of contrast – the bright, ringing lyric, a fountain of life and gladness, in the midst of a nature that suggests mournful analogies – autumnal decay and wintry death.[44]

———

The first of January was popularly known as New Year's Day despite not being endorsed by either sacred or secular authorities. Although the Roman year originally began in March, New Year festivities around 1 January were already entrenched in pre-Christian times, and in the sixth century AD churches in Gaul and Spain adopted the 'Octave of Christmas' on the reasoning that adhering to Jewish Law would make 1 January the day on which Jesus was circumcised.[45] More practically, the Church recognized that New Year celebrations had some status and so needed to be accommodated within the Christian year.

In England, 1 January did not officially become the first day of the new year until 1752, when, as we have seen, it replaced 25 March. John Macky, a Scottish secret agent in the eighteenth century, wrote a description of England in the form of letters to a foreign correspondent. Letter IX, dated 'January 1st, 1714', commences:

> I begin this Letter with wishing you a Happy New-Year, though the Year does not begin in this Kingdom till the 25th Day of March. I have asked several Learned Men the Reason why they do here differ from all

Kingdoms of *Christendom* in the beginning their Year; but could never have any tolerable Account given, except, that the 25th *March* being the Day of the Blessed Virgin's Conception, they date the *Æra* of our Lord from thence.[46]

Beginning the new year on 1 January was adopted by Scotland in 1600. Nevertheless, the English did popularly refer to 1 January as the new year far earlier: the thirteenth-century poet Orm, author of the *Ormulum*, a collection of homilies and biblical exegesis noted:

> tatt daʒʒ iss New ʒress daʒʒ
>> Many Enngleþeode nemmnedd
>
> [that day is called New Year's Day
>> among the English people].[47]

This popular perception that the new year begins on 1 January was acknowledged, too, in the use of an interim dating system for the English year: the dates 1 January to 24 March were generally numbered, for example, in the transitional form '1713–14' or '171¾'.

The day was marked in other ways as well. The salutation 'Compliments of the Season' is recorded from 1669.[48] Pepys kissed his family come one o'clock, not midnight, on New Year's morning and he mentions New Year's gifts several times, especially those given and received in his official capacity at the Navy Office.[49] The tradition of giving gifts on this day, called *strenae*, goes back to Roman times; they were known as 'handsels' – 'hondselle' is mentioned in the fourteenth-century Middle English romance *Sir Gawain and the Green Knight*. Monarchs received and gave gifts until the reign of James II, and public dignitaries such as the Lord Chancellor also received hampers of wine and food from lawyers, and in later years gifts of money. This custom lasted throughout the eighteenth century, and presents were still given to children on New Year's Day in the early nineteenth century, despite it not being an English holiday and the day's celebrations falling into neglect.[50] Nevertheless, New Year's Day wassailing was noted in 1838 by 'A Gastronome', who also provided a recipe for the wassail bowl:

> Simmer a small quantity of the following spices in a teacup-full of water: – cardamoms, cloves, nutmeg, mace, ginger, cinnamon, and coriander. Put the spices, when done, in two, four, or six bottles of port or Madeira, with a pound and a half of fine lump sugar to four bottles, and set all on the fire in a clean saucepan, meanwhile have your noblest china bowl ready, and, for four bottles, the yolks of twelve and the whites of six eggs well whisked up in it. Then, when the wine is a little warm, take out a teacup-full, and mix it in the bowl with the eggs; when a little warmer, another teacup-full, and so on for three or four; after which, when it boils, add the whole of the remainder, stirring it briskly all the time, so as to froth it. The moment a fine froth is obtained toss in twelve fine soft roasted apples, and send it up hot.[51]

Other seasonal treats included 'Pop Ladies', also known as 'Pope Ladies' – nutmeg cakes not unlike hot cross buns but roughly shaped into the female form with currants for eyes. They were sold on New Year's Day in St Albans throughout the nineteenth century and possibly earlier.[52]

Meanwhile, first-footing was adopted from Scotland in some parts of England in the nineteenth and twentieth centuries, and there were many superstitions, often with Scottish origins, that acknowledged the power of the turning year. The first water drawn from a well on New Year's Day was lucky – the 'cream of the well' – and good luck or marriage would come to the drinker of the last glass of wine on New Year's Eve or Day; likewise, the rustic poet John Clare noted that

> On the first moon in the new year young men & maids look through a silk hankerchief (that has been drawn through a ring) at the New moon & as many moons as each person sees through it as many years will they be ere they are married.[53]

It was believed that the activities followed on New Year's Day would be representative of the whole year, and that randomly dipping into the Bible could predict the year's fortunes in general. It was bad luck to sweep dust out of the house rather than driving it to the hearth (old dust effectively signifying good fortune), or to take fire from a neighbour, or to do the washing: 'Pray don't 'ee wash on New Year's day, / or you'll wash one of the family away'.[54]

Needless to say, outspoken Puritans such as William Prynne had thought all this an abomination:

> If wee now parallell our grand disorderly Christmasses, with these Roman Saturnals and heathen Festivals; or our New-yeares day (a chiefe part of Christmas) with their Festivity of Janus, *which was spent in Mummeries, Stage-playes, dancing, and such like Enterludes, wherein Fidlers and others acted lascivious effeminate parts, and went about their Towns and Cities in womens apparel: whence the whole Catholicke Church (as Alchuvinus, with others write) appointed a solemne publike fast upon this our New-yeares day,* (which fast it seemes is now forgotten) *to bewaile those heathenish Enterludes, sports, and lewd idolatrous practises which had beene used on it: prohibiting all Christians under paine of excommunication, from observing the Kalends or first of January (which wee now call New-yeares day) as holy, and from sending abroad New-yeares gifts upon it, (a custome now too frequent;) it being a meere relique of Paganisme and idolatry, derived from the heathen Romans feast of two-faced Janus; and a practise so execrable unto Christians,* that not onely the whole Catholicke Church; but even the 4 *famous Councels ... have positively prohibited the solemnization of New-yeares day, and and* [sic] *the sending abroad of New-yeares gifts, under an anathema & excommunication, as unbeseeming* Christians, *who should eternally abolish, not propagate, revive, or recontinue this pagan festivall, and heathenish ceremonie, which our God abhors.*[55]

———

The Monday after Twelfth Day, 6 January, is Plough Monday, which was when agricultural labourers returned to work and began four weeks of intensive ploughing. It was also known as St Distaff's or St Rock's Day, to mark when women started spinning again – both distaffs, which held the unspun wool, and rocks, which weighted the wheel, were used in early spinning.[56] Plough lights – candles kept burning in church to bless farmers – were lit from at least the fifteenth century and a common plough was sometimes kept in church and used when needed. By the fifteenth century this plough was being carried hither and thither as part of Plough Monday rituals – a customary practice that, like plough lights, embedded the community in the earth and that, also like plough lights, was prohibited by the Reformation. However, plough-carrying revived in the late eighteenth century as part of seasonal mumming, although by this time it seems to have had a more aggressive, radical, anti-Enclosure aspect. This mumming sometimes developed into the relatively sophisticated 'plough play' – more sophisticated, that is, than the 'hero combat' or St George dramas that characterize mummery at other times of the year. The plough play was based around wooing scenes between a lady and a farmer's man and then a fool, sometimes with the added complication of a recruiting officer. They seem to have been confined to the East Midlands – Lincolnshire, Nottinghamshire, Leicestershire, and Rutland – and date from about the 1820s, suggesting a possible political impulse behind them. The plough play was conceivably a covert response either to enlistment during the Napoleonic Wars of the previous decade, or to new farming practices: large, modern farms needed a new workforce of young farm workers, thereby denying work to older labourers.[57]

Plough Monday was followed by Straw Bear Tuesday in some parts of the country. This survives as a village festival in Cambridgeshire and Huntingdonshire, as well as in Grimsby in Lincolnshire, and features a 'straw bear' – a man completely wrapped in straw sheaves – dancing around the town. Attempts to ban the straw bear under begging laws in 1907 proved unsuccessful, but the practice seems to have declined around the time of the First World War. It was revived in Whittlesey in 1980 and now takes place on the Saturday before Plough Monday, and the straw costume is ceremonially burnt on the day after. In 1990 the localist arts and environment group Common Ground, which supports various arboreal customs, launched Tree-Dressing Day in London at this time of the year, a new festival to draw attention to individual trees in a locale.[58] Old New Year's Day, 13 January, coincided with the Feast of Fools, an event more associated with France and the Low Countries, but celebrated with enough vigour in Lincoln in 1236 and 1238 to be suppressed: according to Bishop Grosseteste, 'it was replete with vanity and foul voluptuosity'.[59] This day is also St Hilary's Day; the saint gives his name to the university Hilary Term, and his day is traditionally the coldest day of the year.

The Eve of St Agnes, patron saint of girls, 20 January, is perhaps the best-known night for love divination in the English festive calendar, due in part to Keats's poem 'The Eve of St Agnes':

> St. Agnes' Eve – Ah, bitter chill it was!
> The owl, for all his feathers, was a-cold;
> The hare limp'd trembling through the frozen grass,
> And silent was the flock in woolly fold:
> Numb were the Beadsman's fingers, while he told
> His rosary, and while his frosted breath,
> Like pious incense from a censer old,
> Seem'd taking flight for heaven, without a death,
> Past the sweet Virgin's picture, while his prayer he saith.[60]

Keats would have been familiar with the tradition if only from the Renaissance scholar Robert Burton's encyclopaedic *Anatomy of Melancholy*, first published in 1621:

> 'Tis their only desire, if it may be done by art, to see their husbands picture in a glasse, they'le give any thing to know when they shall be married, how many husbands they shall have, by *Cromnyomantia*, a kind of Divination with onions laid on the altar on Christmas Eve, or by fasting on St Annes Eve or night, to know who shall bee their first husband, or by *Amphitomantia*, by beans in a Cake, &c. to burne the same.[61]

There are, however, many variations of the rituals to be observed, which are, like most preparations for love divination, combinations of trifling mortifications of the flesh and sympathetic magic. Fasting for the evening was popular, as was taking a vow of silence, which was sometimes accompanied with the ritual making of 'dumb cake' to inspire dreams of a future husband. *Aristotle's Last Legacy: or, his Golden Cabinet of Secrets Opened, for Youth's Delightful Pastime* (1711) gives a highly elaborate set of instructions for St Agnes's Day itself, 21 January, in which sprigs of rosemary and thyme need to be urinated upon, then each laid in a shoe, before the same shoes are placed at the head of the bed and an incantation to the saint is repeated.[62]

A very different occasion was commemorated on 30 January: the martyrdom or execution – depending on one's politics – of Charles I in 1649. The feast of King Charles the Martyr was established at the Restoration in 1660 and ran until 1859; several churches were dedicated to him during this period. For nearly two centuries the day was observed as a fast day and pulpits were covered in black cloth, and since 1980 the day has been partially revived by the Anglican Church.[63] Republicans, on the other hand, celebrated 30 January by symbolically eating a calf's head and singing radical songs.[64]

FEBRUARY

Februarius is derived from *februa*, 'means of cleansing', referring to the Roman rituals of purification associated with the month. However, the archbishop of Seville, later St Isidore – the 'last scholar of the ancient world' – invented Februus, the pagan god of the underworld, in order to account for the origins of the name. It is certainly an ill-favoured month in weather lore, and despite being the shortest month, February is both notorious and valued for having the worst weather: 'All the months in the year curse a fair Februeer'.[65] Good weather on Candlemas, 2 February, meant that winter would be prolonged – weather prognostication at Candlemas was noted by John Skelton in 1523: 'How men were wonte for to discerne / By candlemes day, what wedder shuld holde'.[66] Rain is hoped for in February – without it, crops are in danger, for 'When it does not rain in *February*, there's neither good Grass nor good Rye'.[67] It can also snow, which is considered the sign of a good summer – 'Much February snow / a fine summer doth show' – but snow and ice in February are likely to persist.[68] A severe frost on St Matthias's Day, 24 February, will last several days: 'St. Matthias breaks the ice; if he finds none, he will make it'.[69]

Despite all this, the thrall of winter seems to be broken. Snowdrops traditionally appear around Candlemas:

> The snowdrop, in purest white array,
> First rears her head on Candlemas day.[70]

Cowslips and daffodils emerge around the feast of Peter's Chair, 22 February, which celebrates Christ's command to the apostle Peter, 'Feed my sheep'.[71] Such flowers are therefore named after Peter: the cowslip is Peterwort, and daffodils, in Welsh, *cennin Pedr* ('Peter's leeks'). St Matthias also 'sends sap into the tree' and 'shut[s] up the Bee'.[72] As Thomas Hardy wrote of this sylvan wisdom, addressing the birds and the crocuses in his poem 'The Year's Awakening', 'How do you know?'[73]

For Breton, February was a month when the natural world, from frogs to rooks, stirred; lambs were born, trees budded, and the sap rose. Fishmongers prepared for Lent – which begins in February when Easter is earlier than 17 April – but the weather was still very bad: 'the waters now alter the nature of their softnes, and the soft earth is made stony hard: The Ayre is sharp and piercing, and the winds blow cold: the Tavernes and the Innes seldome lack Guests'. It was 'the time of patience', with 'hope of a better time not farre off'.[74]

The novelist and nature writer Richard Jefferies also noted a rumpus among the rooks and a change in the water in his essay 'Out of Doors in February' (1885):

In the slow dull cold of winter even these noisy birds are quiet, and as the vast flocks pass over, night and morning, to and from the woods in which they roost, there is scarcely a sound. . . . But so soon as the waters begin to make a sound in February, running on the ditches and splashing over stones, the rooks commence the speeches and conversations which will continue till late into the following autumn.[75]

There is a sense of correspondence here between the chatter of the freshly thawed waters and the garrulous crowfolk, and a strong indication of a seasonal cycle: when the ice melts, the birds announce this change. In milder winters, however, there may be no ice, and therefore no such change. As a result, there is no sense that the year is about to begin again and an increasing apprehension about the approach of spring.

The sound of melting ice and running water is strongly associated with the break of spring as described by Jefferies. In another essay, 'Haunts of the Lapwing' (1885), he begins a passage on spring with its elusive mutter:

A soft sound of water moving among thousands of grass-blades – to the hearing it is as the sweetness of spring air to the scent. It is so faint and so diffused that the exact spot whence it issues cannot be discerned, yet it is distinct, and my footsteps are slower as I listen. Yonder, in the corners of the mead, the atmosphere is full of some ethereal vapour. The sunshine stays in the air there, as if the green hedges held the wind from brushing it away. Low and plaintive come the notes of a lapwing; the same notes, but tender with love.[76]

This in turn inspires Jefferies to challenge the traditional allegorical representations of winter and its associations with old age, decay, and death. He argues that it is rather a season of hope, not grim despair:

The withered leaf, the snowflake, the hedging bill that cuts and destroys, why these? Why not rather the dear larks for one? They fly in flocks, and amid the white expanse of snow (in the south) their pleasant twitter or call is heard as they sweep along seeking some grassy spot cleared by the wind. The lark, the bird of the light, is there in the bitter short days. Put the lark then for winter, a sign of hope, a certainty of summer. Put, too, the sheathed bud, for if you search the hedge you will find the buds there, on tree and bush, carefully wrapped around with the case which protects them as a cloak. Put, too, the sharp needles of the green corn; let the wind clear it of snow a little way, and show that under cold clod and colder snow the green thing pushes up, knowing that summer must come. Nothing despairs but man.[77]

It is a remarkable passage, keenly scrutinizing the season as it is, not the season that has been built from the strata of literature, folklore, and culture. There is a challenge here to rethink the landscape and the weather, to reconnect with the environment. Yet what does it mean today? The lark, Jefferies's 'sign of hope', is in drastic decline. Moreover, trees are budding earlier and the corn shows sooner, and so the idea of winter that Jefferies seeks to dispel has in fact all but disappeared. Jefferies's own winter has gone too, and his sweet vision has been replaced by an unearthly movement in which autumn seems to bleed into spring.

———

The first day of February is Candlemas Eve, traditionally the time to take down seasonal sprays of greenery to mark the season's change from Christmas to Easter, which has its own flora. The seventeenth-century traditionalist poet Robert Herrick's 'Ceremonies for Candlemasse Eve' advises as follows:

> Down with the Rosemary and Bayes,
> >   Down with the Mistelto;
> In stead of Holly now up-raise
> >   The greener Box (for show).

The Holly hitherto did sway;
    Let Box now domineere;
Untill the dancing Easter-day,
    Or Easters Eve appeare.

Then youthfull Box which now hath grace,
    Your houses to renew;
Grown old, surrender must his place,
    Unto the crisped Yew.

When Yew is out, then Birch comes in,
    And many flowers beside;
Both of a fresh, and fragrant kinne
    To honour Whitsontide.

Green Rushes then, and sweetest Bents,
    With cooler Oken boughs;
Come in for comely ornaments,
    To re-adorn the house.
Thus times do shift; each thing his turne do's hold;
New things succeed, as former things grow old.[78]

The superstition that not clearing the seasonal herbage would bring enough bad luck to cause a death in the family remained until the nineteenth century.

Candlemas, 2 February, is the day on which Mary visited the Temple, forty days, counting inclusively, after the birth of Christ, and is therefore also called the Purification of the Blessed Virgin; this meant that the image of the Blessed Virgin Mary could now be taken down in churches. Although purification and cleansing rituals have disappeared and 2 February is now known as the Presentation of the Lord, the popular name 'Candlemas', first recorded in 1014, still survives. The emphasis of the festival shifted to celebrate the growing powers of the sun, 2 February being midway between the winter solstice and the spring equinox. The name Candlemas perhaps comes from blessed candles being carried in procession, symbolic of Jesus' powers of spiritual illumination. The wax, it has been suggested, represents his earthly body, the wick his soul, and the flame his divine nature. The festival in this form was suppressed by the Reformation and declined after the 1540s, but the day also had agricultural significance: until the Enclosure Acts eradicated common land, Candlemas was the day on which Lammas meadows were fenced to keep them free of stock and bring on the hay, which was mown at Lammastide, 1 August. This attention to animal husbandry continued the day after Candlemas – St Blaise's Day. St Blaise, a fourth-century Armenian physician who in his *Life* describes attending to sick sheep, suffered as a martyr by being abraded with iron combs – hence he is a patron of flocks and in particular wool-carders. The parson James Woodforde describes a St Blaise procession held at Norwich on 24 March 1783 – Norfolk being a mainstay of wool production in the early modern period.[79]

Despite the singing of mistle thrushes and robins, mediaeval calendars record that the first day after winter on which birds sing was either 12 or 13 February, on which day, incidentally, Hell was made. This supposition is associated with St Valentine's Day, 14 February – there was a belief established by the fourteenth century that birds chose their mates on this day, and indeed tawny owl cries are at their loudest in February, when the birds are marking their territory.[80] There is a possibility that there was a shared tradition that St Valentine's Day was the first day of spring, which would also account for the birds' behaviour. John Lydgate applied the tradition to humankind in his early fifteenth-century poem 'A Valentine to Her that Excelleth All', as did Herrick in 'To his Valentine, on S. Valentine's Day' (1648):

> Oft have I heard both Youths and Virgins say,
> Birds chuse their Mates, and couple too, this day:
> But by their flight I never can divine,
> When I shall couple with my Valentine.[81]

There is some confusion over St Valentine himself: there were possibly two St Valentines martyred, but neither has a particular reason to be associated with birds, or with the coming of spring, or with lovers. In fact, in 1756 Alban Butler, in *Lives of the Fathers, Martyrs, and Other Principal Saints*, claimed that St Valentine's Day was linked to the Roman festival of cleansing and fertility, Lupercalia, which took place on 15 February.[82] During the Lupercalia, men would don wolf masks and loin-cloths and race through the streets flailing strips of goatskin. Any women seeking to fall pregnant would hope to be hit by the skins. This popular festival survived the Roman transition to Christianity, despite attempts to suppress it, although claims that link the Lupercalia with springtime customs are, as Butler's speculation suggests, a relatively recent invention. Nevertheless, Shakespeare's play *Julius Caesar* begins during the festival, so it would have been a familiar reference to Elizabethan and Jacobean theatre audiences in the seventeenth century.

Shakespeare also refers to the Eve of St Valentine, 13 February, in *Hamlet*. This is another potent time for divining true loves, and so adds a disturbing level of irony to a bawdy song sung by the deranged Ophelia, which begins:

> Tomorrow is Saint Valentine's day,
> > All in the morning betime,
> And I a maid at your window,
> > To be your Valentine.[83]

The French travel-writer Henri Misson noted the custom in 1698 among English couples on the eve of the day:

> An equal Number of Maids and Batchelors get together, each writes their true or some feign'd Name upon separate Billets, which they roll up, and draw by way of Lots, the Maids taking the Mens Billets, and the Men the Maids; so that each of the young Men lights upon a Girl that he calls his Valentine, and each of the Girls upon a young Man which she calls hers:

By this means each has two Valentines: but the Man sticks faster to the Valentine that is fallen to him, than to the Valentine to whom he is fallen. Fortune having thus divided the Company into so many Couples, the Valentines give Balls and Treats to their Mistresses, wear their Billets several Days upon their Bosoms or Sleeves, and this little Sport often ends in Love.[84]

Traditionally, then, Valentines were either chosen by lot on the preceding evening, or designated as the first person of the opposite sex one met on the morning of the day itself. From evidence in Pepys, who mentions the tradition of drawing lots and its consequences some two dozen times, this seems to have been a gentle social custom, but it was also an opportunity for domestic witchcraft in order to identify and seduce one's heart's desire.

The modish eighteenth-century writers George Colman and Bonnell Thornton wrote a paper on love charms in their periodical *The Connoisseur* (1755), which appraised divination techniques as various as reading coffee grounds and tea-leaves and even hairs in a shoe, fashioning little midsummer dolls that corresponded to a preferred union, and tying knots in a garter and sleeping with wedding cake under the pillow. On St Valentine's Eve in particular, their supposed informant, the lovestruck 'Arabella Whimsey', took five bay-leaves and pinned them to her pillow, ate a boiled egg full of salt before bedtime, took a vow of silence, and wrote her beloved's name on a billet, rolled it into a clay ball, and suspended it in water.[85]

The sending of paper Valentines dates from at least the sixteenth century in England, and in the nineteenth century Charles Lamb's 'Elia' essay on the subject (1819) recorded the shift from Valentine tokens to cards:

> this is the day on which those charming little missives, ycleped Valentines, cross and intercross each other at every street and turning. The weary and all forspent twopenny postman sinks beneath a load of delicate embarrassments, not his own.[86]

Anonymous gifts were also left for the beloved, as described by the poet John Clare in 'The Midsummer Cushion' (1832). There were other customs too: 'Valentining' was another children's begging pursuit, which involved going from house to house and reciting a nonsense rhyme in return for a donation, a practice also noted by Parson Woodforde; and there was an East Midlands cake tradition of 'valentine buns' in Leicestershire, Rutland, and Northamptonshire – they are also known as 'plum shuttles' since they are reminiscent in shape of a weaver's shuttle, and are essentially currant buns, sometimes with caraway seeds added.[87]

St Valentine's Day was inevitably commercialized and simplified in the Victorian age by the availability of printed cards, and the day's customs also feature as a plot device in Thomas Hardy's novel *Far from the Madding Crowd* (1874). However, by 1894, according to one journalist, it was felt that St Valentine's Day 'attracts very little attention nowadays in England, but across the Atlantic the Saint is still honoured'.[88] Cards continued to be furtively sent, but the whole folklore of St Valentine's Eve and Day was forgotten. In recent years, the American influence has reshaped Valentine's Day into a major money-spinner for any establishment that can host a candle-lit dinner, to which it is increasingly an obligation to take one's partner or spouse. But for those who want to get off the relationship merry-go-round and join a different sort of circus, Britain's travelling-fair season traditionally starts on St Valentine's Day.[89]

St Matthias's Day, 24 February, was the original leap day of the Julian calendar and was consequently counted twice every four years – the second date being the *bissextus* or the leap day. This later caused confusion over when St Matthias's Day should be celebrated. In the Middle Ages, St Matthias's Day was the sixth day before the Kalends of March, hence in leap years the feast day became 25 February, which meant that 24 February became the leap day, and this formulation was eventually stipulated in the Gregorian reform of 1582. In England mistakes were made in the Julian dating in both 1680 and 1684, prompting the archbishop of Canterbury to order that the date of 24 February be kept thereafter.[90]

Nowadays, of course, *dies mensis* (numerical dating) has completely replaced reckoning by kalends, nones, and ides, and consequently 29 February is leap day, which occurs every four years unless the year is divisible by 100 but not by 400. Since 1582 these Gregorian adjustments have been made in 1700, 1800, and 1900, and are next due in 2100. By convention, and law, 'leaplings', those born on 29 February, treat the 28th as their birthday, but those born on 1 March in a leap year gain no advantage – in other words, they would not come of age at sixteen on 29 February, but rather on 1 March. Leap Day is a traditional day on which women can ask for a hand in marriage in England. This seems to have at one time applied to the whole of the leap year – the playwright John Lyly notes in *The Maydes Metamorphosis* (1600), 'Maister be contented, this is leape yeare, / Women weare breetches, petticoats are deare' – but was subsequently reserved for Leap Day itself, either 24 or 29 February.[91] Traditionally, if a man refused such an offer, he had to pay a forfeit, such as buying the frustrated suitor a new dress.

So winter gets the benefit of the leap day, and every four years or so is a little longer. But this late in the season the anticipation of spring is strong, and so it is perhaps that season that really gains the day. For the dying moments of winter are the tidings of spring, brought on the winter wind. As Percy Shelley wrote in his 'Ode to the West Wind':

> The trumpet of a prophecy! O Wind,
> If Winter comes, can Spring be far behind?[92]

13 CHRISTMAS AND THE TWELVE DAYS

The twelfth day of Christmas, / My true love sent to me
Twelve lords a leaping, / Eleven ladies dancing,
Ten pipers piping, / Nine drummers drumming,
Eight maids a milking, / Seven swans a swimming,
Six geese a laying, / Five gold rings,
Four colley birds, / Three French hens,
Two turtle doves, and / A partridge in a pear-tree.

'The Twelve Days of Christmas', *Mirth Without Mischief*

Although Easter remains the major Christian festival, Christmas has developed an overwhelming popular appeal – particularly in England, where it is celebrated with huge relish and at vast expense. Christmas today is more a global capitalist enterprise than a Christian festival, and it is revealing that the paraphernalia required for a 'traditional' Christmas tend to be Victorian commodifications of the season rather than the materials of older customs that might not be packaged so readily and sold quite so conveniently. Some of Old Christmas does survive, however, and it might be worth reviving other elements to restore to us a celebration that is more mysterious, more humane, and less blandly commercial – and which reconnects us with the rich heritage of the nation's history.

Christmas developed surprisingly late in the sacred calendar. The festival that celebrates the birth of Jesus was initially only celebrated in the Eastern tradition, while the Western Church busied itself with discussing various dates for the anniversary. Eventually, after 250 years the Church of Rome adopted the solar festival of 25 December – the date chosen being the winter solstice of the Julian calendar, therefore emphasizing the profound terrestrial significance of Christ. In 274 the emperor Aurelian established this day as *dies natalis Solis Invicti*, 'the nativity of the Unconquerable Sun', although ironically by this time the Julian calendar had already slipped and so was no longer in co-ordination with the solar year.[1]

The festival gradually spread, although the name of 'Christmas' itself only became widespread in England after the Norman Conquest in 1066. Midwinter had been the Old English festival of the season, and Bede describes the winter solstice as *modranect*, from Mōðraniht, 'the Mothers'

Night'. This may have referred to making a seasonal cake, so Christmas cake is perhaps the oldest English Christmas tradition.[2] Moreover, the season was celebrated with a twelve-day feast known as 'Yule', a word which has its roots in ancient Germanic languages and which survives today in the tradition of the Yule log.[3]

With Christmas symbolically at the head of the solar year, the first twelve days, which included the 25th, were therefore treated as prophetic, predicting the weather and events of the following twelve months of the year. This prognostication also combined with days of the week, and as such this faith in forecasting remained well into the sixteenth century. The pseudonymous 'Godfridus', in *The Boke of Knowledge of Thynges Unknowen* (1554), detailed the Christmas-tide divination:

> Yf the Nativitie of our Lord come on Sonday, wynter shalbe good, Uer shall be windy, swete and hote, vintage shalbe good[,] Oxen wareth, Shepe shalbe multyplyed, Honny and Mylke, and all goodes shalbe plenteous. Olde men and women shal dye, peace, and accorde shall be in the lande. . . . Who that ben borne shalbe stronge, great and shynynge, Who that flyeth shalbe founde.
>
> . . .
>
> Yf it come on ye saturdaye wynter shalbe darke, snow be great, fruit shalbe plenteous[,] Uer shall be wyndy, sommer evyll, vyntage evyll by places[,] Otes shalbe dere, men shall waxe sycke, and bees shall dye. . . . theft done shall be founde, he that flyeth shal turne againe to his owne[,] they that is sycke shall longe wayle, and unneth they shall leape, that theyne shulde dye.[4]

Elsewhere in the kingdom, confidence in this system lasted for another two hundred years – the eighteenth-century naturalist and travel writer Thomas Pennant noted that in Scotland the weather for the next twelve months was anticipated in the twelve days from 31 December – and vestiges of the belief even remained into the nineteenth century: 'If Christmas day be bright and clear / there'll be two winters in the year'.[5]

Christmas Eve, or Christmas Night, is 24 December. This is Adam's Day, in anticipation of Christ. Midwinter mass is celebrated on 24 December, and many countries celebrate Christmas Eve in preference to Christmas Day. This is the night when horses and oxen knelt in their stalls and bees briefly emerged from hibernation to hum the Hundredth Psalm – another belief held as late as the nineteenth century.[6] In the seventeenth century there was no doubt of the piety of farm animals, which were consequently permitted to rest on the Sabbath – 'mercy and compassion is to be extended to the dumbe creature, that it may sometimes be spared, and have some rest from labour,' declared Edward Elton in 1648.[7] The corollary of this was that some 'simple-minded [and] conscientious' clergymen insisted that livestock should be made to observe fast days.[8] Like the Holy Thorn of Glastonbury's supposed coming into bloom on Old Christmas Day, the behaviour of devout farm animals at this time of the year could be interpreted as another indication that the Gregorian calendar reform was ungodly. Thus the eighteenth-century antiquarian John Brand noted the belief that the Old Style dating was carefully adhered to by livestock:

> A superstitious notion prevails in the western parts of Devonshire, that at twelve o'clock at night on Christmas Eve, the Oxen in their stalls are always found on their knees, as in an attitude of devotion; and that (which is more singular) since the alteration of the stile they continue to do this only on the Eve of old Christmas Day.[9]

Such convictions could lay one open to accusations more serious than whimsical superstition: in the sixteenth and seventeenth centuries, celebrating the flowering of the Holy Thorn at Christmas was regarded as an example of idolatry by zealous Puritans. But equally, all such phenomena were of interest to scholars and scientists, and the sixteenth-century alchemist and inventor Hugh Plat ingeniously argued that the seasonal bloom of the Holy Thorn was due to manuring the bush with 'a graine or two of the great Elixir applied to the roote': it was an exotic plant 'brought from such a climat, as where it did blossome at the same time of the yeere'.[10]

Christmas Eve was thought a safe time for fortune-telling because spirits and fairies were powerless, and love auguries at this time of the year were therefore particularly popular and powerful, and strongly associated with bringing Christmas greenery into the house, symbolic of renewal. This practice of decorating interiors with evergreen foliage has no evident pre-Christian or pagan background, and has been permitted by the Church in England from the seventh century, although for centuries these seasonal adornments only went up on Christmas Eve, never beforehand. Holly and ivy were favoured, and mistletoe emerged in the mid-seventeenth century as a popular ornamental wild plant, although it was deemed unlucky in some places.[11] The London chronicler John Stow recorded in 1598 that:

> Against the feast of Christmas every mans house, as also their parish churches, were decked with holme, Ivie, Bayes, and what soever the season of the yeare aforded to be greene: The Conduits and Standardes in the streetes were likewise garnished.[12]

This enthusiasm for decking the halls with greenery lasted well into the eighteenth century: 'the Rooms were embower'd with Holly, Ivy, Cyprus, Bays, Laurel and Misseltoe, and a bouncing *Christmas* Log in the Chimney, glowing like the Cheeks of a Country Milk-maid'.[13] Kissing games are alluded to in the fourteenth-century poem *Sir Gawain and the Green Knight*, but kissing under the mistletoe is a comparatively recent custom first recorded by the American novelist Washington Irving in *The Sketch Book* (1819–20).[14]

Burning the Yule log or ashen faggot was an almost universal tradition for at least three centuries. Thomas Dudley Fosbroke recorded that on Christmas Eve 'candles of uncommon size, called Christmas-candles, were lit up, and a log of wood, called a Yule-clog, or Christmas block, was laid upon the fire to illuminate the house, and, as it were, turn night into day'.[15] The remains of this log were kept as charms against fire and lightning, and as kindling to light the next year's Yule log. The poet Robert Herrick gives particulars in his 'Ceremonies for Christmasse' in his collection *Hesperides* (1648):

> Come, bring with a noise,
> My merrie merrie boyes,
> The Christmas Log to the firing;
> While my good Dame, she
> Bids ye all be free;
> And drink to your hearts desiring.

> With the last yeeres brand
> Light the new block, And
> For good successe in his spending,
> On your Psalteries play,
> That sweet luck may
> Come while the Log is a teending.[16]

The anthropologist James George Frazer suggests that this may be a relic of ancient oak-tree worship.[17] In fact, it could equally be interpreted as a celebration of St Boniface chopping down the sacred pagan oak of Thor in the eighth century. Or it may be neither. At Taunton in Somerset in the eighteenth and nineteenth centuries the custom of the Yule log was gentrified in the form of the Ashen Faggot Ball, the 'ashen faggot' being a local version of the Christmas log in the form of ash-tree sticks bound tightly together.[18] Of course, in today's centrally heated England the Yule log has been replaced by a chocolate log with red candles to signify flames.

As the great day drew near, church bells were rung and doors opened to 'welcome Christmas in', and in some parts of the country mummers and hobby-horses still roam about, paying unexpected visits to households – a lucky event.[19] Kent mummers retain the 'Hooden Horse', and in Derbyshire there is the 'Old Horse', as well as 'Old Tup' and the 'Derby Ram'. Stockings are hung up, and sherry and a mince pie left out. And then it is Christmas Day.

CHRISTMAS DAY

The earliest description of an English Christmas is probably the account given of King Arthur's court in *Sir Gawain and the Green Knight* (*c.*1340):

> This king lay at Camelot at Christmas-tide
> with many a lovely lord, lieges most noble,
> indeed of the Table Round all those tried brethren,
> amid merriment unmatched and mirth without care.
> There tourneyed many a time the trusty knights,
> and jousted full joyously these gentle lords;
> then to the court they came at carols to play.
> For there the feast was unfailing full fifteen days,
> with all meats and all mirth that men could devise,
> such gladness and gaiety as was glorious to hear,
> din of voices by day, and dancing by night;
> all happiness at the highest in halls and in bowers
> had the lords and the ladies, such as they loved most dearly.
> With all the bliss of this world they abode together,
> the knights most renowned after the name of Christ,
> and the ladies most lovely that ever life enjoyed,
> and he, king most courteous, who that court possessed.
> For all that folk so fair did in their first estate abide,
> > Under heaven the first in fame,
> > their king most high in pride;
> > it would now be hard to name
> > a troop in war so tried.[20]

Christmas in the mid-fourteenth century therefore consisted of merriment, sports of martial prowess, singing and dancing ('carols to play'), and feasting – all lasting just over a fortnight.[21] Seasonal mummers' or guisers' traditions developed, often in the north being based around sword-dancing – in fact, only Norfolk and Suffolk lack evidence of such traditions. Christmas Waits were groups of travelling musicians gathered for the season, and from at least 1300 to 'keep wassail' was the social custom of drinking the health of the assembled company. More formally, communal wassail bowls began and ended the season, and seasonal drinks such as 'lamb's wool' – hot ale, spices, sugar, roasted apples, possibly eggs and cream – were shared from Christmas Eve to Twelfth Night. The traditional toast was 'Wassail' – from the Old English '*wæs hail*', wishing health or good luck to your companions; to which the courteous reply was, unsurprisingly, '*drinc hail*' – 'Let us drink health' or 'Good luck'. This was the definitive Anglo-Saxon toast: Harold's army caroused with much wassailing and drink-hailing on the night before the Battle of Hastings.[22] Centuries later, these traditions continued to bind communities together by spreading good cheer.

The Lord of Misrule was also a Christmas tradition in large households, including the royal residence, and performances of Shakespeare's seasonal play *Twelfth Night* may have been framed by activities presided over by this master of the riots, who ruled from All-Hallows, 1 November, to Candlemas, 2 February. John Stow describes the scene in 1598:

> at Christmasse, there was in the Kinges house, wheresoever hee was lodged, a Lorde of misrule, or mayster of merie disporters, and the like had ye in the house of every noble man, of honor, or good worshippe, were he spirituall, or temporall. Amongst the which the Maior of *London*, and either of the shiriffe, had their severall Lordes of Misrule, ever contending without quarrell or offence, who should make the rarest pastimes to delight the beholders. These Lordes beginning their rule on Alhollon Eve, continued the same till the morrow after the Feast of the *Purification*, commonly called *Candlemas* day: In all which space there were fine and

subtle disguisinges, Maskes, and Mummeries, with playing at Cardes for Counters, Nayles and pointes, more for pastimes then for gaine.[23]

The Puritan Philip Stubbes was, predictably, enraged by such conduct:

But specially in Christmas tyme there is nothing els used but cards, dice[,] tables, masking, mumming, bowling, & such like fooleries: And the reason is, they think they have a commission and prerogative that time, to do what they lust, and to folow what vanitie they will. But (alas) do they thinke that they are privileged at that tyme, to do evill? . . . But what will thei say? Is it not Christmas? must we not be mery? truth it is: we ought both than, and at all tymes besides to be merie in the Lord, but not otherwyse, not to swil and gull more that time than at any other time, not to lavish foorth more at that time, than at another times.

But the true celebration of the Feast of christmas is, to meditat . . . uppon the incarnation and byrthe of Jesus Christ. . . .[24]

Stubbes and his fellow Puritans were extremists – yet they did succeed in abolishing Christmas for a few years, and they were able to do so because there is no scriptural authority for its celebration. Consequently, any festivities held after the Reformation at what was then known as 'Christ-tide' (thus avoiding the term 'mass' and its papist associations) occupied an ambiguous position in the sacred year. The Puritan polemicist William Prynne had in 1633 declared the use of decorative evergreens at Christmas to be idolatrous, and so following 'An Ordinance for Abolishing of Festivals' declared by Parliament on 8 June 1647, the Lord Mayor of London traversed the city in December of that year to pull down the holly and ivy of his citizens.[25] Despite this, the abolition of Christmas was resisted, and on 24 December 1652 Parliament was obliged to reiterate the prohibition. Still it continued: indeed, in 1657 the diarist John Evelyn was arrested in church on Christmas Day at gun-point for celebrating the Nativity.[26] The upshot of this suppression was that 'Old Father Christmas' promptly became a rallying figure for the Royalists, and so Christmas was eventually restored with and by Charles II in 1660.[27] Nonetheless, the Puritan settlers of New England managed to suppress Christmas well beyond the 1660s, and the effects of the Presbyterian Scottish Kirk are still felt today, centuries on. For years, Christmas was a normal working day in Scotland and the Scots referred to the English holiday as 'their Christmas'; even after Christmas became a bank holiday in Scotland in 1871, it was long considered as merely entertainment for children.

As it was, Christmas during the Restoration developed into a highly convivial affair in which the hierarchy of socializing was in inverse proportion to one's station: the gentry dined the poor first, and guests increased in social rank through the days of Christmas until eventually the lord and lady of the manor were dining with their equals. It was a mild and genial version of the Lord of Misrule tradition. This was also the case with the exchange of gifts in the period. As the French visitor Henri Misson put it in 1698, giving little treats was not so much a social custom observed 'from Friend to Friend, or from Equal to Equal, . . . as from Superior to Inferior'. He specifically notes that 'In the Taverns the Landlord gives Part of what is eaten and drank in his House that [Christmas Day] and the next two Days; for Instance, they reckon you for the Wine, and tell you there is nothing to pay for Bread, nor your Slice of *Westphalia*'.[28] This custom perhaps survives in the free pint that decent publicans still provide for their locals at Christmas lunchtime. The toast and salutation 'I pray god send you a merry christmas and a happy new year' seems to date from the late seventeenth century.[29]

Economic relations and social stability were reinforced by these customs: they had a clear political agenda following the Civil War and Commonwealth – there is even a hint of feudal responsibilities in such entertaining. But the social make-up of the country was already shifting to a more class-based metropolitan capitalism in which the quaint ties of an earlier age had no place, and despite its Restoration revival, the celebration of Christmas rapidly went into a 150-year decline. Christmas Waits, mummers' plays, and carol-singing seem to have continued, if somewhat fitfully: mumming was perhaps in part superseded by pantomimes, which were first performed as classical pastiches in England in 1717 and drew on both the European Harlequinade tradition and native mummers' plays, but carol-singing remained strong due to the huge English repertoire of delightful Christmas carols.[30] Pantomimes in fact grew greatly in popularity throughout the eighteenth century and so are still strongly associated with Christmas today. They are the accepted establishment face of the carnivalesque, consisting of unapologetically clichéd plots derived from a hotchpotch of time-honoured elements, contemporary pastiche, innuendo, and topical satire; they always include stock cross-gendered characters such as princes and dames and masquerading animals (arguably the cross-dressed figures and hobby-horses of tradition), and encourage riotous audience participation, heckling, and general disorder. They are of course great fun for children and adults alike.

From the earliest times in England, Christmas was also a time for seasonal feasting and domestic entertainments and games. Boar's head was the Christmas dinner par excellence, but until the nineteenth century most who could afford it dined on roast beef. Turkey was first imported from the New World in about 1530 and from the mid-sixteenth century was being reared in England; initially it appealed to those with exotic tastes, but by the eighteenth century it was already considered traditional by commentators such as the poet and playwright John Gay.[31] Goose was only for the poor, if they could find any birds left over from Michaelmas. Until the nineteenth century mince(d) pies had real meat in them; they were oblong and known as 'coffins' and eating them was lucky for the forthcoming year: 'As many mince pies as you taste at Christmas, so many happy months will you have'.[32] Plum pottage (or porridge) also contained meat until the end of the fifteenth century, thereafter suet. Rich and lavish fare was the watchword: 'Beef, Pudding, Plumb-Porridge, and Mince-Pies in abundance'.[33] In the early eighteenth century, 'Sirloins of Beef, the Minc'd-pyes, the Plumb-porridge, the Capons, Turkies, Geese, and Plumb-puddings' were consumed in quantity, and the household danced, sang, masqueraded, performed little dramas, and played blind-man's buff, puss in the corner (a kissing game), questions and commands (a truth or dare game), hide and hoop (hide and seek), as well as cards and dice.[34] As the evening wore on, members of the family would tell ghost stories, the 'curious memoirs of Old Father Christmas'.[35]

Christmas pie was a spiced meat pie of ox tongue, poultry, and game birds. The dish was described by Henri Misson: 'It is a great Nostrum the Composition of this Pasty; it is a most learned Mixture of Neats-tongues, Chicken, Eggs, Sugar, Raisins, Lemon and Orange Peel, various Kinds of Spicery, &c.'.[36] In 1769–70 Sir Henry Grey, the MP for Northumberland, made a vast Christmas pie from:

> 2 bushels of flour, 20 lbs. of butter, 4 geese, 2 turkies, 2 rabbits, 4 wild ducks, 2 woodcocks, 6 snipes, and 4 partridges; 2 neats' tongues, 2 curlews, 7 blackbirds, and 6 pigeons. . . . It was near nine feet in circumference at bottom, weighs about twelve stones, will take two men to present it to table; it is neatly fitted with a case, and four small wheels to facilitate its use to every guest that inclines to partake of its contents at table.[37]

Christmas cake, meanwhile, was usually reserved for Twelfth Night.

Despite the Christmas amusements and the sumptuous feasting, by 1807 the poet Robert Southey had just cause for complaint when he lamented that Christmas was not what it had once been.[38] Through the eighteenth century, Christmas was increasingly kept only as a religious holiday and a day on which quarterly rents were due. Rent could be received in kind – 'Wheat, Barley or Malt, Oxen, Calves, Sheep, Swine, Turkeys, Capons, Geese, and such like' – but there remained a considerable amount of accounting and book-keeping on the day, and this was common until well into the nineteenth century.[39] Within a generation, however, the season had been completely revived.

In the 1820s, a new Father Christmas emerged from New York, where he had been inspired by immigrant Dutch traditions of St Claas. England had had her Lords of Misrule – a 'Sir Christmas' is mentioned in the six-teenth century – and the figure of Old Father Christmas was enlisted as a defender of Royalist festive values against the repressive Commonwealth of the Puritans. But these archaic incarnations of Christmas as a carnivalesque figure bedecked with holly were superseded virtually overnight by the American Santa Claus. This seasonal personage was formulated in the poem 'A Visit from St. Nicholas', first published on 23 December 1823 in New York. It is perhaps better known as 'The Night Before Christmas', and describes Santa Claus as follows:

> He was dressed all in fur, from his head to his foot,
> And his clothes were all tarnished with ashes and soot;
> A bundle of Toys he had flung on his back,
> And he looked like a pedlar just opening his pack,
> His eyes – how they twinkled! his dimples how merry!
> His cheeks were like roses, his nose like a cherry!
> His droll little mouth was drawn up like a bow,
> And the beard of his chin was as white as the snow;
> The stump of a pipe he held tight in his teeth,
> And the smoke it encircled his head like a wreath;
> He had a broad face and a little round belly,
> That shook when he laughed, like a bowlfull of jelly.
> He was chubby and plump, a right jolly old elf,
> And I laughed when I saw him, in spite of myself,
> A wink of his eye and a twist of his head,
> Soon gave me to know I had nothing to dread.[40]

Santa Claus popularized the exchange of gifts at Christmas. Previously tenants had tended to give a goose to landlords at Michaelmas, a capon at Christmas, and some small present at New Year; but Santa Claus eclipsed all that by identifying Father Christmas with St Nicholas, patron saint of children. He was characterized by giving away toys, which were left in woollen stockings hung by the fireside. He is also, in this poem, tiny, elfish, sooty, and a smoker – pipe smoke was indeed a major feature of the earliest depictions of this 'St Nick', and in one of the immediate sources for 'The

Night Before Christmas' St Nicholas smokes a magic pipe and wreathes the countryside in hallucinatory smoke.[41] Old Father Christmas was thus wholly overtaken by Santa Claus, who gradually developed into a larger, more colourful, and more avuncular embodiment of the season – and, arguably, more representative of American commercial values. The most striking example of this transformation was the introduction of Santa's red robes and white fur trim. Earlier St Nicks and Old Father Xtmases had often been green to harmonize with winter decorations, or white for snow, or even a jolly shade of blue, and it was only after 1862 that he began to appear in a red coat in some illustrations. But it was a Coca-Cola advertising campaign in 1931 that effectively established his modern look. The drinks company restyled Santa's outfit to match the design of their own product, and now all depictions appear in the same red-and-white uniform.[42] And the trans-Atlantic and European influence on the English Christmas does not stop there: several favourite carols are American, such as 'Away in a Manger' and 'We Three Kings', while 'Silent Night' is Austrian.[43]

The tradition of decorated boughs for the English Christmas was revived in the nineteenth century but soon overtaken by the German Christmas tree tradition. It is possible that the custom of a decorated fir tree, like the Yule log, originates with St Boniface chopping down the pagan oak, after which a fir tree reputedly grew in its place, but seasonal fir trees were established in England in 1840 by Prince Albert, and popularized by an engraving of the royal family gathered around their tree in the 1848 Christmas supplement to the *Illustrated London News*; in fact, Queen Victoria had grown up with the tradition as her mother was German. Candles were originally used to light Christmas trees, but fairy lights are now more usually used; these decorations may also hint at the ancient celebration of *Sol Invictus*, the re-emergence of the sun, but they are really simply a way of brightening up the tree on long, dark evenings. Victorian decorations were genteel and elaborate – greenery was trimmed and ornamented with birds and berries – but their preparation could also be thrifty and resourceful: the *Girl's Own Paper* suggested dyeing peas red if there were no berries on one's holly, and even sprinkling Epsom salts onto wadding draped around the room to give the effect of hoar-frost (for more vigorous girls an alternative to using Epsom salts in this way was to crush old bottles under a garden roller and use the pulverized glass).[44] But soon there was, predictably, a healthy business in commercially produced baubles. Christmas was the only time that holly could be brought into the house, otherwise it was not only unlucky but potentially fatal to a family member; mistletoe, in contrast, was another way of foretelling among lovers and could bring dreams of a future spouse. Until 1860 it was usual to burn decorations, especially mistletoe, after Christmas, but a superstition against that also subsequently developed.

In 1843 Charles Dickens published A *Christmas Carol*, which contributed greatly to the popular image of Christmas, particularly of a white Christmas. In fact, the prevalence of snow at Christmas in Dickens's novels stems from his memories of childhood. Dickens was born in 1812, and the first decade of his life was the coldest decade since the 1680s, which was when the first proper frost fairs had begun. It snowed on Christmas Day on six out of the first nine years of the young Dickens's life, including 1816 – the 'Year Without a Summer' – and so inevitably memories of winters of snow and ice influenced his later writings. The characteristic seasonal weather of the ever-snowbound Dickensian winter is a sentimentalization of his childhood winters dating back to the 1810s – weather conditions caused in part by the volcanic explosion of Mount Tambora in 1815.

Coincidentally, in the same year that A *Christmas Carol* appeared, the first Christmas card was sent by the civil servant Henry Cole. Cole, who was to be instrumental in organizing the Great Exhibition and subsequently the foundation of the Victoria and Albert Museum, had worked with Rowland Hill on the penny post and commissioned John Calcott Horsley, a Royal Academician, to design the first seasonal Christmas card – published as a hand-coloured lithograph in 1843 at the costly price of one shilling.[45] Horsley's inaugural image depicted a family Christmas, but cards soon started using greenery, seasonal food, robins, and snow and ice as shorthand for winter, and therefore for Christmas itself.[46] The first Christmas crackers were also developed at around the same time by confectioners competing to make their bon-bons more appealing. Mottoes were included in the packaging, and then, around 1841, a 'snap' was added to sound when the wrapper was pulled off, allegedly inspired by a confectioner hearing a log crackling on the fire. Crackers subsequently developed through the nineteenth century, including party hats and small novelty gifts, and eventually adopting the now familiar tube design.[47]

The modern celebration of Christmas therefore owes much to Victoriana, from cards and crackers to trees and snow. What we have perhaps forgotten, though, is the charitable impulse of the nineteenth century: Victorian enthusiasm for Christmas was not simply fired by the runaway success of A Christmas Carol and the popularity of Prince Albert's festive tree, but by anxiety about the condition of the labouring classes and the possibility of giving direct financial aid to alleviate the sufferings of the poor. Consequently the ethos of the Victorian Christmas drew profoundly on the charitable lessons of a Church that was taking an increasingly decorative and traditional direction – one driven not only by the architectural Gothic Revival based on the recovery of mediaeval arts and crafts but also by its active recuperation of the calendar's liturgical detail in collections such as the poet-theologian John Keble's The Christian Year (1827), the best-selling poetical work of the century.[48] In that sense, then, the Victorian Christmas is almost a communal reparation for the years of Enclosure Acts, urbanization, and industrialization – a reinvention of seasonal customs and traditions now based around donations, alms, and charity boxes. In short, the Victorians restored humanity to Christmas.

THE TWELVE DAYS

The Council of Tours determined the duration of Christmas festivities in AD 567 as twelve days, a period during which no one should work, although these days most people finish their Christmas holiday by 2 January. Twelfth Day was technically the commemoration of the Magi, who visited Christ when he was two years old. In early representations the number of Magi visiting varies between two and four, but eventually a consensus was reached on three. Their thousand-strong retinue and accompanying army are usually left out of the story today. Not surprisingly, Twelfth Day is the traditional gift-giving day in some countries, but this never appears to have been the case in England. The Twelfth Day of Christmas is now reckoned to be 6 January, but in previous centuries 'Twelfth Night' meant the night before the Twelfth Day – in other words, the Twelfth Day's eve; after 1752 this coincided with Old Christmas Day and probably gave momentum to celebrating that date, which between 1753 and 1800 was 5 January. The sixth of January is also Epiphany – the day of Christ's baptism, which was adopted as a festival by the Western Church in the fifth or sixth centuries – and the beginning of Christ's forty days and forty nights' temptation by the Devil.[49] Until 1772, gambling at court was suspended for Christmas and renewed again come Epiphany.

Twelfth Night was also a major secular occasion for festivities until the Victorians reorganized Christmas, but today it is almost entirely eclipsed by New Year celebrations. Christmas carols were traditionally sung during the twelve days of Christmas and culminated in a play; nowadays carols virtually cease after Christmas Day itself, which – bearing in mind the wonderfully rich canon of English carols – is a great shame. Twelfth-night cakes had single beans or figures of Christ in them to bring luck or elevate the recipient to king (or queen) for the night, as mentioned by Herrick in 'Twelfe Night, or King and Queene'.[50] More elaborate games were also played in which various tokens were added to the cake to designate particular parts for the night – for example, a clove indicated who would play the knave. This harmless fun is mentioned by Pepys, who in 1666 found a clove in his portion, but rather than admit to the discovery, he spirited it away onto someone else's plate – a most knavish act in itself. Another variation was to designate character role-playing by billets inserted in the cake. The Victorians moved this tradition to Christmas Day by filling the plum pudding with charms, often of silver, and today coins are generally the preferred supplement to the dish.[51] Other seasonal cakes were jam puffs, which were triangular puff pastries filled with mincemeat

– the triangular shape corresponding to the Trinity. These treats were given by godparents on Twelfth Night and may have originated as Coventry God cakes. Similarly, in Nottinghamshire Twelfth Night was celebrated with a Southwell galette – a rich layered pastry.

The wassail bowl was also drunk during the twelve days of Christmas, sometimes as late as Old Twelfth Night (17 or 18 January) for the tradition of wassailing.[52] At its most simple, this custom involved sprinkling fruit trees with ale, hanging toast in the branches, and firing shots, as noted by Herrick:

> Wassaile the Trees, that they may beare,
> You many a Plum, and many a Peare:
> For more or lesse fruits they will bring,
> As you doe give them Wassailing.[53]

The ritual could become more involved. One account describes how the wassailers meet after dusk on Old Twelfth Night with lights, guns and horns, and cider. They gather around 'Apple Tree Man' – the most fruitful tree. Apple Tree Man is fed with cider or beer, and toast or cake is placed on its boughs to attract robins as the guardians of the orchard. The tree is showered with cider and wassailing songs are sung:

> Old apple tree, old apple tree,
> We've come to wassail thee,
> To bear and to bow apples enow,
> Hats full, caps full, three bushel bags full,
> Barn floors full and a little heap under the stairs.[54]

Wassailing was also an occasion for lighting bonfires. The *Gentleman's Magazine* for 1791 describes how

> On the eve of Twelfth-day, at the approach of evening, the farmers, their friends, servants, &c. all assemble, and near six o'clock, walk all

together to a field where wheat is growing. The highest part of the ground is always chosen, where 12 small fires and one large one are lighted up. The attendants, headed by the master of the family, pledge the company in old cyder, which circulates freely on these occasions. A circle is formed round the large fire, when a general shout and hallooing takes place, which you hear answered from all the villages and fields near; as I have myself counted 50 or 60 fires burning at the same time, which are generally placed on some eminence. This being finished, the company all return to the house, where the good housewife and her maids are preparing a good supper which on this occasion is very plentiful. A large cake is always provided with a hole in the middle.[55]

On Brough Holly Night a holly or ash branch was festooned with lit torches and paraded through the village of Brough in Westmorland, now Cumbria. Twelve fires were lit for the twelve apostles and the twelve days of Christmas, and to wassail the crops. The tradition lasted until the nineteenth century, by which time a whole flaming holly tree was carried, accompanied by a procession. John Aubrey recorded that seasonal cake – 'Twelve-cake' – and a wassail bowl were also traditionally shared among ploughmen.[56]

Some places in England do still celebrate the last day of Christmas, however. The Haxey Hood game is played on the Twelfth Day – or the day before if 6 January is a Sunday – by the villagers of Haxey and Westwoodside in Lincolnshire. This was first recorded in 1815, although legend has it that it began in the fourteenth century. It is essentially a ball game, the aim being to carry 'the hood', three feet of leather-covered rope, to one of four local pubs, but the Haxey Hood has some very curious features, including a Fool who is smoked in a fire, ten 'Boggins' dressed in red, and the Chief Boggin and the Lord who appear in hunting pink and decorated top hats. The Lord is the referee of the game, and the Boggins supervise it. What happens is that an immense scrum is formed around the hood, known as the 'sway', which over the course of several hours eventually makes its way to one of the pubs, whereby the hood is claimed by the landlord for the year and free drinks are provided.

For the rest, Twelfth Night is distinguished only as the last day by which Christmas decorations should be taken down, and can be seen as a way of containing the festive transition from Christmas to the New Year. Winter seems to be passing as the days grow noticeably longer: 'At twelfth-day the days are lengthened a Cock's-stride'.[57] Again, it was the Victorians who nominated Twelfth Night as the end of Christmas: in Herrick's day in the seventeenth century, the greenery would stay up until Candlemas, 2 February. But it was in the interest of nineteenth-century commercial society to get everyone back to work promptly. Today, decorations can go up alarmingly early – even in the first week of October – although there seems to be a common consent that after Bonfire Night is an appropriate time. But they also come down much earlier too. The season of Christmas-tide has, in other words, shifted forward as if it now expresses an impatient and premature desire for gratification. The result is that there are two cold months of winter following Christmas. It is a bleak time and there is little cheer, and spring seems far away – which perhaps accounts for the rising popularity of Valentine's Day. Nevertheless, the turning of the year is the first reminder of the life and hope of spring, despite the depths of winter and however distant that life and hope may seem. The seasons turn again, and we are, as Samuel Taylor Coleridge wrote while watching over his sleeping babe one frosty midnight, perpetually reminded of our place in the real world, in the experience and the culture of the weather:

> Therefore all seasons shall be sweet to thee,
> Whether the summer clothe the general earth
> With greenness, or the redbreast sit and sing
> Betwixt the tufts of snow on the bare branch
> Of mossy apple-tree, while the nigh thatch
> Smokes in the sun-thaw; whether the eave-drops fall

Heard only in the trances of the blast,
Or if the secret ministry of frost
Shall hang them up in silent icicles,
Quietly shining to the quiet Moon.[58]

14 PAST, PRESENT, AND FUTURE

And thus the whirlgig of Time brings in his revenges.
_____

William Shakespeare, *Twelfth Night*

Throughout the long history of the English festive year there has been a persistent tension on the one hand between the people who work the land and the culture that emerges from their local communities, and on the other those who are either visitors to the countryside or who actually own the land and impose on it their notions of what is to be done. As we now face bigger challenges – climate change, population growth, and our unerring ability to pollute ever greater areas and volumes of the planet and its atmosphere – it is my firm belief that culture can and must be enlisted in the defence of the environment.

Culture in this context can mean anything from, say, a familiarity with the English folk-ballad tradition – that extraordinary canon of songs of love and desire, of loss and death, with all their rich topical references to weather, flora, and fauna – to an understanding of how climate change and agri-business are threatening the survival of many of our native and migrant birds, which have been celebrated for generations as part of the panorama of the English seasons. And although it might appear to some as a woefully inadequate response in the face of the imminent 'ecopalypse', we should be learning those ballads – or at the very least going to hear them sung, since in doing so we reinvigorate them, and crucially ourselves, and restore the abiding sense of the history of our land. Likewise, we should also be watching those birds, if not necessarily with a twitcher's obsessiveness: we should make a point of marking and celebrating their presence in the landscape, and do everything we can to ensure that corncrakes and curlews, skylarks and song thrushes, cirl buntings and barn owls remain an integral part of the life of the countryside. We should be active agents in sustaining all this rich culture in all its precious abundance. The generations of verses, songs, and proverbial sayings that have been in different ways passed down to us represent the accumulated story of our relationship with the natural environment recorded over millennia. For better or worse, it is our natural heritage. But a sense of what is actually happening – the land as it now lies, the necessities of farming – is also imperative. We can use culture to promote the reinvention and redevelopment of that environment – to repossess it, if you will – by conserving, maintaining, reviving, and also inventing traditions that celebrate both the seasons and the calendrical year, and our place within them.

The worry, of course, is that we will be left only to grieve over what has been lost. The poet John Clare remembered on 25 October 1824:

> Old Shepherd Newman dyd this Morning an old tenant of the fields and the last of the old shepherds   the fields are now left desolate and his old haunts look like houses disinhabited   the fading woods seem mourning in the autumn wind   how often hath he seen the blue skye the green fields and woods and the seasons changes and now he sleeps unconscious of all   what a desolate mystery doth it leave round the living mind [1]

The implications of the death of Old Shepherd Newman are what this book is trying to prevent. Landscapes are not just physical spaces but layer upon layer of personal, local, and regional identity. And while it is obvious that not everything can be preserved, the secret is surely to remind ourselves of how we can dwell in a place and involve ourselves with it, both socially and practically. It is no longer good enough to spectate; we need, as I have said, to participate.

Take May Day, probably the richest English festival, but now falling into ruin and dereliction. Its cause has recently been taken up by anti-capitalist and anti-globalization groups in a 'Reclaim the Streets' campaign of guerrilla gardening. The Lions Part, meanwhile, is a drama group that runs an annual May pageant with elements that date back to the 1470s: as Sue Clifford and Angela King of Common Ground explain, 'The aim is to reintroduce celebrations of the seasons on urban streets as a way of connecting with the natural world'.[2]

My own contribution to this rehabilitation takes place the week before on a day that was later combined with Maying celebrations: William Shakespeare's traditional birthday, St George's Day, 23 April. I play the part of St George himself in chain-mail weighing some 40 pounds in a traditional pace-egging play, which has been performed in the village where I live for as long as anyone can remember, and yet which is never the same from one year to the next. The festivities may be different, but the message is mutual: the English people, just like the Scots or for that matter the French, need to share the rhythms of their festive year.

Much more could be said about ballads and birds and May Day, about how to fight for a new and revivified idea of the countryside – a countryside reconstructed by communities in order to make it a reality. But as I have suggested, the English countryside continues to be a landscape imagined and to a degree constructed by commercial interests and modern media.[3] Radio, telephone, television, and digital forms of communication have largely replaced writing and painting – and even gardening – as the means through which homogenizing urban standards are being imposed on the countryside. Although the land is still in parts surprisingly and gratifyingly unruly, the media have proved to be highly efficient as instruments of oppression, or at least of redefinition. The Archers, for example, first broadcast in 1950, has successively reinvented English rural life through a series of versions of the pastoral, from the incomer Lynda Snell's attempts to protect picturesque vermin to the affluent Nigel Pargetter's Poundbury-inspired and environmentally aware country estate.[4] The programme does balance such farcical meddling with the opinions of old-guard farmers and their dwindling agricultural labour force, but they speak as though they inhabit another world – which in a sense they do. So despite the working farms of Ambridge, the countryside is less significant in the national imagination as a means of production – of food and of livestock – than it is as a place of leisure and an opportunity for commercial development and colonization. It has become something to be consumed.[5]

But it is not only the content of neo-pastoral television and radio that encourages this perception of the countryside; the very form of the media is prejudiced against rural life. It was precisely through television and radio that urban culture became more and more dominant in the 1950s and 1960s, and as agricultural communities declined due to rural depopulation and mechanization, living in remote areas, according to the rural historian Jeremy Burchardt, 'no longer meant merely accepting a more limited rural culture in place of a more varied urban one, but accepting exclusion from national culture as a whole'.[6] Precisely the same thing is happening today as the media moves into new digital formats.

Rates of rural internet connection remain pedestrian and many areas still have no mobile-telephone reception – including my own village on Dartmoor. This not only limits the ability of those who still live and work full-time in the country to contribute to mainstream culture but also alienates them from it. In effect, this means that we now live in a country of two nations – not the familiar two nations of rich and poor, or of north and south, but of the urban centre and the rural periphery. Yet there are dangers and inherent contradictions here: the perception of the countryside as some sort of parkland in need of technological improvement brings with it unsavoury echoes of the history of Enclosure, the pastoral, and the picturesque. If satisfied, the demand for media connectivity may well risk annihilating what remains of local heritage and identity. We must tread carefully. Whatever happens, and however many mobile-telephone masts we do, or do not, erect, we need to cherish, and to succour, our rural culture at a grass-roots level.

We inhabit strange, contrary times. Just as the tendency to treat our countryside as merely a pleasant, problem-solving diversion from the stresses and strains of urban life has grown, so recognition and acknowledgement of the importance of our indigenous agriculture have diminished. It is not that the volume of food produced on our land has necessarily declined, although worryingly we now import an increasing amount of what we eat, but that capital investment in farming has cata-strophically decreased, as have both the percentage of the population working on the land and consequent government interest in agricultural affairs. (The department of state currently responsible for farming, DEFRA – the Department for Environment, Food and Rural Affairs – remains a byword for incompetence.) Indeed, there is very little awareness these days of what farming and countryside management actually entail, although paradoxically there is still plenty of intrusion from the state, just as there is from both well-meaning but often misguided do-gooders and unscrupu-lous speculators who buy up perfectly decent working land that has been farmed for generations by local people and then allow it to fall derelict – a practice equivalent to buying up accommodation during a housing shortage and allowing it to collapse, or purchasing a row of labour-ers' cottages in a still sustainable village community and knocking them together into one huge weekend residence. These are new forms of envi-ronmental vandalism – and they will destroy the integrity of the nation.

The late pioneer of restoration ecology Tony Bradshaw argued in the *Handbook of Ecological Restoration* that

> people from many different disciplines are likely to be involved in resto-ration, from the ecologist to the engineer, from the landscape architect to the community worker, and indeed from the politician to the ordinary person. Successful restoration can only be achieved if many different disciplines are involved in the process.[7]

It should be evident now that culture too must be a part of this process: it is integral to the conservation of landscape, wildlife, and resources because it explains how people have understood and managed the land-scape in the past, and therefore what their expectations of it are today. In the meantime, there are specific schemes that can help individual species and reform detrimental practices. The cirl bunting, red grouse and yel-lowhammer have, for example, all benefited as a result of such initiatives. There is a campaign to reform the Common Agricultural Policy (CAP) and decouple links between subsidies and quantity, thus ensuring that Single Farm Payments are paid however much or little is produced, provided that land is kept in 'agricultural order'. Other matters are also in urgent need of attention, among them the effects of pesticides, herbicides, rodenticides, and other forms of chemical farming, and the impact of high-yield agribusiness methods on flora and fauna, ecosystems, and the food chain.[8] The intention is not to return farming to some imagined golden age that has never existed, to stop autumn and winter sowing, or to limit access to the countryside, but to adapt the demands of farming to the need to preserve biodiversity, thereby guaranteeing that we have a countryside that is ultimately as sustainable, culturally and environmentally, as it is productive. In doing so, we will be restored to the living world. It is late in the day to do so but not, I hope, too late.

––––––––

Any account of the traditional festive year and the passing culture of the seasons could be criticized as mere nostalgia – a morbid affection for the remembrance of times past, an elegiac form of cultural genealogy, an unhealthy fascination with roots and origins; in short, a typical symptom of the English malady of melancholia. I could also be accused of being more sentimental than analytical in my attitude towards folk traditions. Yet even now those same traditions remain fluid as well as knowing and, sometimes, ironic. The festive calendar is diverse and often antithetical, always changing and perpetually reinvented, elusive and fugitive; I trust I have reflected as much.[9]

As by now must be apparent, I have my own agenda in writing this book: I want more people to join in local festivities. The authenticity of tradition does not reside in its antiquity, or in dutifully following an ancient template, or even in what day of the year or where precisely it takes place – although all these factors may be of interest to the academic. The authenticity of a particular custom lies simply in the fact that it happens.[10] Fifty years ago, the radical French thinker Guy Debord gave this warning about 'the society of the spectacle':

Although the present age presents itself as a series of frequently recurring festivities, it is an age that knows nothing of real festivals. The moments within cyclical time when members of a community joined together in a luxurious expenditure of life are impossible for a society that lacks both community and luxury. Its vulgarized pseudo-festivals are parodies of real dialogue and gift-giving; they may incite waves of excessive economic spending, but they lead to nothing but disillusionments, which can be compensated only by the promise of some new disillusion to come.... The reality of time has been replaced by the *publicity* of time.[11]

It is not hard today to grasp what Debord feared. Festivals – festivities, the 'luxurious expenditure of life' – are vital elements of human society, and never more so than in reaffirming our relationship with the natural environment. Our landscape and countryside have changed and are changing, and climate change threatens to alter them further in ways we cannot yet imagine. But what we think and feel about them, about the weather and the seasons, remain a colossal and inescapable part of what we have been, what we are now, and what we will become. And if we deny nature and our living relationship to it, we deny our deepest selves. R. S. Thomas, poet of the land and landscape, felt this keenly, and so should we all:

The rhythm of the seasons: wind and rain,
Dryness and heat, and then the wind again,
Always the wind, and rain that is the sadness
We ascribe to nature, who can feel nothing.
The redwings leave, making way for the swallows;
The swallows depart, the redwings are back once more.
But man remains summer and winter through,
Rooting in vain within his dwindling acre.[12]

NOTES

Particular use has been made of the following collections and studies of English folklore and calendrical customs:

Bonnie Blackburn and Leofranc Holford-Strevens, *The Oxford Book of Days* (2000).

Bonnie Blackburn and Leofranc Holford-Strevens, *The Oxford Companion to the Year: An Exploration of Calendar Customs and Time-Reckoning* (1999).

Sue Clifford and Angela King, *England in Particular: A Celebration of the Commonplace, the Local, the Vernacular and the Distinctive* (2006).

David Cressy, *Bonfires and Bells: National Memory and the Protestant Calendar in Elizabethan and Stuart England* (2004).

Duff Hart-Davis, *Fauna Britannica: The Practical Guide to Wild & Domestic Creatures of Britain* (2002).

Ronald Hutton, *The Rise and Fall of Merry England: The Ritual Year 1400–1700* (1994).

Ronald Hutton, *The Stations of the Sun: A History of the Ritual Year in Britain* (1996).

Iona Opie and Moira Tatem (eds), *A Dictionary of Superstitions* (1989).

Steve Roud, *The English Year: A Month-by-Month Guide to the Nation's Customs and Festivals, from May Day to Mischief Night* (2006).

Jacqueline Simpson and Steve Roud (eds), *A Dictionary of English Folklore* (2000).

A. R. Wright, *British Calendar Customs: England*, ed. T. E. Lones, 3 vols (1936–40).

Repeated references to these central texts are not included except where the authors or editors make specific interpretative points or are directly quoted, or occasionally as a matter of courtesy when broader points, such as proverbial sayings, are discussed in detail. Full bibliographical details are given below.

Foreword

1. Adapted from the last line of Milton's Sonnet XVI ('They also serve who only stand and wait'), ed. Carey (1971), 328.
2. A word from the wise: disguise is everything when it comes to bestial or cross-gendered impersonation – it moves the performance from pantomime to the 'uncanny'.

1 Introduction

1. Johnson (1761), i. 59 [Johnson's emphasis] (24 June 1758).
2. Hunt (1817), 801 and Hunt (1824), 37; see Roe (1997), 257–63.
3. See Friedrich Nietzsche, 'human art appears as a means to knowledge of nature, since nature itself is artistic creation': quoted by Hadot (2006), 297.

2 The Year

1. In Tusser (1557) the agricultural year commences in August.
2. See Blackburn and Holford-Stevens (1999), 739.
3. For a more contemporary take on these activities see Bennett (1993), 95–103. Interviewing her mother about the interwar years in Coreley village, Clee Hill, Bennett records Mrs W. L. remarking that:

> We didn't used to divide our year into

months, but more into seasons. . . . So you had the church festivals but on top of that we made our own seasons. Didn't used to talk about *months* . . . we talked about 'lambing time', 'haymaking time', 'cider time', and 'pigkilling time' (96).

4. Macrobius, trans. Davies (1969), 89–91 (bk I, chapters 12–13); see Feeney (2007).

5. Shakespeare, *Julius Caesar*, I. ii. 18. The rhyme emerged in nineteenth-century public schools as a useful aid to memory: see Ovid, ed. Pearce (1914), xxxi. There is also an earlier version in a popular but abstrusely convoluted book of mnemonics: Grey (1730), 94.

6. Suetonius, ed. and trans. Graves (2007), 'Divus Julius', para. 40, p. 19.

7. Duncan (1998), 50.

8. Pedersen (1983), 41.

9. Schaff and Wace (eds) (1900), 'On the Keeping of Easter', xiv. 55. See also St John Chrysostum, who commented on the ensuing 'hubbub' in the Church at Easter: Homily xxix, 'A Commentary on the Acts of the Apostles', Schaff, *et al.* (1980), xi. 186.

10. See Pedersen (1983), 17–74.

11. See North (1983), 75–113.

12. North (1983), 82–4.

13. Bacon, ed. Burke (1962), i. 301–2.

14. *Kalender of the Shepherdes* (c.1500).

15. North (1983), 97–9; however, Proverbio (1983) argues that Copernicus' role was limited: 129–34.

16. Duncan (1998), 251; see also 273–5.

17. Pedersen (1983), 62.

18. Butler (ed.) (1909), 513–35.

19. North (1983), 102–4.

20. Bodl., MS Ashmole 1789, folios 1–62: see Poole (1998), 48–59.

21. North (1983), 102–3; see Hughes and Larkin (eds) (1964–9), ii. 497–9.

22. There were occasional remarks on reform: John Greaves, professor of astronomy at Oxford, proposed a change in 1645, while the Puritan mathematician John Wallis strongly objected to any change that would bring the country into line with Catholic nations (*Philosophical Transactions*, xxi (1699),

356–9): see Hoskin (1983), 255–64; and Poole (1998).

23. Chesterfield, ed. Roberts (1992), 224 (18 March 1751, OS).

24. Chesterfield, ed. Roberts (1992), 223–4.

25. The duke of Newcastle advised against the measure: see Chesterfield (1777), i. 198; the Act was passed as 24 Geo. II, *c*.23.

26. This piece of apocryphal history derives from an engraving by William Hogarth, *An Election Entertainment*, which dramatized the Oxfordshire election of 1754 when Macclesfield stood for Parliament. Unlike most eighteenth-century elections, which were pre-arranged to avoid unnecessary conflict, this election was keenly contested. The Tories invoked the recent calendar reform, declaring 'So he like *Old Christmas* shall too be turned out' ('A New Ballad', *The Oxfordshire Contest* (1753), 56; see also a similar line in 'Another New Song', 20), while the Whigs responded with reminders of the supposed Catholic sympathies of many Tories: 'IN Seventeen Hundred and Fifty-three / The Style it was chang'd to P--p--y [i.e., 'Popery'] (*The Jew's Triumph, A Ballad* (1753), 3: quoted with variations by Poole (1998), 9; see also *The Old and New Interest* (1753), 42). This is the origin of the 'Give us back the eleven days we were robbed of', which appears on a discarded placard in Hogarth's illustration. Poole confirms that there were no calendar riots; the riots at the time were against the naturalization of Jews (1–16, 102–19, 136–50); see also Gingerich (1983), 265–79; and Dagnall (1991).

27. See Thompson (1993), 352–403; see also Bushaway (1982).

28. See Mullan and Reid (eds) (2000), 214–36, collecting much of this material; Poole (1998), 129; the New Forest information was reported in *The Salisbury Journal*, 15 January 1753.

29. *The London Magazine: or, Gentleman's Monthly Intelligencer* (1752), 487.

30. Quoted by Poole (1998), 129.

31. Cowper (1800), i. 312 (lines 8–9).

32. Leather (1912), 95.

33. *All the Year Round: A Weekly Journal* (1875), 29.

34. See Russo (1983), 287–97.

3 Months and Days

1. The Stevins Manuscript (sometimes misspelled 'Stevens') is BL, Sloane MS 261; the rhyme is at fol. 17r [Sloane's foliation].

2. Grafton's text is titled 'A rule to knowe how many *dayes euery Moneth in the yere hath*', part of a kalendar prefaced to his *Abridgement* (1570), sig. 1 ¶ iv. There is a sophisticated variation in Irish (1701): 'Thirty days hath *November, April, June*, and *September*, / All the rest have Thirty one, except *February* alone, / Which always has but Twenty Eight days here, / When it is not *Bissextile* or *Leap-Year*' (78). An earlier, rudimentary version of the rhyme is noted by Blackburn and Holford-Stevens (1999), 564, from BL Harley MS 2341, fol. 5r.

3. Tusser (1557), D1r–v.

4. This is a skit on the French revolutionaries' 'calendar of reason', in which the months were renamed *Vendémaire, Brumaire, Frimaire, Nivôse, Pluviôse, Ventôse, Germinal, Floréal, Prairial, Messidor, Thermidor*, and *Fructidor*: see Gingerich (1983), 274. Most of these words are of course 'nonce' words.

5. Flanders and Swann (1960) parody Sara Coleridge's 'January Brings the Snow' (1834); Wendy Cope, 'The English Weather', from *Serious Concerns* (London: Faber & Faber, 1992).

6. Shakespeare, *As You Like It*, IV. i. 147–9.

7. See, for example, Ashton (1959) and Mingay (ed.) (1981).

8. See Baker (ed.) (1854), i. 181–2.

9. Baker (ed.) (1854), i. 246, ii. 152, 203.

10. Baker (ed.) (1854), ii. 203, 295, i. 138.

11. Shakespeare, *The Winter's Tale*, IV. iii. 32.

12. See Thomas (1971), 384; see also Harley (1885) and Petherwick (2010). The moon had various curative and protective qualities: women being 'churched' (blessed after childbirth) traditionally called for protection from the sun and moon, and indeed women are advised that it is traditional to curtsey before the new moon, declaring 'Yonder's the Moon, God save her grace'.

13. See, for example, Goad (1686), 17.

14. It is, however, possible that King Edwin of Northumbria had an astrological military adviser: see Thomas (1971), 301.

15. Ovason (2005), 95.

16. Thomas (1971), 285.

17. Dickens, ed. Tambling (2004), 452. See also the death of Falstaff in Shakespeare, *Henry V*, II. iii. 13: 'ev'n at the turning o' th' tide'; and Goad (1686), 17. Thomas (1971) notes that the condition of the tide at the time of death was recorded in at least one Elizabethan parish register (334).

18. Goad (1686): 'this must not be look'd upon as a *superstitious* Doctrine ... especially when our Age hath been taught that our *Blood circulates in our Body every twenty four hours*' (17).

19. Raleigh (1628), 12 (see Thomas (1971), 333, and Tillyard (1948), 51).

20. Thomas (1971), 383–4.

21. Hooper, ed. Carr (1843), 333.

22. Stubbes [1583], ed. Furnivall (1877–82), ii. 58, 61 [renumbered after first part].

23. See Blagden (1958), 107–16 and Capp (1979); see also Fox (2000) and Jensen (2008), 64–114. Henry Season edited *Speculum anni* from 1733–74; it was taken over by Thomas Wright on Season's death and in 1798 was into its sixty-fifth impression (*Oxford Dictionary of National Biography*).

24. Campbell (1743).

25. 'Poor Robin' (1664), A6r.

26. 'Poor Robin' (1702), C3r: this of course quotes from Shakespeare, *Othello*, II. i. 109–12.

27. 'Poor Robin' (1702), C8r.

28. 'Poor Robin' (1702), C6v.

29. Swift, ed. Greenbank and Piper (1973), 'Predictions for the Year 1708', 426–33; 'The Accomplishment of the First of Mr. Bickerstaff's Predictions', 434–6; and 'A Vindication of Isaac Bickerstaff', 436–41.

30. *Gentleman's Magazine* (1826), 64. The anonymous 'Prognostications of the Weather'

(1844), 154–9, attribute these verses to Erasmus Darwin; however, the *Gentleman's Magazine* and Steinmetz (1866) attributes them to 'Dr Jenner' (141).

31. Ashton (1959), 4–8.

32. Merle, ed. Symons (1891). The manuscripts of Merle's other two works, *De pronosticatione aeris* and *De futura temperie aeris pronosticanda*, are held in the Bodleian Library and remain unpublished: see ODNB.

33. Josselin, ed. Macfarlane (1977), 125. Three centuries on, such fundamentalist readings of the weather were still about: G. F. Vallance privately printed *The War[,] The Weather & God* in about 1942, attributing the miracle of the Dunkirk evacuation to a National Prayer Day that had ensured that God set the weather fair; other divine meteorological interventions were apparent in the historical defeat of the Spanish Armada, and the more recent halt of the German field marshal Erwin Rommel (7–50).

34. Hooke (1702), 173–9; see Ashton (1959), 2.

35. Jones (ed.) (1759), iv. pt II. 49.

36. St Benedict, trans. Parry (1990), 30.

37. Jones (2007), 15.

38. Quoted by Lapidge, 'The Saintly Life in Anglo-Saxon England', in Godden and Lapidge (eds), 243–63, 248; see Jones, ed. Stevens (1994).

39. Tusser (1557), CIV.

40. Shakespeare, *Henry V*, IV. iii. 40–60.

41. See Best, ed. Robinson (1857). Best's calendar is structured through saints' days:

> The usuall saying is, 'ATT ST. LUKE, LET EWE GOE TO TUPPE;' which is aboute the eighteenth of October; but wee, that have succour for our lambes, finde the most ease and profitte in forward and timely lambes, and therefore doe wee putte our tuppes to our ewes aboute Michaellmasse, or howsoever within a weeke after, and att that time allsoe doe wee give our sheepe freshe stubbles.

The remark is footnoted with another North of England saying, 'On St. Luke's day / Let the tup have his play' (27).

42. Ehrenreich (2007), 78.

43. Shakespeare, *The Merchant of Venice*, II. v. 28–33.

44. Ehrenreich (2007), 17.

45. Hutton (1994), 65; see also Cawte (1993), 37–56.

46. Ehrenreich (2007) argues that Europeans associated collective ecstasy with the barbarian 'Other' (9).

47. Thompson (1993), 21; see also Stallybrass and White (1986):

> In the long-term history from the 17th to the 20th century … there were literally thousands of acts of legislation introduced which attempted to eliminate carnival and popular festivity from European life.... Everywhere, against the periodic revival of local festivity and occasional reversals, a fundamental ritual order of western culture came under attack – its feasting, violence, processions, fairs, wakes, rowdy spectacle and outrageous clamour were subject to surveillance and repressive control. (176)

48. Weber, trans. Parsons (1958), 168; see Duffy (1992), especially 11–52.

49. Quoted by Ekrich (2005), 152.

50. Hill (1964), 121.

51. Ehrenreich (2007), 100.

52. Thompson (1993), 47: see Malcolmson (1973), 71.

53. See Darby (2004), 41–6.

54. Thompson (1993), 68.

55. Twycross (ed.) (1996), 20.

4 The Weather

1. Watts (1999), 38–9.

2. Stirling (1997), 3–4.

3. Mumbai (Bombay) has an annual average rainfall of 1809 mm (71.2 in), London has an annual average rainfall of 599 mm (23.6 in).

4. See the rainfall table in Stirling (1997), 51; notwithstanding this, April 2012 was the wettest on record.

5. Inwards (1893), 94.

6. Howard (1865), 2; see Hamblyn (2001) and Pretor-Pinney (2007).

7. Matt. 16: 2–3.

8. See Young's *Literal Translation of the Bible* (1898), which confirms the antiquity of the saying.

9. Gen. 1: 14; 2: 6; 3: 23.

10. Rev. 22: 2. Likewise, arrival in the 'Celtic' Earthly Paradise is marked by a 'warbling of unknown birds' and by a shift in the seasons: 'it is winter with us in our land now, and it is summer here in this land' (Jackson (ed.) (1971), no. 145 (p. 176), from O'Grady (1892), I, 346–7).

11. Gen. 3: 18–19; 41: 29–57; 7: 21, 4; 8: 22.

12. Deut. 28: 12.

13. Gen. 19: 16, 24; Exod. 9: 18–34.

14. Luke 24: 45; see also Matt. 27: 51; Rev. 6: 12–14; see also 11: 19.

15. John 3: 8.

16. Calvin, trans. King (1948), i. 177.

17. 'Pseudo-Defoe' (1704), 180: letter from one 'Frist. Chave'.

18. Milton, ed. Fowler (1967), bk X, lines 651–6.

19. Milton, ed. Fowler (1967), bk X, lines 677–80.

20. For the springtime before the Fall, see bk IV, line 268; for the coming of spring on other worlds, see bk VIII, lines 144–8; for the role of the Graces in the spring, see Wind (1958), 101, in which the dance of the Graces reflects natural rhythms.

21. For the classical account of the seasons beginning in the Silver Age (under Zeus), see Ovid, ed. Kenney (2008), bk I, lines 116–24.

22. See Aristotle, trans. Lee (1952), I. vii. 344a (p. 49).

23. For an alternative taxonomy, see Bacon, trans. R. G. (1671), 6–7.

24. Grant (2007), 95.

25. See Watts (2007), 17.

26. Lucretius Carus, trans. Geer (1965), lines 98–124. Theophrastus also studied thunder and concluded that it came from clouds crashing together and was therefore a random phenomenon.

27. See Rochester's unfinished attempt to translate *De rerum natura*: Rochester, ed. Vieth (1968), 34–5.

28. Aristotle's theories were developed by Seneca, whose *Natural Questions* was inspired in part by Aristotle's *Meteorologica*, via Posidonius' work on meteorology, and *On the Heavens*, and which considered comets, meteors, rainbows, thunder, and lightning, as well as earthquakes: see Grant (2007), 96.

29. Themon Judaeus, *Questions on the Four Books of Aristotle's Meteors*: see Grant (1974), 207–8.

30. Fulke (1571), folios 18r, 19r [contractions expanded].

31. Bacon, trans. R. G. (1671), 18.

32. Bacon, trans. R. G. (1671), 3.

33. Burnet (1684); Janković (2000), 29; see also Boia, trans. Leverdier (2005).

34. Janković (2000), 47–50; see Childrey (1661); 'R. B.' (1684); Whiston (1696); and the Royal Society papers in Jones (ed.) (1759) and in Sprat (1702).

35. Short (1749).

36. See Laurentius, ed. Larkey (1938), 104, 96.

37. See Spitzer (1963).

38. Aston (1996), 216–17.

39. Foucault (1970), 17.

40. Oswald Crollius, *Traité des signatures*: quoted by Foucault (1970), 27.

41. 'Hedgehogs, swallows, owls, cattle and cats, all gave out signs of a future change in the weather' (Thomas (1971), 75): Thomas quotes, among others, Swainson (1873), 228–57; Markham (1635), 11; Patrick, ed. Taylor (1858), viii. 636.

42. Shakespeare, *Macbeth*, IV. i. 1–2.

43. Shakespeare, *Richard III*, I. i. 1–4.

44. Shakespeare, *The Tempest*, II. ii. 1–2.

45. Shakespeare, *Hamlet*, I. ii. 129–30; I depart from the Riverside reading here of 'sallied' for 'solid': see Mazzio (2009), 153–96.

46. *Hamlet*, III. ii. 376–82.

47. Shakespeare, *Antony and Cleopatra*, IV. xiv. 2–8.

48. More (1655), 66.

49. Sterne, ed. Petric (1986), 89.

50. Keats, ed. Garrod (1982), 423.

51. The Romantic reception of Shakespearean weather is noted briefly by Reed (1983), 19–20n.

52. Quoted from Wordsworth, 'Lines Written a Few Miles above Tintern Abbey', Wordsworth and Coleridge, ed. Brett and Jones (1991), lines 101–3 (p. 116).

5 Spring

1. Spenser, ed. Hamilton (1977), bk VII, canto vii, st. 28.

2. White, ed. Greenoak (1986–9), i. 242.

3. Jones (2007), 181.

4. Jefferies, 'Out of Doors in February' (2008), 188. Jefferies may be alluding to Laurence Sterne's memorable line, 'God tempers the wind ... to the shorn lamb' in A Sentimental Journey, ed. Jack and Parnell (2003), 96.

5. Shakespeare, As You Like It, V. iii. 16–21.

6. Tennyson, ed. Ricks (1987), lines 17–20 (vol ii, p. 121).

7. Howard, 'Description of Spring, wherin eche thing renewes, save onely the lover' (1557), B2v.

8. Herrick, 'To Violets', ed. Moorman (1947), 83.

9. Herbert, ed. Wilcox (2007), 316.

10. Sweet [sweat]: life-blood, to lose one's life-blood (OED).

11. Breton (1626), B4v–C1r.

12. Spenser, ed. Hamilton (1977), bk VII, canto vii, st. 32.

13. Most folklorists erroneously give the source of Aubrey's remarks as Remaines of Gentilisme and Judaisme, first published 1881: in fact, they derive from The Natural History of Wiltshire, ed. Britton (1847), 51 (a variant 'raisins' is also offered by the editor, Britton).

14. Quoted by Blackburn and Holford-Strevens (1999), 100.

15. Tolkien (2005), 1106 (Appendix D).

16. A version, omitting March, is recorded in the beautifully printed English Irish Dictionary (1732), 34. Likewise, Ray has many March sayings, such as: 'March grass never did any good. / March wind and May sun, make clothes white and maids dun. / March many weathers.' Ray (1737) also gives 'April showers bring forth May flowers' (34). Coupling March winds with April showers would appear therefore to be of a later date.

17. Wright, ed. Lones (1936–40), ii. 159. Chad (Ceadda, d. 672) was the first bishop of Mercia and Lindsey, and patron saint of medicinal springs – his feast day is 2 March. See also Sts David and Chad Days gardening advice in 'Poor Robin' (1684), A7v.

18. See Ray (1670), 41.

19. 'J. S.' (1765?), 25. This is another problematic reference: Peacock (1853), 50, quotes Thomas Passenger, The Shepherd's Kalender (London, c.1680), a book that appears not to exist. It is worth considering Lisle (1757), 119, which ponders the March weather and its effect on crops, but Lisle does not do so in this divinatory way. Consequently, 'J. S.' is the authority here; one must hope that earlier editions of his Shepherd's Kalender are found. Roud (2006), while accepting Passenger's Shepherd's Kalendar, also usefully quotes a proverb with exactly the opposite advice (77).

20. Beaumont and Fletcher, A Wife for a Moneth (1624; first published in Comedies and Tragedies (1647), 6G2r (II. i. 34–40, p. 51 [pages numbered from The Queene of Corinth]):

> Menallo. I would chuse March, for I would come in like a Lion.
>
> Tony. But you'ld go out like a Lamb, when you went to hanging.
>
> Camillo. I would take April, take the sweet o' th' year.
> And kisse my wench upon the tender flowrets,
> Tumble on every Greene, and as the birds sung,
> Embrace and melt away my soul in pleasure.
>
> Tony. You would go a Maying gaily to the gallowes.

See too Ray (1670), 41: 'March hack ham comes in like a lion, goes out like a lamb'; 'hackande' means 'annoying'.

21. Erasmus, trans. Udall (1542), fol. 237v [contractions expanded].

22. Shakespeare, 1 *Henry IV*, V. ii. 19; 'Lewis Carroll' [Charles Dodgson], ed. Haughton (1998), 58. For more on hares, see Evans and Thomson (1987, 1994).

23. Quoted by Clifford and King (2006), 218.

24. See Isobel Gowdie, ODNB.

25. Shakespeare, *Henry V*, IV. vii. 97–105, V. i. 21–79; Henry was born in Monmouth and as heir to the throne was made Prince of Wales.

26. Schellinks, ed. Exwood and Lehmann (1993), 75 (1 March 1662, OS).

27. Pepys, ed. Warrington (1953), ii. 418 (1 March 1667, OS). Several commentators quote lines supposedly from *Poor Robin's Almanack* for 1757: 'But it would make a stranger laugh / To see th' English hang poor Taff; A pair of breeches and a coat, / Hat, shoes and stockings. And what not; / All stuffed with hay to represent / The Cambrian hero thereby meant; / With sword sometimes three inches broad, / And other armour made of wood, / They drag hur to some publick tree, / And hang hur up in effigy.' The source of this reference appears to be Hone, *The Every-Day Book* (1828), i. 161 [as quoted]; Hone possibly found the lines in *Time's Telescope*, an early nineteenth-century almanac, but they do not occur in extant eighteenth-century almanacs. There is mention in 'Poor Robin' (1682): 'March. The first Day wear green Leeks, if thou beest the Off-spring of the ancient *Britains*, in honour of that great Hero St. *Taffy*' (C5r); see also 'Poor Robin' (1674), A7r.

28. See e.g. Cole (2007), 47; Hutton (1996), 174–7 and (1994), 20.

29. Herrick, 'To Dianeme. A Ceremonie in Gloucester': 'I'le to thee a Simnell bring, / 'Gainst thou go'st a *mothering*, / So that, when she blesseth thee, / Half that blessing thou'lt give me' (ed. Moorman (1947), 232). A simnel cake was either a bread bun made from very fine flour, or a currant cake (OED). Herrick, incidentally, had the following pets: a cat, a spaniel, a lamb, a sparrow, and a pig; the pig could drink beer out of a tankard (Thomas (1983), 118, citing Sells (1955), 96–100).

30. Ray (1737), 270; Ray (1670), 43. The advice for St Chad is sometimes conflated with and corrupted with advice for rearing geese: 'Before St. *Chad* every goose lays good and bad' (Ray (1737), 39).

31. See Groom (2006), 55–6.

32. Tusser, 'Februaries husbandrie' (1580), fol. 37r. Tusser also recommends lunar planting for peas and beans in the succeeding stanza, the waning moon being the optimum time to do so.

33. Ray (1737), 40.

34. Lean (1902–4), i. 377.

35. Cameron (1998), 51; Lady Day at Axbridge was also the tanning fair (see 143).

36. This has implications for later dates: for example, if the Crucifixion was reckoned to have taken place on 25 March AD 29, then Ascension Day would fall on 5 May.

37. Ælfric, ed. Clemoes (1997), 229.

38. In other traditions, such as the Gaulish and Alexandrian, 17 March was the date on which Eve was seduced by the serpent, followed by Adam's primal sin on 18 March. And 17 March was also the anniversary of Noah boarding the ark; he disembarked on 29 April.

39. Breton (1626), C1v.

40. Chaucer 'General Prologue', ed. Robinson (1974), lines 1–12.

41. Breton (1626) describes the effect on the young: 'the youthfull cheeks are as red as a cherry'; to be 'chuffed' is literally to have rosy red cheeks (C1v).

42. Tusser (1573), fol. 44r; see also Ray (1670), 41: 'April showers bring forth May flowers'. While writing this book, I visited Okehampton Show and saw an embroidered sampler quoting the proverb in the Women's Institute craft tent. See above, n. 16.

43. Shakespeare, *Antony and Cleopatra*, III. ii. 43–4.

44. 'Poor Robin' (1672) has 'April's a fickle month, now it doth rain. / Then clears, soon showers, and strait sun shines again / Just

like unto a woman, who doth lowre, / And laugh, and cry, and all in half an hour' [italics reversed] (A7r); the account of the quarter of spring here is derived from Breton (1626), B3r.

45. Clare, 'The days of April', ed. Robinson and Summerfield (1964), 214; 'pilewort' was indeed used to treat haemorrhoids.

46. Clare, 'Larks and Spring', ed. Robinson and Powell (2004), 372.

47. Shakespeare, Sonnet 98 (p. 1767); Shakespeare, *Romeo and Juliet*, I. ii. 27.

48. Shakespeare, *The Two Gentlemen of Verona*, I. iii. 84–7.

49. Pope to John Caryll, July 1713: quoted by Mack (1985), 232.

50. Coleridge, 'Dejection: An Ode (Written April 4, 1802)', ed. Beer (1983), lines 104–7 (p. 282).

51. Coleridge, 'Christabel', ed. Beer (1983), lines 16–22 (p. 195).

52. Keats, 'Ode on Melancholy', ed. Garrod (1982), lines 11–14 (p. 220). Keats also wrote of 'chilly finger'd Spring' in *Endymion*: 'their smiles, / Wan as primroses gather'd at midnight / By chilly finger'd Spring' (bk IV, 969–71, p. 156).

53. See Reed (1983), 218–20.

54. Coleridge, 'The Rime of the Ancient Mariner', ed. Beer (1983), line 268 (p. 180).

55. Eliot, *The Waste Land* (1969), line 1 (p. 61). When in India Rudyard Kipling thought of the English spring, he wished for a more desolate season: 'I am sick of endless sunshine, sick of blossom-burdened bough. / Give me back the leafless woodlands where the winds of Springtime range – / Give me back one day in England, for it's Spring in England now!' (Kipling, ed. Jones (2001), 83).

56. Browning, 'Home-Thoughts, from Abroad', ed. Jack, *et al.* (1991), lines 1–8 (vol. iv, p. 63).

57. Waterhouse (2004), 58. Sir Edward, Viscount Grey, noted 5 February as a date for chaffinches; Grey is perhaps best known for the remark he made on the eve of the First

World War, 'The lamps are going out all over Europe. We shall not see them lit again in our time.'

58. Quoted by Cocker and Mabey (2005), 378.

59. Sir Edward, Viscount Grey (1927), 170.

60. Waterhouse (2004), 22, 44.

61. Garriott (1903), 42.

62. White, ed. Greenoak (1986–9), i. 359 (wryneck), also 9 April 1774 (ii. 30: ring-ousel, and iii. 456: bank-martins).

63. Richard, bishop of Chichester, was born in Droitwich and canonized in 1262.

64. See Groom (2006), 42–80; Hutton (1996), 214–17 and (1994), 55.

65. Cheddar also had a St Luke's Day fair (18 October); the fairs survived until the 1700s.

66. Woodward (1896), i. 305.

67. There is some evidence that 23 April was observed as a national feast day from 1222.

68. The more mysterious and anarchic mummers traditions may have been developed by the common folk as a sort of 'anti-riding'.

69. See Schama (1994), 329; see also 353.

70. Shakespeare, *1 Henry VI*, I. i. 153–4.

71. Groom (2006), 229.

72. Despite the thoroughly English iconography of the White Cliffs of Dover, St Paul's Cathedral, and so forth.

73. Roud (2006), 138.

74. See Clifford and King (eds) (1993).

75. Line based on Roud (2006), 139; see Clare, ed. Robinson, Powell, and Dawson (1993), 138–9 (letter to William Hone, April 1825).

76. Lean (1902–4), ii. pt 1. 362: attributed to the *Poor Robin* apocrypha (1770).

77. Quoted by Blackburn and Holford-Strevens (1999), 170.

78. Blakeborough (1898), 80–1.

79. Keats, 'The Eve of Saint Mark', ed. Garrod (1982), lines 5, 7, 39 (pp. 357–8).

80. See also Pearson, 'The Vigil of St. Mark' (1800), 19–23: 'All of the Hamlet, who this year / Shall yield their mortal breath, / Walk through the Porch a grisly train, / Wrapt in the garb of Death' (20); see also Montgomery, 'The Vigil of St. Mark' (1806), 137–46 – a

possible source too for Keats's 'La Belle Dame Sans Merci'.

81. Child (1957), 140B (iii. 180); also known as 'Robin Hood and the Widow's Three Sons': see Quiller-Couch (ed.) (1910), 621.

82. Floralia was a week-long festival dedicated to Flora, the goddess of springtime and flowers; it was therefore celebrated by naked prostitutes acting in gladiatorial duels and by similar saucy performances; after 45 BC the first day of the ancient Roman Floralia was 28 April. Note that this Maia was not the mother of Hermes.

83. Malory, ed. Cooper (1998), bk XVIII, chapter xxv, p. 443; Chaucer, 'The Legend of Good Women', ed. Robinson (1974), lines 36–9 (p. 483) – this is Text G; Text F has 'Whan that the month of May / Is comen, and that I here the foules synge, / And that the floures gynnen for to sprynge, / Farewel my bok and my devocioun!'

84. Sage was proverbially good for health: 'He that would live for ay must eat Sage in May' (Ray (1737), 28).

85. Breton (1626), C2r.

86. Spenser, ed. Hamilton (1977), bk VII, canto vii, st. 34.

87. Clare, 'May', ed. Robinson, Powell, and Dawson (1996–8), i. 58–74 ['mozzled' means 'mottled'; 'bum barrels' are long-tailed tits; 'princifeathers' lilacs; and a 'cuckaball' is a spherical bouquet of May flowers]. Clare lists very many of the seasonal wildflowers and hedgerow plants – lilies of the valley, corn poppies, charlocks, ironweed, pimpernels, forget-me-nots, knopweed, fennel, daisies, mallow, henbane, buttercups, watercress, mint – remarking that 'My wild field catalogue of flowers / Grows in my ryhmes [sic] as thick as showers' (lines 193–4).

88. Browning, 'Home-Thoughts, from Abroad', ed. Jack, et al. (1991), lines 9–10 (vol. iv, p. 64).

89. Tusser (1573), fol. 46r; and Ray (1670), 42; see 'Antient Meteorological Prognostics' from Time's Telescope, reprinted in Atheneum (October 1819–April 1820), vi. 365–6, 366;

see also, however, Lowthorp (ed.) (1716): 'A green Christmas makes a fat Church-yard' (ii. 20) – similarly, Ray (1670) also has 'A green winter makes a fat Church-yard' (42).

90. Another violent hailstorm followed the same year in Herefordshire on 17 June. The Silver Jubilee of George V in May 1935 was very cold and frosty; on 16 May the temperature dropped to –8.6 °C at Rickmansworth, Hertfordshire, and it snowed from Yorkshire to the Scilly Isles.

91. Quoted by Blackburn and Holford-Strevens (1999), 220; it is not clear why this should be the case.

92. Sowter (1733), 47; Sowter also records, for instance, 'A May Flood, / Never did Good, / Sheer your Sheep in May, / And clear them all away' (see Ray (1670), 41).

93. With regard to forgoing the winter wardrobe, see Blackburn and Holford-Strevens (1999): 'Till April is dead / change not a thread' (140).

94. See 'Lincolnshire Folklore: Calendar Customs' (1933), 279.

95. Lloyd (1590), 147.

96. See Blackburn and Holford-Strevens (1999), 183–93.

97. Cameron (1998), 165–6.

98. Dickens, 'Greenwich Fair', ed. Slater (1994), 112.

99. 8 May is the eve of the earliest possible date for Pentecost (Whit Sunday) and the forty-ninth (seven times seventh) date from 21 March (which is itself the earliest date for Easter, following the first full moon of the spring equinox: see Jones (2007), 76). Furry Day is held on the Saturday before 8 May if that date is a Sunday or a Monday.

100. Peter, ed. Jones (2006), 27; see also Baring-Gould and Sheppard (1895), 50–1. The phrase 'Hal-an-Tow' has been subject to much speculation; it is probably simply a corruption of the dance step, heel-and-toe.

101. Gentleman's Magazine 60 (June 1790), 520; note that the event was nevertheless moved to the feast day of the Apparition of St Michael the Archangel.

102. Cameron (1998), 126.

103. Nevertheless, I have it on excellent authority that the sea on the Jurassic Coast still harbours impressive shoals of mackerel.

104. Lucas (1903), 174; see Simpson (1973).

105. Whittingstall (2001) gives a recipe for this delicacy, 377–8.

106. See *Notes and Queries*, 2nd series, 12 (19 October 1861), 303.

107. Kightly (1986), 176; in addition to May Day, Kightly suggests that Oak Apple Day absorbed Grovely Rights Day and Neville's Cross Commemoration.

108. It was once held between Maundy Thursday and Whit Monday.

109. See Kightly (1986), 128.

110. Tusser (1557), C3v.

111. Herrick, 'The Argument of his Book', ed. Moorman (1947), 5; I am indebted to Ayesha Mukherjee for several of these points.

6 Easter

1. If Easter falls on 22 March in a leap year, the earliest possible date for Septuagesima is 19 January. This last occurred in England under the Julian calendar in 1668; it will not be repeated until 2872.

2. The number forty was significant: it was also the number of hours spent in the tomb.

3. Despite ferocious debate, the educated consensus is that the traditional forty days of Lent do not include Sundays, which are days of celebration; whether this means that Christians are permitted to break their abstinence every Sunday during Lent is a matter of personal conscience.

4. The Easter Triduum actually begins with evening prayers on Maundy Thursday and runs to the evening prayers of Easter Sunday.

5. For which they are accused of being drunk on 'new wine': Acts 2: 2–4, 13.

6. Gal. 4: 10–11; Col. 2: 17.

7. 'From the Letter of the Emperor to all those not present at the Council', Eusebius, *Vita Constantini*, bk III, 18–20: see Schaff and Wace (eds) (1900), xiv. 54.

8. Muhammad declared that the Muslim calendar should be purely lunar to distinguish it from the luni-solar calendar of the Jews and the solar calendar of the Christians. Each month begins about two days after the new moon, when the crescent moon is first glimpsed. There is some evidence from the names of the Muslim months that it was originally a solar calendar corresponding to the seasons.

9. See Mosshammer (2008), 3–58.

10. The Second Vatican Council (1962–5) also made a similar proposal to fix Easter to a particular Sunday.

11. See Mosshammer (2008), 59–108.

12. Bede, ed. McClure and Collins (1994), 153; see also Bede, *De temporum ratione* (*The Reckoning of Time*) on the progress of time.

13. Hutton, for example, is sceptical: see Hutton (1996), 180.

14. See Cole (2007), 43.

15. As collected by Baring-Gould.

16. Salaman describes this practice as 'almost universal' in Ireland: Salaman, rev. Hawkes (1985), 117.

17. The eighteenth-century scholar George Steevens, the 'Puck of Commentators', produced a *tour de force* of pedantic potato lore as a tongue-in-cheek note to Shakespeare: see Shakespeare, ed. Groom (1995), ix. 166–70.

18. See Wright, ed. Lones (1936–40), i. 1, 8: Wright notes that these names are recorded by the sixteenth-century poet Barnabe Googe; for collops, see Langland, ed. Schmidt (1984), passus VI. l. 285.

19. Warner (1597), 121.

20. Shakespeare, *All's Well That Ends Well*, II. ii. 23–4.

21. Taylor (1619), D1v; see Capp (2003), 346.

22. Manning (1903), 167: the children go on with another rhyme if they are not paid. Hutton gives a rich sampling (1996), 164–6. A South-west alternative is recorded by Wright, beginning 'Lent crock, give a pancake, / Or a fritter, for my labour' (Wright, ed. Lones (1936–40), i. 4–5).

23. Thomas (1983), 76.

24. See Wright, ed. Lones (1936–40), i. 1–2, who claims that one team consists of everyone named Tom, Will, and John, while the other team is made up of the rest of the world.

25. Carew (1602), 75r-v [contractions expanded].

26. For an idiosyncratic account, see Taylor (1620). See also Burning Judas and especially the Black Knight of Ashton, in Roud (2006), 108–9, 124–5. Wright notes that in the North Country Wednesday was 'Fruttis' or 'Fritter Wednesday' (Wright, ed. Lones (1936–40), i. 4).

27. Quarles, 'Eglogue VIII' (1646), 79.

28. See Thomas (1983), 75.

29. OED: Poor Robin (1733), A7r. There is a mid-eighteenth-century mention of 'hot cross buns' in George Colman's fashionable journal, The Connoisseur for 20 March 1755, Dublin edition (Colman and Thornton (1756), ii. 76); the street cry 'One a penny, two a penny hot cross buns!' also appears in the anonymous and picaresque Adventures of Oxymel Classic (1768), ii. 233.

30. Smith (1753), 8–9.

31. Hone (1826), i. 202–3; reprinted as 'Hot Cross Buns', The Saturday Magazine (10 April 1841), 144. There is a collection of such buns in the Widow's Son pub (Devons Road, Bromley-by-Bow).

32. Pepys, ed. Warrington (1953), i. 408 (15 February 1667).

33. Gay (1716), 10; see Power (2009), 353: 'The change of season, then, is indicated by human behaviour, a direct inversion of the situation in the Georgics'.

34. The Ulverston Pasche Egg event was shamefully cancelled due to bad weather in 2010 – gamely, some families turned up and rolled their eggs anyway; it has continued annually since then.

35. There are, for example, several nineteenth-century chapbook versions of the anonymous The Peace Egg, or, St. George's Annual Play, some of which include material to make it a book for all seasons.

36. See Palmer (1985), 219, 126–8.

37. See Brand, rev. Ellis (1813), i. 155n., quoting Gentleman's Magazine (1784), 96; see also Monthly Magazine (April 1798), 273.

38. Quoted by Hutton (1996), 245.

39. See Hutton (1996), 204–13, for an exemplary account.

40. A lamb fair was held at London Leadenhall on Holy Thursday (Ascension Day, being forty days after Easter). See Cameron (1998), 69; also Owen (1780 [six editions, 1780–99], and Stevenson (1661). See also Blake's 'Holy Thursday', ed. Keynes (1970), 19, 33 [Blake's pagination].

41. In 1998 there was torrential rain on Good Friday and there were blizzards in Scotland and Devon.

42. The Church House of St Andrews in South Tawton on Dartmoor, for example, has a Church Ale beer brewed by the Exe Valley Brewery.

43. Shakespeare, Henry V, II. iv. 25. The Sunbury 1758 text is quoted by Wright, ed. Lones (1936), i. 161, transcribed from a printed cutting dated May 1758 in the antiquarian and book-collector Joseph Haslewood's copy of Brand's Observations. See also Clare, ed. Robinson, Powell, and Dawson (1993), 139 (letter to Hone, April 1825).

44. Robert Dover's Cotswold Olimpicks: www.olimpickgames.co.uk; see Haddon (2004).

7 The Cuckoo

1. Wordsworth, 'To the Cuckoo', ed. Hayden (1994), line 4 (p. 137).

2. Wordsworth (1823), 91.

3. See the dated but still valuable article by Hardy (1879), 47–91.

4. Gregory (ed.) (1976).

5. British Library, MS Harley 978, fol. 11v. The most notorious rendition of this is in a version by Paul Giovanni at the climax of the film The Wicker Man (dir. Robin Hardy, 1973): see 'Ballads of Seduction, Fertility and

Ritual Slaughter', *The Wicker Man: The Original Soundtrack* (1973; 2002).

6. Spenser, Sonnet XIX (1595), B3v; as Wordsworth recognized two centuries later, Spenser thrills 'that all the woods theyr echoes back rebounded / as if they knew the meaning of their layes'.

7. Nashe (1600), B3r.

8. Thomson, *Spring*, ed. Sambrook (1972), lines 579–80 (p. 18).

9. 'Poor Robin' (1682), C5r. 'Poor Robin' (1664) notes in 'Observations on April' that 'In this month (if the weather prove warm) we may expect the coming of the Cuckow; but some will say, it is no matter whether he come or no; truly I say so too, as good not come, as come for no good', before going on to attribute the cuckolding of men at this time to the 'vivification' of the sun (A8r).

10. Quoted by Clifford and King (2006), 121; for a rich and concise account, drawn upon here, see Buczacki (2002), 300–4; see also Gibson (1904), 53–7.

11. Kipling, ed. Jones (2001), 519. The poem has the following preface: 'Spring begins in Southern England on the 14th April, on which date the Old Woman lets the Cuckoo out of her basket at Heathfield Fair – locally known as Heffle Cuckoo Fair.'

12. Harte (1986), 29; citing L. M. G. Bond, *Tyneham, A Lost Heritage* (Longmans: Dorchester, 1956), 112.

13. Northall (1892), 267, attributed to *The Athenæum* (1846) and *Gardener's Chronicle* (1850); there are several variants of this rhyme.

14. Northall (1892), 268; see also Iona and Peter Opie (1977), 74.

15. Northall (1892), 236, 242, who gives two further verses: 'The cuckoo sucks the birds' eggs, To make her sing so clear, / And then she sings "Cuckoo," Three months in a year. // I love my little brother, And sister every day, / But I seem to love them better, In the merry month of May.' See a variation in Palmer (1985), 229–30.

16. Bett (1952), 121. Pershore Fair is held on 26 June (NS) or 15 June (OS).

17. Field (1913).

18. See Buczacki (2002), 303, quoting a National Trust press release (spring 1999).

19. Thomas (1983), 83.

20. Ray (1670), 43; see Armstrong (1958).

21. 'Poor Robin' (1682), C5r.

22. John Gay, Fourth Pastoral (1714), lines 15–18 (p. 32): 'When first the year, I heard the cuckow sing, / And call with welcome note the budding spring, / I straitway set a running with such haste, / Deb'rah that won the smock scarce ran so fast'; Roud (2003), 127–30.

23. Brand (1777), 400n–1n.

24. Opie and Tatem (1989), 112.

25. Logan, 'Ode to the Cuckoo' (1781), 2: the ode was first printed in 1770 by Bruce (109; vii).

26. Baring-Gould, ed. Hitchcock (1974), 32–3.

27. 'Peter Puzzlecap' (*c*.1820), 10; it is illustrated by Thomas Bewick.

28. Shakespeare, *King Lear*, I. iv. 214–16.

29. Chaucer, 'The Parliament of Fowls', ed. Robinson (1974), line 358 (p. 314) (note that 'The Cuckoo and the Nightingale' or *Book of Cupid*, frequently quoted by folklorists, is not part of the Chaucer canon but is by Sir John Clanvow, ODNB); Milton, ed. Carey (1971), Sonnet I, line 9 (p. 90), perhaps alluding to Clanvow.

30. Shakespeare, *Love's Labor's Lost*, V. ii. 894–902.

31. Brand, ed. Ellis (1813), ii. 113–18.

32. 'Poor Robin' (1686), A7v [italics reversed].

33. See 'Observations on April', 'Poor Robin' (1682): 'This is the *Cuckow* month, which is the reason that some People after their wives have run away 2 or 3 years together with other men, yet take them again, and for a we[l]come home, treat them with musick, wine, and a plentiful Supper' (A8r).

34. Swainson (1886; 1998), 121.

35. Aubrey, ed. Britten (1881), 10; 'Poor Robin' (1692): 'This is the Month, of all the rest, /

That Fools they are in great request' (A7v
[italics reversed]).

36. Lean (1902–4), i. 360.

37. White, ed. Allen (1900), 473.

38. Buczacki (2002), 302.

39. Ockendon, Hewson, Johnston, and Atkinson (2012), 111–25.

40. Waterhouse (2004), 80–1.

8 May Day

1. Peter (2006), 7, 15.

2. 'I will pay to the hobby-horse' / And her comrades': *Beunans Meriasek*, cd. Stokes (1872), lines 1061–? (p. 61).

3. The 'Lord of the Summer Country' dresses in green leaves and is a younger suitor than Guenevere's [sic] husband Arthur, a spring to his winter; he is also known as Melwas or Sir Mellyagraunce.

4. *One Day's Journey* (1784), 9, 9n; see also Macpherson (1771), 164–6; and Pennant (1771), viii, 90–1, 159–60.

5. Robertson, 'Parish of Callander', in Sinclair (ed.) (1791), xi. 621: gleefully quoted by Frazer (1933), 619; being 'devoted ' or 'fey' meant moving into another world, for example with only twelve months to live.

6. See entry for Sanas Chormaic in Maier (ed.) (2000).

7. Quoted by Frazer (1933), 621.

8. See Hodgson, part II, vol. ii, p. 425: 'walked over the water called Bowls-green Steps to the bounder stones set to ascertain Morpeth bounder'.

9. Tusser (1557), C2v.

10. St Helen's Day-in-the-Spring should be distinguished from St Helen's Day (18 August).

11. See Jones (2007), 202.

12. John Grant, 'Parish of Kirkmichael', Sinclair (ed.) (1791), xii. 465–6.

13. Kilvert, ed. Plomer (1977), i. 119–20 (30 April 1870).

14. Shakespeare, *Love's Labor's Lost*, III. i. 29; *Hamlet*, III. ii. 135: 'the hobby-horse is forgot', meaning that days of merriment are passed.

The Mari Lwyd has recently been revived; there are also several Welsh Morris sides: borders are porous.

15. See Kille (1999).

16. For example, Banbury in Oxfordshire now has an annual hobby-horse festival.

17. Quoted by Hutton (1996), 226.

18. Forni (ed.) (2001), 72–3.

19. Whitelock (ed.) (1979), 'Extracts from the Laws of Cnut (1010–1023)', p. 455, para. 5.1; p. 475, para. 54.

20. See Hall, 'The VII. Yere of Kyng Henry the VIII.' (1809), 582.

21. Shakespeare, *All's Well That Ends Well*, II. ii. 23–4; see also Kemp (1600).

22. The earliest recorded reference to Morris dancing is 1448: Heaney (2004), 513–15; see also Garry (1983), 219–28; Shakespeare mentions a Whitsun Morris in *Henry V* (II. iv. 25). Bampton Morris, which has the longest continuous history of any English Morris side, was first described in 1847.

23. Morley, Cantus XVIII (1594), E3v–E4r [contractions expanded].

24. Stubbes (1583), title-page.

25. Stubbes (1583), 92v–93r [contractions expanded].

26. Thomas (1983), 747–8, 215.

27. Spenser, 'Maye' (1579), fol. 16v.

28. Stow (1598), 72.

29. Now known as 'The Mummer's Dance', quoted by Frazer (1933), 121.

30. *Gentleman's Magazine* 24 (1754), 354.

31. See 'Isaac Bickerstaff', *The Tatler* 166 (29 April–2 May 1710) [1].

32. Southey, ed. Warter (1856), 4 May 1820, iii. 193; see also Southey (1807), i. 146 (Letter xiii). A folk tune named 'Jack in the Green' is mentioned by Smart in *The Nonpareil* (1757), 181: this is probably 'Jack of the Green' – see *Thompson's Compleat Collection* ([c.1775]), 7 ('Jack o' the Green' was also a jockey of the time: see i. 141 of Swift (1777), 13). For more on May Day in this period, see Joshua (2007).

33. Jefferies, 'Out of Doors in February' (2008), 189.

34. Coles (1656), 67. Richard Moore-Colyer assures me that flies of all sorts also steer well away from elder, noting that one often finds elder bushes planted alongside the outdoor privy, and that it was also affixed to the reins or the collars of horses to deter flies.

35. Chapple and Pollard (eds) (1966), 30.

36. Shakespeare, *A Midsummer Night's Dream*, IV. i. 132–3: 'No doubt they rose up early to observe / The rite of May'. However, some critics argue that Shakespeare deliberately mixes different seasonal aspects, as summarized by Jensen (2008), 103–4.

37. Morley, Cantus III (1595), B2v [repeats omitted].

38. Rollins (ed.) ii. 11; see Judge (2000).

39. Herrick, ed. Moorman (1947), 'Corinna's going a Maying', 69.

40. Robert of Brunne, ed. Furnivall (1901), lines 4681 (p. 156), 997–1004 (p. 36).

41. Fetherston (1582), D7v; *Vox Graculi* (1623), 62.

42. Stubbes (1583), 94r–v [contractions expanded].

43. Thomas (1983), 78: see Hall (1661); and Fisher (1650).

44. Hobbes, ed. Macpherson (1985), 681 [366]; Hobbes also compares Rogation with the Roman festival of Ambarvalia.

45. Evelyn (1670), 207.

46. Fletcher (1800), 99; quoted in part by Thompson (1993), 54.

47. Hutton (1996), 93 (see also 233–6, 81ff., 270); he goes on to say that 'Likewise, in societies in which most of this formalized misbehaviour is carried on by young men, young women are always going to be the favourite objects of attention.'

48. Prynne (1633), 892; Thomas (1983) cites Cawte (1978), esp. 21, 79, 181, 209.

49. See, for instance, *A New Description of Merryland* (1740).

50. It has also been suggested that in the sixteenth century St George 'ridings' or pageants were moved by a week to become part of May Day celebrations, in part because it was often cold in April.

51. See Laslett and Oosterveen (1973), 255–86. As the satirist Charles Churchill put it (1764): 'APRIL with fools, and MAY with bastards blest' (19).

52. Traditional; regularly quoted by Garth Gibbs in his columns for the *Daily Mirror*.

53. Hill (1964), 154.

54. See *Come Lasses and Lads* ([*c*.1885]), *passim*; claims that this dates from 1670 are hopeful.

55. See Irving (1822), ii. 54, 123–5, 130–1. Frazer (1933) inevitably suggests that the custom was far more ancient (131), and Joshua (2007), 20, 66–7, and *passim*, gives a somewhat credulous account. See also Clare, ed. Robinson, Powell, and Dawson (1993), 139–40 (letter to Hone, April 1825).

56. Tennyson, ed. Ricks (1987), lines 25–8 (vol. I, p. 460).

9 Summer

1. Tennyson, 'The Throstle, ed. Ricks (1987), lines 1–4 (vol. iii, p. 102).

2. Shakespeare, *The Tempest*, V. i. 88–94.

3. Marvell (1681), 49–50.

4. Shakespeare, Sonnet 18 (p. 1752).

5. Tennyson, *Tithonus*, ed. Ricks (1987), lines 1–4 (vol. ii, p. 607).

6. See also, for example, Shakespeare's Sonnet 94 (p. 1766).

7. Breton (1626), C2v.

8. *A Supplement to all the Common Almanacks* (1730), 9 [italics reversed]; this publication appears to have been a promotion for a patent remedy: 'This Book is Given Gratis Up One Pair of Stairs at the Sign of Dr. *Chamberlen's* Famous Anodyne Necklace For *Children's* Teeth, FITS, Fevers, Convulsions, &*c*.' (title-page).

9. Tusser (1557), C3v.

10. Inwards (1869), 30.

11. Denham (1846), 49. St Vitus is associated with Sydenham's chorea, a nervous disease, but the original St Vitus' dance which the saint inspired and calmed might have instead been an example of mass-hysteria.

12. Simons (2008), 91.

13. Hardy (1879), 50.

14. Waterhouse (2004), 228.

15. Thomas (1983), 230: quoting Wilson, ed. Linnell (1964), 241; for St Barnabus Day roses, see Andrews (ed.) (1898), 235.

16. Ray (1737), 39. 'Barnaby the bright' appears in Spenser's sonnet 'Ring ye the bels, ye yong men of the towne': 'This day the sunne is in his chiefest hight, / With Barnaby the bright' (1595, H3r); there is also reference made to a birth on a 'Barnaby-bright in the Morning' in Rowe's play The Biter (1705), 39; and see also the anonymous peregrination The Comical Pilgrim (1722): 'the longest Day in the Year, call'd Barnaby bright' (99).

17. Daily Telegraph, 21 June 2010.

18. See Hill (2008), 177–83.

19. www.new-age.co.uk.

20. Dickens mentions Stonehenge in The Uncommercial Traveller: Dickens, ed. Slater and Drew (2000), 28, 255.

21. See Bosworth and Toller (eds) (1898), 720: 'Nigon nihtam ǽr middum sumere' (nine nights of midsummer).

22. From Kemble (1849), i. 361–2, quoted from Homans (1991), 369.

23. Aubrey, ed. Britten (1881), 96–7.

24. Blackburn and Holford-Strevens (1999), 259.

25. Shakespeare, 1 Henry IV, II. i. 87; see Aubrey, ed. Britten (1881), 53–4.

26. See Aubrey, ed. Britten (1881), 97.

27. Shakespeare, Twelfth Night, III. iv. 56.

28. Strutt, ed. Cox (1801), 284.

29. Stow (1603), 102.

30. Plat (1653 [1652]), 44–50.

31. Stow (1598), 75.

32. Puttenham (1589), 128.

33. Frazer (1933), 655.

34. Bottrell (1870), 54–6; see also Bottrell (1880), 179–80 and Bottrell (1873), 283, 287–8.

35. Cameron (1998), 87, 18, 65. Dorchester also had fairs on Holy Trinity, to the memory of St James, and Candlemas Day.

36. See Davey (2008).

37. Cameron (1998), 16–17.

38. See Appleton Thorn Primary School (www.appletonthornprimary.org.uk). The song is attributed to the nineteenth-century fox-hunter and poet Rowland Eyles Egerton-Warburton; not all the verses are here transcribed.

39. Miller (2006), 19.

40. Spenser (1579), fol. 72v.

41. See, for example, Tusser's 'A Sonet, or brief rehersall of the properties of the twelue monethes afore rehersed', which includes the line: 'As July bid all thing, in order to ripe' (1557, D11r); and, more explicitly, 'And Puppy-like there told him truly, / First leap he had was but last July' (Poems on Affairs of State (1704), iii. 195).

42. Ray (1670), 41.

43. Breton (1626), C3r.

44. Gadbury (1696), B3r; Ephemeris was regularly published from the mid-seventeenth to the mid-eighteenth century.

45. Marston, 'A Cynicke Satyre' (1598), Lib II, Sat. vii, sig. F3v.

46. Simons (2008), 64.

47. Denham (1846), 52, who concludes the saying with the Mummerset diction 'na mair'; see Denham (52–4) for an account of St Swithin's Day rhymes; Denham also records 'St. Swithin is christening the apples' (50). 'Poor Robin' (1697) records the wisdom thus: 'In t[h]is Month is S. Swithin's' day, / On which if that it Rain, they say / Full forty Days after it will, / More or less, some Rain distill' (B2v). The poet and dramatist John Gay, meanwhile, scorned the superstition: 'How, if on Swithin's Feast the Welkin lours, / And ev'ry Penthouse streams with hasty Show'rs, / Twice twenty Days shall Clouds their Fleeces drain, / And wash the Pavements with incessant Rain. / Let not such vulgar Tales debase thy Mind; / Nor Paul nor Swithin rule the Clouds and Wind' (1716, 12–13).

48. William of Malmesbury, ed. Hamilton (2012), 162: 'Jam vero vitæ præsenti valefacturus, pontificali auctoritate præcepit

astantibus ut extra ecclesiam cadaver suum humarent, ubi et pedibus prætereuntium et stillicidiis ex alto rorantibus esset obnoxium.'

49. ODNB. Interestingly, a Welsh rain-saint, St Cewydd, is also celebrated on 1, 2, or 15 July. His relationship with St Swithin has yet to be properly established.

50. Quoted by Blackburn and Holford-Strevens (1999), 278.

51. 'Antient Meteorological Prognostics', Atheneum (1819–20), vi. 365.

52. Opie and Tatem (eds) (1989), 337.

53. There is, however, a St Bartholomew's Day proverb that bears out the dating of St Swithin's Day to 15 July (see note 107 below).

54. Times Online, 15 July 2005.

55. Gadbury's almanac Ephemeris (1696) gives an astrological explanation of the phenom-enon: 'To make Saint Swythin weep, the Potent Sun / Doth Chronus smite by Opposition, / And, Venus too frowns with the same Aspect / Upon him also, heightening the Effect' (B2v).

56. Campbell (1902), 277; see Scott, The Abbot (1870), xi. 142.

57. For another comparable tradition, see the feast of St Vitus (note 11 above).

58. See Churchill (1764): 'JULY, to whom, the Dog-Star in her train, / Saint JAMES gives oysters, and Saint SWITHIN rain' (19).

59. 'T. Q. M.', 'Notes on a Tour, chiefly Pedestrian, from Skipton in Craven, Yorkshire, to Keswick, in Cumberland', in Hone (1828), Table-Book, ii. 279 (quoted at length in Blackburn and Holford-Strevens (1999), 301–2). Roud (2006) gives Grasmere rush-bearing as 5 August (being St Oswald's Day, the church's dedication), but this evidently varied over time (264–5).

60. 'A Gest of Robyn Hode', Knight and Ohlgren (eds) (2000), lines 1757–60 (p. 146).

61. See Jones (2007), 182.

62. Chambers (ed.) (1832), ii. 122; Roud (2006) doubts all of this (259).

63. Ray (1670), 44. Tusser (1557) also recommends reaping on St James's Day (C4v).

64. Cameron (1998), 70–1.

65. Brewer (1988), 735.

66. Spenser, ed. Hamilton (1977), bk VII, canto vii, st. 37.

67. Lean (1902–4), i. 189: this is misattrib-uted, see Notes and Queries for Somerset & Dorset 3 (1893), 115.

68. Tusser (1570), fol. 22r.

69. Breton (1626), C3v.

70. See Stevenson (1661), who notes that 'the new Wheat makes the Gossips Cake' (37); however, the recipe appears to be lost.

71. Young (1771), 290.

72. The first sheaf of corn had a ritual signifi-cance in the Scottish Hebrides, for example: the harvest began on 15 August (the festival of the Assumption of the Virgin Mary) and the first corn was made into a special 'ban-nock' bread.

73. See Brand, ed. Ellis (1849), i. 348; this fancy possibly originated from Scottish ver-nacular spelling: see Spotiswood (1715), 195.

74. Wright, ed. Lones (1936–40), iii. 43; this land did not, however, survive the Enclosure Acts. For 'Lord Livingston' see Child no. 262; these lines are actually taken from 'The Battle of Otterburn', which was fought at this time of the year: 'Yt fell abowght the Lamasse tyde, / Whan husbondes wynnes ther haye' (Child no. 161).

75. The Anglo-Saxon Chronicles, 102 (AD 921).

76. Cossins (1877), 18.

77. OED: 'Gule' is pronounced with a hard g.

78. Ray (1737), 275.

79. Hone, The Every-Day Book (1827), ii. col. 1071. This was also the opening of the legal season which closed on 15 June.

80. Likewise, since the 1831 Act it has been illegal to shoot partridge before 1 September.

81. The Nativity of Mary (8 September) was similarly known as 'Little Mary in Harvest'.

82. Jones (2007), 179, 83; Roman agrarian festivals had also taken place in mid-August, and these merged with Marian celebrations.

83. Cameron (1998), 14, 17.

84. Quoted by Blackburn and Holford-Strevens (1999), 333.

85. Quoted in *Notes and Queries*, 4th series, 10 (23 November 1872), 411.

86. Frazer (1933), 406–8, 429.

87. Hone (1837), ii. col. 1171; the refrain is simply a slow crescendo and diminuendo on the same note, F.

88. Milton, ed. Fowler (1967), bk IX, lines 838–42 (p. 487).

89. Frazer (1933), 411; Frazer cannot resist, however, arguing that the Corn-mother and Harvest-maiden are prototypes of Demeter and Persephone.

90. Writing in 1598, Hentzner noted that, 'As we were returning to our inn, we happened to meet some country people *celebrating their Harvest-home*: their last load of corn they crown with flowers, having besides an image richly dressed, by which, perhaps, they would signify Ceres, this they keep moving about, while men and women, men and maid servants, riding through the streets in the cart, shout as loud as they can till they arrive at the barn' (trans. Walpole (1757), 79; for a full account of 'harvest home', see Hutton (1996), 332–47.

91. See Langland, ed. Schmidt (1984): 'By that it neghed neer harvest and newe corn cam to chepyng; / Thanne was folk fayn, and fedde Hunger with the beste – / With good ale, as Gloton taghte – and garte Hunger to slepe' (passus VI, lines 299–301, p. 76).

92. See Jones (2007), 217.

93. Fielding (1751), 7–8.

94. Duck, 'The Thresher's Labour' (1730), 25.

95. The Hammonds (1911, 2003), 181–2: see Crabbe on an English Sunday in *The Village* (1783), 26.

96. *The Parliamentary Register* (1800), xi. 237 (18 April 1800).

97. In Scotland, August Bank Holiday is the first Monday in August; note that Scotland and Northern Ireland have additional bank holidays to England and Wales.

98. Reading Rock festival was established in 1971 as 'The National Jazz, Blues, and Rock Festival'; it was banned for two years in 1984–5 and is now twinned with the Leeds Festival. The first Glastonbury festivals were in 1970 and 1971, and have been running more or less continuously since 1978.

99. Jonson ([1735?]; first performed 1614), V. iii (p. 96). Pope notes in *The Dunciad* that the actor Elkanah Settle 'kept a booth at Bartholomew-fair, where, in the droll called St. George and for England, he acted in his old age in a Dragon of green leather of his own invention': see Pope, ed. Rumbold (2009), bk III, line 283n. (p. 254).

100. Brathwaite (1631), 200.

101. Cameron (1998), 153–9; Pepys, ed. Warrington (1953), ii. 48 (7 September 1664).

102. See Green (2010).

103. Wordsworth, ed. Wordsworth, Abrams, and Gill (1979), 1805 text: bk VII, lines 685–721 (pp. 262–3). Wordsworth's poem should be compared with the song 'Bartleme Fair' written by George Alexander Stevens (1772): 'Here's fiddling and fluting, and shouting and shrieking, / Fifes, trumpets, drums, bag-pipes, and barrow-girls squeaking … Here are drolls, hornpipe dancing, and shewing of postures; / Plum-porridge, black-puddings, and op'ning of oysters; / The tap-house guests swearing, and gall'ry folks squawling, / With salt-boxes, solos, and mouth-pieces bawling; / Pimps, pick-pockets, strollers, fat landladies, sailors, / Bawds, baileys, jilts, jockies, thieves, tumblers, and taylors …' and so on, and on (69–71; quoted in full in a modernized form by Blackburn and Holford-Strevens (1999), 344).

104. Fairs at Smithfield in London, Newbury in Berkshire, and Ubley in Somerset were also held on St Bartholomew's Day: see Cameron (1998), 33–4.

105. 'The Doggerel': www.burningbartle.org.uk/tradition.php.

106. Several other suggestions are given on the Burning Bartle website; see Kightly (1986), 59–60.

107. Inwards (1869), 32, who also notes of St Bartholomew's Day: 'If it rains this day it will rain the forty days after'. A Prayer for Fair Weather was supposed to be delivered from the pulpit on 20 August 1860; Charles Kingsley refused to do so.

108. Grey (1927), 139.

109. Kipling, 'The Long Trail', ed. Jones (2001), 172.

110. Dickens, 'London Recreations', ed. Slater (1994), 97.

10 A Land Enclosed

1. Goodridge (2012), 20.

2. Thomson, ed. Sambrook (1972), 'Summer', lines 165–79.

3. See Rawlinson (1878), iv–v.

4. Thomson, ed. Sambrook (1972), 'Spring', line 495 (p. 16); Thomson (1730), 23 [later revised].

5. See the Hammonds (1911, 2003); see also their studies 1917 and 1919.

6. Young (ed.) (1796), xxv. 488.

7. Young (ed.) (1804), xlii. 27; reprinted in Batchelor (1813), 235, and see also 223.

8. Young (ed.) (1804), xlii. 28.

9. See Thompson (1975), 22–4 and *passim*; see also Groom (ed.) (1999), i. vii–x.

10. Linebaugh (1991), 80.

11. Emsley (1987), 209–12.

12. The Hammonds (1911, 2003), 154–5; this severity was repealed in part the following year.

13. Landry (2001), however, argues against the 'Enclosure Act Myth' that the English landscape is an artificial creation of the last 250 years as land required for fox-hunting and pheasant-shooting precisely in defiance of agricultural capitalism. Hunting and shooting are therefore conservationist and consequently potential allies for green politics (24–5).

14. See Salaman, rev. Hawkes (1985), 506–17.

15. Apocryphal, of course.

16. Eden, *The State of the Poor or An History of the Labouring Classes in England*, vol. i, 533.

17. Salaman, rev. Hawkes (1985), 453, 486.

18. See Salaman, rev. Hawkes (1985), 120. It has also been suggested that the Inca name 'papa' meant that the potato became the 'pope's fruit', or even the 'pope-ato': see Allen (2002), 137, 21 [no source given].

19. Salaman, rev. Hawkes (1985), 120, 437.

20. See Gallagher (2000), 113–14.

21. Salaman, rev. Hawkes (1985), 112, 114, 116.

22. Young (1801), 12–13; also Young (ed.) (1801), xxxvi. 508.

23. Rawlidge has – or had – his apologists: see the defence offered on the eve of Prohibition by Graves (1920), 41–7.

24. Rawlidge (1628), 12–13 ['hunting' may be read for 'haunting'].

25. The only people to benefit were publicans: 'I have never seen more taverns and ale-houses in my whole life than in London', remarked Platter, trans. Williams (1937), 189.

26. Clare, ed. Robinson and Powell (2004), lines 123–34 (p. 4).

27. 'Portraitures of Modern Poets: No. XIV, John Clare', *The Ladies' Monthly Museum; or, Polite Repository of Amusement and Instruction* 18 (1823), 83.

28. Goldsmith (1770): 'Even now the devastation is begun, / And half the business of destruction done; / Even now, methinks, as pondering here I stand, / I see the rural virtues leave the land' (25); for a detailed account of this poem, see Lonsdale (ed.) (1989), 669–74.

29. Goldsmith (1770), 18–19 (Lonsdale (ed.) (1989), lines 275–86 (p. 388)).

30. Goldsmith (1770), 19 (Lonsdale (ed.) (1989), line 302 (p. 388)).

11 Autumn

1. Donne, ed. Smith (1996), 'Elegy 9 *The Autumnal*', lines 1–2 (p. 105).

2. Chatterton, ed. Taylor and Hoover (1971), 'Ælla', i. lines 296–7 (p. 186).

3. Keats, ed. Garrod (1982), 218–19.

4. See McGann (1985), 15–65; Wolfson (1986);

Roe (1997), 254–7; and, for an enhancement of the point based around Winchester politics, see Turley, Archer, and Thomas (2012), 797–817.

5. See, for example, Vendler (1983), 244.

6. Tennyson, 'In Memoriam A. H. H.', ed. Ricks (1987), canto lxix, lines 1–2 (vol. ii, p. 383).

7. Larkin (1990), 'Autumn', 75.

8. Milton, ed. Fowler (1967), bk IX, lines 158–9, 180, 635–6 – God of course is the sun that can dissolve mist.

9. Looker (ed.) (1948), 65.

10. See Langford (2000), 287–8.

11. Shakespeare, *Henry V*, III. v. 15–22.

12. See Chandler (1998).

13. See Reed (1983), 10.

14. Locke (1690), bk III, chapter 9, pp. 238–9.

15. Twining (1856), ii. 133–4; see also Twining (1849). See Boutell (1877), 233–6.

16. See Boutmy, trans. Bodley (1904), 12.

17. Walton and Cotton, ed. Buxton (1982), 74.

18. Swinburne (1868), 'Itylus', 63.

19. Grey (1927), 136–7.

20. Charcoal-burning occurs in August and September, protected by St Theobald; as his feast is 30 June or 1 July, this perhaps indicates some earlier practice or tradition: see Jones, 193.

21. Tusser (1570), 22r; see also Fuller (1732), no. 6214 (p. 278): 'September, blow soft, / Till the Fruit's in the Loft'.

22. Spenser, ed. Hamilton (1977), bk VII, canto vii, st. 38.

23. 'Poor Robin' (1676), B4v [italics reversed; note the rhyme 'truly'/'July'].

24. Plot (1686), 434.

25. See Heaney (1987), 359–60; see also Shipman (1982).

26. Shakespeare, *As You Like It*, IV. ii. 10–18.

27. Green (1991):

A series of interwoven steps with dancers in a line is followed by the formation of a circle, and then the teams of dancers skip off in opposite directions. The stag dance follows when the dancers with antlers mime the fighting clash of rutting stags, advancing and retreating three times. The other characters snap their sticks or bows or bang a ladle in time to the music, which now is a variety of folk tunes, because the original 'genuine' Horn Dance tune was lost at the end of the 1880s. The dancers meet and cross over three times and 'fight' three times, then form a line and continue on their way, repeating the pattern countless times during a long day of dancing (97).

28. Greenwood (1867), 198–9.

29. Cameron (1998), 15.

30. Tusser (1573), 54v.

31. 'Poor Robin' (1673) B5r. The Devil also spits on blackberries while he's out; see McMichael (1910), 33–4; the practice is noted in *The London Magazine* 2 (1733), 421. The 'Devil's nutting bags' were traditionally extremely black (see Ward (1721), 24), although the slang lexicographer Francis Grose unexpectedly defines the phrase as 'DANDY GREY RUSSET' (1788, I2r); there is surely bawdy innuendo here.

32. Clare, ed. Robinson, Powell, and Dawson (1993), 140 (letter to Hone, April 1825, spelt thus).

33. Tusser (1573), 18r; the nursery rhyme 'Here we go gathering nuts in May' is clearly anachronistic – May is not known for 'cold and frosty mornings' either.

34. Defoe (1734), [46–7].

35. Orange (1840), i. 248; see Cameron (1998), 30–1, 60, 34, 132.

36. Quoted by Manship, ed. Palmer (1854), 6.

37. Camden, rev. Gibson (1753), i. col. 466.

38. Trythall (1912), refrain ['And it's, "Oh, then, where be he going, and what be he doing of there? / Heave down your prong and stamp along, to Tavistock Goosey Fair"'; a 'prong' is a pitchfork].

39. See Garbet (1818), 227–8.

40. Hardy, ed. Falck-Yi (2008), 43.

41. Cameron (1998), 123.

42. See Wright, ed. Lones (1936–40), iii. 84.

43. Gascoigne (1575), 'Flowers', xl.

44. Tusser (1573), 18r.

45. Tusser (1573), XIV ('The Points of Huswifrie', fol. 13v).

46. Spenser, ed. Hamilton (1977), bk VII, canto vii, st. 39.

47. Breton (1626), C4v.

48. Baring-Gould (1876), 226; Baring-Gould mistakenly claims that 1 October was Lammas Day.

49. See Hone, *The Every-Day Book* (1827), ii. cols 1307–10.

50. Brewer (1998), 1207.

51. St Ethelreda's Day is 23 June.

52. Sitwell (1927), 9.

53. Cobbett (1825), ¶ 507.

54. See Clifford and King (2006), 13–14.

55. Defoe (1724), Letter II, i. 6 [new pagination].

56. Hardy, ed. Gibson (1979), no. 673 (p. 709).

57. St Crispin is the patron saint of cobblers and leather-workers; Middleton (1611), C2r.

58. For a detailed account, see Rogers (2002).

59. Frazer (1933), 634.

60. Blackburn and Holford-Strevens (1999), 436.

61. The *Daily Mail* (31 October 2011) claimed that 22 per cent of the population would support a ban on trick-or-treating following the 2011 summer riots (www.dailymail.co.uk/femail); on 23 October 2009 the *Daily Telegraph* reported that Waltham Forest Council had introduced measures against the wearing of masks for Hallowe'en and that local shops would not be selling eggs (www.telegraph.co.uk); for a moderate Anglican attitude towards Hallowe'en, see Harding (2006).

62. Eliot (1969), 'Murder in the Cathedral', 239.

63. The first of November was also the traditional date to start growing Yorkshire forced rhubarb, although milder winters have meant that this can now be delayed as late as Christmas.

64. Gadbury (1696), B7r: 'They were in form about the bigness of a *Two-Penny Cake*: And every Visitant took one of them'; see also Aubrey, ed. Britten (1881), 23.

65. Northall (1892), 218 [includes variant line, 'Three for the little lad under the wall']; see also Wright, ed. Lones (1936–40), iii. 139.

66. Inwards (1898), 43; see also Lean (1902–4), i. 307 and Dunwoody (1883), 102. This proverb is explained thus: 'When the ice before Martlemas bears a duck / then look for a winter of mire and muck' (Lean (1902–4), i. 382).

67. Dove (1664), C5r–v; see also Addy (1895), 118.

68. Shakespeare, 1 *Henry IV*, I. ii. 158–9.

69. Westwood (?), 'Upon the Fifth of November', in 'The Blind-Man's Meditations' (1744), 80 – the verse continues for another fifty-six lines.

70. Pepys notes bonfires and fireworks on 5 November 1660 (ed. Warrington (1953), i. 109).

71. For a detailed account, see Hutton (1996), 393–407.

72. See Northall (1892), 244–50 for variants, including 'King George's sake'; a 'coil' is a 'coal'.

73. Howitt (1841), 80. Howitt also recorded the rhyme 'Pray remember / The Fifth of November! / A stick or a stake / For King George's sake, / Timber or coal / For the bonfire pole' (81).

74. See www.lewesbonfirecouncil.org.uk; visitors were discouraged in 2010.

75. See Cressy (2004), 81–2.

76. Flaming barrels are also carried in Hatherleigh at 5 a.m. on the morning of 5 November.

77. See 'Turning the Devil's Boulder: Primitive Rite in a Devon Village', *The Times*, 4 November 1952, 8; the correspondent notes: 'The oldest inhabitant [of the village], a blacksmith 87 years of age, has given his boyhood memories of the custom. He told me that in his time the custom took place later in the evening, and torches and lanterns were used to illuminate a square that is now lit by electricity.'

78. Stevenson (1661), 53.

79. Clare, ed. Robinson and Powell (2004), 'St Martins Eve', 174–5; see Goodridge (2012), 149.

80. Hood, ed. Jerrold (1906), 'No!' (1844), 364.

81. Lean (1902–4), i. 382; Lean notes that this was verified 1881–2.

82. Brewer (1998), 816; see also Dryden, ed. Hammond and Hopkins (2007), 'The Hind and the Panther', pt iii, line 565n (p. 488).

83. Spenser, ed. Hamilton (1977), bk VII, canto vii, st. 40.

84. Inwards (1869), 33.

85. Shakespeare, 1 Henry VI, I. ii. 131–2.

86. Dorothy Wordsworth, ed. Woof (2002), 31.

87. Evelyn (1729), 301; see Campbell-Culver (2006).

88. Another severe storm in January 1990 killed forty-seven.

12 Winter

1. Carlyle, ed. Goldberg, Brattin, and Engel (1993), 9.

2. Shakespeare, Sonnet 97, 1766–7; Sonnet 98 continues the theme, but glories in the revival of spring.

3. Andrewes (1629), Sermon 15 (25 December 1622), 'Sermons of the Nativity', 139–47, 143–4.

4. Eliot (1969), 'Journey of the Magi', 103.

5. Seneca, 'De providentia', trans. Davie (2007), 12–13. Schama points out that the intimate proximity of the German peoples to their natural environment not only questioned Roman metropolitanism, but seemed to Stoic philosophers such as Seneca an indication of moral decline (86).

6. Brooke, 'The Soldier', in Braithwaite (ed.) (1919), 141; Brooke is buried on the Greek island of Skyros.

7. Evelyn, ed. Dobson (1996), i. 120–1.

8. Clifford and King (2006), 435.

9. 'Icedore Frostifacc' (1740), 16.

10. 'Icedore Frostiface' (1740), 17; Frost Fair (23 January 1740) [italics reversed].

11. Frostiana (1814) ('Printed and published on the ICE on the River Thames, February 5, 1814'), 18.

12. Frostiana (1814), 24.

13. Stirling (1997), 286.

14. The winter of 1962–3 was the coldest since 1740, and saw the longest duration of snow covering lowlands (sixty-seven days); forty-nine people died of exposure. This winter was popularly seen as the herald of a new ice age.

15. Keats, ed. Garrod (1982), 'Stanzas', 436; Cowper (1785), 144.

16. Breton (1626), D1v–D2r.

17. Jones (2007), 183.

18. Aubrey, ed. Britten (1881), 40–1.

19. Machyn, ed. Nichols (1848), 160.

20. Sternberg (1851), 183–4; the first published book to have 'folk-lore' in its title.

21. Lean (1902–4), i. 367, 383. Clare notes that the Eve of St Thomas is also a time for love divination: see Clare, ed. Robinson, Powell, and Dawson (1993), 140 (letter to Hone, April 1825).

22. Ray (1678), 52.

23. Lean (1902–4), i. 383.

24. The bird is more properly the 'alcyon': see the account in Blackburn and Holford-Strevens (1999), 499.

25. Tayler, ed. Wise (1962), 78.

26. See Frazer (1933), 536–7.

27. See Herd (ed.) (1776), ii. 210–11, beginning 'Will ze go to the wood? quo' FOZIE MOZIE' (it is also known as 'Green Banks'); there may also be a link to the nursery rhyme 'Who Killed Cock Robin?' first published in 1744 (see Opies (1997), 130–3, and Roud (2006), 408).

28. Carew (1723), 32.

29. Lamb (1923), 'New Year's Eve', 47.

30. Chambers (ed.) (1832), ii. 787.

31. See Woodforde, ed. Beresford (1978), 167 (31 December 1780); and Hawthorne (1900), xx. 22 (vol. ii of Notes of Travel, 4 vols) (Liverpool, 1 January 1856).

32. Lamb (1923), 'New Year's Eve', 47.

33. Gunter (1830), 126, 133.

34. Breton (1626), B4r; A Propre New Booke of Cokery (1545), A2v.

35. Breton (1626), B4r.

36. Lloyd (1590), B3r–D2v [20].

37. Pater (1540), B4v–B5r.

38. Balfour (1904), 174; Pater (1540), B7v–B8r; for a later, modernized version from Cornwall, see *The Western Antiquary; or Devon and Cornwall Note-Book* 3 (1884), 193. Note the Conversion of St Paul is represented in early calendars by a sword, although this is not the day of his martyrdom by that weapon.

39. Forster (1824), 15.

40. Breton (1626), B4r.

41. Grey (1927), 15–16.

42. 'He is not of the winter singers that wait for a gleam of spring-like sunshine to inspirit them, but is loudest in wet and rough weather; and it is this habit and something in the wild and defiant character of the song, heard above the tumult of nature, which have won for him the proud name of storm-cock' (Hudson (1921), 40).

43. Brathwaite (1634), D12r–v; see Brand (1813), ii. 533; the goose's breastbone is also used in weather lore.

44. Hudson (1921), 60.

45. Confirmed by Luke 2: 21.

46. Macky (1714–23), i. 106.

47. Orm, ed. Holt and White (1878), lines 4230–1 (i. 146).

48. Temple (1731), ii. 17 (letter dated 2 January 1669, NS).

49. See Pepys, ed. Warrington (1953), iii. 328 (1 January 1669).

50. See Brady (1812), i. 136–7.

51. *The London and Paris Observer* (7 January 1838), 80 [reprinted throughout the century]. Blackburn and Holford-Strevens (1999) add spices for each bottle of wine from the recipe in Chambers's *Book of Days*: 10 grains of mace, 26 grains of cloves, 27 grains of cardamums, 28 grains of cinnamon, 12 grains of nutmeg, 48 grains of ginger, 49 grains of coriander seeds [= 3 g mace, 12 g cloves, 10 g cardamom, 7.5 g cinnamon, 3 g nutmeg, 12.5 g ginger, 13 g coriander seed; use whole spices] (13).

52. Spicer (1948), 2–3; the cakes may be linked with the apocryphal Pope Joan – the Lady Pope.

53. See Jamieson (1808), ii, entry under 'YULE' [no pagination]; Clare, ed. Robinson, Powell, and Dawson (1993), 140 (letter to Hone, April 1825).

54. Lean (1902–4), i. 373; Herrick adapted this in 'The New-Yeeres Gift, or Circumcisions Song, sung to the King in the Presence at White-Hall', ed. Moorman (1947), 355: 'Cast Holy Water all about, / And have a care no fire goes out'.

55. Prynne (1633), 755–7. Alchuvinus is Alcuin.

56. See Herrick, ed. Moorman (1947), 'Saint Distaffs Day, or the Morrow after Twelfth Day', 308. See also Clare, ed. Robinson, Powell, and Dawson (1993), 142–3 (letter to Hone, April 1825).

57. See Howkins and Merricks (1991), 187–208; and Cass and Roud, ed. Taylor and Rowe (2002).

58. Clifford and King (2006), 415.

59. Quoted by Henricks (1991), 34.

60. Keats, ed. Garrod (1982), 'The Eve of St Agnes', 195.

61. Burton, ed. Faulkner, Kiessling, and Blair (1989–94), iii. 191.

62. *Aristotle's Last Legacy* (1711), 50.

63. For example, in Plymouth, Falmouth, and Tunbridge Wells; the Society of King Charles the Martyr was founded in 1894 and since then has published the journal *Church and King*.

64. See Lacey (2003), and contemporary accounts such as Edward ('Ned') Ward (1703), which ran through three editions in one year (retitled for the eighth and ninth editions, 1713–14).

65. Ray (1670), 40.

66. Skelton, ed. Dyce (1856), 'Garlande of Laurell', ii. 234; see Skelton, ed. Brownlow (1990), 231.

67. Stevens (1706), Aa2r; see also Swainson (1873), 39: 'If in February there be no rain, / 'Tis neither good for hay nor grain'.

68. Lean (1902–4), i. 355.

69. Inwards (1898), 22.

70. Horwood (1919), iii. 114.

71. John 21: 15–17.

72. Ray (1678), 50, 52.

73. Hardy, ed. Gibson (1979), no. 275 (p. 335).

74. Breton (1626), B4v.

75. Jefferies (2008), 'Out of Doors in February', 185.

76. Jefferies (2008), 'Haunts of the Lapwing', 201.

77. Jefferies (2008), 'Out of Doors in February', 188.

78. Herrick, ed. Moorman (1947), 277–8.

79. Woodforde, ed. Beresford (1978), 198–200.

80. Chaucer, ed. Robinson (1974), 'Parliament of Fowls', lines 309–10 (p. 314): 'For this was on seynt Valentines day, / Whan every foul cometh there to chese his make'.

81. Lydgate, ed. MacCracken (1911), 'A Valentine to Her that Excelleth All', 304–10; Herrick, ed. Moorman (1947), 'To his Valentine, on S. Valentine's Day', 149.

82. Butler (1756), i. 295, 192.

83. Shakespeare, *Hamlet*, IV. v. 48–51.

84. Misson, trans. Ozell (1719), 330–1.

85. Colman and Thornton (1758), 129–31 [misnumbered] (20 February 1755); I would not recommend eating a boiled egg full of salt under any circumstances.

86. Lamb (1923), 'Valentine's Day', 121.

87. See Woodforde, ed. Beresford (1978), e.g. 1782 (p. 181), 1785 (p. 243), 1786 (p. 263), etc.

88. 'Scraps', *The Graphic* (17 February 1894), 190: 'At one house supper was served on heart-shaped tables lighted by Cupids holding a candle as torch shaded with delicate pink paper'.

89. Cameron (1998), 8.

90. In the Roman Catholic calendar of saints, St Matthias' feast is now 14 May.

91. Lyly (1600), F1r.

92. Shelley, ed. Reiman and Powers (1977), 'Ode to the West Wind', lines 69–70 (p. 223); in Thomson's *The Seasons* the words of the poet are creative as they are in the Book of Genesis, and the last line of 'Winter' invokes spring again: see Thomson, ed. Sambrook (1972), 'Winter', lines 1042–6, 1068–9 (pp. 156–7).

13 Christmas and the Twelve Days

1. Based on Blackburn and Holford-Strevens (1999), 515; Christmas is still to be recognized by the Armenian Church.

2. For a comprehensive account, see Hutton (1996), 1–33; see also Hervey (1888, 2000).

3. OED derives 'yule' from earlier forms in Old Norse, Old Anglian, and Gothic; *guili*, *geōla*, or *jiuli* were names of the Saxon month that began and ended the year.

4. 'Godfridus' (1554), B2r, B3r–v. 'Uer' is an Anglicization of the ancient Greek word for spring, *éar* or *wêr*; 'unneth' is an archaic form of 'uneath', meaning 'with difficulty'.

5. Pennant (1776), 48; Lean (1902–4), i. 383.

6. Harland and Wilkinson (1867), 253.

7. Elton (1647), 109.

8. For example, the Revd Morris of Exeter in 1839: see Mozley (ed.) (1891), ii. 291.

9. Brand (1813), i. 354; Sternberg (1851), 186; and Wright, ed. Lones (1936–40), ii. 74–5: see Gen. 9: 10.

10. Plat (1608), 4, 150.

11. Herrick records mistletoe display in 'Ceremonies for Candlemasse Eve' (ed. Moorman (1947), 277 – although he advises taking it down for Christmas, perhaps alluding to local customs, for example in Herefordshire, which deem mistletoe unlucky if brought into the house before New Year's Day.

12. Stow (1603), 98.

13. *Round About Our Coal-Fire* (1730?), 1.

14. Irving (n.d.), 'Christmas Eve', 181 (1 January 1820); its pagan associations are recorded by the Roman historian Pliny the Elder.

15. Fosbroke (1825), ii. 587.

16. Herrick, ed. Moorman (1947), 'Ceremonies for Christmasse', 258.

17. Frazer (1933), 636–7.

18. See Thorn (1795), 13, 15.

19. Thomas Hardy (ed. Slade (1999), 122) writes of the reluctance of tradition in *The Return of the Native* (1878), describing the Egdon mummers' play. Its authenticity lay in its very deficiency:

A traditional pastime is to be distinguished from a mere revival in no more striking feature than in this, that while in the revival all is excitement and fervour, the survival is carried on with a stolidity and absence of stir which sets one wondering why a thing that is done so perfunctorily should be kept up at all. Like Balaam and other unwilling prophets, the agents seem moved by an inner compulsion to say and do their allotted parts whether they will or no. This unweeting manner of performance is the true ring by which, in this refurbishing age, a fossilized survival may be known from a spurious reproduction.

20. *Sir Gawain and the Green Knight*, trans. Tolkien (2006), 18.

21. For 'carols', the original line in *Gawain* is 'Justed ful Jolile þise gentyle kniȝtes,/ Syþen kayred to þe court, caroles to make' (line 43): see OED. For seasonal morris dancing and mumming see Clare, ed. Robinson, Powell, and Dawson (1993), 140–1 (letter to Hone, April 1825).

22. See OED under 'wassail'.

23. Stow (1598), 72.

24. Stubbes (1583), O7v–O8r.

25. Prynne (1633), 21: '*or to decke up their Houses with Laurell, Yvie, and greene boughs*, (as we Use to doe in the Christmas season) *because all this observation is descended of Paganisme*'; and Stow, ed. Strype (1720), i. 253. In compensation, the second Tuesday of every month became a day of thanksgiving; the first of these took place on 13 July 1647.

26. Evelyn, ed. De Beer (1955), viii. 204.

27. See 'T. H.' (1647); 'Simon Minc'd Pye' (1646); and King (1658).

28. Misson (1719), 34 ('*Westphalia*' refers to bacon or ham).

29. Clarendon (1765), ii. 128 (18 December 1686).

30. Weaver (1717); for carols, see Dearmer, Vaughan Williams, and Shaw (eds) (1964): of the 197 carols in this collection, by far the majority are for the Christmas season.

31. Gay (1716), 58.

32. Denham (1846), 62; Denham stuffily observes that this is 'A trite observation, general through the whole of Westmorland and Cumberland'.

33. Dorman (1740), 7.

34. *Round About Our Coal-Fire* (1730?), 3.

35. *Round About Our Coal-Fire* (1730?), 8–10.

36. Misson (1719), 34–5.

37. Hone, *The Table Book* (1827), 667; Hone assigns this to the *Newcastle Chronicle*, 6 January 1770 – there is no reason to doubt this, but no copy of the relevant newspaper appears to be extant.

38. Southey (1807), iii. 102–3 (Letter lviii). Southey puts this down to urbanization and the sale of country estates to those 'who have no feeling connected with times and seasons' (103). He also mentions Valentine cards, i. 284 (Letter xxiv).

39. *Round About Our Coal-Fire* (1730?), 6.

40. Moore (1849) [13]–[15]; the authorship of the poem is disputed between Clement Clarke Moore and Henry Livingston, Jr.

41. See Irving (1873), 144–5, in which Oloffe Van Kortlandt dreams of a similar St Nicholas.

42. See Hutton (1996), 112–23; also www. thecoca-colacompany.com/heritage/ cokelore_santa.html.

43. See, for example, Dearmer, Vaughan Williams, and Shaw (eds) (1964), no. 195.

44. 'Hints for Christmas Decorations', *Girl's Own Paper* (11 December 1880), 109–10.

45. See ODNB.

46. Some recipients of early cards, however, remained superstitious about wild birds entering the house, which extended to the depictions of robins on Christmas cards.

47. The OED entry for the 'cracker bonbon' erroneously attributes its first mention to Sir Andrew Smith in the skit 'Delightful People', in *The Mirror of Literature, Amusement, and Instruction* 37 (1841), 404; 'Delightful People' was in fact written by Albert Richard Smith, and appears in *Comic Tales and Sketches* (1852), 30–45, 41. Tom Smith, a Norwich confectioner, is popularly considered the

innovator of the English cracker in 1847: see the account at www.tomsmithcrackers.co.uk.

48. Keble (1827).

49. The Devil eventually left Jesus on 15 February.

50. Herrick, ed. Moorman (1947), 'Twelfe Night, or King and Queene', 310.

51. In the green room at Drury Lane Theatre the traditional St Baddeley's Cake is eaten, established by Robert Baddeley by a bequest in 1794.

52. The wassail bowl was also drunk on St Catherine's Day (25 November); Catherine was called upon by unmarried women.

53. Herrick, ed. Moorman (1947), 'Christmasse-Eve, another Ceremonie / Another', 259.

54. Traditional: see Christian (1972), 113.

55. *Gentleman's Magazine* 61 (1791), 116. 'The hole in the cake allows it to be placed on the horn of an ox, who is then ticked and tosses it one way or the other, by which prognostication it becomes the property of either the master or the mistress of the house.'

56. Aubrey, ed. Britten (1881), 40.

57. Ray (1768), 40.

58. Coleridge, ed. Beer (1983), 'Frost at Midnight', lines 65–74 (p. 139).

14 Past, Present, and Future

1. Clare, ed. Robinson and Powell (2002), 189.

2. Clifford and King (2006), 276.

3. See Cloke (1993), 53–67.

4. At least until Nigel fell off the roof of his stately home, Lower Loxley.

5. Burchardt (2002) argues that in the twentieth century 'the countryside as an object of consumption rather than as a means of production ... has more significantly affected English society' (2, see also 204).

6. Burchardt (2002), 165.

7. Bradshaw (2002), i. 7; see also White, Jr (1967), 1203–7; Steward (1972), 120–9; Higgs (1997), 338–48; Cairns, Jr (1994).

8. See Carson (1962, 2000); Shoard (1980); Donald, Green, and Heath (7 January 2001), 25–9; and Lovegrove (2007).

9. See, for example, Rowe (2006).

10. See Hamos, ed. Josephson (1962), 172–9: cited by Ehrenreich (2007), 250.

11. Debord, trans. Knabb (2004), ¶ 154 (p. 50).

12. Thomas, 'The Minister' (1956), 91.

BIBLIOGRAPHY

Manuscripts

John Dee, 'A playne Discourse and humble Advise for our Gratious Queen Elizabeth, her most Excellent Majestie to peruse and consider, as concerning the needful Reformation of the Vulgar Kalendar for the civile years and daies accompting, or verifyeng, according to the time truely spent', Bodleian Library, MS Ashmole 1789, folios 1–62.

Stevins Manuscript: Walter Stevens, 'G. Chaucer's Conclusions of the Astrolabe, amended by W. Stevins' [*c*.1553–4], British Library, Sloane MS 261.

'Sumer is icumen in', British Library, MS Harley 978, fol. 11v.

Works cited

Sidney Oldall Addy, *Household Tales with Other Traditional Remains collected in the Countries of York, Lincoln, Derby, and Nottingham* (London: David Nutt; Sheffield: Pawson & Brailsford, 1895).

Ælfric, ed. Peter Clemoes, Early English Text Society, Second Series 17 (London: Oxford University Press, 1997).

Stewart Lee Allen, *In the Devil's Garden: A Sinful History of Forbidden Food* (Edinburgh: Canongate, 2002).

William Andrews (ed.), *The Church Treasury of History, Custom, Folklore, etc.* (London: privately printed, 1898).

Lancelot Andrewes, XCVI. *Sermons by the Right Honorable and Reverend Father in God,* Lancelot Andrewes, late Lord Bishop of Winchester (London, 1629).

Anon., *The Adventures of Oxymel Classic, Esq; once an Oxford Scholar,* 2 vols (London, 1768).

Anon., *The Anglo-Saxon Chronicles,* trans. and ed. Michael Swanton (London: Phoenix, 2000).

Anon., *Aristotle's Last Legacy: or, His Golden Cabinet of Secrets Opened, for Youth's Delightful Pastime* (London, 1711).

Anon., *Come Lasses and Lads,* Randolph Caldecott's Picture Books (London: Frederick Warne, n.d. [*c*.1885]).

Anon., *The Comical Pilgrim; or, Travels of a Cynick Philosopher, thro' the Most Wicked Parts of the World, namely, England, Wales, Scotland, Ireland, and Holland* (London, 1722).

Anon., *English Irish Dictionary. An focloir bearla Gaoidheilge. Ar na chur a neagar le Conchobar o Beaglaoich mar don le congnamh Aodh bhridhe mac Cuirtin agus fós* (bPairis, 1732).

Anon., *Frostiana: or A History of the River Thames, in a Frozen State; with an Account of the Late Severe Frost; and the Wonderful Effects of Frost, Snow, Ice, and Cold, in England, and in Different Parts of the World; interspersed with Various Amusing Anecdotes* (London: G. Davis, 1814).

Anon., *The Jew's Triumph, A Ballad* (London, 1753).

Anon., *The Kalender of the Shepherdes* (London, *c*.1500).

Anon., 'Lincolnshire Folklore: Calendar Customs', *Folklore* 44.3 (1933), 279–95.

Anon., *May-Day: A Poem* (London, 1769).

Anon., *Mirth Without Mischief* (London, 1800).

Anon. [Thomas Stretser?], *A New Description of Merryland* (Bath, 1741 [1740]).

Anon., *The Old and New Interest: or a Sequel to The Oxfordshire Contest* (London, 1753).

Anon., *The Oxfordshire Contest: or the Whole Controversy between the Old and New Interest* (London, 1753).

Anon., *The Peace Egg, or, St. George's Annual Play: For the Amusement of Youth* (London: William Willis, 1835).

Anon., *The Potent Ally: or, Succours from Merryland* (Paris, 1741).

Anon., 'Prognostications of the Weather', *Robert Merry's Museum* (Nov. 1844), 154–9.

Anon., *A Propre New Booke of Cokery declaryng What Maner of Meates bee best in Ceason for all Tymes of Ye Yere and how thes ought to bee Dressed and Served at the Table bothe for Fleshe Daies and Fisshe Daies: with a Newe Addicion, veri necessarye for all them that Delighteth in Cokery* (London, 1545).

Anon., *Round About Our Coal-Fire: or Christmas Entertainments* (London, 1730?).

Anon., *Sir Gawain and the Green Knight*, trans. J. R. R. Tolkien, ed. Christopher Tolkien (London: HarperCollins, 2006).

Anon., *A Short Description of the Roads which lead to that Delightful Country called Merryland* (London, 1743).

Anon., *A Supplement to all the Common Almanacks containing Things for Every Month in the Year, which all the Common Almanacks ought to mention, and yet None of Them Speak a Word Of* (London, 1730).

Anon., *Vox Graculi, or Jacke Dawes Prognostication* (London, 1623).

Aristotle, *Meteorologica*, trans. H. D. P. Lee, Loeb Classical Library (Cambridge, Mass. and London: Harvard University Press, 1952).

Edward A. Armstrong, *The Folklore of Birds* (London: Collins, 1958).

T. S. Ashton, *Economic Fluctuations in England, 1700–1800* (Oxford: Clarendon Press, 1959).

Margaret Aston, *The Panorama of the Renaissance* (London: Thames & Hudson, 1996).

John Aubrey, *The Natural History of Wiltshire*, ed. John Britton (London: Wiltshire Topographical Society, 1847).

John Aubrey, *Remaines of Gentilisme and Judaisme* (1686–7), ed. James Britten (London: Folk-Lore Society, 1881).

Francis Bacon, *The Natural and Experimental History of Winds &c. written in Latine by the Right Honourable Francis Lord Verulam, Viscount St. Alban; translated into English by R. G., Gent.* (London, 1671).

Roger Bacon, *The Opus Majus of Roger Bacon*, ed. Robert Belle Burke, 2 vols (New York: Russell & Russell, 1962).

Anne Elizabeth Baker (ed.), *Glossary of Northamptonshire Words and Phrases*, 2 vols (London: John Russell Smith, 1854).

M. C. Balfour, *County Folklore*, vol. 4: *Northumberland* (London: David Nutt, 1904).

Sabine Baring-Gould, *Folk Songs of the West Country*, ed. Gordon Hitchcock (Newton Abbot: David & Charles, 1974).

Sabine Baring-Gould and H. Fleetwood Sheppard, *Songs and Ballads of the West* (London: Methuen, 1895).

Sabine Baring-Gould, *The Vicar of Morwenstow: A Life of Robert Stephen Hawker, MA* (London: Henry S. King & Co., 1876).

Thomas Batchelor, *General View of the County of Bedford* (London: Sherwood, Neely, and Jones, 1813).

Francis Beaumont and John Fletcher, *Comedies and Tragedies* (London, 1647).

Bede, *The Ecclesiastical History of the English People*, ed. Judith McClure and Roger Collins (Oxford: Oxford University Press, 1994).

Bede, *The Reckoning of Time*, trans. Faith Wallis (Liverpool: Liverpool University Press, 1999).

St Benedict, *The Rule of Saint Benedict*, trans. Abbot Parry (Leominster: Gracewing, 1990).

Gillian Bennett, 'Tales My Mother Told Me: The Relevance of Oral History', Theresa Buckland and Juliette Wood (eds), *Aspects of British Calendar Customs*, Folklore Society Mistletoe Series 22 (Sheffield: Sheffield Academic Press, 1993), 95–103.

Henry Best, *Rural Economy in Yorkshire in 1641, being the Farming and Account Books of Henry*

Best, of Elmswell, in the East Riding of the
County of York, ed. C. B. Robinson (Durham:
Surtees Society, 1857).

Henry Bett, English Myths and Traditions
(London: Batsford, 1952).

Beunans Meriasek. The Life of Saint Meriasek,
Bishop and Confessor, ed. and trans. Whitley
Stokes (London: Trübner & Co., 1872).

The Bible: Authorized King James Version (Oxford
and New York: Oxford University Press,
1998).

Bonnie Blackburn and Leofranc Holford-
Strevens, The Oxford Book of Days: Being a
Voyage through the Calendar (Oxford: Oxford
University Press, 2000).

Bonnie Blackburn and Leofranc Holford-
Strevens, The Oxford Companion to the Year:
An Exploration of Calendar Customs and Time-
Reckoning (Oxford: Oxford University Press,
1999).

Cyprian Blagden, 'The Distribution of
Almanacks in the Second Half of the
Seventeenth Century', Studies in Bibliography
11 (1958), 107–16.

Hugh Blair, Lectures on Rhetoric and Belles
Lettres, 2 vols (London, 1783).

William Blake, Songs of Innocence and of
Experience, ed. Geoffrey Keynes (Oxford:
Oxford University Press, 1970).

Richard Blakeborough, Wit, Character, Folklore
and Customs of the North Riding of Yorkshire
(London: Frowde, 1898).

Boethius, Anicius Manlius Torquatus Severinus
Boetius his Consolation of Philosophy, in Five
Books translated into English, trans. William
Causton (London, 1730).

Lucian Boia, Weather in the Imagination, trans.
Roger Leverdier (London: Reaktion, 2005).

Joseph Bosworth and T. Northcote Toller
(eds), An Anglo-Saxon Dictionary (Oxford:
Clarendon Press, 1898).

William Bottrell, Stories and Folk-Lore of West
Cornwall (3rd series) (Penzance: privately
printed, 1880).

William Bottrell, Traditions and Hearthside
Stories of West Cornwall (Penzance: privately
printed, 1870).

William Bottrell, Traditions and Hearthside
Stories of West Cornwall (2nd series)
(Penzance: privately printed, 1873).

Henry Bourne, Antiquitates Vulgares; or, The
Antiquities of the Common People (Newcastle,
1725).

Henry Bourne, see John Brand.

Charles Boutell, 'Symbols of the Seasons
and Months represented in Early Art', The
Art Journal 3 (1877), 233–6.

Émile Boutmy, The English People: A Study of
their Political Psychology, trans. J. E. C. Bodley
(New York and London: G. P. Putnam's
Sons, 1904) [originally published as Essai
d'une psychologie politique du peuple anglais au
XIXe siècle (Paris: Libraire Armand Colin,
1901)].

Anthony D. Bradshaw, 'Introduction and
Philosophy', in Martin R. Perrow and
Anthony J. Davy (eds), Handbook of Ecological
Restoration, 2 vols (Cambridge: Cambridge
University Press, 2002).

John Brady, Clavis Calendaria; or, A Compendious
Analysis of the Calendar: illustrated with
Ecclesiastical, Historical, and Classical Anecdotes,
2nd edn, 2 vols (London: London, Hurst,
Rees, Orme, & Brown, 1812).

John Brand, Observations on Popular Antiquities:
including the Whole of Mr. Bourne's Antiquitates
Vulgares, with Addenda to Every Chapter of that
Work: as also, An Appendix, containing such
Articles on the Subject, as have been omitted by
that Author (Newcastle upon Tyne, 1777).

John Brand, Observations on Popular Antiquities:
chiefly Illustrating the Origin of our Vulgar
Customs, Ceremonies, and Superstitions,
rev. Henry Ellis, 2 vols (London: F. C. &
J. Rivington, 1813).

John Brand, Observations on Popular Antiquities:
chiefly illustrating the Origin of our Vulgar
Customs, Ceremonies, and Superstitions, ed.
Henry Ellis, 2 vols (London: Charles
Knight, 1841).

John Brand, Observations on the Popular
Antiquities of Great Britain: chiefly illustrating the Origin of our Vulgar Superstitions
and Provincial Customs, Ceremonies, and

Superstitions, ed. Henry Ellis, 3 vols (London: Bohn, 1849).

Richard Brathwaite, *Whimzies: or, A New Cast of Characters* (London, 1631).

Richard Brathwaite, *A Strange Metamorphosis of Man, Transformed into a Wildernesse Deciphered in Characters* (London, 1634).

William Stanley Braithwaite (ed.), *The Book of Modern British Verse* (Boston: Small, Maynard, & Co., 1919).

Nicholas Breton, *Fantasticks: Serving for a Perpetuall Prognostication* (London, 1626).

E. Cobham Brewer, *The Dictionary of Phrase and Fable*, Classic Edition (London: Galley Press, 1988).

Robert Browning, *The Poetical Works*, ed. Ian Jack, *et al.*, 15 vols (Oxford: Clarendon Press, 1983–2009): vol. iv. *Dramatic Romances and Lyrics*, ed. Ian Jack, Rowena Fowler, and Margaret Smith (Oxford: Clarendon Press, 1991).

Michael Bruce, *Poems on Several Occasions* (Edinburgh, 1770).

Theresa Buckland and Juliette Wood (eds), *Aspects of British Calendar Customs*, Folklore Society Mistletoe Series 22 (Sheffield: Sheffield Academic Press, 1993).

Stefan Buczacki, *Fauna Britannica* (London: Hamlyn, 2002).

Jeremy Burchardt, *Paradise Lost: Rural Idyll and Social Change since 1800* (London and New York: I. B. Tauris, 2002).

Thomas Burnet, *The Theory of the Earth containing an Account of the Original of the Earth, and of All the General Changes which it hath already Undergone, or is to Undergo, till the Consummation of All Things* (London, 1684: English translation).

Robert Burton, *The Anatomy of Melancholy*, ed. Thomas C. Faulkner, Nicolas K. Kiessling, and Rhonda L. Blair, 3 vols (Oxford: Oxford University Press, 1989–94).

Bob Bushaway, *By Rite: Custom, Ceremony and Community in England, 1700–1880* (London: Junction Books, 1982).

Alban Butler, *The Lives of the Fathers, Martyrs, and Other Principal Saints: compiled from Original Monuments, and Other Authentick Records: Illustrated with the Remarks of Judicious Modern Criticks and Historians*, 4 vols (London, 1756).

Arthur John Butler (ed.), 'Elizabeth: December 1582, 21–31', *Calendar of State Papers Foreign, Elizabeth*, vol. 16: *May–Dec. 1582* (London: Institute of Historical Research, 1909).

John Cairns, Jr, *Ecological Restoration: Re-examining Human Society's Relationship with Natural Systems*, The Abel Wolfman Distinguished Lecture (Washington DC: National Research Council, 1994).

John Calvin, *Commentaries on the First Book of Moses called Genesis*, 2 vols, trans. John King (Grand Rapids, Mich.: Eerdmans, 1948).

William Camden, *Britannia: or, A Chorographical Description of Great Britain and Ireland, Together with the Adjacent Islands*, rev. Edmund Gibson, 2 vols (London, 1753).

David Kerr Cameron, *The English Fair* (Stroud: Sutton, 1998).

John Campbell, *Hermippus Redivivus, or, The Sage's Triumph over Old Age and the Grave* (London, 1743).

John Gregorson Campbell, *Witchcraft & Second Sight in the Highlands & Islands of Scotland: Tales and Traditions collected entirely from Oral Sources* (Glasgow: MacLehose & Sons, 1902).

Maggie Campbell-Culver, *A Passion for Trees: The Legacy of John Evelyn* (London: Eden Project Books, 2006).

Bernard Capp, *Astrology and the Popular Press: British Almanacks, 1500–1800* (London and Boston: Faber & Faber, 1979).

Bernard Capp, *When Gossips Meet: Women, Family, and Neighbourhood in Early Modern England* (Oxford: Oxford University Press, 2003).

Richard Carew, *The Survey of Cornwall* (London, 1602).

Richard Carew, *The Survey of Cornwall. And an Epistle concerning the Excellencies of the English Tongue. Now first Published from the Manuscript* (London, 1723).

Thomas Carlyle, *On Heroes, Hero-Worship, & the*

Heroic in History, ed. Michael K. Goldberg, Joel J. Brattin, and Mark Engel, The Norman and Charlotte Strauss Edition of the Writings of Thomas Carlyle (Berkeley, Los Angeles, and Oxford: University of California Press, 1993).

'Lewis Carroll' [Charles Dodgson], Alice's Adventures in Wonderland and Through the Looking Glass and What Alice Found There, ed. Hugh Haughton (London: Penguin, 1998).

Rachel Carson, Silent Spring (1962) (London: Penguin, 2000).

Eddie Cass and Steve Roud, Room, Room, Ladies and Gentlemen . . . : An Introduction to the English Mummers' Play, ed. Malcolm Taylor and Doc Rowe (London: English Folk Dance & Song Society, 2002).

E. Christopher Cawte, 'It's an Ancient Custom – But How Ancient?', Buckland and Wood (eds), 37–56.

E. Christopher Cawte, Ritual Animal Disguise: A Historical and Geographical Study of Animal Disguise in the British Isles (Cambridge: D.S. Brewer, 1978).

Robert Chambers (ed.), The Book of Days: A Miscellany of Popular Antiquities in Connection with the Calendar including Anecdote, Biography, & History, Curiosities of Literature, and Oddities of Human Life and Character, 2 vols (London and Edinburgh: Chambers, 1832).

Robert Chambers (ed.), The Book of Days: A Miscellany of Popular Antiquities in Connection with the Calendar, 2 vols (London and Edinburgh: W. & R. Chambers, 1864).

James Chandler, England in 1819: The Politics of Literary Culture and the Case of Romantic Historicism (Chicago: University of Chicago Press, 1998).

J. A. V. Chapple and Arthur Pollard (eds), The Letters of Mrs Gaskell (Manchester: Manchester University Press, 1966).

Thomas Chatterton, Complete Works, ed. Donald Taylor and Benjamin Hoover, 2 vols [continuously paginated] (Oxford: Clarendon Press, 1971).

Geoffrey Chaucer, The Works of Geoffrey Chaucer, ed. F. N. Robinson (Oxford, Melbourne, and Cape Town: Oxford University Press, 1974).

Lord Chesterfield, Letters, ed. David Roberts (Oxford and New York: Oxford University Press, 1992).

Lord Chesterfield, Miscellaneous Works of the late Philip Dormer Stanhope, Earl of Chesterfield, 2 vols (London, 1777).

Francis James Child (ed.), The English and Scottish Popular Ballads, 5 vols (New York: Folklore Press and Pageant Book Company, 1957).

Joshua Childrey, Britannia Baconica, or, The Natural Rarities of England, Scotland & Wales (London, 1661).

Roy Christian, Old English Customs (Newton Abbot: David & Charles, 1972).

Charles Churchill, Gotham. A Poem (London, 1764).

John Clare, By Himself, ed. Eric Robinson and David Powell (Manchester: Carcanet, 2002).

John Clare, Cottage Tales, ed. Eric Robinson, David Powell, and P. M. S. Dawson (Manchester: Carcanet, 1993).

John Clare, The Later Poems of John Clare, ed. Eric Robinson and Geoffrey Summerfield (Manchester: Manchester University Press, 1964).

John Clare, Major Works, ed. Eric Robinson and David Powell (Oxford: Oxford University Press, 2004).

John Clare, Poems of the Middle Period, 1827–1837, ed. Eric Robinson, David Powell, and P. M. S. Dawson, 4 vols (Oxford: Clarendon Press, 1996–8).

Earl of Clarendon, The State Letters of Henry Earl of Clarendon Lord Lieutenant of Ireland during the Reign of K. James the Second: and His Lordship's Diary for the Years 1687, 1688, 1689, and 1690, 2 vols (Oxford, 1765).

John Claridge, The Shepheards Legacy, or, John Clearidge, his Forty Years Experience of the Weather being an Excellent Treatise, wherein is shewed the Knowledge of the Weather (London, 1670).

John Claridge, The Shepherd of Banbury's Rules

to *Judge of the Changes of the Weather, grounded on Forty Years Experience* (London, 1744).

Sue Clifford and Angela King, *England in Particular: A Celebration of the Commonplace, the Local, the Vernacular and the Distinctive* (London: Hodder & Stoughton for Common Ground, 2006).

Sue Clifford and Angela King (eds), *Local Distinctiveness: Place, Particularity and Identity* (London: Common Ground, 1993).

Paul Cloke, 'The Countryside as Commodity: New Spaces for Rural Leisure', in Sue Glyptis (ed.), *Leisure and the Environment: Essays in Honour of Professor J. A. Patmore* (London and New York: Belhaven Press, 1993).

William Cobbett, *The Woodlands: or, A Treatise on the Preparing of Ground for Planting; on the Planting; on the Cultivating; on the Pruning; and on the Cutting Down of Forest Trees and Underwoods . . .* (London: privately printed, 1825).

Mark Cocker and Richard Mabey, *Birds Britannica* (London: Chatto and Windus, 2005).

Jennifer Cole, *Ceremonies of the Seasons: Exploring and Celebrating Nature's Eternal Cycle* (London: Duncan Baird, 2007).

Samuel Taylor Coleridge, *Poems*, ed. John Beer (London: Dent, 1983).

William Coles, *The Art of Simpling* (London, 1656).

George Colman and Bonnell Thornton, *The Connoisseur*, 2 vols (Dublin, 1756).

George Colman and Bonnell Thornton, *The Connoisseur*, 4 vols [continuous pagination] (London, 1758).

Wendy Cope, *Serious Concerns* (London: Faber & Faber, 1992).

James Cossins, *Reminiscences of Exeter Fifty Years Since* (Exeter: privately printed, 1877).

William Cowper, *Poems*, 2 vols (London: J. Johnson, 1800).

William Cowper, *The Task, A Poem, in Six Books* (London, 1785).

G. V. Coyne, SJ, M. A. Hoskin, and O. Pedersen (eds), *Gregorian Reform of the Calendar. Proceedings of the Vatican Conference to Commemorate its 400th Anniversary: 1582–1982* (Vatican: Specola Vatican, 1983).

George Crabbe, *The Village: A Poem* (London, 1783).

'George Crayon': *see* Washington Irving.

David Cressy, *Bonfires and Bells: National Memory and the Protestant Calendar in Elizabethan and Stuart England* (Stroud: Sutton, 2004).

H. Dagnall, *Give Us Back Our Eleven Days: An Account of the Change from the Old Style to the New Style Calendar in Great Britain in 1752* (Queensbury, UK: published by the author, 1991).

Jan Darby, 'Robin Hood: The Lord of Misrule', *Renaissance* 9.3 (2004), 41–6.

Alison and Merv Davey, *Snail Creeps and Tea Treats: Clay Country Customs* (Bodmin: Rescorla Festival, 2008).

Percy Dearmer, R. Vaughan Williams, and Martin Shaw (eds), *The Oxford Book of Carols* (Oxford: Oxford University Press, 1964).

Guy Debord, *The Society of the Spectacle*, trans. Ken Knabb (London: Rebel Press, 2004).

Daniel Defoe, *The Compleat English Tradesman*, 2 vols (London, 1727).

Daniel Defoe, *Curious and Diverting Journies, Thro' the Whole Island of Great-Britain* [*A Tour through the Whole Island of Great Britain*] (London, 1734).

Daniel Defoe, *The Storm*: *see* 'Pseudo-Defoe'.

Daniel Defoe, *A Tour thro' the Whole Island of Great Britain, divided into Circuits or Journies*, 3 vols (London, 1724).

Daniel Defoe, *A Tour thro' the Whole Island of Great Britain*, 3rd edn, 4 vols (London, 1742).

Michael A. Denham, *A Collection of Proverbs and Popular Sayings relating to the Seasons, the Weather, and Agricultural Pursuits; gathered chiefly from Oral Tradition* (London: Percy Soc., 1846).

Charles Dickens, *David Copperfield*, ed. Jeremy Tambling (London: Penguin, 2004).

Charles Dickens, *Hard Times*, ed. David Craig (London: Penguin, 1985).

Charles Dickens, *Dickens' Journalism: Sketches by Boz and Other Early Papers, 1833–39*, ed. Michael Slater (London: J.M. Dent, 1994).

Charles Dickens, *The Uncommercial Traveller and Other Papers, 1859–70*, ed. Michael Slater and John Drew (London: Dent, 2000).

Leonard Digges, *A Prognostication of Right Good Effect Fructfully Augmented, contayninge Playne, Briefe, Pleasant, Chosen Rules, to Judge the Wether for ever, by the Sunne, Moone, Sterres, Cometes, Raynbowe, Thunder, Cloudes, with Other Extraordinarie Tokens, not omitting the Aspectes of Planetes, with a Brefe Judgemente for ever, of Plentie, Lacke, Sickenes, Death, Warres &c. openinge also many Naturall Causes, woorthy to be Knowe[n]* (London, 1555).

Leonard Digges, *A Prognostication Everlasting of Ryght Good Effecte Frutefully Augmented by thauthor [sic], co[n]teyning Playne, Brief, Pleasant, Chose[n] Rules to Judge the Weather, by the Sunne, Moone, Starres, Cometes, Raynbowe, Thunder, Cloudes, with Other Extraordinarie Tokens, not omitting the Aspectes of Planetes, with a Briefe Judgement for ever of Plentie, Lacke, Sickenes, Death, Warres, &c. opening also many Natural Causes woorthy to be Knowen* (London, 1556).

P. E. Donald, R. E. Green, and M. F. Heath, 'Agricultural Intensification and the Collapse of Europe's Farmland Bird Populations', *Proceedings of the Royal Society of London* 268, no. 1462 (7 January 2001), 25–9.

John Donne, *The Complete English Poems*, ed. A. J. Smith (London: Penguin, 1996).

John Donne, *The Sermons*, ed. Evelyn M. Simpson and George R. Potter, 10 vols (Berkeley, Los Angeles, and London: University of California Press, 1984).

Joseph Dorman, *Sir Roger de Coverly; or, The Merry Christmas* (London, 1740).

Jonathan Dove, *Speculum Anni à partu Virginis MDCLXIV. An Almanack for the Year of our Lord God 1664* (London, 1664).

Michael Drayton, *Poly-Olbion* (London, 1612).

John Dryden, *Selected Poems*, ed. Paul Hammond and David Hopkins (Harlow: Longman, 2007).

John Dryden (trans.), *The Works of Virgil containing his Pastorals, Georgics and Æneis: adorn'd with a Hundred Sculptures* (London, 1697).

Stephen Duck, *Poems on Several Subjects* (London, 1730).

Eamon Duffy, *The Stripping of the Altars: Traditional Religion in England, c.1400–c.1580* (New Haven and London: Yale University Press, 1992).

David Ewing Duncan, *The Calendar: The 5,000-Year Struggle to Align the Clock and the Heavens – and What Happened to the Missing Ten Days* (London: Fourth Estate, 1998).

H. H. C. Dunwoody, *Weather Proverbs*, Signal Service Notes No. IX (Washington: Government Printing Office, 1883).

Sir Frederic Morton Eden, *The State of the Poor: or, An History of the Labouring Classes in England, from the Conquest to the Present Period*, 3 vols (London, 1797).

Barbara Ehrenreich, *Dancing in the Streets: A History of Collective Joy* (London: Granta, 2007).

A. Roger Ekrich, *At Day's Close: A History of Nighttime* (London: Weidenfeld & Nicolson, 2005).

T. S. Eliot, *The Complete Poems and Plays* (London: Faber & Faber, 1969).

Edward Elton, *Gods Holy Minde touching Matters Morall: which himself Uttered in Ten Words, or Ten Commandements* (London, 1647).

Clive Emsley, *Crime and Society in England: 1750–1900* (London and New York: Longman, 1987).

Paul Ward English and Robert C. Mayfield (eds), *Man, Space, and Environment: Concepts in Contemporary Human Geography* (New York and London: Oxford University Press, 1972).

Desiderius Erasmus, *Apophthegmes that is to saie, Prompte, Quicke, Wittie and Sente[n]cious Saiyinges, of certaine Emperours, Kynges, Capitaines, Philosophiers and Oratours, as well*

Grekes, as Romaines, bothe Verie Pleasaunt and Profitable to Reade, partely for All Maner of Persones, and especially Gentlemenne, trans. Nicholas Udall (London, 1542).

George Evans and David Thomson, The Leaping Hare (London: Thames & Hudson, 1987, 1994).

John Evelyn, The Diary of John Evelyn, in Great British Diarists, ed. Austin Dobson, 3 vols (London: Routledge/Thoemmes Press, 1996).

John Evelyn, The Diary, Now First Printed in Full from the Manuscripts Belonging to Mr. John Evelyn, ed. E. S. De Beer, 6 vols (Oxford: Oxford University Press, 1955).

John Evelyn, Directions for the Gardiner and Other Horticultural Advice, ed. Maggie Campbell-Culver (Oxford: Oxford University Press, 2009).

John Evelyn, Silva: or, A Discourse of Forest-Trees, and the Propagation of Timber in His Majesty's Dominions: as it was delivered in the Royal Society the 15th of October, 1662, upon Occasion of Certain Quaeries propounded to that Illustrious Assembly, by the Honourable and Principal Officers and Commissioners of the Navy, fifth edn (London, 1729).

John Evelyn, Sylva (London, 1670).

Denis Feeney, Caesar's Calendar: Ancient Time and the Beginnings of History (Berkeley, Los Angeles, and London: University of California Press, 2007).

Christopher Fetherston, A Dialogue agaynst Light, Lewde, and Lascivious Dauncing: wherein are refuted all those Reasons, which the Common People use to bring in Defence thereof (London, 1582).

John Edward Field, The Myth of the Pent Cuckoo (London: Eliot Stock, 1913).

Henry Fielding, An Enquiry into the Causes of the late Increase of Robbers, &c. with some Proposals for Remedying this Growing Evil (Dublin, 1751).

Edward Fisher, A Christian Caveat to the Old and New Sabbatarians (London, 1650).

John Fletcher, Posthumous Pieces of the Late Rev. John William de la Fletchere (London, 1800).

Kathleen Forni (ed.), The Chaucerian Apocrypha: A Counterfeit Canon (Gainesville: University Press of Florida, 2001).

T. Forster, The Perennial Calendar, and Companion to the Almanack; illustrating the Events of Every Day in the Year, as connected with History, Chronology, Botany, Natural History, Astronomy, Popular Customs, & Antiquities, with Useful Rules of Health, Observations on the Weather; Explanations of the Fasts and Festivals of the Church (London: Harving, Mavor, & Lepard, 1824).

Thomas Dudley Fosbroke, Encyclopaedia of Antiquities, and Elements of Archaeology, Classical and Mediæval, 2 vols (London: John Nichols & Son, 1825).

Russell G. Foster and Leon Kreitzman, Seasons of Life: The Biological Rhythms that Living Things Need to Thrive and Survive (London: Profile, 2009).

Michel Foucault, The Order of Things: An Archaeology of the Human Sciences (London: Routledge, 1970).

Adam Fox, Oral and Literate Culture in England, 1500–1700 (Oxford: Clarendon Press, 2000).

James George Frazer, The Golden Bough: A Study in Magic and Religion (London: Macmillan, 1933).

'Icedore Frostiface', An Account of all the Principal Frosts for above An Hundred Years Past: with Political Remarks and Poetical Descriptions (London, 1740).

William Fulke, A Goodly Gallery with a Most Pleasant Prospect, into the Garden Of Naturall Contemplation, to beholde the Naturall Causes of All Kind of Meteors, 2nd edn (London, 1571).

Thomas Fuller, Gnomologia: Adagies and Proverbs; Wise Sentences and Witty Sayings, Ancient and Modern, Foreign and British (London, 1732).

John Gadbury, ΕΦΗΜΕΡΙΣ, or, A Diary Astronomical, Astrological, Meteorological for the Year of our Lord 1696 it being the Bissextile, or Leap-Year (London, 1696).

Catherine Gallagher, 'The Potato in the Materialist Imagination', in Catherine

Gallagher and Stephen Greenblatt, *Practicing New Historicism* (Chicago and London: University of Chicago Press, 2000), 110–35.

Samuel Garbet, *The History of Wem* (Wem: G. Franklin, 1818).

Edward B. Garriott, *Weather Folk-Lore and Local Weather Signs*, US Department of Agriculture, Weather Bureau (Washington: Government Printing Office, 1903).

Jane Garry, 'The Literary History of the English Morris Dance', *Folklore* 94.2 (1983), 219–28.

George Gascoigne, *The Poesies of George Gascoigne Esquire* (London, 1575).

John Gay, *The Shepherd's Week. In Six Pastorals* (London, 1714).

John Gay, *Trivia: or, The Art of Walking the Streets of London* (London, 1716).

Frank Gibson, *Superstitions about Animals* (London and Newcastle-on-Tyne: Walter Scott, 1904).

Owen Gingerich, 'The Civil Reception of the Gregorian Calendar', Coyne, Hoskin, and Pedersen (eds), 265–79.

John Goad, *Astro-Meteorologica, or, Aphorisms and Discourses of the Bodies Coelestial, their Natures and Influence* (London, 1686).

Malcolm Godden and Michael Lapidge (eds), *The Cambridge Companion to Old English Literature* (Cambridge: Cambridge University Press, 1991).

'Godfridus', *Here begynneth The Boke of Knowledge of Thynges Unknowen aperteynynge to Astronomye with Certayne Necessarye Rules, and Certayne Speres contaynyng herein compyled by Godfridus super Palladum de agricultura Anglicatum* (London, 1554).

Oliver Goldsmith, *The Deserted Village* (London, 1770).

John Goodridge, *John Clare and Community* (Cambridge: Cambridge University Press, 2012).

Richard Grafton, *Graftons Abridgement of the Chronicles of Englande* (London, 1570).

Edward Grant, *A History of Natural Philosophy: From the Ancient World to the Nineteenth Century* (Cambridge: Cambridge University Press, 2007).

Edward Grant, *A Source Book in Medieval Science* (Cambridge, Mass.: Harvard University Press, 1974).

Thornton S. Graves, 'Richard Rawlidge on London Playhouses', *Modern Philology* 18 (1920), 41–7.

Jonathon Green (ed.), *Green's Dictionary of Slang*, 3 vols (London: Chambers, 2010).

Marian Green, *A Calendar of Festivals: Traditional Celebrations, Songs, Seasonal Recipes & Things to Make* (Shaftesbury: Element, 1991).

James Greenwood, *Unsentimental Journeys: or, Byways of the Modern Babylon* (London: Ward, Lock, & Tyler, 1867).

Kenneth Gregory (ed.), *The First Cuckoo: Letters to The Times, 1900–75* (London: Times Books, 1976).

Sir Edward, Viscount Grey, *The Charm of Birds* (London: Hodder & Stoughton, 1927).

Richard Grey, *Memoria Technica: or, A New Method of Artificial Memory, applied to and exemplified in Chronology, History, Geography, Astronomy* (London, 1730).

Nick Groom (ed.), *The Bloody Register*, 4 vols (London and New York: Routledge/ Thoemmes Press, 1999).

Nick Groom, *The Union Jack: The Story of the British Flag* (London: Atlantic, 2006).

Francis Grose (ed.), *A Classical Dictionary of the Vulgar Tongue*, 2nd edn (London, 1788).

William Gunter, *Gunter's Confectioner's Oracle containing Receipts for Desserts on the Most Economical Plan for Private Families, and all Founded on the Actual Experiments of Thirty Years. With an Appendix, containing the Best Receipts for Pastry-Cooks, and an Elucidation of the Principles of Good Cheer. Being a Companion to Dr. Kitchiner's Cook's Oracle* (London: Alfred Miller, 1830).

Celia Haddon, *The First Ever English Olimpick Games* (London, Sydney, Auckland: Hodder & Stoughton, 2004).

Pierre Hadot, *The Veil of Isis: An Essay on the*

History of the Idea of Nature, trans. Michael Chase (Cambridge, Mass.: Belknap Press, 2006).

Edward Hall, The Union of the Two Noble and Illustre Famelies of Lancastre & Yorke [Chronicle, 1548] (London: Johnson, Rivington, et al., 1809).

Thomas Hall, Funebria Florae The Downfall of May-Games: wherein is set forth the Rudeness, Prophaneness, Stealing, Drinking, Fighting, Dancing, Whoring, Mis-Rule, Mis-Spence of Precious Time, Contempt of God, and Godly Magistrates, Ministers and People, which oppose the Rascality and Rout, in this their Open Prophanenesse, and Heathenish Customs (London, 1661).

Richard Hamblyn, The Invention of Clouds: How an Amateur Meteorologist forged the Language of the Skies (London: Picador, 2001).

John Lawrence Hammond and Barbara Hammond, The Town Labourer, 1760–1832: The New Civilisation (London: Longmans, 1917).

John Lawrence Hammond and Barbara Hammond, The Skilled Labourer 1760–1832, 2nd edn (London: Longmans, 1920).

John Lawrence Hammond and Barbara Hammond, The Village Labourer (1911) (Stroud: Nonsuch, 2003).

Paul Hamos, 'The Decline of the Choral Dance', in Eric and Mary Josephson (eds), Man Alone: Alienation in Modern Society (New York: Dell, 1962), 172–9.

Nick Harding, Better than Halloween: Bright Alternatives for Churches and Children (London: Church House Publishing, 2006).

James Hardy, 'Popular History of the Cuckoo', The Folk-Lore Record 2 (1879), 47–91.

Thomas Hardy, The Variorum Edition of the Complete Poems, ed. James Gibson (London: Macmillan, 1979).

Thomas Hardy, Far from the Madding Crowd, ed. Suzanne Falck-Yi (Oxford: Oxford University Press, 2008).

Thomas Hardy, The Mayor of Casterbridge, ed. Dale Kramer (Oxford: Oxford University Press, 1998).

Thomas Hardy, The Return of the Native, ed. Tony Slade (London: Penguin, 1999).

John Harland and T. T. Wilkinson, Lancashire Folk-Lore: illustrating the Superstitious Beliefs and Practices, Local Customs and Usages of the People of the County Palatine (London: Warne & Co., 1867).

Timothy Harley, Moon Lore (London: Swan Sonnenschein, 1885).

Duff Hart-Davis, Fauna Britannica: The Practical Guide to Wild & Domestic Creatures of Britain (London: Weidenfield & Nicolson, 2002).

Jeremy Harte, Cuckoo Pounds and Singing Barrows: The Folklore of Ancient Sites in Dorset (Yeovil: Dorset Natural History and Archaeological Society, 1986).

Nathaniel Hawthorne, Complete Writings, 22 vols (Boston and New York: Houghton, Mifflin, & Co., 1900).

Michael Heaney, 'The Earliest Reference to the Morris Dance?', Folk Music Journal 8.4 (2004), 513–15.

Mike Heaney, 'New Evidence for the Abbots Bromley Hobby-Horse', Folk Music Journal 5.3 (1987), 359–60.

Thomas S. Henricks, Disputed Pleasures: Sport and Society in Preindustrial England (Westport, Conn.: Greenwood, 1991).

Paul Hentzner, A Journey into England, trans. Horace Walpole (Strawberry Hill, 1757).

George Herbert, The English Poems, ed. Helen Wilcox (Cambridge and New York: Cambridge University Press, 2007).

David Herd (ed.), Ancient and Modern Scottish Songs, Heroic Ballads, etc., 2 vols (Edinburgh, 1776).

Robert Herrick, Hesperides, in The Poems of Robert Herrick, ed. F. W. Moorman (Oxford: Oxford University Press, 1947).

Thomas K. Hervey, The Book of Christmas: Descriptive of the Customs, Ceremonies, Traditions, Superstitions, Fun, Feeling and Festivities of the Christmas Season (1888) (Ware: Wordsworth Editions for the Folklore Society, 2000).

Eric Higgs, 'What is Good Ecological Restoration?', Conservation Biology 11 (1997), 338–48.

Christopher Hill, *Society and Puritanism in Pre-Revolutionary England* (London: Secker & Warburg, 1964).

Rosemary Hill, *Stonehenge* (London: Profile, 2008).

Thomas Hobbes, *Leviathan*, ed. C. B. Macpherson (Harmondsworth: Penguin, 1985).

John Hodgson, *A History of Northumberland*, part II, vol. 2 (Newcastle-upon-Tyne: privately printed, 1832).

Leofranc Holford-Strevens, *The History of Time: A Very Short Introduction* (Oxford: Oxford University Press, 2005).

George Homans, *English Villagers of the Thirteenth Century*, 2nd edn (New York and London: W. W. Norton & Co., 1991).

William Hone, *The Every-Day Book; or, Everlasting Calendar of Popular Amusements, Sports, Pastimes, Ceremonies, Manners, Customs, and Events, incident to Each of the Three Hundred and Sixty-Five Days, in Past and Present Times; forming a complete History of the Year, Months, & Seasons, and a Perpetual Key to the Almanack . . .*, 2 vols (London: Hunt & Clarke, 1826).

William Hone, *The Every-Day Book; or, Everlasting Calendar of Popular Amusements, Sports, Pastimes, Ceremonies, Manners, Customs, and Events, incident to Each of the Three Hundred and Sixty-Five Days, in Past and Present Times*, 2 vols (London: Hunt & Clark, 1827).

William Hone, *The Table Book, of Daily Recreation and Information: concerning Remarkable Men, Manners, Times, Seasons, Solemnities, Merry-Makings, Antiquities and Novelties, forming a Complete History of the Year* (London: William Tegg, n.d. / William Hone, 1827).

William Hone, *The Every-Day Book; or, Everlasting Calendar of Popular Amusements, Sports, Pastimes, Ceremonies, Manners, Customs, and Events, incident to Each of the Three Hundred and Sixty-Five Days, in Past and Present Times*, 2 vols (London: William Tegg, 1828).

William Hone, *The Every-Day Book and Table Book; or, Everlasting Calendar of Popular Amusements, Sports, Pastimes, Ceremonies, Manners, Customs, and Events, incident to Each of the Three Hundred and Sixty-Five Days, in Past and Present Times*, 3 vols (London: William Tegg, 1837).

William Hone, *Table-Book*, 2 vols (London: privately published, 1828).

Thomas Hood, *Whimsicalities: A Periodical Gathering* (1844), in *The Complete Poetical Works*, Oxford Edition, ed. Walter Jerrold (London, Edinburgh, Glasgow: Henry Frowde, 1906).

Robert Hooke, 'A Method for Making a History of the Weather', Thomas Sprat, *The History of the Royal-Society of London, for the Improving of Natural Knowledge*, 2nd edn (London, 1702), 173–9.

John Hooper, *Early Writings of John Hooper*, ed. Samuel Carr (Cambridge: Cambridge University Press, 1843).

Gerard Manley Hopkins, *Poems*, ed. W. H. Gardner and N. H. Mackenzie, 4th edn (Oxford: Oxford University Press, 1970).

A. R. Horwood, *A New British Flora: British Wild Flowers in their Natural Haunts*, 6 vols (London: Gresham, 1919).

Michael Hoskin, 'The Reception of the Calendar by other Churches', Coyne, Hoskin, and Pedersen (eds), 255–64.

Henry Howard, Earl of Surrey, *Songes and Sonettes* (London, 1557).

Luke Howard, *Essay on the Modifications of Clouds* (1803), 3rd edn (London: John Churchill & Sons, 1865).

William Howitt, *The Boy's Country Book: being the Real Life of a Country Boy, written by Himself; exhibiting all the Amusements, Pleasures, and Pursuits of Children in the Country* (London: Longman, Orme, Brown, Green, & Longmans, 1841).

Alun Howkins and Linda Merricks, 'The Ploughboy and the Plough Play', *Folk Music Journal* 6.2 (1991), 187–208.

W. H. Hudson, *British Birds* (Longmans, Green, & Co., 1921).

Paul L. Hughes and James F. Larkin (eds), *Tudor Royal Proclamations*, 3 vols (New Haven: Yale University Press, 1964–9).

Thomas Hughes, *The Scouring of the White Horse: or, The Long Vacation Ramble of a London Clerk* (London: Macmillan & Co., 1859).

Leigh Hunt, 'Christmas and other old National Merry-Makings', *The Examiner* (21 December 1817), 801–3.

Leigh Hunt, 'Christmas and other old National Merry-Makings', *The Nic-Nac, or, Literary Cabinet* 2 (1824), 37–9.

Ronald Hutton, *The Rise and Fall of Merry England: The Ritual Year 1400–1700* (Oxford: Oxford University Press, 1994).

Ronald Hutton, *The Stations of the Sun: A History of the Ritual Year in Britain* (Oxford: Oxford University Press, 1996).

Richard Inwards, *Weather-Lore* (London: W. Tweedie, 1869).

Richard Inwards, *Weather Lore: A Collection of Proverbs, Sayings, and Rules concerning the Weather* (London: Elliot Stock, 1898).

Richard Inwards, *Weather Wisdom: A Collection of Proverbs, Sayings and Rules concerning the Weather* (London: Elliot Stock, 1893).

David Irish, *Animadversio Astrologica: or, A Discourse Touching Astrology* (London, 1701).

Washington Irving ['Geoffrey Crayon'], *Bracebridge Hall; or, The Humourists*, 2 vols (New York: Van Winkle, 1822).

Washington Irving, *A History of New York, from the Beginning of the World to the End of the Dutch Dynasty* ... (Philadelphia: J. B. Lippincott & Co., 1873).

Washington Irving, *The Sketch Book of Geoffrey Crayon, Gent* (n.p.: A. L. Burt, n.d.).

Kenneth Hurlstone Jackson (ed.), *A Celtic Miscellany: Translations from the Celtic Literatures* (London: Penguin, 1971).

Henry Hyde, *see* Earl of Clarendon.

John Jamieson, *An Etymological Dictionary of the Scottish Language* ..., 2 vols (Edinburgh: Edinburgh University Press, 1808).

Vladimir Janković, *Reading the Skies: A Cultural History of English Weather, 1650–1820* (Manchester: Manchester University Press, 2000).

Richard Jefferies, *The Open Air* (Stroud: Nonsuch, 2008).

Phebe Jensen, *Religion and Revelry in Shakespeare's Festive World* (Cambridge: Cambridge University Press, 2008).

Richard Johnson, *The Most Famous History of the Seaven Champions of Christendome Saint George of England, Saint Dennis of Fraunce, Saint James of Spaine, Saint Anthonie of Italie, Saint Andrew of Scotland, Saint Pattricke of Ireland, and Saint David of Wales* (London, 1596).

Samuel Johnson, *The Idler*, 2 vols (London, 1761).

Charles W. Jones, *Bede, the Schools and the Computus*, ed. Weseley Stevens (Aldershot: Ashgate Variorum, 1994).

Graham Jones, *Saints in the Landscape* (Stroud: Tempus, 2007).

Henry Jones (ed.), *The Philosophical Transactions (from the Year 1700, to the Year 1720)*, 4 vols, 3rd edn (London, 1759).

Ben Jonson, *Bartholomew Fair* (London, [1735?]).

Eric and Mary Josephson (eds), *Man Alone: Alienation in Modern Society* (New York: Dell, 1962).

Essaka Joshua, *The Romantics and the May Day Tradition* (Aldershot: Ashgate, 2007).

Ralph Josselin, *The Diary of Ralph Josselin, 1616–1683*, ed. Alan Macfarlane (Oxford: Oxford University Press, 1977).

'J. S.', *The Shepherd's Kalender: or, The Citizen's and Country Man's Daily Companion*, 6th edn (London, 1765?).

Roy Judge, *The Jack-in-the-Green*, 2nd edn (London: Folk Lore Society, 2000).

John Keats, *Poetical Works*, ed. H. W. Garrod (Oxford and New York: Oxford University Press, 1982).

John Keble, *The Christian Year: Thoughts in Verse for the Sundays and Holydays throughout the Year* (Oxford: J. Parker, 1827).

John Mitchell Kemble, *The Saxons in England. A History of the English Commonwealth till the Period of the Norman Conquest*, 2 vols (London: Longman, Brown, Green, & Longmans, 1849).

William Kemp, *Kemps Nine Daies Wonder Performed in a Daunce from London to Norwich* (London, 1600).

Charles Kightly, The Customs and Ceremonies of Britain: An Encyclopaedia of Living Traditions with a Calendar of Customs and Regional Gazetteer (London: Thames & Hudson, 1986).

Herbert W. Kille, West Country Hobby Horses and Cognate Customs (n.p.: Oakmagic, 1999).

Francis Kilvert, Kilvert's Diary, ed. William Plomer, 3 vols (London: Cape, 1960).

Josiah King, The Examination and Tryall of Old Father Christmas at the Assizes held at the Town of Difference, in the County of Discontent (London, 1658).

Rudyard Kipling, The Collected Poems, ed. R. T. Jones (Ware: Wordsworth, 2001).

Stephen Knight and Thomas Ohlgren (eds), Robin Hood and Other Outlaw Tales (Kalamazoo, Michigan: TEAMS, 2000).

Andrew Lacey, The Cult of King Charles the Martyr (Woodbridge: Boydell Press, 2003).

Charles Lamb, 'New Year's Eve', The Essays of Elia: First Series, 1823 (London: Harrap & Co., 1923).

Donna Landry, The Invention of the Countryside: Hunting, Walking and Ecology in English Literature, 1671–1831 (Basingstoke: Palgrave, 2001).

Paul Langford, Englishness Identified: Manners and Character, 1650–1850 (Oxford and New York: Oxford University Press, 2000).

William Langland, The Vision of Piers Plowman: A Complete Edition of the B-Text, ed. A. V. C. Schmidt (London and Melbourne: Dent, 1984).

Philip Larkin, Collected Poems (London: Faber & Faber, 1990).

Peter Laslett and Karla Oosterveen, 'Long-Term Trends in Bastardy in England', Population Studies 27 (1973), 255–86.

M. Andreas Laurentius, A Discourse of the Preservation of the Sight, trans. Richard Surphlet (1599), ed. Sandford Larkey (London: Oxford University Press, 1938).

Ella Mary Leather, The Folklore of Herefordshire collected from Oral and Printed Sources (London: Sidgwick & Jackson, 1912).

Vincent Stuckey Lean, Collectanea: Collections of Vincent Stuckey Lean of Proverbs (English & Foreign), Folk Lore, and Superstitions, also Compilations towards Dictionaries of Proverbial Phrases and Words, Old and Disused, 4 vols (Bristol: Arrowsmith, 1902–4).

Peter Linebaugh, The London Hanged: Crime and Civil Society in the Eighteenth Century (Harmondsworth: Penguin, 1991).

Edward Lisle, Observations in Husbandry (London, 1757).

John Locke, An Essay Concerning Humane Understanding in Four Books (London, 1690).

Lodowick Lloyd, The First Part of the Diall of Daies containing 320. Romane Triumphes, besides the Triumphant Obelisks and Pyramydes of the Aegyptians, the Pillers, Arches, and Trophies Triumphant, of the Graecians, and the Persians, with their Pompe and Magnificence: of Feastes and Sacrifices both of the Jewes and of the Gentils, with the Stately Games and Plaies belonging to these Feastes and Sacrifices, with the Birthes and Funeral Pomps of Kinges and Emperours, as you shall finde more at large in the 2. Part, wherein All Kind of Triumphes are Enlarged (London, 1590).

John Logan, Poems (London, 1781).

Roger Lonsdale (ed.), The Poems of Thomas Gray, William Collins, Oliver Goldsmith (London and New York: Longman, 1989).

Samuel J. Looker (ed.), The Nature Diaries and Note-Books of Richard Jefferies (London: Grey Walls, 1948).

Roger Lovegrove, Silent Fields: The Long Decline of a Nation's Wildlife (Oxford: Oxford University Press, 2007).

John Lowthorp (ed.), Royal Society, The Philosophical Transactions and Collections, to the End of the Year 1700, 2nd edn, 3 vols (London, 1716).

E. V. Lucas, Highways and Byways in Sussex (London: Macmillan, 1903).

Titus Lucretius Carus, On Nature, trans. Russel Geer (New York: Macmillan, 1965).

John Lydgate, Minor Poems of John Lydgate, Early English Text Society, ed. Henry Noble

MacCracken (London: Kegan Paul, Trench, Trübner, & Co., and Oxford University Press, 1911).

John Lyly, *The Maydes Metamorphosis as it hath bene Sundrie Times Acted by the Children of Powles* (London, 1600).

Jerome McGann, *The Beauty of Inflections: Literary Investigations in Historical Method and Theory* (Oxford: Clarendon Press, 1985).

Henry Machyn, *The Diary of Henry Machyn, Citizen and Merchant-Taylor of London, from* A.D. 1550 *to* A.D. 1563, ed. John Gough Nichols, Camden Society 42 (London: J. B. Nichols & Son, 1848).

Maynard Mack, *Alexander Pope, A Life* (New Haven and London: Yale University Press; New York and London: Norton, 1985).

John Macky, *A Journey through England. In Familiar Letters from a Gentleman Here, to his Friend Abroad*, 3 vols (London, 1714–23).

J. Holden McMichael, 'Filberts: "When The Devil Goes A-Nutting"', *Notes and Queries* series 11, vol. 1 (1910), 33–4.

James Macpherson, *An Introduction to the History of Great Britain and Ireland* (London, 1771).

Macrobius, *Saturnalia*, trans. Percival Vaughan Davies (New York: Columbia University Press, 1969).

Bernhard Maier (ed.), *Dictionary of Celtic Religion and Culture*, trans. Cyril Edwards (Woodbridge: Boydell, 2000).

Robert W. Malcolmson, *Popular Recreations in English Society* (Cambridge: Cambridge University Press, 1973).

Thomas Malory, *Le Morte Darthur: The Winchester Manuscript*, ed. Helen Cooper (Oxford: Oxford University Press, 1998).

Percy Manning, 'Stray Notes on Oxfordshire Folklore', *Folklore* 14.2 (1903), 167–77.

Henry Manship, *The History of Great Yarmouth*, ed. Charles John Palmer (Great Yarmouth: Louis Alfred Meall, 1854).

Gervase Markham, *The English Husbandman drawne into Two Bookes, and Each Booke into Two Parts* (London, 1635).

John Marston, *The Scourge of Villanie Three Bookes of Satyres* (London, 1598).

Andrew Marvell, *Miscellaneous Poems* (London, 1681).

Carla Mazzio, 'The History of Air: Hamlet and the Trouble with Instruments', *South Central Review* 26.1–2 (2009), 153–196.

William Merle, *Merle's MS Consideraciones temperiei pro 7 annis [Temperature of the Air at Oxford for Seven Years]: The Earliest Known Journal of the Weather, 1337–1344*, ed. George Symons (London: E. Stanford, 1891).

'Dick Merryman', *see* Anon., *Round About Our Coal-Fire*.

Thomas Middleton, *The Roaring Girle. Or Moll Cut-Purse as it hath lately beene acted on the Fortune-Stage by the Prince his Players* (London, 1611).

Christopher Miller, *The Invention of Evening: Perception and Time in Romantic Poetry* (Cambridge: Cambridge University Press, 2006).

John Milton, *Complete Shorter Poems*, ed. John Carey (London and New York: Longman, 1971).

John Milton, *Paradise Lost*, ed. Alastair Fowler (Harlow: Longman, 1967).

'Simon Minc'd Pye', *The Arraignment, Conviction, and Imprisoning, of Christmas: on St. Thomas Day last* (London, 1646).

G. E. Mingay (ed.), *The Victorian Countryside*, 2 vols [continuously paginated] (London, Boston, and Henley: Routledge & Kegan Paul, 1981).

Henri Misson, *M. Misson's Memoirs and Observations in his Travels over England. With Some Account of Scotland and Ireland*, trans. John Ozell (London, 1719) [originally published as *Mémoires et observations faites par un voyageur en Angleterre, sur ce qu'il y a trouvé de plus remarquable, tant à l'égard de la religion, que de la politique, des mœurs, des curiositez naturelles, & quantité de faits historiques . . .* (La Haye [The Hague]: H. van Bulderen, 1698)].

James Montgomery, *The Wanderer of Switzerland, and Other Poems* (London:

Vernon & Hood; London: Longman, Hurst, Rees, & Orme, 1806).

Clement C. Moore, *A Visit from St. Nicholas* (New York: Spalding & Shepard, 1849).

Henry More, *An Antidote Against Atheism or, An Appeal to the Naturall Faculties of the Minde of Man, whether there be not a God*, 2nd edn (London, 1655).

Thomas Morley, *Cantus of Thomas Morley the First Booke of Balletts to Five Voyces* (London, 1595).

Thomas Morley, *Madrigalls to Foure Voyces* (London, 1594).

Timothy Morton, *Ecology Without Nature: Rethinking Environmental Aesthetics* (Cambridge, Mass. and London: Harvard University Press, 2007).

Alden A. Mosshammer, *The Easter Computus and the Origins of the Christian Era* (Oxford: Oxford University Press, 2008).

Anne Mozley (ed.), *Letters and Correspondence of John Henry Newman during his Life in the English Church*, 2 vols (London: Longmans, Green, & Co., 1891).

John Mullan and Christopher Reid (eds), *Eighteenth-Century Popular Culture: A Selection* (Oxford: Oxford University Press, 2000).

Marjorie Hope Nicolson, *Mountain Gloom and Mountain Glory: The Development of the Aesthetics of the Infinite* (Seattle and London: University of Washington Press, 1997).

Thomas Nashe, *A Pleasant Comedie, called Summers Last Will and Testament* (London, 1600).

J. D. North, 'The Western Calendar – "Intolerabilis, Horribilis, et Derisibilis"; Four Centuries of Discontent', Coyne, Hoskin, and Pedersen (eds), 75–113.

G. F. Northall, *English Folk Rhymes: A Collection of Traditional Verses relating to Places and Persons, Customs, Superstitions, etc.* (London: Kegan Paul, Trench, Trübner, & Co., 1892).

N. Ockendon, C. H. Hewson, A. Johnston, and P. W. Atkinson, 'Declines in British-Breeding Populations of Afro-Palaearctic Migrant Birds are linked to Bioclimatic Wintering Zone in Africa, possibly via Constraints on Arrival Time Advancement', *Bird Study* 59.2 (2012), 111–25.

Standish Hayes O'Grady, *Silva Gadelica* (London: Williams and Norgate, 1892).

Iona and Peter Opie (eds), *The Dictionary of Nursery Rhymes*, 2nd edn (Oxford: Oxford University Press, 1997).

Iona and Peter Opie, *The Oxford Nursery Rhyme Book and English Dialect Dictionary* (Oxford: Clarendon Press, 1977).

Iona Opie and Moira Tatem (eds), *A Dictionary of Superstitions* (Oxford: Oxford University Press, 1989).

James Orange, *History and Antiquities of Nottingham*, 2 vols (London: Hamilton, Adams, & Co., 1840).

Orm, *The Ormulum*, ed. Robert Holt and R. M. White, 2 vols (Oxford: Clarendon Press, 1878).

David Ovason, *The History of the Horoscope* (Stroud: Sutton, 2005).

Ovid, *Elegiac Poems of Ovid, vol 2: The Roman Calendar: Selections from The Fasti*, ed. J. W. E. Pearce (Oxford: Clarendon Press, 1914).

Ovid, *Metamorphoses*, ed. E. J. Kenney, trans. A. D. Melville (Oxford: Oxford University Press, 2008).

William Owen, *Owen's New Book of Fairs, published by the King's Authority* (London, 1780) [six editions 1780–99].

Roy Palmer, *The Folklore of Leicestershire and Rutland* (Wymondham: Sycamore Press, 1985).

The Parliamentary Register; or, History of the Proceedings and Debates of the Houses of Lords and Commons (London: Debrett, 1800).

Erra Pater, *The Pronostycacyon For Ever of Erra Pater: A Jewe borne in Jewery, a Doctour in Astronomye, and Physycke Profytable to kepe the Bodye in Helth. And also Ptholomeus sayth the Same* (London, 1540).

Symon Patrick, *The Works of Symon Patrick, including his Autobiography*, ed. Alexander Taylor, 9 vols (Oxford: Oxford University Press, 1858).

Edward Peacock, 'Weather Rules', *Notes and Queries* 194 (16 July 1853), 50.

Susanna Pearson, *Poems on Various Subjects* (London: Rivington, 1800).

Olaf Pedersen, 'The Ecclesiastical Calendar and the Life of the Church', Coyne, Hoskin, and Pedersen (eds), 17–74.

Thomas Pennant, *A Tour in Scotland. MDCCLXIX* (Chester, 1771).

Thomas Pennant, *A Tour in Scotland. MDCCLXXII, Part II* (London, 1776).

Samuel Pepys, *The Diary of Samuel Pepys*, ed. John Warrington, 3 vols (London: Dent, 1953).

Thurstan Peter, 'The Hobby Horse', *Cornwall's May Folk Festivals: The Complete Guide*, ed. Kelvin I. Jones (n.p.: Oakmagic, 2006).

Tom Petherwick, *Biodynamics in Practice: Life on a Community Owned Farm* (Forest Row: Rudolf Steiner Press, 2010).

Hugh Plat, *Floraes Paradise Beautified and Adorned with Sundry Sorts of Delicate Fruites and Flowers, by The Industrious Labour of H. P. Knight: with an offer of an English Antidote, (beeing a Present, Easie, and Pleasing Remedy in Violent Feavers, and Intermitting Agues) as also of some other Rare Inventions, Fitting the Times* (London, 1608).

Sir Hugh Plat, *The Garden of Eden* (London, 1653 [1652]).

Thomas Platter's *Travels in England, 1599*, trans. Clare Williams (London, 1937).

Poems on Affairs of State, from 1640. to this Present Year 1704 ([London?] 1704).

Robert Plot, *The Natural History of Stafford-shire* (Oxford, 1686).

Robert Poole, *Time's Alteration: Calendar Reform in Early Modern England* (London: UCL Press, 1998).

'Poor Robin', *An Almanack after a New Fashion wherein the Reader may see (if he be not blinde) Many Remarkable Things Worthy of Observation: containing a Two-Fold Kalender, viz. the Julian or English, and the Round-Heads or Fanaticks, with their Several Saints Daies, and Observations upon Every Month: calculated for the Meridian of Saffron-Walden, where the Pole is elevated 52 degrees and 6 minutes above the Horizon* (London, 1664).

'Poor Robin', *Poor Robin 1672 An Almanack after a New Fashion: wherein the Reader may see (if he be not Blind) Many Remarkable Things worthy of Observation: Being the Bissextile, or Leap-Year: containing a Two-Fold Kalendar, viz. the Julian, or English, and the Round-Heads, Or Fanaticks: with their Several Saints Days, and Observations upon Every Moneth* (London, 1672).

'Poor Robin', *Poor Robin 1673 An Almanack after a New Fashion: wherein the Reader may see (if he be not Blind) Many Remarkable Things Worthy of Observation: being the Bissextile, or Leap-Year: containing a Two-Fold Kalendar, viz. the Julian, or English, and the Round-Heads, or Fanaticks: with their Several Saints Days, and Observations upon Every Moneth* (London, 1673).

'Poor Robin', *Poor Robin 1674 An Almanack after a New Fashion: wherein the Reader may see (if he be not Blind) Many Remarkable Things worthy of Observation: being the 2d after Bissextile, or Leap-Year: containing a Two-Fold Kalendar, viz. the Julian, or English, and the Round-Heads, or Fanaticks: with their Several Saints Days, and Observations upon Every Moneth* (London, 1674).

'Poor Robin', *An Almanack after a New Fashion wherein the Reader may see (if he be not Blind) Many Remarkable Things Worthy of Observation ... containing a Two-Fold Kalendar, viz. the Julian or English, and the Round-Heads or Fanaticks, with their Several Saints Days, and Observations upon Every Month* (London, 1676).

'Poor Robin', *Poor Robin 1682 An Almanack after a New Fashion: wherein the Reader may see (having before cleared his Eyesight with a Good Mornings Draught) Many Remarkable Things worthy of Precious Observation: containing a Twofold Kalendar, viz. the Julian, or English, and the Roundheads, Fanaticks, Whimzy-Pated, or Maggot-Head People: with their Several Saints-Days, and Observations upon Every Month* (London, 1682).

'Poor Robin', *Poor Robin 1684 An Almanack after a New Fashion wherein the Reader may find many Remarkable Things Worthy Most Serious Observation: containing a Two-Fold Kalendar* viz. the Julian, English, or Old Account, and the Roundheads, Fanaticks, Paper-Skull'd, or Maggot-Headed New Account, with their Several Saints-Days, and Observations upon Every Month (London, 1684).

'Poor Robin', Poor Robin 1686 An Almanack of the Old and New Fashion: wherein the Reader may find (unless he be Very Dull or Stark Blind) Many Remarkable Things worthy of his Choicest Observation: containing a Two-Fold Kalendar, viz. the Julian English, or Old Account and the Roundheads, Fanaticks, Paper-Skull'd, or Maggot-Headed New Account, with their Several Saints-Days, and Observations upon Every Month (London, 1686).

'Poor Robin', Poor Robin 1697 An Almanack of the Old and New Fashion, or, An Ephemeris both in Jest and Earnest, wherein the Reader may see (with a due regard, and right understanding of what he reads) Many Remarkable Things for his Information: containing a Two-Fold Calendar, viz. the Julian, English, or Old Account, and the Round-Heads, Whimzey-Heads, Maggot-Heads, Paper-Scull'd, Fanaticks, or New Account, with their Several Saints Days, and Observations upon Every Month: being the first after Bissextile, or Leap-Year (London, 1697).

'Poor Robin', Poor Robin, 1702. A Prognostication for the Year of our Lord God, 1702 (London, 1702).

'Poor Robin', Poor Robin (London, 1733).

Alexander Pope, The Dunciad in Four Books, ed. Valerie Rumbold (Harlow: Pearson Longman, 2009).

Alexander Pope, Minor Poems, ed. Norman Ault and John Butt (London: Methuen & Co., and New Haven: Yale University Press, 1964).

Henry Power, 'Virgil, Horace, and Gay's Art of Walking the Streets', Cambridge Quarterly 38.4 (2009), 338–67.

Gavin Pretor-Pinney, The Cloud-Spotter's Guide (London: Hodder & Stoughton, 2007).

Edouardo Proverbio, 'Copernicus and the Determination of the Length of the Tropical Year', Coyne, Hoskin, and Pedersen (eds), 129–34.

William Prynne, Histrio-Mastix The Players Scourge, or, Actors Tragædie, divided into Two Parts (London, 1633).

['Pseudo-Defoe',] The Storm: or, A Collection of the Most Remarkable Casualties and Disasters which happen'd in the Late Dreadful Tempest, both by Sea and Land (London, 1704).

George Puttenham, The Arte of English Poesie contrived into Three Bookes: the First of Poets and Poesie, the Second of Proportion, the Third of Ornament (London, 1589).

'Peter Puzzlecap', Gammer Gurton's Garland of Nursery Songs, and Toby Tickle's Collection of Riddles (Glasgow: Lumsden & Son, c.1820).

Francis Quarles, The Shepheards Oracles delivered in Certain Eglogues (London, 1646).

Arthur Quiller-Couch (ed.), The Oxford Book of Ballads (Oxford: Clarendon Press, 1910).

Sir Walter Raleigh, The Historie of the World In Five Bookes (London, 1628).

Richard Rawlidge, A Monster late Found Out and Discovered. Or the Scourging of Tiplers, the Ruine of Bacchus, and the Bane of Tapsters wherein is plainly set forth All the Lawes of the Kingdome, that be now in force against Ale-House Keepers, Drunkards, and Haunters of Ale-Houses, with all the Paines and Penalties in the Same Lawes (Amsterdam [London], 1628).

'R. B.', Admirable Curiosities, Rarities, and Wonders in England, Scotland and Ireland, or, An Account of Many Remarkable Persons and Places … together with the Natural and Artificial Rarities in Every County … as they are recorded by the Most Authentick and Credible Historians of Former and Latter Ages; adorned with the Lively Description of Several Memorable Things therein contained, Ingraven on Copper Plates (London, 1684).

W. G. Rawlinson, Turner's Liber Studiorum: A Description and a Catalogue (London: Macmillan, 1878).

John Ray, A Collection of English Proverbs digested into a Convenient Method for the Speedy Finding any one upon occasion: with Short Annotations: whereunto are added Local Proverbs with their Explications, Old Proverbial Rhythmes, Less Known or Exotick Proverbial Sentences, and Scottish Proverbs (London, 1670).

John Ray, A Compleat Collection of English Proverbs; also the Most Celebrated Proverbs of the Scotch, Italian, French, Spanish and Other Languages, 3rd edn (London, 1737).

John Ray, A Compleat Collection of English Proverbs; also the Most Celebrated Proverbs of the Italian, Scotch, French, Spanish, and Other Languages, 4th edn (London, 1768).

John Ray, The Ornithology of Francis Willughby of Middleton in the County of Warwick Esq, Fellow of the Royal Society in Three Books: wherein all the Birds hitherto known, being reduced into a Method sutable to their Natures, are Accurately Described: the Descriptions illustrated by Most Elegant Figures, nearly resembling the Live Birds, engraven in LXXVII Copper Plates: translated into English, and enlarged with Many Additions throughout the Whole Work: to which are added, Three Considerable Discourses, I. Of the Art of Fowling, with a Description of Several Nets in two large Copper Plates, II. Of the Ordering of Singing Birds, III. Of Falconry (London, 1678).

Arden Reed, Romantic Weather: The Climates of Coleridge and Baudelaire (Hanover and London: Brown University Press, 1983).

Edward M. Reingold and Nachum Dershowitz, Calendrical Tabulations: 1900–2200 (Cambridge: Cambridge University Press, 2002).

Robert of Brunne, Handlyng Synne, ed. Frederick J. Furnivall, Early English Text Society (London: Kegan Paul, Trench, Trübner, & Co., 1901).

Eric Robinson (ed.), John Clare's Autobiographical Writings (Oxford: Oxford University Press, 1983).

Earl of Rochester, The Complete Poems of John Wilmot, Earl of Rochester, ed. David Vieth (New Haven and London: Yale University Press, 1968).

Nicholas Roe, Keats and Culture of Dissent (Oxford: Clarendon Press, 1997).

Nicholas Rogers, Halloween: From Pagan Ritual to Party Night (Oxford: Oxford University Press, 2002).

Hyder Edward Rollins (ed.), The Pepys Ballads, 6 vols (Cambridge, Mass.: Harvard University Press, 1929–31).

Steve Roud, The English Year: A Month-by-Month Guide to the Nation's Customs and Festivals, from May Day to Mischief Night (London: Penguin, 2006).

Steve Roud, The Penguin Guide to the Superstitions of Britain and Ireland (London: Penguin, 2003).

Doc Rowe, May Day: The Coming of the Spring (Swindon: English Heritage, 2006).

Nicholas Rowe, The Biter (London, 1705).

John Ruskin, Complete Works, 30 vols (New York: Thomas Y. Crowell, 1905).

François Russo, SJ, 'Contemporary Discussions on the Reform of the Calendar', Coyne, Hoskin, and Pedersen (eds), 287–97.

Redcliffe N. Salaman, The History and Social Influence of the Potato, rev. J. G. Hawkes (Cambridge: Cambridge University Press, 1985).

Philip Schaff and Henry Wace (eds), Nicene and Post-Nicene Fathers, 37 vols: second series, vol. 14: The Seven Ecumenical Councils (New York: Charles Scribner's Sons, 1900).

Philip Schaff, J. Walker, J. Sheppard, and H. Browne (eds), A Select Library of the Nicene and Post-Nicene Fathers of the Christian Church, rev. G. B. Steven, 14 vols (Grand Rapids, Michigan: Eerdmans, 1980).

Simon Schama, Landscape and Memory (London: HarperCollins, 1994).

William Schellinks, The Journal of William Schellinks' Travels in England 1661–1663, trans. and ed. Maurice Exwood and H. L. Lehmann, Camden Fifth Series 1 (1993).

Walter Scott, The Abbot being a Sequel to The Monastery, Waverley Novels Centenary Edition, 25 vols, vol. 11 (Edinburgh: Adam & Charles Black, 1870).

Henry Season [Thomas Wright], Speculum anni: or, Season on the Seasons, for the Year of our Lord 1798; being the second after Bissextile, or Leap Year (London, 1798).

Seneca, *Dialogues and Essays*, trans. John Davie (Oxford: Oxford University Press, 2008).

A. Lytton Sells, *Animal Poetry in French and English Literature and the Greek Tradition* (Bloomington: Indiana University Press, 1955).

William Shakespeare, *The Plays of William Shakespeare* (1778–80), ed. Samuel Johnson, George Steevens, and Edmond Malone, ed. Nick Groom, 12 vols (London and Bristol: Routledge/Thoemmes Press, 1995).

William Shakespeare, *The Riverside Shakespeare*, ed. G. Blakemore Evans, *et al.* (Boston: Houghton Mifflin, 1974).

Percy Bysshe Shelley, *Shelley's Poetry and Prose*, ed. Donald H. Reiman and Sharon B. Powers (New York and London: W. W. Norton & Co., 1977).

E. R. Shipman, *The Abbots Bromley Horn Dance* (Rugeley: Benhill Press, 1982).

Marion Shoard, *The Theft of the Countryside* (London: Maurice Temple Smith, 1980).

Thomas Short, *A General Chronological History of the Air, Weather, Seasons, Meteors, &c. in Sundry Places and Different Times*, 2 vols (London, 1749).

Paul Simons, *Since Records Began: The Highs and Lows of Britain's Weather* (London: Collins, 2008).

Jacqueline Simpson, *The Folklore of Sussex* (London: Batsford, 1973).

Jacqueline Simpson and Steve Roud (eds), *A Dictionary of English Folklore* (Oxford: Oxford University Press, 2000).

Sir John Sinclair (ed.), *The Statistical Account of Scotland*, 21 vols (Edinburgh, 1791).

Sacheverell Sitwell, *The Cyder Feast and Other Poems* (New York: George Doran, 1927).

John Skelton, *The Book of the Laurel*, ed. F. W. Brownlow (Cranberry, NJ: Associated University Presses, 1990).

John Skelton, *Poetical Works*, ed. Alexander Dyce, 3 vols (Boston: Little, Brown, & Co., 1856).

Christopher Smart, *The Nonpareil; or, The Quintessence of Wit and Humour: being a Choice Selection of those Pieces that were Most Admired in the Ever-To-Be-Remember'd Midwife; or, Old Woman's Magazine* (London, 1757).

Albert Richard Smith, *Comic Tales and Sketches* (London: Richard Bentley, 1852).

William Smith, *The Trial, Conviction, Condemnation, Confession and Execution of William Smith, for Poisoning his Father-in-Law, Thomas Harper, and William and Anne Harper his Children, at Ingleby-Manor, in Yorkshire, by mixing Arsenick in a Good-Friday Cake, who was Tried on Monday the 13th of August, at the Assizes held at the Castle at York, before Mr. Serjeant Eyre, and Executed on Wednesday the 15th, and afterwards Dissected by the Surgeons of that Place. To which is added, an account of the murder of farmer Harvey, his wife, son and daughter in the Parish of Brent, within Sixteen Miles of Plymouth, who were found murdered, on Friday the 10th of this Month* (London, 1753).

Robert Southey, *Letters from England: by Don Manuel Alvarez Espriella*, 3 vols (London: Longman, Hurst, Rees, & Orme, 1807).

Robert Southey, *Selections from the Letters*, ed. John Wood Warter, 4 vols (London: Longman, Brown, Green, Longmans, & Roberts, 1856).

John Sowter, *The Way to be Wise and Wealthy, or The Excellency of Industry and Frugality: In Sundry Maxims* (Dublin, 1733).

Edmund Spenser, *Amoretti and Epithalamion* (London, 1595).

Edmund Spenser, *The Faerie Queene*, ed. A. C. Hamilton (Harlow: Longman, 1977).

Edmund Spenser, *The Shepheardes Calender conteyning Twelve Aeglogues proportionable to the Twelve Monethes* (London, 1579).

Dorothy Gladys Spicer, *From an English Oven: Cakes, Buns and Breads of County Tradition, with Legends and Festivities Associated with their Origins and Use* (New York: Women's Press, 1948).

Leo Spitzer, *Classical and Christian Ideas of World Harmony: Prolegomena to an Interpretation of the word 'Stimmung'* (Baltimore: Johns Hopkins University Press, 1963).

John Spotiswood, *An Introduction to the Knowledge of the Stile of Writs, Simple and*

Compound, made use of in Scotland (Edinburgh, 1715).

Thomas Sprat, The History of the Royal-Society of London, for the Improving of Natural Knowledge, 2nd edn (London, 1702).

Peter Stallybrass and Allon White, The Politics and Poetics of Transgression (London: Methuen, 1986).

Philip Dormer Stanhope, see Lord Chesterfield.

Andrew Steinmetz, A Manual of Weathercasts: composing Storm Prognostics on Land and Sea; with An Explanation of the Method in Use at the Meteorological Office (London: George Routledge, 1866).

Thomas Sternberg, The Dialect and Folk-Lore of Northamptonshire (London: John Russell Smith, 1851).

Laurence Sterne, The Life and Opinions of Tristram Shandy, Gentleman, ed. Graham Petrie (Harmondsworth: Penguin, 1986).

Laurence Sterne, A Sentimental Journey Through France and Italy, ed. Ian Jack and Tim Parnell (Oxford: Oxford University Press, 2003).

George Alexander Stevens, Songs, Comic, and Satyrical (Oxford, 1772).

John Stevens, A New Spanish and English Dictionary: collected from the Best Spanish Authors, both Ancient and Modern (London, 1706).

Matthew Stevenson, The Twelve Moneths, or, A Pleasant and Profitable Discourse of Every Action, whether of Labour or Recreation, proper to each particular Moneth branched into Directions relating to Husbandry, as Plowing, Sowing, Gardening, Planting, Transplanting (London, 1661).

Julian H. Steward, 'The Concept and Method of Cultural Ecology', in English and Mayfield, 120–9.

Robin Stirling, The Weather of Britain, 2nd edn (London: Giles de la Mare, 1997).

John Stow, A Survay of London contayning the Originall, Antiquity, Increase, Moderne Estate, and Description of that Citie, written in the Yeare 1598 (London, 1598).

John Stow, A Survay of London · conteyning the Originall, Antiquity, Increase, Moderne Estate, and Description of that City, written in the Yeare 1598, 2nd edn (London, 1603).

John Stow, A Survey of the Cities of London and Westminster: containing the Original, Antiquity, Increase, Modern Estate and Government of those Cities, ed. and rev. John Strype (London, 1720).

Joseph Strutt, The Sports and Pastimes of the People of England from the Earliest Period, including the Rural and Domestic Recreations, May Games, Mummeries, Pageants, Processions and Pompous Spectacles, illustrated by Reproductions from Ancient Paintings in which are Represented most of the Popular Diversions, ed. J. Charles Cox (London: Methuen & Co., 1801).

Philip Stubbes, The Anatomie of Abuses containing, A Discoverie, or Briefe Summarie of such Notable Vices and Imperfections, as now raigne in Many Countreyes of the World: but (especiallye) in a Famous Ilande called Ailgna: together, with Most Fearefull Examples of Gods Judgements, executed upon the Wicked for the same, aswel in Ailgna of Late, as in Other Places, Elsewhere (London, 1583).

Philip Stubbes, The Second Part of the Anatomie of Abuses, containing the Display of Corruptions, with a Perfect Description of such Imperfections, Blemishes, and Abuses, as now Reigning in Everie Degree, require Reformation for Feare of Gods Vengeance to be Powred upon the People and Countrie, without Speedie Repentance and Conversion unto God: made Dialogwise [1583], ed. F. J. Furnivall (London: N. Trübner, 1877–82).

Sir John Suckling, The Works (London, 1709).

Suetonius, The Twelve Caesars, ed. and trans. Robert Graves, rev. James Rives (London: Penguin, 2007).

Charles Swainson, A Handbook of Weather Folk-Lore; being a Collection of Proverbial Sayings in Various Languages relating to the Weather, with Explanatory and Illustrative Notes (Edinburgh and London: Blackwood, 1873).

Charles Swainson, The Folklore and Provincial Names of British Birds (1886) (Felinfach: Llanerch Publishers, 1998).

Jonathan Swift, *Writings*, ed. Robert Greenbank and William Piper (New York and London: Norton & Co., 1973).

Theophilus Swift, *The Gamblers, A Poem* (London: privately printed, 1777).

Algernon Charles Swinburne, *Poems and Ballads*, 3rd edn (London: John Camden Hotten, 1868).

William Tayler, *Diary of William Tayler: Footman, 1837*, ed. Dorothy Wise (London: St Marylebone Society Publications Group, 1962).

John Taylor, *Jack a Lent his Beginning and Entertainment with the Many Pranks of his Gentleman-Usher Shrove Tuesday that goes before him, and his Foot-Man Hunger attending* (London, 1620).

John Taylor, *Pasquils Palinodia, and his Progresse to the Taverne where after the Survey of the Sellar, you are presented with a Pleasant Pynte of Poeticall Sherry* (London, 1619).

Sir William Temple, *The Works of Sir William Temple, Bart.*, 2 vols (London, 1731).

Alfred, Lord Tennyson, *Poems*, ed. Christopher Ricks, 2nd edn, 3 vols (Harlow: Longman, 1987).

'T. H.', *A Ha! Christmas, This Book of Christmas is a Sound and Good Perswasion for Gentlemen, and All Wealthy Men, to keepe a Good Christmas* (London, 1647).

Keith Thomas, *Man and the Natural World: Changing Attitudes in England 1500–1800* (London: Allen Lane, 1983).

Keith Thomas, *Religion and the Decline of Magic: Studies in Popular Beliefs in Sixteenth and Seventeenth Century England* (London: Weidenfeld & Nicolson, 1971).

R. S. Thomas, *Song at the Year's Turning: Poems, 1942–1955* (London: Rupert Hart-Davis, 1956).

Thompson's Compleat Collection of 120 Favourite Hornpipes as performed at the Public Theatres (London: C. & S. Thompson, n.d. [*c*.1775]).

E. P. Thompson, *Customs in Common* (London: Penguin, 1993).

E. P. Thompson, 'Time, Work-Discipline and Industrial Capitalism', *Customs in Common*, 352–403.

E. P. Thompson, *Whigs and Hunters* (Harmondsworth: Penguin, 1975).

James Thomson, *Autumn. A Poem* (London, 1730).

James Thomson, *The Seasons and The Castle of Indolence*, ed. James Sambrook (Oxford: Clarendon Press, 1972).

Romaine Joseph Thorn, *Christmas, A Poem* (Bristol, 1795).

E. M. W. Tillyard, *The Elizabethan World Picture* (London: Chatto & Windus, 1948).

J. R. R. Tolkien, *The Lord of the Rings*, 3 vols [continuously paginated], vol. iii: *The Return of the King* (London: HarperCollins, 2005).

C. John Trythall , *Tavvystock Goozey Vair* (London: J. H. Larway, 1912).

'T. Q. M.', 'Notes on a Tour, chiefly Pedestrian, from Skipton in Craven, Yorkshire, to Keswick, in Cumberland', in Hone, *Table-Book* (1828), ii. 279.

Richard Marggraf Turley, Jayne Elisabeth Archer, and Howard Thomas, 'Keats, "To Autumn", and the New Men of Winchester', *Review of English Studies* 63 (2012), 797–817.

Thomas Tusser, *A Hundreth Good Pointes of Husbandrie* (London, 1557).

Thomas Tusser, *A Hundreth Good Pointes of Husbandry lately maried unto a Hundreth Good Poynts of Huswifery: newly corrected and amplified with Dyvers Proper Lessons for Housholders, as by the Table at the latter ende, more plainly may appeare: set foorth by Thomas Tusser Gentle Man, Servant to the Right Honorable Lorde Paget of Beudefert* (London, 1570).

Thomas Tusser, *Five Hundreth Points of Good Husbandry united to as many of Good Huswiferie, first Devised, nowe lately Augmented with Diverse Approved Lessons concerning Hopps[,] Gardening, and Other Needeful Matters together, with an Abstract before Every Moneth, conteining the Whole Effect of the Sayd Moneth with a Table [and] a Preface in the Beginning both Necessary to be Reade, for the Better Understanding of the Booke* (London, 1573).

Thomas Tusser, *Five Hundred Pointes of Good Husbandrie as well for the Champion, or Open Countrie, as also for the Woodland, or Severall, mixed in Everie Month with Huswiferie, over and besides the Booke of Huswiferie, Corrected, Better Ordered, and Newly Augmented to a Fourth Part More, with Divers Other Lessons, as a Diet for the Fermer, of the Properties of Winds, Planets, Hops, Herbes, Bees, and Approved Remedies for Sheepe and Cattle, with Many Other Matters both Profitable and Not Unpleasant for the Reader*, 2nd edn (London, 1580).

Henry Twining, *The Elements of Picturesque Scenery, or Studies of Nature made in Travel with a View to Improvement in Landscape Painting*, 2 vols (London: Chapman & Hall, 1856).

Henry Twining, *On the Philosophy of Painting: A Theoretical and Practical Treatise* (London: Longman, Brown, Green, & Longmans, 1849).

Meg Twycross (ed.), *Festive Drama: Papers from the Sixth Triennial Colloquium of the International Society for the Study of Medieval Theatre, Lancaster, 13–19 July 1989* (Cambridge: D. S. Brewer, 1996).

G. F. Vallance, *The War[,] The Weather & God* (privately printed, c.1942).

Helen Vendler, *The Odes of John Keats* (Cambridge, Mass.: Harvard University Press, 1983).

Izaak Walton and Charles Cotton, *The Compleat Angler*, ed. John Buxton (Oxford: Oxford University Press, 1982).

Edward Ward, *The Merry Travellers: or, A Trip upon Ten-Toes, from Moorfields to Bromley . . . Part I* (London, 1721).

Edward Ward, *The Secret History of the Calves-Head Clubb, or, the Republican Unmasqu'd: wherein is fully shewn the Religion of the Calves-Head Heroes, in their Anniversary Thanksgiving Songs on the Thirtieth of January, by them called Anthems; for the Years 1693, 1694, 1695, 1696, 1697* (London, 1703).

Edward Ward, *The Whigs Unmask'd: being the Secret History of the Calf's-Head-Club*, 8th and 9th edns (London, 1713 and 1714).

William Warner, *Albions England a Continued Historie of the Same Kingdome, from the Originals of the First Inhabitants Thereof: and most the Chiefe Alterations and Accidents there Hapning: unto, and in, the Happie Raigne of our now Most Gracious Soveraigne Queene Elizabeth*, 2nd edn (London, 1597).

Michael Waterhouse, *The Strange Death of British Birdsong* (Ashbourne: Landmark Publishing, 2004).

Alan Watts, *The Weather Handbook*, 2nd edn (London: Adlard Coles Nautical, 1999).

John Weaver, *The Loves of Mars and Venus; A Dramatick Entertainment of Dancing, attempted in imitation of the Pantomimes of the Ancient Greeks and Romans; as perform'd at the Theatre in Drury-Lane* (London, 1717).

Max Weber, *The Protestant Ethic and the Spirit of Capitalism*, trans. Talcott Parsons (New York: Scribner, 1958).

Samuel Westwood (?), *The Modern Miscellany* (London, 1744).

William Whiston, *A New Theory of the Earth, from its Original to the Consummation of All Things wherein the Creation of the World in Six Days, the Universal Deluge, and the General Conflagration, as laid down in the Holy Scriptures, are shewn to be Perfectly Agreeable to Reason and Philosophy: with a Large Introductory Discourse concerning the Genuine Nature, Stile, and Extent of the Mosaick History of the Creation* (London, 1696).

Gilbert White, *The Journals of Gilbert White*, ed. Francesca Greenoak, 3 vols: 1751–1773; 1774–1783; 1784–1793 (London: Century Hutchinson, 1986–9).

Gilbert White, *The Natural History of Selborne*, ed. Grant Allen (London and New York: John Lane at The Bodley Head, 1900).

Gilbert White, *The Natural History of Selborne*, ed. Richard Mabey (London: Penguin, 1987).

Lynn White, Jr, 'The Historic Roots of our Ecological Crisis', *Science* 155 (1967), 1203–7.

Hugh Fearnley Whittingstall, *The River Cottage Cookbook* (London: HarperCollins, 2001).

Dorothy Whitelock (ed.), *English Historical Documents c.500–1042*, vol. 1: English Historical

Documents, ed. David C. Douglas, 2nd edn, 12 vols (New York: Oxford University Press, 1979).

William of Malmesbury, *De Gestis Pontificum Anglorum libri quinque*, ed. N. E. S. A. Hamilton, Rolls Series 52 (London: Longman, 1870; reprinted Cambridge: Cambridge University Press, 2012).

John Wilmot, *see* Earl of Rochester.

Thomas Wilson, *The Diaries of Thomas Wilson, D.D., 1731–37 and 1750: son of Bishop Wilson of Sodor & Man*, ed. C. L. S. Linnell (London: S.P.C.K., 1964).

Edgar Wind, *Pagan Mysteries in the Renaissance* (New Haven: Yale University Press, 1958).

Susan Wolfson, 'Keats and Politics: A Forum', *Studies in Romanticism* 25 (1986).

James Woodforde, *The Diary of a Country Parson: 1758–1802*, ed. John Beresford (Oxford and New York: Oxford University Press, 1978).

John Woodward, *A Treatise on Heraldry British and Foreign*, 2 vols (Edinburgh and London: Johnson, 1896).

Dorothy Wordsworth, *The Grasmere and Alfoxden Journals*, ed. Pamela Woof (Oxford: Oxford University Press, 2002).

William Wordsworth, *A Description of the Scenery of the Lakes in the North of England*, 4th edn (London: Longman, Hurst, Rees, Orme, & Brown, 1823).

William Wordsworth, *The Prelude: 1799, 1805, 1850*, ed. Jonathan Wordsworth, M. H. Abrams, and Stephen Gill (New York and London: Norton, 1979).

William Wordsworth, *Selected Poems*, ed. John O. Hayden (London: Penguin, 1994).

William Wordsworth and Samuel Taylor Coleridge, *Lyrical Ballads*, ed. R. L. Brett and A. R. Jones, 2nd edn (London: Routledge, 1991).

A. R. Wright, *British Calendar Customs: England*, ed. T. E. Lones, 3 vols (London: Folklore Society, 1936–40).

Arthur Young (ed.), *Annals of Agriculture, and Other Useful Arts*, 45 vols (Bury St Edmunds and London, 1784–1815).

Arthur Young, *The Farmer's Kalendar; or, A Monthly Directory for all sorts of Country Business: containing, Plain Instructions for performing the Work of Various Kinds of Farms, in Every Season of the Year* (London, 1771).

Arthur Young, *An Inquiry into the Propriety of applying Wastes to the better Maintenance and Support of the Poor* (Bury St Edmunds: Rackham, 1801).

Robert Young, *Young's Literal Translation of the Holy Bible*, 3rd edn (Edinburgh: G. A. Young & Co., 1898).

Music

Michael Flanders and Donald Swann, 'A Song of the Weather', from *At the Drop of a Hat* (Parlophone, 1960).

Paul Giovanni, 'Ballads of Seduction, Fertility and Ritual Slaughter', *The Wicker Man: The Original Soundtrack* (British Lion Music, 1973; Silva Screen Records, 2002).

Journals and websites are listed under individual references.

INDEX

orpine 190
Ostara, festival of 35, 93
Ottery St Mary, fire festival 260
Oxfordshire election, 1754 330n26
Oyster Day (Old St James's Day) 206
Oyster Festival, Whitstable 200–1
oysters 200–1, 239, 250

pace-egging 139
Pack Monday Fair, Sherborne 249–50
Padstow 'Oss, the 161–2, 165, 166
paganism 62, 169, 175–7, 276–7
Paine, Tom 258
Paleoimerologites (Old Calendarists) 52
Palm Sunday 127, 136
Palmer, Roy 139
pancake day 133–6
pantomimes 308–9
Paradise Lost (Milton) 80–1, 208, 235, 236
Parker, George 47
parkin 263
Parliament, summer recess 76–7, 182
Partridge, John 64
partridge season 240
Paschal Controversy, the 131
Paschal Sunday, the 130
Pasquils Palinodia 133–4
passion flower, the 243
pastoral, the, cult of 26–7
pastoral poetry 26
Pater, Erra, *Pronostycacyon For Ever* 58, 281–2
Paul, St 129, 281
Paul V, Pope 258, 263
pawnbrokers 275
pea-planting 103
Pearly Kings and Queens 208
Peasants' Revolt, 1381 277
Pennant, Thomas 301
Pentecost 70, 127, 337n99
Pepys, Samuel 101, 138, 171, 212–13, 284, 296, 315
Perseids meteor shower 203
Peterloo Massacre, the 234
Peter's Chair, feast of 290
picturesque painting 27
pigs 223
Pilgrim's Progress, The (Bunyan) 72

pinching and punching on the first day of
the month 56
plants
apparently indigenous 28
symbolic use 169
Plat, Hugh 302–3
Plot, Robert 241
plough lights 287
Plough Monday 286–7
plough plays 287
plough-carrying 287
plum pudding 315
plum shuttles 297
Pluto 189
pollution 321
Polwhele, Richard 162
Poor Robin almanac series 63, 63–4, 137, 148,
152, 155–6, 173, 239
Pop Ladies 285
Pope, Alexander 106
Pope Day, New England 258
Pope Ladies 285
Popular Superstitions (Brand) 155
population growth 321
Portugal 44
potato, the 132, 226, 346n18
pre-Christian belief systems, survival of
177–8
premonitions 115–16
Presentation of the Lord, the 293–4
prices 224
Priddy Fair 202–3, 203
printed calendars 42
Processus 197–8
progress 221
Pronostycacyon For Ever (Pater) 58, 281–2
Proserpina 189
Protestants, adoption of the Gregorian
calendar 45–7
Prynne, William 177, 286, 307
Ptolemy 40, 59
public festivities, suppression of 227
puffin, the 110
Punky Night 253
purgatory 255
Puttenham, George 192
Pyefleet Channel, Essex 239